MW01595859

# HOPES of VICTORY

# HOPES of VICTORY

The Sweeping Saga of
a Family at War

# SHAUN CHAPMAN

Library of Congress Control Number:      2018911216
ISBN:          Hardcover              978-1-9845-5452-9
               Softcover              978-1-9845-5451-2
               eBook                  978-1-9845-5450-5

Print information available on the last page.

Rev. date: 01/30/2020

**To order additional copies of this book, contact:**
Xlibris
1-888-795-4274
www.Xlibris.com
Orders@Xlibris.com
775383

# Contents

# DEDICATION

This book is dedicated to the ships and men of the Royal Navy, United States Navy, Royal Canadian Navy and Merchant Navy who sailed the seven seas at a time of war between 1939 and 1945, when only a thin strip of sea stood between all that was right and good and an evil that had swept across Europe wearing jackboots and carrying a flag emblazoned with a swastika, spouting the words, "Heil Hitler!". . . It is especially dedicated to those in the Flower class Corvettes, ships of 1200 tons when fully laden and packed full of high explosive, whose mission was simple: seek and destroy enemy submarines and protect the convoys at all costs. . .

It is dedicated to the men I sailed with, our First Officer Tom Brocus, Lieutenant Alf Cole (Sec.Nav. of the RNZN in the 1960s), Sub-Lieutenant Lunn, and, of course, our ship, HMS Sweetbriar (K209), its captains: Lt. Jack Winston Cooper, Lt. Cdr. Robert Edwards, Lt. Cdr. William Whitfield, Lt. James Grenville Lewis, Lt. John Douglas Gordon Mitchell, and to B2 Group . . . To Lieutenant Nicholas Monsarrat who sailed with HMS Campanula, one of our sister ships in B2 Group . . . To the United States Navy and Royal New Zealand Navy . . . To my wife Elizabeth Katherine Chapman, my son Mark Chapman, my daughter Tina Louise Chapman, Adam, Nathan, Jennifer, Vo and little Logan, and of course, Emma Watson and David & Judy Langridge . . . To my father Ernest Andrew Chapman a Driver/Gunner and corporal of the Royal Field Artillery (L/29187), to my Uncle Albert Chapman of the Gloucestershire Regiment

1st Battalion (38158), who lies asleep at Savy British cemetery, Aisne in France (Plot 11.A.15., Memorial ID: 56406951) . . . To my father's other brothers, Edward, Jack & Kenneth . . . To my mother Elizabeth Chapman (previously O'Sullivan) and my brothers Ernie, Jimmy, Teddy & Alfred and their sons and daughters . . . To my Uncle James 'Jimmy' O'Sullivan who fought in Turkey during the Great War . . . and, to those who have no grave markers, those men, women and children who died at the hands of our enemy in ghettos and concentration camps where the only escape was death . . . *Cdr. Stanley William Chapman*

# Acknowledgements

We would like to thank our many supporters who have helped with not only *Hopes of Victory* but our conservation work and books as well as keeping us alive & kicking, especially Dennis Udoh, Chris Stevens, Ronny Beifus, Christopher Tonoh, Valerie Kirchner, Chris Jones, Ntweng Titus Makhubedu. The following deserve credit for helping me in my research: The Great War Forum members, Margaret Nolan & the Gallipoli Association . . . It has been a long and hard journey, maybe a little too hard at times, but as I sit here and look back on it I am proud to have people such as yourselves join us on the epic quest we have undertaken, and hope that what is written within these pages will make a difference to the world in which we live . . . *Make War No More* . . . Neither to the flora and fauna with which we share our planet and to our fellow man . . . For, it is high time man appreciated the gifts he has inherited . . . But, one man deserves so much credit, and that is my father Stanley William Chapman, whose sense of fun always amused Tina, Mark and I when we were young. His sense of duty, loyalty and honor is unsurpassed. His love and generosity to his children know no bounds . . . Thanks Dad . . . for everything . . .

# FOREWORD

*As I stand here looking back over the years, I have witnessed a wave of uncaring abuse sweep over Britain, destroying and tearing the fleshy parts off the lion that was once our proud emblem. Of central banking institutions with hidden agendas imposing their will in the same manner as Hitler and the Third Reich, a European Union that has sought to enslave the British people with laws and statutes of their own making. Of a political correctness used by unscrupulous men and women devised to destroy and defeat the very principles we held dear to our hearts, principles that an evil personified by Hitler himself, wished to destroy, an evil that would have at its core the destruction of values of distinction and greatness. Were the sacrifices we made worth it? All I can say is the same thought processes and patterns prevalent in sustaining the Third Reich now seem to play a part in the British government and the draconian laws they have institutionalized – In the end, what the Third Reich failed to accomplish is being completed by a corporatocracy sweeping the Earth in the guise of a wooly pelted baying sheep, underneath which is a ravenous wolf seeking to devour the whole world . . . I have witnessed successive British political parties erode the very lives of those bringing them to power – either for self-gain or their own insidious hidden agendas. There is an old saying, 'All politicians are rats, but not all rats are politicians–'*

*Over the years I have lived to see the British people continually abused and lambasted and insulted by individuals and countries even though Britain has given so much to the world – It is these self same individuals and nationalistic entities that quickly forget those sacrifices made by the British people to rescind and wage war against slavery, who sacrificed their lives and those of their loved ones on a pyre of international tumult and angst, a sacrifice to end the hurt and suffering of others on a scale unseen before in the realm of historical fact. One that those same nationalistic entities wish to resurrect enmeshing themselves with the same form of ideologies as the Third Reich . . .*

*By standing up to a bully in a playground on an international scale, the British people have given rise to a whole different chain of events, and, it is up to the whole world to respect and honor their sacrifices . . . For, if this had not been the case the vast majority of those alive today would never have existed and those extant on Earth would be forever more chained to the will and been at the mercy of tyrannical forces such as the world will never see again in this stream of time . . .*

*We stood for all that was right and good in a world gone mad at that time. At the beginning, alone we defended our shores, alone we faced an evil that would have crushed righteousness, light and goodness under its heel as it spread its dark tendrils around the globe . . .*

*I am proud to have been one of those few who stood stalwart and unmoving in the face of danger and a foe intent on the enslavement of all mankind, imposing a will surpassing only the devil himself . . . A diamond is formed by pressure and heat, Hitler had applied both to the British people and a diamond had been formed . . .*

*Present and future wars will always be pale and petty in comparison – and at least I know I was in the war to end all wars and we, our allies, particularly the United States, won . . . Cdr. Stanley William Chapman*

# INTRODUCTION

*When my father and I started Hopes of Victory I wondered how the book would turn out and what the content would be, and would it be good enough for the general public. I write this as the book is nearing completion and I am proud of how it has transformed from a small seed into a wonderful repository of our family's history. More than this though it has shown me how precious each and every member of our family is and was. I have a much greater appreciation of both my mother and father and the sacrifices they made so I can be where I am today. I have seen through the pages of our family's sojourn through time that even the smallest of deviation in the march toward our present future would have given rise to a dramatically different outcome. They coin it the Butterfly Effect. And within this timescape nestles a myriad of instances where our family's fortunes would have improved drastically, which, in turn would have given rise to a multitude of different outcomes. At other times the exigencies of certain time periods proved to be an insurmountable wall onto which our fortunes and dreams were dashed to pieces with little or no chance of escape. And whilst every effort has been made up to the time of publication to make sure that all the information contained in this book is a true and correct interpretation of events, any erroneous details or misinterpretations are purely unintentional . . . Working on our family's history has proved enlightening; working on it with my father has provided me with an immeasurable amount of satisfaction and happiness. It is a project that any father and son would be proud of. It has given me a unique insight both of my father and all those who have gone before. It has shown me the strife and turmoil our family has experienced even up to the point my sister, brother and I came onto the scene. I am indescribably proud of my father, mother, sister and brother. Things may not have turned out the way we wanted, but, we are family . . . and, the love we have for one another shall last for all eternity . . . Cdr. Shaun Chapman*

# CHAPTER 1

## The Great War 1914-18

Some say the Great War started with the assassination of the Austrian Archduke Francis Ferdinand and his wife in Sarajevo on Sunday 28 of June 1914. The Archduke was Kaiser Wilhelm Bismarck's nephew and heir, but his was just one inconsequential human life that really mounted to nothing more than a storm tossed rock lying on a beach strewn with pebbles that all looked the same. Was his life worth the blood of millions spilt on the battlefields of Europe, or was it yet just another petty excuse for the military might of Germany to hold France and the rest of the World accountable for some imagined slight to their nation's manhood and their imperial dreams. Then again maybe they felt everyone else was weak and they could storm through the Low Countries and seize them, standing on their necks and proudly proclaiming, "We are gods, bow down to us now, for you are now our subjects and shall feel the keen edge of our wrath if thou raise thy heads . . ." Gavřilo Prinzip, the Bosnian student, didn't give a thought to his unconscionable action as he pulled the trigger of his firearm. Nor did he give any conscious thought to the repercussions and effect this simple act could cause. His senseless and irrational behavior brought about the deaths of so many on the battlefields of Europe . . . Was Serbia complicit in the crime? Quite possibly, but this was never proved conclusively . . .

But the reason for the war didn't matter, it didn't matter for little Johnny Jones lying in a pool of his blood at the bottom of a trench filled with the stench of rotting corpses and mud; it didn't matter to Henry Baker who now lay in several pieces, courtesy of a German shell, on the field of battle in no-man's land; and it didn't matter to Albert Chapman either, for he had done what he had thought was right and joined the army to make a difference, to fend off the Hun and stop them from taking France and ultimately taking Britain as well. As he lay mortally wounded in a shell hole behind a mass of twisted barbed wire thoughts of home in the village of Leiston and of happier days in Saxmundham flickered through his mind, and he wondered what would become of his brother who was also on this same battlefield. The pain from his wounds was unbearable and he started to hallucinate seeing the face of a young woman he had proposed to and planned to marry when he got home, he called out to her, but it was a fading image, a memory that had impressed itself upon, and replaced, the images around him. He tried to shut the pain and destruction around him out but couldn't, he didn't want to be there, he didn't care for the war anymore, there was no bravado now for he just wanted to live, he didn't want to die, at least not like this. His future was fading fast and so was his beloved, there would be no children, no growing old with the woman he loved and no playing with his grandchildren on grass covered slopes populated by dandelions whose seeds the little children would try and catch as they blew this and that way with the breeze. He didn't want it all to end like this; he had so much to live for, so much to do with his life, this couldn't be happening, it must be some mistake . . . Albert tried to call for help but his cry was more like a croak than a full throated passion-filled yell for assistance and succor . . . Over the steady rhythm of a Hun machine gun there came yet another sound, a whistling noise, an ominous sound that brought death with it . . .

Ernest Chapman loved animals, and horses in particular, and they loved him. Underneath him was *Dolly*, his horse, a war horse of the Royal Field Artillery and underneath her steel shod hooves was the clinging sticky mud and wet soil of France. *Dolly's* nostrils flared as she struggled to breathe, inhaling the stink of cordite and explosives as she did so. The air above was filled with whistling shells and all about were loud explosions that blew pieces of fragmented trees, and that self-same mud and soil, all over the field of battle. Ernest guided *Dolly* over the muddy terrain as fast as he could. Next to *Dolly* was another horse of which Ernest held the bridle, and behind them two more horses and another driver riding on the horse behind Ernest. They were pulling a gun carriage and a medium sized piece of field artillery with two men riding atop the carriage. It was said that you would never hear the shell that killed you . . . All about the horses a barrage of shells erupted with such vehemence and anger Ernest could feel and smell the hot fetid breath of Satan's hordes . . . and out of the deafening clamor and roar of the explosions around them came yet another and even more ominous sound, a whistling noise and it seemed to be coming straight for them. Ernest gave it no thought and urged *Dolly* forward by kicking his heels into her flanks and yelling above the din for even greater speed out of the steeds in his charge. The whistling became louder and louder with each passing second until it seemed to be nearly upon them . . .

Jimmy O'Sullivan had been ordered by the officers in command to surrender, so he did what he was told, he wanted to carry on fighting but an order was an order so what could he do. He had laid down his rifle and stuck his hands up . . . It all seemed like an eternity ago as he pulled back on the oars of the boat as he headed towards Greece. His lips were parched and dry and his tongue felt a little swollen, his face was burnt from the Mediterranean sun beating down upon him. He prayed for

rain but it never came, just the same hot burning sun by day
and the cold stygian black starry sky at night. At the moment
he would have traded his soul for a canteen filled with water.
His meager ration of bread and cheese and spam were gone . . .
and his canteen was empty . . . the scraps of food had been
finished nigh two days ago while he was sitting in a tree . . . *'Still,
things could have been worse'*, he thought, looking up at the stars
to orientate himself . . . The Turks had always treated escaped
prisoners the same way . . . *for, without even blinking an eye, they
would slit your throat if they found you* . . .

* * *

Leiston was a wonderfully quaint little town on the east coast
of Suffolk right next to Saxmundham; it had a pebble beach
and farmland all around. Ernest's father, Alfred, worked for
the railways in Saxmundham and his stepmother, Joan, was a
schoolteacher in a small school, she had originally come from
Wales and her maiden name was Davis. His real mother Ellen
Elizabeth Chapman (ne Peters) had passed away. Summer was
an idyllic time of the year for Ernest; his father had spoken to
one of the farmers in the area who had taken the young lad on
as a part-time farmhand. He loved animals so any farm chore
was just another opportunity to be nearer to nature and his
favorite animal, the horse. He ploughed fields with them, fed
and watered them and brushed them down at the end of the
day. But most of all he loved to talk to them because they were
his best friends and the farmer knew this, which is why, even at
a very young age, he entrusted the boy with work usually done
by an older youth or an adult. The horses under his care would
do anything for him; he only had to ask them with a nod of his
head, a whisper or a calm word. At the time there were really
only five modes of road traffic, travel by foot, by train or by horse
or horse drawn carriage and cycle, like the Penny Farthing.
The horseless carriage was a scarcity and an oddity, and many

thought the strange machine wouldn't last. The summers were long and warm and after finishing his chores Ernest would lie down in the green grass with a straw in his mouth and look up at the clouds above while his equine charges chomped on the blades of grass by him. There was no sound in the skies above and no harsh sounding mechanical engines on the roads, just the gentle swishing back and forth of the long grass. And when the day was done a hot farm cooked meal lay in wait for him on the kitchen table. Come harvest time there were barn dances and parties at many of the farms in the area with Ernest's entire family being invited to many of them . . . As part payment for his work at the farm Ernest was allowed to ride the horses and exercise them, taking them out into the countryside . . .

Ernest had four brothers, Albert, who was older, then Jack, Kenneth and Edward. Life was simple just after the turn of the century, but the *winds of war* were about to turn into a *gale of destruction* as the German military machine began the task of building ships and long range artillery pieces for a future battle unseen to all save a few, for even in the year 1900 the Kaiser and his military advisors had begun to draw up their battle plans . . . In the dark days of the Boer War Queen Victoria, even though aged, stated, "The Queen is not interested in the possibility of defeat . . ." At the end of hostilities and with the Boer War finished and won Britain prided itself on being the greatest and most powerful nation on Earth . . . Germany, however, had eyes on this title and wouldn't rest until it had both the title and had claimed the far flung lands Britain held sway over. The British lion was about to receive a good and proper mauling by the Kaiser's two headed eagle . . . All they needed was an excuse to further their ambitions . . .

\* \* \*

Alfred and Joan Chapman had made their house at Leiston into a warm and happy home for their family, they were all

very happy after moving there from Saxmundham, but war
was about to break out due to the Kaiser's intransigence and
warmongering policies. The safety of Britain and her dominions
was in jeopardy. Boys being boys though, Albert, Ernest, Jack,
Kenneth and Edward took little note of what was happening
on the political scene, their life in the town of Leiston could
not have been happier what with running races in the fields
around the town and riding horses in the green pastures when
they could, and going to school which cost their father a ha'
penny a week for each of them, and of course, getting dressed
in their best clothes for church every Sunday at St. Johns church
in Saxmundham. Their mother took great care of the boys and
loved each and every one . . . In 1911 George V was crowned king
of Great Britain, Ireland, and the British Dominions beyond
the seas, emperor of India, on the 22$^{nd}$ of October . . . Alfred
was the best boilermaker the Great Eastern Railways had, he
was so skilled he was sent all over Britain to repair boilers and
teach others the fine art of boiler making. When their father
was away working for the Great Eastern Railways Albert would
take charge of the household after his mother who made sure
her brood was skilled in reading and writing and all the other
subjects they were taught at school. Like any household full
of boys fights broke out occasionally but nothing ever serious,
just normal sibling rivalry for the affections and favor of their
parents . . . Then war broke out in Europe between Austria and
Serbia in response to the assassination of Archduke Ferdinand,
and as Russia mobilized her forces to the districts closest to
Austria on the 29$^{th}$ of July 1914, Austria moved toward Belgrade
and began bombarding the Serbian capital. The German
fleet was recalled from the Baltic Sea and Germany informed
Russia that because she had mobilized her forces Germany
would do the same. On that same evening the Kaiser and his
council of war decided to declare war on France and Russia
simultaneously. They offered their assurances to the British
government that if they remained neutral they had no intention

of making territorial gains if Germany proved victorious against France. This was rejected by the British Ambassador in Berlin, Sir Edward Grey. He had no intention of embroiling Britain in another war so he delayed advising the cabinet to take such action for as long as possible. Ultimatums and assurances were bandied about all so that German forces could be moved into position, for the Germans had decided to take France in one swift blow which would incapacitate her leaving them to concentrate on the fall of Russia. Britain had obligations to Belgium and asked France and Germany for assurances that her neutrality would be respected. France responded and gave the required guarantee but Germany had no intention to respect the treaty she had been cosignatory to in 1839 . . . The following day German troops crossed the frontier into Luxembourg then on into France where skirmishes between French and German troops took place. In short order the Germans attacked Belgium and France leaving Britain no option other than to declare war after an ultimatum for Germany to remove her troops failed to elicit a response . . . On midnight on Tuesday the 4th of August 1914 a state of war existed between Britain and Germany . . .

\* \* \*

For two days the Belgians kept the Germans at bay from taking the city of Liege until it was occupied on the 7th of August. German artillery continued to pound away at the forts surrounding it until all resistance crumbled. The German forces pushed on through Belgium quickly destroying all in its path on its way to the northern border of France. Britain had mobilized 150,000 troops under Sir John French and deployed them to France. This British Expeditionary Force first came into contact with the Germans on Sunday the 23rd of August that year. Back in Britain the newspapers were full of war reports and the war was on everybody's lips . . . The Chapman boys poured over any newspapers that came their way, devouring every little detail. After dinner was finished in the Chapman household they all they crowded into the living area. Albert and Ernest would sit by their father and read as their brothers sat on the rug by the fireplace, over which, was suspended a kettle. Their mother, knitting sweaters, would correct them if they weren't able to pronounce something correctly. Alfred, their father, had never been taught how to read when he was a youngster while he was growing up, so he sat in rapt attention listening about the war and the efforts of Lord Asquith and Lloyd George in their attempts to stop the conflict widening and stem the German advance. Albert showed a caricature of the Kaiser to his father, who laughed, then noted, "There is no reasoning with the Germans, they're all pig-headed and they won't stop until we're all subjects of the Kaiser . . ."

"Have you seen the posters in the village, father, they need men to fight them. I'd like to join up right now . . ." said Albert loudly and puffing his chest out proudly. "Me too," piped in Ernest, a little more subdued than his brother. Their mother shook her head from side to side and said, "You're both too young right now . . . I'm sure it won't last, the Germans will pull back once our troops get into action. Look what happened in the Boer War . . ."

Alfred turned to the boys, "Hopefully your mother is right and there'll be no need for you to go to war."

"It won't be too long before I'm eighteen and then I can join up . . . it would be a great adventure father . . ." added Albert.

Alfred replied uneasily, "What if you were injured? What then . . ."

"No German's going to harm me father, I'll make sure of that," answered Albert.

"Albert, war is a nasty business and I hope this mess is cleared up before you turn eighteen, besides, the Great Eastern Railways are expecting you to continue your apprenticeship. So we can't have you gallivanting off to France now, can we?" commented the boy's father.

"But father all my friends are wanting to volunteer," said Albert.

"Then, that is something their parents will have to talk to them about, fighting over in France will not put food on the table, or anything else for that matter . . . The politicians started this mess so let them deal with it. It has nothing to do with decent folk trying to make an honest living . . ." stated Alfred with irritation.

"Yes, father," said Albert humbly.

Joan, their mother, put down her row of knitting and got up, "Time for bed now boys, early to bed and early to rise, makes a man healthy, wealthy and wise . . ."

"Yes, mother . . ." chorused the boys as they struggled to rise from the comfortable rug and warm fire they sat next to. After the boys were tucked safely in bed Alfred picked up the discarded newspaper looking at the caricature. Joan sat back down and carried on with her knitting, turning to her husband she smiled, "Would you like some tea?" she asked. "Yes please," answered Alfred pretending to peruse the paper studiously while gently rocking his chair back and forth.

The following day, being a Sunday, meant the boys all went to church with their parents, including Albert who would take the train back to Leytonstone late that day. After church at St. John's in Saxmundham, which was so close to Leiston the villages nearly merged into one another, they changed into play clothing and the boys grabbed some sticks and started marching around like soldiers in the field between their house and the shingle beach behind it, then they started chasing each other with half playing the role of the Hun and the others British soldiers defending a fort they had built near the beach. Ernest shot at one of his brothers with his stick, "Bang!" he said loudly. Jack carried on running toward the fort which he and Albert were defending. "Hey, you can't do that, you're dead!" he shouted crossly. As Jack jumped over a tree stump and jumped on top of Ernest, tackling him and bowling him over. "You're dead I say . . . when you're shot you're dead!" complained Ernest loudly. Jack smiled at him, "The Germans don't follow the rules, you should know that . . ."

Ernest pushed his brother off, "If you can't simply follow the rules of war then I'm not playing!"

Albert turned to Ernest as Kenneth and Edward followed Jack over the stump. "You can't leave me all alone with these rascals Ernest," cried Albert, grabbing the two children by their collars and holding them at arm's length. "I'm going, for if you can't play properly then I sharn't play at all . . . Besides, I have chores to do," said Ernest angrily, storming off.

Later that day while Ernest was mucking out the pigsty near the tomato plant sticks at the back of the house, Albert came over to him and leaned against the fence. "You know you shouldn't be cross with them, they were only playing," apologized Albert for his other brothers' behavior.

Ernest looked at him somewhat sheepishly. "I'm not upset with them, I'm upset with the fact you'll probably be going to France and I won't," replied Ernest.

Albert smiled, "From what everyone is saying the war could go on for a long time . . ."

"But I want to go with you . . ." retaliated Ernest.

"Ernest you're not old enough, even I'm not old enough yet," continued Albert looking at their pig nuzzling his brother's leg. "So don't be pig headed . . ." smiled Albert as the pig nearly bowled his brother over, "Besides, you even have trouble keeping upright with one pig, how would you fare against the Hun?"

Albert turned to leave, but stopping for a second he said, "Don't be wishing for things other men are frightened of and would stay well away from . . ." With that final comment he walked away toward the house.

Ernest shook his head and grumbled, not noticing the pig behind him. As the pig bumped into him Ernest lost his balance and fell backwards into the slimy muck . . . Sitting in the muddy gunk he moaned, "Et tu Brutus . . ."

\* \* \*

A British army non-commissioned officer with two soldiers came to Leiston and Saxmundham one day to put up recruitment posters and collect volunteers for the army. The posters were tacked up at the town hall and local churches, shops and in the local pubs. They had come to gather volunteers and register those old enough for fighting. The soldiers were also on the lookout for horses, commandeering them for the war effort. Ernest breathed a sigh of relief when his two favorite plough horses were passed over. "Too old . . ." they said, plus a couple of other unsavory words which Ernest thought unkind and unnecessary. To Ernest they were steeds akin to the horses of old such as King Arthur rode as he fought the Saxons, in his eyes they were the most beautiful horses ever and he adored them, and they he, for whenever they caught sight or sound of him they would gallop towards Ernest and follow him wherever he went. And every time Ernest visited the farm he would take a little treat for them. Coming up to him they would search him, seeking out an apple or other sweet thing he would hide in his pockets or hold in his hands behind his back. Their ever eager and sensitive noses always found what they sought and Ernest would stroke their long bony noses, kiss them gently and say a quiet reassuring word . . .

With their quota of eligible men filled British army officers led their men to the railway station and from there to a training camp. The village of Leiston stood by their men waving paper Union Jacks on sticks and shouting words of encouragement as they passed by little shops along narrow streets in the village. The children of Leiston marched up and down with toy rifles made of wood and broom sticks, amongst them were Jack, Kenneth and Edward puffing chests out proudly and falling in behind the men with their friends. Ernest looked on disconsolately at the procession, wishing he was going with them . . . Standing next to him Albert saw the pain in his eyes . . . His one wish was that he alone could go and that the war would end before Ernest was old enough to join up . . .

Time waits for no man and the war continued in France on the other side of the English Channel. A year went by leaving Ernest and Albert to fight with wooden swords on the plough horses borrowed under the excuse of exercise and stretching the horses' legs on the weekend. With naught but reins and a bareback Ernest and Albert would chase after each other through green fields and pastures. Stuck in wide belts around their waists were wooden swords their father had fashioned for them years before. They would do nothing against Saxon or German steel but to them they were gleaming blades like Arthur's Excalibur. As they galloped through the fields and countryside around Leiston and Saxmundham they stopped to look at the sea from a hill overlooking the murky grey waters below. Panting atop his horse, Albert drew in a deep breath, "You would never guess that over there," he pointed eastward, "battles are raging and brave men are dying, would you?"

"No you wouldn't," Ernest noted with a hint of wistfulness.

"But, be that as it may," Albert pulled out his wooden sword from his broad belt, "Taste my steel you Saracen dog . . ."

"So you think you can best me, do you?" retorted Ernest gripping his reins tightly.

"Most assuredly," answered Albert tensing his legs and steadying himself as he struck out with his sword. Ernest parried the blow and their wooden swords clashed. And as wood struck wood the clashing slowly turned to steel on steel, bayonets against bayonets, German bullets against the flesh and blood of good men who died in the mud whence they stood, men who wished only to defend their countries and the lives of the innocent . . .

\* \* \*

David Lloyd George, 1st Earl of Dwyfor, was born in 1863 at Chorlton-on-Medlock in Manchester. His father, William George, a schoolmaster, was a native of Fishguard in South Wales. He left teaching for farming before George reached his first year, but died shortly afterwards on their farm not far from Haverfordwest. Richard Lloyd, a shoemaker and William's brother-in-law, looked after the family in Llanystumdwy, Caernarvonshire, where he lived and worked. George went to the village school and was eventually articled to a firm of solicitors in Portmadoc. In 1884 he started practicing law at Criccieth but was a very outspoken liberalist with strong views. In 1890 he became an elected representative and replaced a Conservative Parliamentarian. He was a great orator and stuck up for his constituents arguing against an unfair Local Taxation Bill and even stood up against Joseph Chamberlain in Parliament. When it came to protecting the Welsh people and their interests he was always at odds with his own Liberal Party, but he stuck to his guns nonetheless. During the South African War he became very unpopular at home because he outwardly supported the Boers in their quest to break from British governance. He loved Wales and purchased a house in Pwllheli, near Portmadoc. He strove for Welsh independence and it was largely through his efforts that it became an issue within the Liberal Party. Even so, he was not popular with the patriotic crowd that saw him as a traitor because of his views in the 1901 election. In Birmingham, where he spoke in the town hall, the police insisted he be disguised as one of them to leave because of the crowd's patriotic fervor.

All through his career as a parliamentarian he was an uncompromising idealist who could not stand for fools, and in his mind parliament was full of them . . .

At the outbreak of hostilities Lloyd George was a leading debater in the House of Commons and coined terms which stuck in the minds of the electorate, such as, 'the silver bullet,' when he was referring to war loans. In May of 1915 he became minister of munitions when the government was reorganized due to the war, now there was no delineation between the Liberal, Tory and Labour Parties. Everyone had a role to play in countering the aggression of the Kaiser and the German military forces invading the Low Countries, France and Russia. They had to be stopped at any cost . . . It wasn't long before he succeeded Lord Kitchener as war minister but shortly afterwards he resigned because of disagreements with the Prime Minister, Lord Asquith, over the way in which the war was being fought. By December of 1916 Asquith resigned as Prime Minister and his post was filled by Lloyd George. He was now able to put into practice the strategies that he hoped would change the tide of the war . . .

* * *

Jimmy O'Sullivan had volunteered to fight the Hun scourge, there had been no pushing or cajoling, he thought his country was in dire need of men to fight in the trenches over in France. He gave no thought as to whether he would survive the war or the fact that he would be fighting seasoned professional soldiers. Like most men who volunteered he wanted to serve his country. Many wars had been fought in Europe, Russia, Asia and the Near East but none quite like this. Most had been limited to one country or another, however, this was vastly different; nations were struggling to retain their national identity against a foe intent on ruling the entire world. And the method of war was different; Otto Lilienthal had been the first to get airborne in a heavier-than-air-craft, a glider, while Richard William Pearse, an inventor of home-made aero planes, motor bicycles and agricultural machinery, achieved controlled sustained propeller driven flight early in 1902 along the Waitohi main road outside Auckland, New Zealand; the Wright brothers, a pair of pioneering bicycle mechanics, took a leap into the skies one grey day near Kitty Hawk, South Carolina, in December 1903 with their motorized and propeller driven aircraft. Now, in a short period of time, aircraft ruled the skies above the trenches photographing them and dropping bombs on the troops below in much more complex fabric and wood machines. The Germans had even developed the MG-1914, an air-cooled 1200 round per minute machine gun that could cut down advancing troops. These guns were placed at regular intervals along the trenches producing an enfilading cross-fire that ripped apart anyone caught in it. The British Vickers water-cooled machine gun and the Lewis machine gun used by the Allies were not as effective. The rest of the world had stagnated while the Germans had forged ahead developing and devising new and better ways for killing men . . . Added to this carnage was a new terror on the field of battle, that of poisonous gas, gas that could blind a soldier and destroy his lungs, leaving him on the ground rolling in searing pain gasping for one last breath . . . Jimmy thought nothing of this, as he proudly boarded his ship wearing his itchy thick wool khaki uniform with bandage type leggings above his brown leather boots that still smarted and gave him blisters on his heels and toes. On his back was a small rucksack with a bedroll strapped on to it and an entrenching tool. He carried his Lee Enfield rifle proudly and wore his tin hat at a jaunty angle. His parents had left Ireland for London so that their children could have a better life. A little part of him questioned his reasons for joining up, had it been true patriotism for a country that looked down on him because of his Irish decent, or did he truly feel he was a British citizen fighting for King and Country in the Royal Munster Fusiliers. He didn't know. The answer seemed to elude him. Irrespective of the true motives for him joining he was a proud man at this moment in time, going off to fight a common enemy of both the upper and lower classes of Britain. Though he wondered, by what right did those with titles and money have to lord it over those less fortunate. At heart he believed in an egalitarian society in which all were equal and equally blessed with opportunities and financial rewards . . .

Jimmy looked below as he climbed up the steep gangplank. He saw his mother. Maria Coughlin-O'Sullivan, and his sisters, Elizabeth, Ellen May, whom they had nicknamed Ester, and Mary, who were holding tightly on to his half-sister Margaret, while his half-brother Daniel held the hand of his mother. They were proud of him and smiled and waved gleefully with the children waving their little Union Jacks. There had been no nay saying at home, just good wishes for him on this adventure of a lifetime. He returned their smiles and quickly found a space by the rail so he could bid them *'Bon Voyage'.* For some reason he didn't feel apprehensive at all, for he just knew he would be returning home someday. Elizabeth, his sister whom had been given the nickname Betty, had that same feeling and told him so at home. She was absolutely certain he would return back into the welcoming arms of his family. So, as the ship pulled away from her berth at London's dockside, Jimmy felt no regret, no pinning for the home that was fast disappearing into the distance. Someday in the near future he would return a hero, well, maybe not a hero, but nonetheless he would return . . .

\* \* \*

When Ernest was ten his mother would ask his brothers, "Where is Ernest?" They would sing out, "You know where he is mummy, he's at the stables . . ."

Ernest loved horses and would help the stablemen clean the stalls and if a horse was sick he would stay with it for hours and hours, there was nothing he would not do for them. Even when he was a young boy he said to his father, "When I grow up I want to go and work in the stables . . ." His father, Alfred, would give him a condescending scolding look and reply, "That job has no future, son, you are going to work on the railways like your brother, and myself, for you are going to be an engine driver and that is that. I want to hear no more of this stable poppycock my boy . . ." His father really wanted him to be an engine driver, in fact, he wanted him to be the youngest driver in all Britain. This saddened Ernest for his every thought was of the venerable horse and how he could be near them. Even so, Ernest started as a cleaner with the Great Eastern Railways just after his fourteenth birthday. His father, Alfred, had got him a position with them at the London Stratford Railway Works and told him when he started, "Now you can earn your keep and give something back to your mother for all her hard work nurturing you throughout the years . . ." It would take him many years, but, eventually, he would become a railway locomotive engineer and engine driver, though his love for flesh and blood horses was never replaced by the steel horse that rode on lines made of steel. He and Albert shared lodgings at Leytonstone and Ernest joined the local running club and won many races. Albert was already an apprentice in the railway engine maintenance section but he yearned for more, he yearned to be on the front line and being a hero, he wanted it desperately, all his friends ever talked about now was joining up and giving the Hun what for. Some of the older boys he had known at home had already joined the Suffolk Regiment and done their training and would be on their way to France shortly. Albert envied them and so did Ernest, when he saw a khaki clad soldier the young boy would always salute him smartly and stand to attention. When Albert saw this he always chided and ribbed his brother. But he understood the young lad's yearning, he too was disgusted with what the Germans had done in Belgium, and how the Kaiser had manipulated, twisted and exploited the situation in Serbia and Russia to attack Belgium and then France. Their duplicity had been without rival. And because of this the men, women and children of Europe had tasted German steel in the form of bullets, artillery shells and the sharpened edges of bayonets. Throughout Britain nationalistic fervor was rising. There was much banter at lunch between the apprentices at the railway works in Stratford while they sat and consumed their vitals . . . "We would really teach those Hun a good lesson or two if we were over there," sneered one of the lads out the corner of his mouth as he chomped down on his sandwich.

"Yes, they wouldn't last more than a day with all the food coming out o' yer' gob matey," replied a tall boy in coveralls called James.

"Are you joining up then?" asked Albert of him.

"Of course, as soon as I turn eighteen . . . And you . . . when are you going over?" noted James.

"The same, but I'll be joining up next month though, that's when my birthday is . . ." said Albert reservedly, for now that he was going to join up his bravado and cocky assuredness were now fast disappearing. He had seen the lists of the dead and had heard of the carnage the Germans had wrought upon the Allied forces, even though the papers and government tried to hide it. He had begun to have second thoughts. There was a lot of talk from Lord Asquith and Kitchener but this war was beyond them, the world had moved on and so had the art of war, the all out conflict Britain was enmeshed in had them totally outfoxed, they were way out of their depth . . . Lloyd George knew this, and it was his firm hand that was needed at the helm . . .

Albert had a sweetheart in Saxmundham, he had known her all his life and her parents' house was not too far away. He had travelled up from Leytonstone one weekend where he lived while working as an apprentice for the railway . . . Albert stood in the pasture behind their house next to the sea, grey waves with frothy foam attacked the shoreline and the wind blew his hair all over the place. Small droplets of water from the grey clouds above struck his face as he held on to his girlfriend Meredith in a warm loving embrace. "Albert, I don't want you to go . . ." said Meredith softly.

"Neither do I, now that I'm actually going," he answered.

"Can't you talk to them, tell them we're planning to get married. I mean, it is what you want as well, isn't it?" she continued in her Suffolk home country lilt.

"Of course, there is no one else I would rather spend my life with . . ."

"Then tell them you can't go," pleaded Meredith, her black long skirt and white ruffled blouse getting a tad wet and windblown even though Albert held her close to him. Her dark hair was tied in a bun with two attractive ribbons entwining it.

"They can't do this to us, Albert. That Kaiser is a very nasty man and who knows what may happen to you once you're in France," continued Meredith.

"Nothing will happen to me my dearest, you'll see, I'll be back in no time and we can have our engagement party then . . ." said Albert smiling.

Meredith looked crossly at him. "Don't look at me like that," Albert said with a look of mock hurt on his face. "Besides, I have something for you . . ." he added, pulling something small from his pocket. Meredith's quizzical look turned to one of glee when she saw what it was, a ring!

"It's not the best but it's all I can afford now, I promise you I'll get you a better one when I get back from the front . . ."

Meredith put her arms around his neck and gave him the biggest most slobbery kiss he'd ever had. "It's the most wonderful ring in the world Albert, and don't you dare ever think of replacing it . . ." she said as Albert got down on one knee and slipped the ring on her finger. "Will you marry me?" he asked.

"Of course Albert . . ." said Meredith wrapping her arms around his neck once more as he stood up. In the upstairs window of his parents house Albert caught sight of his younger siblings mocking him. He turned back to the woman in his arms and kissed her on the lips as the rain started to fall. The little droplets had now turned into a proper North Sea rain storm so he grabbed Meredith's hand and ran with her through their garden past the big apple tree, the cherry tree and rows of tomato plants on sticks to the back door of his parents' house and the warm fire in the living room he knew waited for them . . .

* * *

Albert and Ernest had taken the train home to visit their parents, and, for Albert, it was the last chance for him to see them before he headed off to France. He had been given leave so he had decided the trip home would be the thing to do. Besides, his sweetheart was waiting for him, and he couldn't leave without telling her he loved her . . . It was a dark day when Albert left his Leiston home in his khaki green wool uniform, his family didn't want him to go and neither did Meredith, especially Meredith, who couldn't keep the tears from falling down her face. "I will come back, Meredith, I promise. Not all the Kaiser's horses and all the Kaiser's men could stop me from returning and holding you in my arms once more . . ." said Albert holding her one last time before he left the house. His father, Alfred, shook his hand, and whispered, "Make us proud son . . ."

"I will father, have no fear of that . . ." replied Albert.

His stepmother, Joan, kissed him on the cheek, "Be careful Albert, don't take any unnecessary risks."

"Of course not mother," Albert answered. He rumpled up the hair of his younger siblings and added, "You boys take care of mother and father now. Don't let me come back and hear you've been naughty . . ."

"Yes Albert," chorused the boys, with tears in their eyes. As Albert strode for the door all the boys surrounded him and gave him a hug. Ernest stood to one side of the room with a sour expression on his face. Breaking away from the boys he went over to him and shook his hand. "Goodbye Ernest, till we meet again . . ." Ernest nodded his head. Sensing his unhappiness Albert stated, "Ernest, you're still too young, don't rush into it, for your time will come . . ."

"Yes, but when, the war will probably be over soon . . . and, I'll, I'll miss all the fun . . ." said Ernest. Albert shook his head, "My little brother I fear that it will be anything but fun, nor even an adventure if that is what you think. Trench warfare is hard and horrible . . . Don't be in such a hurry . . ."

Albert turned and eked his way through his family to the front door which was open. Meredith pulled him aside to plant one more kiss on his lips before he left to join a few other men in the street all dressed in khaki. Albert waved to them and headed off to the town hall were the men were to assemble. Along the road as they went men and women shouted words of encouragement and little children waved flags to see them off . . . Albert's chest swelled with pride, and so did those of the soldiers next to him. They all felt very important and let any fearful feelings fall behind them with every hobnailed boot step on the cobbled roads of Leiston.

After Albert had left, Joan hustled and mustered the children together all in their Sunday best. She called upstairs, "Are you ready Ernest?"

"Yes mother, I'll be down shortly . . ." he replied.

"Well, don't tarry now, we don't want to miss seeing off Albert at the station, now, do we?" shouted his stepmother standing with her hands on her hips, her black dress swishing as she turned to help her youngest child with his buttons. Ernest stood looking out at the sea from the boys' bedroom, he looked at the waves breaking and the foam washing up on the shingles, his mind was in turmoil, he wanted to join up and go with his brother but there was an issue with his age . . . His stepmother called out once more, "Ernest we have to go now, ready or not, we'll meet you at the station . . ."

His family left the house and closed the door behind them. Ernest was going to stay another two days then go back to Leytonstone and the Stratford Railway Works, but instead he pulled a small suitcase from under his old bed and then opened his drawer. He pulled out the few clothes he had brought with him and put them in the case. Out of another drawer he retrieved his railway concession ticket and slipped it into his pocket book. Working for the Great Eastern Railways did have its perks, especially when it came to travel on the rail networks around Britain. Ernest left a short note on his dresser for his parents and went downstairs with suitcase in hand. He opened the door and stepped outside and headed down the pathway to the road. His heart quickened as he took one last look at home before he hurried up the road to the railway station . . .

* * *

At the town hall khaki clad men formed up for a non-commissioned officer and began their march to the railway station. It was a proud day for the people of Leiston and the town mayor who had given a speech in honor of the men had wished them all Godspeed and a safe journey to France. Their route was lined with the residents of the town now festooned with bunting. Flags were waved by all and sundry as the men marched past with chins held high and arms swinging. Yes, it was a proud day for Leiston as Ernest quietly gave his ticket to the collector on the platform to be clipped. He slipped on board without anyone noticing and took a seat at the rear of the train . . . On the platform the men quickly boarded the train and Albert found a seat by a window next to the platform. He slid the window open and leaned out trying to catch the attention of his family who were on the busy platform. He waved and they all rushed over just as the conductor blew his whistle. "Look after Ernest!" he shouted above the din as he looked up and down the platform trying to spot his brother. "Don't you worry about him," said his mother giving him a kiss as the train jolted forward, "He's going nowhere until he's eighteen . . ."

Meredith managed to grab hold of Albert's hand as he leaned out the window and ran with the train until it picked up speed. When she eventually stopped running Meredith stood there on the platform watching it disappear down the railway tracks as the people around her gradually left and the platform emptied.

All, that is, except Albert's mother who had sat patiently on a wooden bench waiting for her . . .

As the pair left the station Meredith turned to Joan, "What if something bad happens to him Aunt Joan?"

"Don't worry dear, he'll be alright, we Chapmans are a hardy and strong bunch. So don't trouble yourself with such thoughts . . ."

Meredith sniffed and took out a little handkerchief and wiped the tears from her eyes. She felt much better now . . . unnoticed by her was the look on Albert's stepmother's face, for in her eyes was reflected both dread and worry of things to come, she couldn't help it, she loved Albert, once a boy not short years past and now all grown up and heading off to war . . .

When the family arrived home the boys looked for their brother but could find neither head nor tail of him, until, that is, Kenneth found the note on their dresser addressed to their parents. He took it down to the living room and presented it to his mother. When she opened it a look of dread came over her face. "He's gone back to London to join the army," she said, shocked.

Alfred, her husband, shook his head from side to side, "They'll never take him my dear, he's too young, they'll see it and send him packing off home and back to work at the railway works in Stratford . . ."

"I hope you're right Alfred, I do hope you're right . . ." said Joan as she slumped down in a chair feeling a bit faint. She had just sent one son off to France and had no intention of sending another one as well . . .

* * *

At a recruiting station in London Ernest stood in line waiting for his turn to sign up. Behind the sergeant sitting at a large desk a poster with the image of Kitchener pointing seemingly at Ernest, had the words 'WE NEED YOU!' in large bold letters. Ernest shuffled his feet and looked down at the floor, not wanting to be noticed, the men around him all looked much older than he but he had done his best to assume the same gruff mannerisms. When at last he got to the table the sergeant pushed some papers in front of him, "Sign these, with your full name, place of birth and age and place of residence . . ." he grunted.

As Ernest filled out the paper the sergeant motioned to an officer standing nearby, "He seems a bit young, doesn't he?"

"A little, hard to tell though, ask him if he has any experience with horses, we need more drivers and gunners in the Horse and field Artillery" said the officer.

The sergeant turned to Ernest and asked, "Do you have any experience with horses?"

At the mention of horses Ernest's face lit up, "Of course, I have plenty," he replied.

"In that case," the sergeant stamped his form and gave it to the officer to sign, "Welcome to the army . . ."

* * *

While in training Ernest spent any free moment with the horses of the regiment, brushing them, feeding and watering them and keeping their tack oiled and in good order. The officers of the regiment took note of his great affinity to them and were greatly impressed by his actions toward them. In the end he won not only the praise of his officers but the love of all the regiment's four legged equine beasts of burden as well . . . One horse, a mare, had an even greater affinity to Ernest, and that was *Dolly*. She became his in mind body and soul, for she was very affectionate towards the young man and jealous of his affection toward other horses in the regiment. When Ernest was busy cleaning tack *Dolly* would come over and put her head over his shoulder to see what he was up to. Naturally, as with the horses around Leiston and Saxmundham, Ernest always had a little treat for her. His training as a driver and gunner went well and the officers of the regiment thought he was a natural when it came to horses and gunnery practice. He eventually became their team leader and they were amongst the top gunners in the regiment. His training didn't last forever though, for men were needed at the front, especially gunners and their very mobile medium sized cannon. Only four horses were needed to pull it with the lead driver on the left front horse and another driver behind him on another horse while the gun carriage that contained the shells carried two men atop with the gun behind. In a battlefield situation moving the cannon from one place to another was hazardous, leaving the gun crews and their charges in the open most of the time, a prime target for shelling and they were at the mercy of German bombardments. For Ernest and his gun crew their time in England was fast coming to an end, for they would be shipped to the front the following day with their horses, carriage and gun . . . They decided to spend their last night in the local pub near to the barracks for their leave ended at 2000 hours. Inside the smoky bar Ernest had a pint of frothy beer and two darts in his left hand while in the other he had a single dart which he was about to launch at the dart board against the wall. Some of the other gunners of his regiment entered and sat themselves down at the bar counter. "A pint fer' each o' me mates, barkeep!" shouted one of the men.

"Righty ho' sport," answered the barkeep as he reached for some beer tankards under the counter. As he pulled the lever down to fill up a tankard one of the newcomers spotted Ernest. "Hey," he pointed to Ernest and tapped the bloke next to him on the shoulder, "He's too young to drink, ain't even eighteen yet . . ."

"Take the pint away from the young lad, barkeep, yonder lads a young un' . . ." said one of the men. Ernest threw his dart which hit the red bull in the center of the board. He turned to the men at the counter, "If that's the case how come I have one stripe on my arm and you have none Bertrand?" The men at the counter laughed. "Besides, if I'm old enough to fight in France," he threw another dart at the board, "I'm old enough to drink, isn't that right, Harry . . ."

"Too right, Ernest, would you like another?" asked the bar tender.

"Now, who's up for a game of *Round the Clock* boys?" added Ernest.

"You're too good for us, Ernest," spat William, one of the other gunners at the bar, "I'd hate to be the poor Hun that comes under fire from your gun in France . . ." he continued laughing and spitting half of the beer from his mouth out. Bertrand got up from the bar and grabbed hold of Ernest, "Time to toss the little bugger," he smiled mischievously.

"Not on yer' life mate," cried Ernest trying to slip past him. William slipped in front of him and blocked his path to freedom, "Not so fast me matey . . . wasn't so long ago you had your birthday so it's up in the air with you . . ."

A few of the other men surrounded him and threw him up towards the ceiling. "Mind the lamps you morons!" shouted Harry, the bar tender.

"One!" shouted all the men in the bar in unison . . . "Two!" they continued as they heaved the slight form of Ernest up again . . . Behind them others chorused, "Bumps! Bumps! Bumps!"

The shouts of joy and mayhem in the bar continued as a barrage of shells landed amid the British trenches in France at that same moment. The shouts of joy were overtaken by cries of pain as soldiers, torn asunder, tried to pick themselves up and face the German onslaught they knew would come . . . and then, there were those that couldn't rise, those that just lay there, ripped and pulled apart, broken and smashed bodies never to rise again . . . *For all the King's horses and all the King's men couldn't put Humpty Dumpty together again . . .*

\* \* \*

"Easy girl! Easy . . ." said Ernest as he led *Dolly* up a gangplank into the hold of a transport ship.

William, another gunner, shouted to Ernest, "You think more of the horses than you do of us!"

"If you had four legs and a tail I'd give you some sugar and an apple, Will," returned Ernest.

"Make that a beer and I'll neigh for you, Ernest . . ." joined in Bertrand.

Their regimental sergeant major, clambering up a ladder, shouted, "Enough talk you slackers, get the horses stowed away and get your sorry asses on deck for inspection, I'll not let a rabble like yourselves spoil the regiment's good name . . ."

"Yes, Sah!" piped up three voices.

As the sergeant turned to leave Bertrand said out the corner of his mouth, "I hope the Hun get him first . . ."

As the sergeant continued up to the next deck he spat out, "I heard that Bertrand . . . Don't worry though, I'll be at the front with you . . . and I'll be right behind you, just to make sure those Hun know where to aim . . ." Not being a man of great mirth, or any mirth for that matter, nary a smile crossed his lips, just a chilling comment as he departed, "You'll be laughing on the other side o' yer' face soon me boyo, it'll be no laughing matter when ye get to the front . . ."

Ernest led his charges into their respective stalls and got the horses settled in. The other three members of his gun crew had already departed topside to wave at the crowd of well-wishers on the dock. While cheerful soldiers waved goodbye and threw kisses to their loved ones Ernest reassured the horses down below, since no one he knew had come to bid him *Bon Voyage*, he preferred it that way. His mother and father had not been pleased with him when they found out he'd volunteered and joined up; for by the time they did it was too late . . . Stable lad, driver or gunner in charge of a gun crew, he was happy, he was where he always wanted to be, with the one thing he loved more than anything else in the world, the venerable horse . . .

He kissed *Dolly* on the nose gently and gave her an apple he had secreted in his pocket. If the other lads saw this, the ribbing would know no bounds and he would never hear the end of it . . . He felt the ship move away from the dock, he thought, *'Soon we will be in France and on our way to the front.'* He caressed *Dolly's* flanks, "I hope you'll be alright old girl," he said softly.

Back at the barracks he had a photograph taken with him atop *Dolly*; to Ernest it was worth more than all the gold and diamonds found in King Solomon's mines. Something to treasure for an eternity . . . The horses shifted uneasily as he went from stable to stable in the cramped confines of the hold. He looked affectionately at them, then said, "Don't worry, I'll do my best to look after all of you . . ."

\* \* \*

A bullet zipped over Jimmy O'Sullivan's helmet as he hunkered down in the sand on a beach somewhere in Turkey. "I'm running out of ammo," he shouted to the man next to him over the din of battle, "Have you any spare?" he continued.

The other soldier crouched down and opened an ammo box by him, "No, nothing, nothing in here either . . ." he answered. "I wonder when the supplies will come," noted Jimmy.

"Maybe never, I feel like we've been hung out to dry in this horrible place . . ." said the soldier.

"How's your food, got any bully beef for supper?" asked Jimmy.

"That's all you ever think about Jim," noted the soldier as artillery fire exploded just in front of them throwing up sand and soil and rocks which cascaded all over them. "We need to get off this damned beach before we're all killed . . ." commented Jimmy as he dusted some sand off his already soiled uniform.

"At least the place is hot," said the soldier taking aim with his Lee Enfield .303 and drawing in his breath. He squeezed off a round at a Turkish soldier he'd spotted, breathing out as he did so. The round hit its mark dropping the soldier in his tracks. "Good shot, Fred!" exclaimed Jimmy, smiling, "One less of the buggers . . ."

"Nearly down to my last round," said Fred.

"What do we do when we run out, throw rocks at them?" laughed Jimmy.

"Well, I presume that's what you do in Ireland, Jim. How good a shot are you?" added Fred.

Jim, ignoring the comment stuck his head up and called out loudly over the din of battle, "Anyone got any ammo, we're nearly out!"

Cries of, "None here, mate!" and, "Nor here!" were bandied down the roughly dug fox holes and trenches on the beach. "Brilliant, what next, surrender, that would be daft," mused Jimmy, more to himself than to Fred lying prone beside him. Fred looked at him, "I wonder what daft idiot put this mission together?"

"Take your pick, I'm sure there are plenty of them," piped in Jimmy rolling his eyes upwards.

"I sure could do with some more water; my canteen's nearly dry . . ." complained Fred.

"Mine too," said Jimmy shaking his head from side to side . . . "This is going to be a long hot dry day for us if we can't move up instead of being pinned here like butterflies to a board . . ." he noted. Jimmy looked down the beach to the shoreline and caught sight of a trawler offloading supplies . . . "Maybe we can have something nice to eat later on," he noted with a smile, "Looks like our supplies have arrived and we can move on . . ."

"I think they should print postcards with, 'Welcome to Sunny Gallipoli!' on them . . ." noted Fred with a broad smile squeezing off another round to celebrate the arrival of their supplies . . .

On the 22nd of November British troops reached Ctesiphon. Not having adequate forces to take the strongly prepared positions they retreated and by the 3rd of December what was left of the British force reached Kut al Amara. A five month siege ensued and the town was surrounded by four Turkish divisions. The Turkish commander, Nur-ed-Din, called for the surrender of the British. Major General Townshend, in charge of the forces, refused, this led to a heavy bombardment of the town by the Turks. With relief forces failing to break through because of severe flooding, Townshend, low on food and ammunition, had no option but to surrender or sign the death warrant of every man there . . .

* * *

On a muddy road somewhere in France Ernest and his gun crew were busy making final preparations before heading to the front. In the distance the loud reports of canon discharging shells filled the air followed not long afterward by even louder explosions as the shells hit the British lines. *Dolly* shifted uncomfortably as she stood next to the other horses. "Easy girl, there'll be plenty of that where we're going . . ." said Ernest, trying to comfort her.

Mud was everywhere as the road, jam packed with vehicles and men, going to and fro, filled every inch of the road. A line of injured men filed past the gun carriage and artillery piece. Ernest grimaced; half the men had bandages over their eyes and held onto the shoulder of the man in front. Some of the men had canes and were trying to keep pace with the injured, hobbling as fast as they could. Each man had a tag placed over their necks. Blood seeped from some of the bandages. Others had been burned badly. Still others had bullet wounds. Ernest looked down at the cinch as he tightened it, thinking, *'And those are the lucky ones . . .'* As an ambulance passed them Ernest finished with his checking and climbed up on *Dolly* glancing back at the carriage in front of his gun and the men atop it, unconsciously he fingered the Enfield revolver in a holster attached to his belt and made sure his bandolier was secure around his shoulder, just in case . . .

"Are you ready?" he said turning to the men.

"As ready as we'll ever be . . ." voiced a gunner sitting on the carriage in a somber and subdued tone. "Then we'd best be off . . ." said Ernest slapping his reins at *Dolly's* sides and setting the horse beside and those in front of the gun carriage off. As they made their way slowly through the mud each man took note of the wounded and the expressions they wore on their faces, horror and uncomprehending acceptance of their fate and what was to become of them after reaching the medical tent or hospital, or wherever they went for that matter. They didn't seem to care, they just plodded through the mud . . .

"I'd hate to end up like those poor buggers . . ." commented a gunner sitting on the carriage.

Ernest Chapman nodded in agreement and dug his heels into *Dolly's* flanks as the mud started to clog the wheels of their field gun and bog down the horses' hooves. With every foot of mud crossed the noise of the artillery bombardment got louder and louder becoming a deafening roar that set the horses nerves on edge. The men on the carriage shifted uneasily, for them too it was the first time in actual combat, not some training exercise, for this, was the real thing . . . The thunder at the front caused the ground to shake beneath the wheels of the carriage as the wounded still filed past. Ernest's stomach began to sink; this was the real face of war, the stink of explosives and the stench of death following the men filing past . . . and, willingly, he had volunteered for it . . . At the back of his mind he wondered how long it would be before they ended up like these poor souls, if indeed they survived at all . . .

\* \* \*

A line of soldiers marched toward the sound of artillery fire and shells detonating in the distance, they sang, *"We're here, because we're here, because we're here . . ."* to the tune of Auld Lang Syne . . . it was a marching song that reflected the utter pointlessness of what was happening around them and what they would be thrown into within a short period of time. The men had resigned themselves to whatever fate threw at them, life or death, it was all the same . . . The war had reigned supreme, with the battles of Mons, Marne and Ypres leaving thousands and thousands of men dead on the fields of battle. When the whistle blew a soldier had two choices, go over the top and face the burning red hot shells fired at them by the Germans, or, prepare to be shot by a British officer for cowardice if they refused the order to attack and place oneself at the fore in the heat of battle . . . even if a soldier seemed to hesitate at the urgings of an officer the result would be the same–a bullet! Summary executions were held in front of troops as a lesson to those who entertained thoughts of leaving the field of battle. Even officers were not immune to such treatment. Sub-Lieutenant Edwin Dyett was found in a dazed state wandering behind the lines just after the Ancre offensive. On the 5th of January 1917 he was shot for cowardice by a naval firing squad. The true nature of the conflict was soon realized by the men who faced the murderous onslaught of the Hun and this new way of solving political arguments and spats. Patriotism was fast becoming a thing of the past, and with each year the war raged volunteers became scarcer. In the first three weeks of the Dardanelles campaign there were 40,000 British casualties. On the Western Front men dropped like flies in front of German machine guns. Officers were now in short supply as they too fell facing the Hun in ill-conceived charges from their entrenched positions . . . And as chlorine and mustard gas preceded the attacks by the Hun, blinded men made long lines from the front to medical stations . . . It was a brutal war and a brutal foe the British soldiers faced as the roar of 600 artillery pieces fired on them all at once ripping the very soil away from beneath their feet . . . But, the new recruits kept coming bringing fresh meat to the slaughter, and lines of troops sang out in happy tune,

*"It's a long way to Tipperary,*
*It's a long way to go,*
*It's a long way to Tipperary to the sweetest girl I know,*

*Goodbye Piccadilly, farewell Leicester Square,*
*for my heart is still there . . ."*
. . . for they knew not what was in store for them . . .

* * *

Guns thundered from behind the British positions as tinker, tailor, soldier and candlestick maker prepared themselves. They stood by long ladders leading to the tops of their trenches and the barren flattened and shell pockmarked land that lay without. "Ready lads!" cried an officer with his revolver drawn as the shelling stopped as suddenly as it began. Whistles blew and men with bayonets attached to their rifles poured over the top of the trench. The officers led the charge over barbed wire, broken shattered trees and shell holes littering the ground in front of them. Immediately to the fore of them lay the German lines and their machine-gun fire. In front of the British soldiers cries of "Achtung!" broke the relative silence of the Western Front as Hun guns sounded out a deadly chatter. Men fell in mid-stride and crumpled to the ground, pieces of flesh and bone were trampled underfoot as British troops tried desperately to get to the German positions. Men hung entwined in the deathly grip of barbed wire jiggling like so many puppets on strings manipulated by an unseen puppet master as bullets ripped their flesh apart piece by piece. Gradually the men were pushed back as so many were cut down and slaughtered by the machine gun fire. It seemed pointless to Albert as the remnants retreated back to their trenches. Gunfire raked those that were left on the field of battle above as the pain filled cries of friend and compatriot filled no-man's land. As night began to fall, the injured and dying men cried out, "Water! Water!" as they lay in the mud cut to pieces with their life's blood slowly oozing from wounds inflicted by a merciless foe. It was all too much for Albert as he sat on a wooden box trying to eat something in an effort to keep up his strength. He held his hands over his ears in an attempt to block out the plaintive soulful cries, but it didn't work. Albert made up his mind to do something about it, he climbed up a ladder and was about to climb over into no-man's land when burly hands pulled him back . . . "You can't do that, Albert, the Hun will finish you off for sure!"

"We can't leave those poor buggers out there like that," cried Albert, his voice full of pain and disgust. "Nothing we can do about it, orders is orders . . ." replied one of the soldiers. "Take it up with the sergeant if you want to . . ." noted another soldier jerking his thumb towards the three-striper sitting on a crate and probing into a can of bully beef. Before Albert could do anything hundreds of German artillery pieces started to rain death from above onto their positions cutting any thought out of mind save life's own preservation . . . The ground rocked and men dived for scant cover. Some men were not so lucky as their body parts littered what was left of the French countryside, and as the shells stopped falling on Allied positions another and more ominous threat wafted their way – Mustard Gas!

A soldier cried out, "GAS!" and every soldier fumbled for his gas mask, putting it on as quickly as they could. Those that were slow or did not have them at hand writhed in the mud whence they found themselves, screaming in pain as Germans reached the British trenches . . . In short order Albert donned his gas mask and found himself confronted with a foe he had never come face to face with . . . Fighting for his life and the life of the man next to him he emptied the contents of his clip at the Hun now in their midst. When his Lee Enfield was empty and there was no room to wield rifle and bayonet he reached for the trench knife stuck in his belt to continue fighting for both his and his compatriots' lives . . . There was no fair play and no sense of patriotism compelling him, just the survival of both he and his friends around him in the muddy rat filled trench they found themselves quartered in . . . The fight was short and bloody leaving Albert standing over the prostrate forms of his square helmeted foe; the Hun finding the British soldiers no mere pushovers. There was no celebration and no well done lad as he once more sat down and attempted to eat the bully beef in the can he had found discarded in the muddy trench as the cries of the dead and dying called out to his very soul . . .

\* \* \*

Ernest was exceptionally proud to be in the Royal Field Artillery and when he and his gun crew first tasted the heat of battle he soon realized how ill-equipped the British forces were compared to the Germans, but then, they had been long preparing for this conflict. He felt sorrow for the dead British and French soldiers they found at the front gripping their old fashioned rifles in lifeless hands. He pitied their families and loved ones. He could do nothing for them as there were so many. They littered the ground about as though so much flotsam on a restless sea. The stench of rotting corpses filled the air as they set up their gun time and time again. His sense of decency cried out from the depths of his being, crying, *'Bury them! Bury them!'* but he and his men could do naught as shell fire rained down on them while they manhandled their artillery piece into position at the front line and loaded it, all the while German shells exploded about filling the air with the rancid scent of gunpowder. Ernest and his crew fired at the German positions until their ammunition was finished and not one shell remained. Shouted orders by officers went unheard, for over the roar of their artillery piece German shells pounded them with regularity . . . The sound of shell and gunfire resonated over the battlefield in a continuous onslaught of the senses leaving both Ernest and his gun crew deaf to all save the Hun shells that pounded French soil close by . . . but it was the scent of death and the rotting sweet corpses that troubled the young man more than anything else . . . He felt the pain they had experienced and their final moments of life on these stark and desolate blood soaked fields of what was once barley and wheat . . .

\* \* \*

Once again the whistles blew and Albert climbed up a ladder to reach the top of the trench and the German guns beyond. His legs felt leaden and tired as he screamed at the top of his voice trying to give courage to himself and the others around him. The British soldiers charged over the rough shell pocked ground as bullets zipped past and mortars exploded all around them. A Hun bullet hit his leg causing him to tumble to the ground. Another round from a machine gun hit him in the side, then, another found its mark on his now bleeding body. Albert lay in the mud as men charged past him only to be blown apart by mortar fire or torn asunder by machine gun fire. The call for retreat sent the men back to the cover of the trenches running helter-skelter dodging bullets and bombs. Little pieces of earth were thrown into the air as the men reached the safety of the trenches . . . All that is except Albert and other poor unfortunate souls from his unit, he tried to reach out for them as they passed him by but he remained unnoticed by all save death . . . His mouth became uncommonly dry as he tried to call out but no words escaped his lips . . . Finally he forced out a croak that was barely discernable to him let alone anyone else . . . As his life's blood seeped away Albert pulled out a letter from his sweetheart, he convulsed as he held the letter in a bloody hand trying to open it one last time . . . From high above the scream of an artillery shell filled the air around him . . . As Albert's soul drifted away he dreamt of the life he could have had with his sweetheart who waited for his return in England – and, nearby, his comrades in arms lay dead, not on a field of valor but on a field of ignominy . . .

\* \* \*

It normally took the gun carriage twenty minutes to reach the front line, but this time Ernest had guided the horses this and that way as shells rained from the heavens above on them. The road erupted constantly with percussive force frightening the horses and sending the gun carriage off the road, if one could call it that. In the end Ernest struggled to stay on the back of *Dolly* as shells rained down upon them. And through it all he guided the gun carriage behind him, entreating the men behind to stay the course and not be fazed by the bombardment. As they continued towards the front line the scream of a shell filled the air above – the scream of the shell grew and grew and the men on the carriage bowed their heads all praying that this one wouldn't be the last they ever heard . . . 'KABOOM!' The blast blew Ernest off *Dolly* sending him flying and knocking the other three horses down – Dazed, Ernest looked up from the ground where he lay. His ears and nose were bleeding; there was a constant ringing and buzzing in his head coming from his ears. He felt his forehead which was covered in a red stickiness that was trickling down his face into his eyes. Through the haze he now inhabited he saw the shattered remains of both gun and carriage. His men were nowhere to be seen as he struggled to stand, he looked at his left hand which was in pain, it hung on shreds and pieces of sinew and flesh, nearly severed from his arm by shrapnel. He grimaced as he unhitched the horses from the shattered remains of the gun carriage with his right hand as shell after shell continued to explode all around them. All about carnage ruled with an air of indifference. Holding onto the leather straps he led them into a gulley whence they would be spared the constant explosions and searing heat of German shells. As he tried to settle them he heard cries of pain above and dragged himself up the steep sides. Some way away he caught sight of his men who had been thrown away from carriage and gun. While shells exploded around him, sending French soil erupting skywards, Ernest struggled to the men's sides. One was surely dead, of that he had no doubt, unless of course it was possible for him to live without a head. Of the other two only one was conscious. He dragged both, one at a time to the gulley and collapsed as he tried to keep his hand from falling off . . . His last conscious thought for some time was that of *Dolly* nuzzling his face trying to awaken him . . . When at last he came to he just lay where he was not knowing what to do, for he knew not even where he was . . . After two hours of pain and recrimination a soldier bearing a Red Cross insignia on his arm slipped down into the gulley . . . Ernest could just remember being dragged to safety by the man as he slipped in and out of consciousness from blood loss and the injury to his head . . .

\* \* \*

Many leagues away in an Eastern country James O'Sullivan, formally a British soldier and combatant, now sat behind barbed wire in a Turkish prison camp. He stared out through the wire yearning for his freedom, for no more could he sit and wait for the scraps of food proffered by his captors to the prisoners, no more did he wish to suffer in silence and feel the vicious kicks and beatings from his captors, no, no more . . . Others who escaped and had been brought back had their throats slit in front of the other prisoners as an example of what lay in wait for those wishing ill-conceived freedom. With that in mind, Jimmy, as everyone called him, planned his escape . . . With what little in the way of water and food Jimmy O'Sullivan could find, he picked an opportune moment, avoiding detection he climbed the barbed wire fence and bolted off into the night to rejoin the fight against an evil empire to be . . . Jimmy put as much distance as he could between him and his ex-captors, and as dawn neared he spotted a tree, it was big and tall enough for him to escape detection so he quickly climbed up it. For two days and nights Jimmy stayed up in the tree as Turkish soldiers searched below for him . . . When at last they left to search another area Jimmy breathed a sigh of relief and climbed down. His first priority was to find a stream and fill his bottle with the precious water; since his water bottle was as dry as a bone . . . Avoiding his Turkish captors he made his way to the coast. It was early morning when the salty scent of the Mediterranean filled his nostrils way before he arrived at the crossroads between sea and sand. He breathed a sigh of relief and found a place to hide in enemy territory until evening. When night came the starry sky above spread out like a coverlet calming his restless heart; steeling himself the young soldier set out northwards along the beach. After travelling several miles he came across an abandoned boat. Taking charge of the fishing boat Jimmy pushed it into the water and rowed far out to sea in the direction of Greece . . .

The Sun beat down mercilessly upon the Irishman as Jimmy pulled back on the oars, it had been three days and nights now with not another boat or soul in sight. He wondered what would happen to him if a ship failed to appear. Pulling back on the oars Jimmy laughed to himself and voiced loudly, "Then I shall row all the bloody way back to England!"

With rations and water now finished a dry mouthed Jimmy O'Sullivan just rowed and rowed and rowed, until on the seventh day he heard a hooting. Forcing his head up Jimmy peered into the distance and spied a ship, a destroyer with a Royal Navy ensign proudly fluttering in the wind at its stern . . . Standing up Jimmy waved his arms back and forth, but his efforts and dry mouthed shouts were not necessary for the crew of the British destroyer had seen him through their glasses and had no intention of leaving the disheveled man with a beard and torn British uniform to the mercy of sea, storm and sun . . . *let alone the vicious Turks . . .*

* * *

At Etaples Ernest lay on a stretcher with a ticket on his chest in a Red Cross hospital. "When can I go back to the front?" Ernest asked the doctor quite seriously. "Never!" the doctor replied looking at Ernest's shrapnel wounds and his nearly severed hand. "You'll be on the next ship to Blightly, so consider yourself lucky. By all accounts you should be dead . . ."

Ernest took a second to digest the doctor's comment, then said, "Is my horse *Dolly* alright, I need to get back to the front to get her . . ."

"You are going nowhere," said the doctor checking the dressings on Ernest's head and his pulse.

Ernest looked away as he continued his examination. "You nearly lost your hand, normally we would have just cut it off but we're going to leave it on for the time being and let the doctors in the hospital at London decide. They will try to save it if they can, they are doing wonderful things there I hear . . ." Then the doctor added, "As I said, consider yourself very fortunate. I understand the shell killed one of your men outright and badly injured the other two. We managed to save one of them. So, as I said, consider yourself lucky to be alive . . ."

As the doctor walked to the next bed Ernest just lay still looking up at the fan in the ceiling. His hand was all bandaged up and pained him terribly. A nurse walked past him, he called out to her, "Nurse, do you have anything for the pain, my hand is awfully sore . . ."

The nurse walked over to the doctor and spoke to him, he nodded and she strode over to a medicine cabinet and pulled out a syringe and a small bottle of morphine . . . Withdrawing the liquid she walked back to Ernest and injected it into his arm . . . Ernest stared at the ceiling as he grew drowsy and eventually slipped into a deep sleep . . .

\* \* \*

Lying in a hospital bed in London, Ernest contemplated the ceiling above, the doctors had saved his hand by stitching the veins, muscles, nerves and tendons back together again. It was groundbreaking work and the surgery had been long, but well worth it, for now, Ernest would not have to go through life missing a hand. It was true that he would have to have his hand strapped to a board for a long time, probably months, but that was better than losing it. A pretty dark haired Irish nurse was tending to his other wounds and changing his bandages. His arm was uncomfortable being strapped to the board which prevented him from moving it much if at all. "How long must it be like this?" he asked her. "A couple of years the doctor says . . ." answered the young and beautiful dark haired nurse. Ernest gulped but then smiled, and thought, *yes, things could be worse.* He looked into her eyes and said, "Excuse me, but what is your name?"

"Elizabeth O'Sullivan," responded the nurse returning his smile. She walked over to the nurses' station and pulled out some medicine. Another nurse came over to her and spoke to her, as they stood there they both glanced over at Ernest and giggled a little. Ernest turned away and thought, *'I hope it wasn't something I said . . .'*

* * *

Ernest spent a long time in the hospital, a very long time as his wrist and injuries slowly healed, and with the passing of each day he grew more in love with the pretty dark haired nurse, and so had she for him, for she returned his affections with equal intensity and would sit next to him during the night when the ward was quiet reading the newspapers telling of the war in Europe, Turkey and East Africa. In a world of turmoil they had found something to cling to, the love of each other. And as Ernest grew stronger he was able to get out of bed and walk with her to the garden outside where they would sit holding hands on a bench and contemplate everything but the war. Ernest had never forgotten *Dolly* though and it was his sincerest wish to get better and search for her at the front, even if that meant getting fit enough to join his unit once again. While sitting together in the garden one day Elizabeth said to Ernest, "I know you have strong feelings for me Ernest, but who is *Dolly*?"

Ernest looked shocked and replied, "Where did you hear that name?"

Elizabeth wore a somber expression on her face, "When you are asleep you say her name all the time . . ." then she added, "is she your sweetheart?"

Ernest laughed which caused even more pain within Elizabeth's chest, "No, nothing like that, she's my horse, my special woman, a mare, I looked after her ever since I joined up . . ." he looked into her eyes and said apologetically, "You have nothing to worry about, besides, she's probably dead by now, horses don't last long on the front . . ."

Ernest gazed up at the white clouds and blue sky above, mumbling, "Yes . . . she is probably dead by now," his eyes watered, "it is truly the worse place on Earth at the moment, France . . ."

As days turned to months Ernest and Elizabeth fell more and more in love with each other until one bright day, as the pair sat on the bench Ernest got down on one knee and asked her, "Will you do the honor of marrying me, Elizabeth?" He took a ring out of his pocket and slipped it on her finger. Elizabeth stared at the ring then up to the window of the ward where Ernest had his bed. The other nurses stood at the windows craning their necks trying to see the proposal and Elizabeth's reaction. "Of course, Ernest, I would love to . . ." With those words she cupped Ernest's face in her hands and kissed him on the lips . . .

* * *

Ernest Andrew Chapman and Elizabeth O'Sullivan got married in Bow church, London. Ernest and his friends and comrades were all in their regimental military uniform and it was a fine affair with Elizabeth's family and friends all there . . . The war on the Western Front and all hostilities ended on the 11th of November 1918 with an armistice between the Central Powers of Europe, Germany and the Allied Forces . . .

Ernest was now a married man and had responsibilities to his new wife and the Great Eastern Railways, soon to be the London North Eastern Railways, where he worked, but inside he felt pain, a pain that never left him, not the constant pain of his stiff wrist, about which he never complained, but one that left him with nightmares and cold sweats during the middle of the night . . . and as the days passed he became more and more restless, until one day he left work early and went to his old regimental barracks in the hope of seeing an old friend . . .

"I'm looking for my horse?" said Ernest to a sergeant on duty that he had never come across before.

The sergeant smiled apologetically, "Sorry, can't help you . . . there are so many of them and I'm rather busy right now . . ."

The sergeant didn't seem to be the least bit interested in what Ernest had to say when he opened his mouth . . . he just looked down at the paperwork on the desk in front of him and ignored the man standing in front of him. Ernest turned dejectedly and walked outside. As he headed back to the entrance a stable lad walked past leading a noble looking steed. Ernest smiled at him, and then asked, "Do you have a horse here by the name of *Dolly*?"

The lad gave him a quizzical look, "Funny you should ask that, we have a horse from the front by that name . . ."

"May I see her," said Ernest with excitement.

"Sure thing guv'nor, don't see if'n it'll do no harm . . ." with those words he led Ernest to the stables and pointed to the horse called *Dolly* in a stall at the back. "Probably not the one you're looking for, not many came back, but she's over there, so go take a gander . . ."

Ernest walked slowly through the familiar stable to the back of the building, and as his feet trod softly over the cobbles a familiar whinnying came to his ears and a familiar face greeted him from over a stall's wooden supports–*Dolly*!

Ernest's heart was beating quickly and he felt a sense of finality to all the pain he had experienced on the front when he got to her stable and took *Dolly's* head in his hands and kissed her on the nose. He then pulled something out of his back pocket as she nuzzled him–an apple–

As Ernest stroked *Dolly's* nose he thought of Albert, his comrades in arms and those thousands and thousands of men who had lost their lives. Ernest struggled to hold back the tears as a song came to mind, one that he and his men would sing as they headed to the front to set up their artillery gun, he choked out the song,

> *"Pack up your troubles in your old kit bag,*
> *And smile, smile, smile,*
> *What's the use of worrying as it never was worthwhile,*
> *So pack up your troubles in your old kit*
> *bag and smile, smile, smile . . ."*

So many good men lost their lives in pointless scrambles for mere feet consisting of nothing but mud in France and Belgium during the Great War. Amongst them were many extended family members of the Chapman's . . . Albert Chapman, born in King's Lyn, joined up in Norwich and became a corporal in the 8th Battalion Norfolk Regiment. He led many patrols into no-man's land to the German trenches and was awarded the DCM for his bravery and intelligence. He never made it back and was killed in the line of duty against the Hun on the 26th of September 1916 . . . Some families lost one son, some two, some three sons out of four . . . and other families lost every male member lying in the trenches where they died under fields of poppies . . . 18 million souls lost their lives and 23 million were wounded. But the figures alone cannot describe the carnage that had ensued on the battlefields of Europe and other parts of the world. So many had died in agonizing pain, sacrificed on the pyre of international angst and vanity . . .

But, duty is duty . . . Corporal/Driver/Gunner Ernest Andrew Chapman, #L/29187, was with 34 Division from its landing in France in January 1916 and through till the war's end. He initially served with Divisional Ammunition Column before joining 176 Brigade RFA for a short period and then 160 Brigade RFA. The London Gazette published on the 23rd of February 1918, Supplement 30540, page 2414, posted that, 'His Majesty the KING has been graciously pleased to confer the Military Medal for Bravery in the Field to Dvr. Ernest Andrew Chapman (Wigston) for Bravery in battle, for conspicuous acts of gallantry and devotion to duty under fire . . .'

Pvt. Albert Chapman, #SR/144947, joined on the 1st of November 1915 and was assigned to the Royal Army Service Corps ending up in the bakery. He requested a transfer to a front line unit and was given a new service number, #38158, with a new enlistment date of June 1917. When his division arrived in France they mustered at the Infantry Base Depot on the 17th of June 1917 and were transferred to the Gloucestershire Regiment, 1st Battalion, joining them in the field on the 18th of June 1917 . . . Pvt. Albert Chapman was killed in action on the 15th of September 1918 near grid reference: 62c, R.35.b.7.7 where he was buried. After hostilities had ended his body was exhumed and transferred to Savy British Cemetery in Aisne, France, where he lies to this day . . .

Pvt. James O'Sullivan, #6665, 1st Royal Munster Fusiliers, was with 29th Division, 86th Brigade in Gallipoli. He was born on the 17th August 1895 at number 12 Mary Street, Cork, County Cork. Group Registration number #9859270. The 1901 Census records the O'Sullivans were at number 2 Cove Street, Cork, and in the 1911 Irish Census the O'Sullivans were resident at Tyrone Place, Cork, with a now burgeoning family. Jeremiah and Maria O'Sullivan were both 40 years of age, James was 15 yrs, John 13 yrs, Elizabeth 11 yrs, Ellen May 9 yrs and Mary Josephine 4 years old. All the children were born in Cork City. Sometime afterwards they moved to London . . . James had no doubt in his mind he would return home, his father, Jeremiah, would always say, "James has the luck of the Irish . . . of course he'll come back!"

# Chapter 2

## Our family

Long ago in the mists of time mum's family, the O'Sullivans, were once called Sulliban. The Sulliban chiefs ruled Cork and the surrounding areas. As the sands of time marched forward the power of the Sullibans waned and the warriors of the clan turned to growing crops and animal husbandry, and, of course, fishing, which has always been a staple in Ireland. Famine, war and strife, and the English invasion reduced a once proud war-like clan to tenant farmers, laborers and fishermen. The land they once owned was taken forcibly from them by Cromwell and his army in a frenzy of bloodletting. There were those that fought and died and those that left seeking greener pastures away from the Emerald Isles, never to return. My mother's father, Jeremiah O'Sullivan, had been a farmer in Ireland and was born in County Cork along with my grandmother. They lived in a croft, a one roomed stone building, but had run into financial difficulties due to poor harvests and the potato famine. The land they tilled had been taken over by so-called royalty. With no harvest, no potatoes and no money to pay for the land on which they lived the landed gentry came and knocked down the croft forcing them off the land. They had few avenues open to them, either fight the self-imposed overlords or move to England or the United States. Of course they could have stayed and died of starvation with their children or been put up against a wall and shot as so many were for standing up for their birthright and historical ownership of the land. My mother kept her pride and sorrow carefully hidden but even so she retained a fierce resentment of what the English had done to Ireland, and even though she married an Englishman the hurt still remained . . . In the 19th century there was a certain landowner in Ireland called Boycott and it was there that the term boycott first came into the English language after tenant farmers refused to pay Mr. Boycott, or get off the land, during the potato famine. They stayed where they were much to the chagrin of those holding sway over large stretches of the Emerald Isles incurring the wrath of those in power . . .

\* \* \*

My father's forebears certainly had a tale to tell starting at the time of Arturius and his knights around 480 – 537 AD battling the invading Saxons, to the time of the Knights Templar 840 years later fighting the Mameluke hordes to secure Jerusalem from the Moslems and to protect the routes of Christian pilgrims from bandits and barbarians. In the passage of time all I have are tales and bedtime stories passed down in oral tradition from generation to generation, some original names of the principle characters have parted from my memory and disappeared into the firmament from the lips of our ancestors over the intervening centuries. Part of our family branch of the Chapman clan had moved down from Scotland over two hundred years before and one of my great grandparents was from Denmark, but that is another story . . . The very old rendition of our surname is *Chaucer* which is the archaic form of Chapman used hundreds of years ago. Chapman was a freeman, a merchant, a trader, a person who bought and sold goods and travelled widely around Briton . . .

\* \* \*

My mother was born in Cork in the year 1899 on the 10th of October at number 2 Cove Street to Maria and Jeremiah O'Sullivan. Maria's family name was Atkinson. My father was born in Suffolk on the 15th of February just before the new century. My parents had five boys in all. Ernest was the oldest being born in February of 1921, James Edward, or Jimmy as we always called him, was born on November the 11th 1922, and I was born on November 30th 1924 and given the name Stanley William Chapman. We three arrived borne by storks to No: 52 Colegrave Road in Leytonstone, Essex. Edward, or Teddy, as we renamed him, arrived in the month of May in the 1930's. While Alfred, my youngest brother, referred to as Alfie by the family, came by way of a stork in June of 1936 when we lived at No: 352 Becontree Avenue, Dagenham in Essex . . . We went to Colegrave Road Infants School, Grafton Road Infants School and Loxford Central School all in Ilford, Essex. We lived at No: 52 Colegrave Road, Leytonstone; No: 352 Becontree Avenue, Dagenham; No: 116 Richmond Road, Ilford, and No: 1 Meath Road, Ilford, all in Essex. When war was declared in 1939 we were still at No: 1 Meath Road in Ilford.

My earliest memory was that of my mother singing me a lullaby in my cot as I would look out the cold misty window at the man lighting the gas street lamps without in the darkness while I held on tightly to my Teddy bear. Her voice was calming and reassuring, she would sing:

> *"If you ever go across the sea to Ireland,*
> *it may be at the closing of my days,*
> *just to see the ripple of a trout stream,*
> *and watch the sun go down in Galway Bay.*
> *Too-ra, too-ra, too-ra,*
> *Too-ra, too-ra, lay,*
> *Hush now go to sleep now . . .*
> *Too-ra, too-ra, too-ra,*
> *Too-ra, too-ra, lay.*
> *Hush now go to sleep now . . ."*

When I was little I looked the splitting image of 'Bubbles', a character immortalized in both drawings and paintings distributed around the globe. I had the same buttoned emerald green velvet jacket and shorts with black chrome highly polished shoes with two silver buckles on them. I had matching emerald green socks with white tops and white silk shirts with ruffled collar and cuffs which turned back over the ends of my sleeves. My mother was very proud of her children and always wanted the best for the family. One day I had my photograph taken in front of a scaled down steam engine, also emerald green with a touch of blue adorning the boiler. My mother was really proud of that, just as she was of the picture of my father on his horse called *Dolly* taken during the First World War. That picture in his military riding attire and riding boots always graced pride of place in our living room, that and his boots, cap and riding crop. My father was a very proud man and took great pride in his achievements during the Great War. The fact that he even survived is testament to his courage and fortitude after being blown off his horse and nearly having his whole hand ripped off. It used to bother him a bit during winter and he never quite got full mobility of his wrist, but he was fortunate to have it at all. To me dad was a war hero first, a locomotive engineer second and a long distance runner third, even though he won many races and was treated with the utmost respect in his running club. One of my father's brothers, Uncle Albert, hadn't been so lucky, he never made it back from France, dying a heroes death in the trenches cut down in his prime by German guns . . .

My grandfather on my mother's side, James O'Sullivan, since no one called him Jeremiah, said I reminded him of the laughing cavalier, a picture at that time that was also distributed around the world. He would say I would end up as chief judge in County Cork and be the savior of all the O'Sullivans, this he would say oft with a jug of ale in his hand. Times were hard in the 20s and 30s; Mother had the vision of where we were going, she wanted a beautiful house in a decent area and for her children to all have a good life. We moved five times because of our burgeoning and growing family and each time it would be to a better area and a bigger house, all except once, mother hated that one house, and being rather psychic she felt it had too much of an unseen presence in it, we only stayed there a week before mum found a better home for us. And every house we moved into mum would have it scrubbed from top to bottom with Life Buoy soap, with the windows spotlessly cleaned. She took pride in our appearance and pride in her home making improvements wherever she could. Dad let her do what she wanted, he would put his feet up at the end of the day and close his eyes; he worked hard and deserved a break at day's end. My Uncle Jim bought a house in Wembly, Uncle Dan bought one in London, but dad wasn't so interested in houses or anything related to them since he was so focused on his work as an engineer, it was in his blood, for without a huge iron locomotive monster belching out steam under his control life just wasn't life to him. He really enjoyed what he was doing. All the locomotive engineers that I met were all exactly the same. It was a calling few attained and required a certain stick-to-it-ness of character . . .

My Aunt Margaret never married but looked after Granma O'Sullivan. My Uncle John was a hard worker and brother of my Aunt Ester who was a beautiful young lady. I remember her putting me on her knee and saying to my mother, "He's going to be a king one day." Aunt Ester died tragically of pneumonia at the young age of 26. Mum was with her in hospital when it happened one summer's day. Mum said when she passed away the curtains next to her bed fluttered open. There was no wind or breeze of any sort just Ester's spirit leaving, mum said . . . As time went by my Aunt Mary had to rely on my mother for food and other things, she had seven children, and as I said, times were tough back then. Her girls were called Marie, Violet, Jessie and Doreen. Then there was Michael and Martin. One of her boys, John, lost his eye playing cricket in Letchworth. One of

Aunt Mary's sons had to be placed in Dr. Banardo's, a children's home and was sent to New Zealand. I met him before he went when we lived in Dagenham . . .

Mother would send her little son, Stanley, to the pawnbroker shop down the road with her wedding ring for money to cover any housekeeping shortfall during the month. She would always give me the money at the end of the month to get it back. The little Jewish proprietor of the store would always smile at me and give me a sweet, a sticky bun or something. He would always greet me pleasantly, with, "Hello Stanley, how is your mother today?" Issy was short, with a grey ring of hair and wore a waistcoat like my father with his watch hanging on a chain slipped into his pocket. He would have his reading glasses hanging around his neck with what I referred to as a rope, at which my two older brothers would always laugh. One day I hid behind my mother holding onto her skirt as she walked into the store. Issy asked, "Where's Stanley today?" I pulled mum's skirt to one side and peaked at him from behind it. He said, "I know what you want . . ." He put his hand into a jar full of sweets on the counter and pulled some out then handed them to me. "Is that what you want, Stanley?" I nodded my head and smiled . . . Issy liked my company and treated me like a family member, I reminded him of his son when he was young, and he would put me on a stool to watch while he took care of his clients. Many times mummy would come in and say, "Stanley, is this where you've been all this time?" I would nod my head and try to hide a sticky bun behind my back . . . Times were harsh and work was scarce, Aunt Mary had little option but to rely on her relatives to put food on the table. It was hard on my mother but she did what she had to do with a smile on her face.

Grandmother Maria and Grandfather Jeremiah O'Sullivan were both from County Cork. My mother's father loved birds and animals, building an aviary out of a window on the third floor of his tenement building. He lived for his birds and raced his pigeons come hell or high water, snow or storm. He died, still young, catching pneumonia in the course of looking after his doves and pigeons. He and my Grandmother O'Sullivan had five children, my mother Elizabeth O'Sullivan, Aunt Ester, Aunt Mary, Uncle Dan and Uncle Jim who served in the army during the First World War like my father. But he was captured by the Turks during the battle for Turkey. He managed to escape from them and climbed up a huge tree, he stayed up there eating, sleeping and drinking what sparse rations he had on him. Eventually the Turks gave up searching for him and left the area. Making his way to the coast he stole a small boat and rowed out into the Mediterranean heading up the coast to Greece and the Greek islands, after a week when far out to sea he was picked up by a British destroyer operating in the Med. Uncle Jim was also a good artist, his son took after him and was commissioned to produce both murals and oil paintings around London before WWII.

Grandmother Maria O'Sullivan remarried to Grandfather Daniel Coughlin and had two children, Margaret & Daniel. Uncle John's pastime was going to the dogs, he loved betting on them. He never lost and always had cash in his pockets since he had a good eye for spotting the winners. Like Uncle Dan he made a success out of becoming a scrap merchant. Uncle Dan started out with a cart, then a donkey and cart in the 20s, then a horse and cart. Dan eventually ended up with a fleet of trucks. He even said to my mother, "Elizabeth, you have five sons, so why don't you let Stanley come and live with us?"

Uncle Dan had two small daughters; they always invited me over to their home in Leytonstone High Road. Their house was much bigger than ours. Pamela was my favorite cousin; she was fair headed just like her mother who was very Scandinavian in appearance. Both daughters were so much like their mum with blonde fair hair and Nordic looks. Their house wasn't far from ours in Colegrave Road, and when we moved Uncle Dan was upset the most since my mother was his favorite sister out of the four. When I did visit on my bike when I was older they always wanted me to stay longer, especially during our school holidays.

My Aunt Margaret had very dark hair and looked like the schoolteacher she was. Both she and Uncle John lived with grandmamma. When I visited I would love the sound of grandmother's chiming clock on the mantle. Aunt Mary lived in the same tenement building on the 4th floor. The building was blown up during the Blitz, but Grandma O'Sullivan had died before the war started. My cousin Marie was badly injured in that bomb blast and had her nose nearly completely blown off, the surgeons at the time used the breast bone of a bird to reconstruct it. They stayed with my mum in Buntingford for a while after their tenement building was destroyed.

Uncle Percy O'Sullivan, Aunt Mary's husband, had been to Canada working on the Canadian Pacific Railways, cutting through mountains, building tunnels and bridges. During the excavation of one mountain dynamite and nitroglycerin charges were set nearly bringing the whole mountain down on the men. Uncle Percy dug and pulled himself out of the rocks minus one eye. After that incident he had to wear a patch for the rest of his life. His pride and joy was his handlebar moustache which he use to twirl at the ends like an old fashioned soldier in the King's Grenadiers . . . The O'Sullivans are a tough lot and not even a whole mountain managed to kill Percy, but the German bombs . . . that is another story . . .

It wasn't only Aunt Mary who needed help at that time, our extended family knew that mummy would help if they were in a bind and needed food or money. Our family always did its best to assist one another. Because we had a house and my father had a good job with the railways we were viewed as well off in those days. We never lacked for food, mum was way too good a homemaker for that, she would go down Sugar House Lane picking up bargains at the food and fruit stalls. There was one place that made beautiful fruit and mince pies, the size of a side plate. They were three pence each. When the war started and rationing started to bite the price jumped up to 6d, six pence. One day when I was three I became so engrossed with the different wares on offer that I slipped away from mummy. The aromas from freshly made mince pies, mashed potatoes, pork and beef pies that would melt in your mouth and animals from way off places, it was like Aladdin's cave to me. I wandered down the two isles that stretched down on both sides of Sugar Hill Lane not realizing I had lost my mummy in the process. On the other hand my mother was panic stricken running around everywhere trying to find her young boy. I didn't know what to do so I headed home without her. While mummy was searching for me she met Mrs. Crouch who said she had seen me sitting on the doorstep to our house. She told mum she'd asked me where she was and said I'd pointed down the street towards the corner where Sugar Hill Lane was. She said, "If I'd known you were halfway down the lane I would have taken him with me."

When mummy came home I was next door with our neighbor having tea and cake. I, at least, was a happy young lad. Then, on the other hand, my mum was ecstatic that I was safe . . .

When I visited Grandmamma O'Sullivan as a young boy Uncle John would take me to the dog races which started at about 4:30 pm and go on till 11:00 pm. Granma would complain about him keeping me out so late but I didn't mind, he would always carry me on his shoulders until we got back home.

My father originally came from Saxmundham and Leiston in Suffolk, the two villages were so close they merged into one another, and in those days, between the years 1800 and 1900, the area was known for its farming and fishing. It was said that hundreds of years ago our family had moved from the north of Scotland down to Suffolk. Grandfather Chapman had a Welsh wife, a school teacher from Cardiff; I only met Grandmother Chapman on two occasions when she was about sixty something years of age, she was really very beautiful even at that time of her life, she was also quiet, unassuming and had a lovely personality. She would sit me on her lap and tell me wondrous tales of our forebears in long forgotten times. Grandfather Chapman was well known in the London North Eastern Railways for his expertise in boiler making and construction. He was sent all over the British Isles to repair broken and damaged boilers for the railways . . .

* * *

I was four years old when I nearly had my first brush with the law, leaving the house one day I had decided to take a ride on a tram to see my grandma. I had always been intrigued by the tram lines crisscrossing the roads around London and dreamed of the wondrous places they all went to. The trams had two decks with the top one being open to the elements and sun in front. My grandmamma lived in Bow in a high rise building surrounded by canals. It was really quite a distance, especially when you're only four years old, but it didn't bother me one bit, I looked forward to the adventure. I had slipped out of the house without anyone seeing me and made a beeline for the nearest tram stop. I stood there like I belonged to someone. When the first tram pulled up at the stop I waited for people to disembark and then climbed aboard. The conductor who collected the fares looked at me quizzically and asked me where my mother was. I said she was just behind me and climbed up the caged in stairs to the top deck like I owned the place. Scrambling to the front of the tram between the rows of seats and tram riders I squeezed myself into the front so the conductor could not see me. Sitting atop the open deck I pretended I was the driver of the tram as it crossed other rails going in different directions, swinging the big imaginary steering wheel I had between my hands this way and that, all the while thoroughly enjoying myself. I guess I was just plain lucky that the tram was headed for Bow so when we got to bow bridge I knew it was time to get off. As the tram pulled to a stop I was already at the bottom of the stairs waiting expectantly, the conductor kept looking behind me and up the stairs from whence I had bounded down. My imaginary mother never appeared and I jumped off and ran down the road toward my grandmother's flat as fast as my little legs could carry me, all the while thinking the conductor was hot on my heels. As I fled other children playing in the street were laughing at my appearance, the dark curly haired little boy in the purple velvet suit, me being much better attired than the pack of them. Undaunted I climbed the three flights of stairs to granny's place and knocked on the door.

Aunt Margaret answered, she opened the door looked down at me and said, "Hello Stan, where's mummy?"

I replied, "At home."

It took some time to convince her I really was on my own and grandmamma made such a fuss of me I stayed the rest of the day and night, sleeping with my auntie in her bed. The following morning Uncle John said he would take me home since he wasn't working that day. When we arrived home boy was mummy cross, but in the end, upset as she was, mum just voiced her concern and simply said, "Stanley, you have a wandering spirit like that of a true Irishman . . ." I must say it was nice to be back in my own bed that night as I closed my eyes and said a silent prayer to myself and God up above who I thanked for looking after me . . . *All's well that ends well . . .*

\* \* \*

My mother was very straight forward with her children and would accept no monkey business. One day I was playing with some kids and we ended up behind Woolworths in Ilford. There were piles of packets with teapots in them and my playmates each picked up one. I also took one home with me, when I entered the front door and mum caught sight of the pot in my hands, she said, "Where did you get this?"

"Behind Woolworths, where we were playing," I replied.

Mum was furious, "Take it back immediately," she fumed.

Dad came downstairs and gave me a sharp uncompromising look, "I'll take you now," he said pursing his lips forcefully.

When we got back to Woolworths I snuck around a side street that led to the back alley behind the store. I was too embarrassed to take it back where I'd found it so I left it by the corner and made off to the front of the building where my father stood waiting. I felt hot under the collar and vowed that I would never incur the wrath of my mother by doing something like that again.

The Prudential insurance man used to come every week to pick up mum's one shilling insurance policy money. One day when he came to make his regular pickup, he noted, "I've been collecting from you for such a long time but have you ever made a claim?"

"No," replied mummy.

"Well, I've been collecting from you for the past three years now and that carpet runner of yours is starting to look worn especially with five boys running up and down it . . ." noted the Prudential man as he pulled a lighter from his pocket walked over to the carpet knelt down and set the corner alight. Blowing out the little fire he had started he said to mum, "Not to worry, I'll allow you to buy a new one now . . . the Prudential will pay as soon as you find out how much one costs." As he was leaving he turned to mum and added, "Now don't you choose a cheap one by the way, get a decent quality carpet runner."

Not long afterward a beautiful thick pile 36 inch wide and 10 foot long runner graced the passageway floor courtesy of the Prudential.

Life was very safe back then and as a five year old I would pop down to the bakery each day to pick up a loaf of bread for mummy. On one particular day the baker asked me to wait since he was very busy with his baking. When at last he finished he gave me a huge box with a Christmas style fruit cake in it and a dozen buns from the batch he'd been busy with. "Give these to your mother . . ." he said. We used to buy the buns for a half penny and sometimes he would take a farthing from me, especially when our neighbor asked if Stanley was going to the bakery. One evening my mother sent me to the shop as the sun had just set and it was getting dark. I was halfway there, about three blocks, when I glanced up at the rising moon. It seemed to be following me and I got the shock of my young life, I turned and ran back home as fast as my legs could take me. When I arrived I burst through the front door with a worried look on my face. Mummy came out of the kitchen and asked, "What's wrong Stanley?"

"The moon is following me," I stammered.

Mummy took me by the hand and led me back to the bakery. She told the baker what had happened and he looked out the window and shook his fist at the moon. Kneeling down next to me, he said, "If it follows you again I'll pull him down here and give that naughty moon a spanking, Stanley." With a smidgeon of disbelief I wondered, *'Could he really do that?'*

The lady and her husband across the road were very fond of birds and had a whole lot of them in cages inside their house. I would go over just to sit down and admire their beautiful and varied colors. Sometimes she would give me cake and tea. After a year or so she approached my mother asking if she could adopt me as they couldn't have children. My mother was fiercely jealous of her family and each one of her boys, and in no uncertain terms gave her an emphatic, "No!"

It wasn't long afterward that she and her husband moved to Russia. We never saw or heard of them again . . . We also moved a few months later to No: 352 Becontree Avenue in Dagenham. Becontree Ave was quite some distance from town so my parents decided to find a much nicer house, which they did, No: 16 Richmond Road, Ilford in Essex. It wasn't too far from my school, Loxford Central School. Mum was very proud of her home and we always moved to a better house eventually ending up at No: 1 Meath Road in Ilford.

My mother really loved her children as all Irish mothers do. While living in Becontree Ave my mum had built up a reputation of being straightforward and honest who feared no-one. Even the local constabulary asked her for advice and opinion on things. One day, the big broad shouldered woman called Mrs. Crouch, who lived round the corner in Hitherfield Road, decided she would rough house Ernie because he had inadvertently said something to upset one of the older boys he had been playing with. As trivial and innocent as Ernie had thought the comment to be it was not the case with Mrs. Crouch who came out of her house and gave Ernie such a clout it knocked him off his feet and sent him flying to the pavement. Ernie was still a young boy, and when he came home with grazes on his knees and elbows and a swollen cheek my mother flew into a furious rage and stormed round to the woman's house. Mum knocked on the door and Mrs. Crouch answered, she stood a head and a half above mum, a few angry words were passed between the pair, an insult flew from the mouth of Mrs. Crouch, a closed fist from mummy smacked the bad tempered woman so hard in the face she verily lifted off the steps and fell down the steps to the coal cellar some distance behind her. No-one in the neighborhood liked Mrs. Crouch very much; she was a bully through and through. After that incident no-one took advantage of Elizabeth O'Sullivan-Chapman's children, she had gained the healthy respect of one and all.

\* \* \*

I think mummy was told many times by our neighbors that Stanley was both naughty and nice. My grade school teacher, a Miss Davis from Wales with short dark hair, at my Grafton Road Dagenham school; used to put me on her lap and make a fuss of me. When I first started school there my effervescent personality and love of the Irish blarney made me a firm favorite with the children. I had a group of about ten of them at my beck and call and they would follow me everywhere I went. One day the 10:00 am bell rang for break and I thought it was the end of the school day bell. I told my young group I knew of a nice place where we could all play, some 'chalk pits' a little way away. Well off we went with me leading them like the Pied Piper in the Hans Christian Anderson story. When we got to the pits there were little rivers we had to jump across. Some of them were a little too wide for our young legs so much of the time we ended up to our waists in dirty white water. It didn't take long for all of us to be coated in the white calcium carbonate dust from head to toe. What we didn't know was that search parties including teachers, parents and children were searching all over for us. About three hours later our group of about nine children, including me, came ambling up Becontree Avenue. Outside of our house stood a crowd of worried parents, mum was at the forefront as we waltzed up covered in white chalk dust. Their faces turned pale when they saw us for we all looked like ghosts. When they realized we were alright there was a huge sigh of relief, my mother ran up to me and blurted out, "Stanley, where on earth have you been!"

Of course I got all the blame, I told them, "When the bell rang I thought it was time to go home." My mother wasn't very cross and she was so relieved I was home in one piece she ended up laughing as she put me in the bath tub and scrubbed all the white chalk off. Jimmy, my older brother came in and said, "Mum, you can't trust Stanley, he's too young to go to school, make him stay at home!" Mum continued to send me but told Jim and Ernie to keep a close watch on me and make sure I didn't get into trouble. There were advantages to this as no bully in school ever dared touch me because they'd have to deal with my older siblings.

\* \* \*

My lust for adventure and exploration continued, whether I was three, four or five years of age, I would never stand still. I was likened to the Scarlet Pimpernel, they would see me here, they would see me there, and they would see me everywhere. I made little matchbox boats with matchstick masts and paper sails, these I would put in the gutters around the streets outside our house and let the rushing water from the rain take them to places I could just dream of. In my imagination I was the captain of these little ships, a pirate, an adventurer coming across wild beasts and mountainous seas, just like a character in *Homer's Odyssey.* My boat was always the fastest and strongest and able to contend with anything my adventures and nature threw at us.

I managed to acquire a little tent around this time and decided that venturing forth to Hainault forest would be the beginning of an adventurous life. Two of my young friends and I decided we would camp that night in the forest; we had no money or food with us just some blankets and the tent. The forest was about seven miles from where we lived. It was a lovely summer's day when we set off but on the way we got hungry. Passing fields with fruit trees and potatoes in we availed ourselves of nature's bounteous fruits. It wasn't long before we had cabbage, some potatoes, plums and apples, trouble was, nothing was ripe, but, as the saying goes, *anything in a storm.*

Some of the plums were so green and bitter we gave them to a couple of donkeys in a field. Their eyes started to water not long afterwards. The cabbage was somewhat raw and hard but we ate it anyway. Walking in the hot sun was hard on our little legs so by the time we reached the forest we were all very tired. We pitched the tent on the edge of the forest near a field. There was no ground sheet so we just placed our blankets on the grass inside the tent and fell asleep nearly immediately . . . At around five the following morning I woke up with a start, a strange noise had disturbed me. Being only six years of age in a tent seven miles from home my imagination started to run wild, inflaming the thought of fearsome creatures prowling around outside our canvas fortress. The weird noise got louder and louder, I stood up nearly knocking the poles over. The noise without sounded like a hundred galloping horses about to bring the tent down and crush us beneath their hooves. By now my two friends were up and also shaking in fear. Then the tent shook violently. I peered between the fly sheets and saw a big bull grazing next to us and rubbing himself against the tent. We verily flew from the tent grabbing it and our blankets and headed for the safety of the road. Halfway we changed our minds and started for the forest instead. Just then a farmer saw us and came over, he asked what were we doing and where were we going. We mumbled something unintelligibly. He smiled and said, "Why don't you boys come with me–"

He took us to a shed and gave us some fresh bread and even fresher milk from the cow he had just been milking. After that experience we decided it was time to head home, we were all a little shaken and frightened by imagined fears. Within the hour we had wrapped up the tent and our blankets and made haste in home's direction . . .

When I got to the front door of our house mummy was standing on the porch looking very worried. "Where have you been? I sent Jimmy and Ernie to look for you. I thought you would pitch the tent up in the garden or the park behind the house."

I was hustled to the bathroom where I was washed and scrubbed down, next was a set of clean clothes and something to eat and drink. As always dad heard about my escapade when he got home from work, he never hit us, no matter what, though he would pretend to take his belt off and go through the motions just to frighten us back into line. But mum, she was ready for a fight anytime, woe betides anyone who got on her wrong side, if she lost her temper she was highly dangerous. If ever she saw tears in her children's eyes she would want to know all about it and the culprit would probably be torn limb from limb. She was well known in Becontree Avenue and elsewhere. During election times politicians would come to her for advice and wisdom . . . Like my father, I was an early riser, dad would be off at 5:00 am in the morning and I would get up at the same time he did. I would make a cup of tea for mum while she was still in bed then sit there snuggled up next to her and listen to tales of Ireland and County Cork . . . At one time our family put up a paddy from Poldine, Thurles in Tipperary by the name of Martin O'Shannahan. He was very stocky and full of muscle with very square shoulders, but a little flat-footed. He would walk with his feet slightly out-turned. Eventually he returned to Ireland and we left Colgrave Road and moved to Bel Avenue in Dagenham. After which we moved back to Leytonstone to a big old house. The place was dark and dingy and full of rats. Mum improved every house we moved into but she found another one quickly in Ilford, number 116 Richmond Road . . . And then we shifted to Meath Road where we stayed until I left school . . .

* * *

As a railway engine driver my father had the privilege of travelling anywhere the railway could take him in Great Britain, and with five boys to contend with he would always book interesting holidays for the whole family at the most popular holiday resorts the British Isles had each summer. I was eight years old when we went to Scarborough that year. We stayed at a lovely guest house and received a wonderfully warm reception from the proprietors as we entered the large reception hall. Jim, being older than me, decided to take me on a jaunt to Scarborough castle, a sturdy defensive stone mass built to deter the invading Normans and put a stop to their sacking and pillaging in that area on the east coast of England. When we arrived we went straight up to the gate keeper and asked if we could go in and look around. He let us through without even asking for the price of a ticket, *boy were we chuffed*. Maybe he'd

taken a liking to our southern country accents, I don't know . . .
at any rate we were very fortunate. We walked over the draw
bridge fighting each other with imaginary swords and pole
arms, me with an imaginary suit of armor on. Going into the
courtyard through the keep we came across a pit twelve feet deep
and about seven feet wide covered with a steel grill. It was used
to put prisoners in before their execution either by hanging,
beheading or some other painful death. Having enough of
the castle's interior walls we decided to poke around outside
as young boys are wont to do in such places. There were plenty
of rock strewn nooks and crannies for a pair of young lads to
explore, places where adults and even older children couldn't
get to. Because I was slim Jimmy asked me to squeeze through
a crevasse that had the promise of intrigue and adventure.
Squeezing into the narrow entrance I found myself in a small
cave-like opening. I ventured in as far as I could and found a
dagger standing up stuck between two rocks; I gripped the bone
handled hilt and withdrew it slowly from the rocks. Holding it
I could see it was very old, the blade was about eight inches in
length and stopped at a golden colored quill which stopped the
hand sliding onto the blade. A beautifully crafted bone hilt with
jewels set in it finished the knife off. I couldn't believe my luck
and was beaming from ear to ear when I squeezed myself back
out into the sunlight. Seeing the dagger in my hand a jealous
Jimmy took it off me before I could say anything. I was so upset
when he gave it to the gatekeeper for a shilling; in fact I decided
then and there never to show Jimmy anything I found or had
ever again. I had discovered my very own *Sword in the Stone* only
to have it snatched from my grasp with the same haste with
which the invading Normans had taken the goods, farms and
women folk of the land hereabouts. We continued to scour the
area around the castle for the rest of our holiday but never
found anything else. The summer sun was hot that year and we
all wanted to swim in the sea but mum and dad warned us not
to go too deep for both tide and currents were strong whipping

any unwary swimmer out into the sea never to be seen again. The thought of Jimmy venturing a little further out more than once crossed my mind . . .

* * *

When I was around ten years of age we lived at No: 1 Meath Road, Ilford, Essex, I used to help the United Dairies milkman on his rounds early each morning from 4:00 – 6:00 am. After school I would go out with a bucket and spade collecting horse manure, selling it for two pence a bucket. I started this little business when I was around seven years old. Most people had either an allotment or a small garden at the back of their house. I use to sell up to twenty buckets of manure each week. I would give mummy sixpence and kept sixpence for myself including tuppence for the cinema matinee on Saturday morning. Mum was happy with the extra money from my milk rounds and during the extremely cold winter months when I got home she would sit me by the fire and rub my hands until the circulation got going again. I never complained for we always had a nice clean and warm home with lots of good food on the table. One cold morning the horse got a bit of a fright while I sat with the reins and the milkman was selling large duck eggs for a half penny each to one of his private clients. The horse reared and nearly tipped the cart over spilling some of the milk crates as it bolted down the road. Lucky for me a man saw what had happened and jumped into the road grabbing the bridle and put a stop to the runaway animal . . . Money wasn't all that good though, for when we lived in Colegrave Road my father's career with the railways was still in its infancy, railway engineers all had to start at the bottom as an engine cleaner and then fireman . . . With the money I had left I would spend a tuppence on sweets for school for the following week and a tuppence on my bike which I had made myself out of old bike parts I'd found and scrounged. Dad helped me put it together and bought any parts

I didn't have. All the kids in the area looked forward to the Saturday morning flicks which were for children only. I used to get there early to sit near the front while others would run up to the gallery to throw sweets, paper and nutshells on those below. At first we had silent movies which started with the funnies and Charlie Chaplain accompanied with music and even an organist. Shortly afterwards sound incorporated into the movies was introduced putting many organists out of work. Serials like Flash Gordon enthralled the cinema goers as did Tarzan with Johnny Weissmuller. We always had cowboys and Indians on at the cinema and I enjoyed those the most. Stars like Tom Mix and Buck Jones didn't sing but just fought the injuns, others like Roy Rogers, Ken Maynard and Gene Autry were singing cowboys. Out of the lot Tom Mix was my favorite; his films were the most exciting with Indians scalping those having fallen off horses after being shot with arrows. One of my most memorable moments came when Tom Mix came to town with a host of Indians and his horse. That day the streets of Ilford were bereft of trams as Tom, astride his huge chestnut and white horse, *Silver*, clip-clopped down the main road wearing a big Stetson, beautifully tooled cowboy boots, a big leather fringed holster with a pair of silver six guns, reflecting brightly in the sunlight, and fringed leather shirt and pants. There was both a whip and lasso hanging from the pommel. It was a scene right out of the movies and I made sure I had a front row seat at the side of the road. In truth there was standing room only but I had the best spot, he was my hero. There was nothing fake about Tom Mix, both his and the Indians' faces were weather beaten and sun bronzed as if he and they had been out on the range since the day they'd been born. He had on a big red bandana which contrasted starkly with his buck skin suit. The extra leather on his pants between his legs was so worn you could see he spent a lot of time in the saddle. There weren't any stunt men around then so the actors would have to do all their own stunts, even if that meant both horse and rider had to leap off a cliff into a raging river some twenty feet below. Both the Indians and Tom had faces lined by the merciless Wild West sun. Tom's saddle was a proper western saddle, magnificently hand tooled, and his horse was beautiful beyond words, with a shiny trimmed dark mane and long tail. The sides of his steed shimmered in the British summer sun. I had never seen a real life Indian before and my mouth hung agape as two tall Indian chiefs walked past me, they too were attired in buck skin with fringes and wore big eagle feather war bonnets on their heads. The one closest to me had two long braided pony tails hanging down on either side of his chest. His buck skin jacket was ornamented with brightly colored beads and on his back was a quiver full of arrows, in his hand he carried a bow with the ends curled out and feathers attached to the ends. He wore moccasins and had a tomahawk tucked into his waist belt. I couldn't believe my eyes; Tom even smiled at me as he passed by. What I would've given to be astride the horse with Tom . . . Two songs from my favorite westerns came to mind:

*"Mule train – Mule train,*
*Clipperty, Clipperty – Clipperty clop,*
*Clipperty clop – Clipperty clopping along,*
*Over the hills, over the trails,*
*Soon they're going to reach the top,*
*Clipperty clop,*
*Clipperty clopping along . . .*

*Roll along covered wagon, roll along,*
*Roll along covered wagon, roll along,*
*Pretty ladies maybe fine,*
*But give me that girl of mine,*
*Roll along covered wagon, roll along . . ."*

I didn't have a chance to ride with Tom Mix but later that week dad asked me if I'd like to ride on the footplate of his steam locomotive and I jumped at the offer. It was forbidden to take anyone on a railway engine, but I got to ride upfront with my dad anyway. Mummy got me dressed and off I went with dad at 5:00 am in the morning. When I climbed up the steel steps of the large iron locomotive engine my mind immediately went into movie mode, as dad, with his engine driver's cap looked like an engineer ploughing the Wild West through Indian country. His fireman, shoveling coal into the burner and covered in black soot, looked like an extra playing in the cowboy movie in my head. Dad put his cap on my head and let me pull the train's whistle as we approached small stations in the English countryside. The day was a real hoot for a young lad. It was a little while after this in 1935 that dad got the *Silver Link*, no. 2509, a beautiful A4 locomotive with a livery of three different shades of grey. The front of the smoke box, before the boiler, was painted a dark charcoal grey which went over the smoke stack, with the wheel skirts battleship grey and the rest of the locomotive's boiler and the cab and coal tender a silver grey. The *Silver link* was the first of the A4s to be built and was made especially for the 'Silver Jubilee', and took only 12 weeks to complete. It was delivered three days before the 'Silver Jubilee' and reached just over 112 miles per hour in a publicity run. The A4s eventually captured the World Speed Record for Steam Traction which has never been broken since. Dad was really proud when he was given the honor of being one of the first engineers to drive the A4. During the war the svelte three tone grey livery was replaced by a coal black paint scheme. It wasn't as nice as the grey livery but I guess it kept the German fighter bombers guessing, especially at night.

Both Jimmy and I had skates which we would tear around the streets on, normally we never had a problem with stopping, until that is, Jimmy decided one day he'd stick out his arm to stop him colliding into a lamppost rapidly approaching him down the street he was rolling on. It didn't do him much good as his arm broke and mum had to rush him to hospital. I was left to look after my two baby brothers, Teddy and Alfie. There was nothing more loved by Alfie than to dig up and eat worms from our little garden at the back of the house . . . Sometimes I would put the gramophone on with Primo Escala's accordion band and stand against the window in my bedroom holding a small suitcase and pretend to play it. The children in our street were all very impressed and thought I could play the accordion very well. I always had a little giggle about that. When I had nothing else to do I would go to Chadwell heath Railway Bridge and watch the fast passenger trains go by. I loved the first-class Pullman saloon and dining cars which were so beautifully made and furnished and looked so posh, but were very expensive to ride in. It proved to be the seed that took root and moved me to apply for an apprentice's position as a coachbuilder with the railways. Of course dad also had a say in it as well, him being an engineer with the railways n'all . . .

Jimmy and Ernie always wanted their own room away from the younger ones in the family, and when we moved to Meath Road they got their wish. I shared a room with Teddy and Alfie, it was smaller than theirs but it had a nice big window to play my 'accordion' in. One day I decided to play a prank aimed at my older brothers. I set up the deck chair outside in the garden with the back frame just resting on the notches so it would collapse if someone sat on it. Murphy's Law held true and instead of my older brothers sitting on it Alfie, the youngest did, sending him crashing to the ground and catching one of his fingers between the two frames as they closed together causing horrendous screaming and my mother to lose her temper at me, boy, was she cross! Hell hath no fury compared to my mother . . .

# CHAPTER 3

## A Young Pirate & Family Tales

**M**other and her relatives would always talk about our family's origin and how a certain Spanish sea captain called de Croix had landed on the south coast of Ireland in County Cork. He had headed there to avoid vicious storms driven by Southwest winds pounding what was left of the Spanish Armada in 1588 AD as it tried to escape around Scotland and Ireland heading for the Bay of Biscay after its battles with the English fleet led by Lord Howard of Effingham and Sir Francis Drake. This fateful clash of warships extended from Cornwall to the Dutch coast, culminating in the Battle of Gravelines. The action, lack of provisions and storms took a heavy toll on the Spanish fleet, leading to the destruction of nearly the entire Armada. Captain de Croix stayed in Irish waters for some time afterward harassing English shipping in piratical fashion. Legend has it that the blood of Captain de Croix runs through the veins of the O'Sullivans and Spanish blood in the Coughlins . . . "Stanley," they said, "has more Irish and Spanish pirate blood in him than anyone else in the family . . ." Grandma Chapman would also sit me on her lap and tell her tales of the past and how the Chapmans and her family had made their mark in the mists of time . . .

\* \* \*

I was about eight years old when we had Mr. Hall as one of our teachers. We use to call him Votcha Hall because every time he caned someone he would cry out *"Votcha"* with each strike. I was busy one morning filling the ink wells in his classroom with a large teapot-like container filled with blue ink when I caught my leg and foot on a ladder that was lying by the windows against the wall. I went flying downwards trying to keep the pot level, all to no avail since most of its contents ended up all over me. I was sent home to bath and change. We had a play to put on the following day so after mummy had taken my clothes and put them in the wash bucket and I had cleaned up and put on fresh clean clothes I then hastened back to school for a rehearsal. The play was about *Tristram and Iseult* and I would be playing the Irish king, whom our drama teacher thought I would portray quite nicely. I had a cardboard crown, a wooden sword and a velvet robe. *Iseult* was played by one of my schoolmates that I liked a lot, Mary Cornwall. I was sweet on her and thought of her as my little girlfriend, well, both her and Pat Smith. They were a year younger than me but I was smitten with both of them. On the day of the play it was raining and cold outside, the hall was a little chilly but the assembled children took away any thought of that. We had done quite a few rehearsals and pretty much all knew our lines. The King of Briton whom I had to deliver my daughter *Iseult* to had a reputation of being a bit rough, so to say, me, I had no love of him and thought he was a pushy little brat. On the stage everything had started perfectly and one of our teachers was playing the piano down below, that is, until the King of Briton tried to kiss Iseult. I had to defend my lady's honor so I stepped between them and put a stop to it, and with drawn swords we battled to the death on the stage in front of the whole school. It ended with the King of Briton being trounced by the King of Ireland and him being left sprawled flat on his back on the stage floor. My warriors and followers behind me rushed the King of Briton's men chasing them off the stage. With all her work, effort and coaching behind the play our drama teacher wasn't too chuffed with my actions and my error in judgment and hasty reaction. This put an end to my dreams of becoming a thespian and taking up acting as a full time profession on the stages of Londinium, well, not quite. All the kids loved my version of the play, however, even if I did end up with an appointment with *'Votcha'* at day's end.

* * *

The Tale of Gwendolyn and Arturius the Younger: In a land of good and evil, in a time long ago, there was a good king by the name of Arturius, he fought for the rights of the people of Briton against a wicked enemy, the Saxons. Arturius was a Christian man who feared God and did his utmost to bring peace and security to the lands under his dominion. There were many greedy kings at that time who were jealous and wanted to depose such a noble person as King Arturius, they would commit any vile act in order to achieve their grandiose desires. King Maelgwn of Gwynedd was one of them. Around that time the North Irish, the Scotti, were settling in Scotland and becoming one people with the Picts. Many Saxons and other Germanic people had invaded Briton and settled on the Eastern seaboard. During the earlier part of the fifth century the heathen Angles and Saxons had come to Briton by invitation from King Vortigern the usurper, he used them as auxiliaries to swell his own forces in his battles for dominion over those who stood against him. Because of Vortigern's invite the Angles and Saxons, now emboldened, thought they could conquer and settle Briton with their own people killing and forcing the Bretons from their own lands. This period in Briton's history is known as the Dark Ages, it was a period when very few literary works were put down on paper due to constant war and strife. Most of its history was reduced to fables and tales, sung by minstrels and told as stories around campfires on the dark cold misty nights of those times. These stories were passed down from generation to generation through Welsh and Cornish families. Even though the Roman Empire was crumbling, its days drawing to a close, a phoenix had risen from its ashes in the form of Christianity. It was within this turmoil and uncertainness that a great leader had been born and bequeathed as a savior for all Briton, Arturius, son of Uther Pendragon and Ygerne. Uther had fallen in love with Ygerne while she was still wed; their union produced a son, Arturius, who was born in Tintagel, Cornwall. It was not long afterward that Ygerne's husband died in battle leaving her free to marry Uther and legitimize Arturius. At least this is the version told in the medieval romances by Geoffrey of Monmouth and Sir. Thomas Mallory. There were many kings of that period and they could be likened to tribal chieftains holding sway over large areas of land. Was Arturius a real person, yes, but he lived in the Dark Ages between 460 – 540 AD. Was he one of the kings of Briton or a war chief, we will never know? Was he an ancestor of ours, I would like to think so . . . Evidence of the characters spoken of in tales of that period are rife in Cornwall, the tale of Tristram and Isolde for instance. Was Tristram, the male protagonist in the story, an actual person, yes, was King Mark, his father, adopted or a true sire, we will never know . . . On a stone monument, a seven foot high monolith, near Fowey an inscription in old Latin reads: DRUSTANUS HIC IACIT CUNOMORI FILIUS. Translated into English it reads: **HERE LIES TRISTRAM SON OF CUNOMORI**. Drustanus, Drustans, Tristram and Tristan are one and the same person, just different expressions and spellings at different periods of time. The name Cunomori refers to King Marcus Cunomori, or, King Mark in the old tale. The monument was moved some hundred yards from its original position so is not exactly above Tristram's final resting place. Castle Dor, at least what remains of its earthen embankment defenses, lies in a field two miles away as the crow flies. Historians have ignored the abundance of information relating to Arthur's existence even though there is far more empirical evidence relating to him than that of

Jesus Christos . . . The following family bedtime story about the period after Arthur's death was handed down from generation to generation through the mists of time and narrowly escaped the pyre of forgotten and discarded tales forever joining those in the dark abyss of the past . . .

In the orange groves of Avalon a wounded Arturius lies mortally wounded, his person having been carried on his shield to safety and healing hands from the battlefield. Arturius had faced his enemies at Camlann and received a mortal wound. The house of our Lord in the refuge of Avalon, surrounded by marsh and water, was at least defensible having one road leading to it, an embankment raised above the marsh around. Those knights who remained his loyal followers crowded around as the monks did their best to stem the blood flowing from him. Modred, an arch enemy of Arturius, had been killed in the Battle of Camlann, but there were many more wishing to take advantage of the demise of Arturius. Many men searched for Arturius, riding roughshod over the country and peasants alike in search of him. Arturius had been taken from the field of battle before any more harm could befall him, for his knights seeing him succumb to a series of sword blows had surrounded him in an effort to preserve his life. There were many who wished to take what Arturius had, including Guinevere, Camelot and the lands surrounding it. Amongst the chieftains and kings of Briton not one held the people of Breton in such high regard as Arturius did. Their petty jealousies and hatred of one another had weakened their forces and lost this last battle keeping the Angles and Saxons at bay. And now, Arturius lay dying in the Vale of Avalon. In the preceding years it was Arturius and his men who had led the way, forging forth in the heat of battle to seize the day and push their foes back and win the fight at hand through sword, arrow and spear. His fame in battle though, had won him many enemies in those he thought were allies. His fairness to those subjected to him was also a contentious issue for those railed against him, for the people loved Arturius . . .

And now, as his lifeblood flowed from his body, Guinevere was brought to him to say her final goodbyes. Arturius's two oldest sons were still at Camelot with his youngest son, Arturius. Guinevere had brought their only daughter, Gwendolyn, still in swaddling, who still suckled at her bosom. With Guinevere was a handmaiden, Gwyneth, who looked after young Gwendolyn when Queen Guinevere was otherwise occupied. The wooden castle of Camelot (Cadbury Castle) was not too distant from Avalon (Glastonbury). As Arturius was administered to by the monks Guinevere's tears rolled freely upon her King's chest. However, Maelgwn, thinking to exploit the situation and steal away Guinevere for him to gain legitimacy in claiming both Camelot and the lands around it, had sent his agents forth to kidnap her and kill her offspring borne of Arturius. His agents had made their way to both Camelot and Avalon, and through deception gained access to both. A scuffle ensued and blades were drawn and blood spilt as Arturius's men fought the agents of Maelgwn. Guinevere thrust a dagger into her chest not wishing to be dragged from her beloved King and husband. Bedevere thrust a sword into the hands of Gwyneth and said, "Take this blade, my Lord's, and defend thyself against all comers, go to Camelot where you will be safe and yonder child will find life . . ."

With that Gwyneth fled on her horse slashing at any who dared interfere with her mission. The baby in swaddling tucked firmly in the folds of her mantle. With her travelled two stout knights in leather armor . . . When Camelot they arrived turmoil reigned resolute with all fearful of the days to come having lost their king and chieftain, Arturius. An assassin's dagger had already found the heart of his oldest son. And the middle one, having not the experience to draw upon and thrust into kingship, fell short in his duties to protect Camelot. For inside the castle redoubt mayhem had gripped the people and agents of Maelgwn ran amok spreading false rumors and striking down the best amongst them in the dark recesses of the castle and in their beds as they slept. During this time both Arturius and Guinevere were laid to rest in a hewn log and buried at Avalon. Bedevere had placed his own sword in the hands of Arturius to bode him well in the afterlife should there be any who sallied forth with intent to smite him down. In the eyes of Lancelot it was not well to send him so into the ground without means of defending himself . . .

A snake-like Maelgwn presented himself at the court of Arturius in an attempt to sway the young king and let him manage the lands around enabling him to swell his own coffers and become lord over all. But by this time Arturius's surviving oldest son had composed himself and met Marelgwn as an equal with the handmaiden Gwyneth, Arturius the younger, and Gwendolyn, still in swaddling; and against the wooden throne upon which the eldest surviving son sat rested Excalibur, the sword of Arturius. Maelgwn's eyes widened and he cursed the young boy who would be king inwardly. He must have both sword and seat of power, whence he would appoint a puppet to rule in his stead. Maelgwn's oil-soaked tongue coated in honey praised the youngster fully, nere letting one compliment fall upon his ears before another was cast as though it were a fishing line with honey coated biscuits on the hook. Maelgwn's men had encamped on the plains below waiting for a signal from their lord. Guinevere's handmaiden advised the young king not to trust the man before him but Maelgwn's honey had slid down his throat and tasted so good to the young boy he refused to listen to her. Maelgwn pleaded that his men should not suffer the cold outside on the plain and they should be let in to experience the comforts and safety of Camelot. Permission was given, ere the words had escaped his lips and the die was cast . . . Maelgwn had succeeded where armed men and enemies of the righteous had failed. Maelgwn's men marched and rode into Camelot as King Maelgwn led Arturius's eldest onto the ramparts. As they watched, Maelgwn's dagger sought the breast of the young lad as he held a large hand over his mouth so as not to arouse suspicion in anyone. When dead, the boy, who had been king scant hours, days and weeks, was thrown over the wooden ramparts . . . Maelgwn smiled as he headed for his quarters to lay his head down, secure in the knowledge that his plans, whilst not fully implemented yet, would be done so shortly in the days to come . . .

In the morning just before Maelgwn rose from a deep untainted slumber, for he was a wicked man and no amount of evil would cause him the slightest discomfiture, a great cry rang shrilly from without, for the new king's body had been discovered. A broad grin spread over Maelgwn's face as his men struck down all those who stood against them. Maelgwn got out of bed and dressed slowly for his breakfast which his servant had brought him, along with warm water to bathe his face. After his toilet was done Maelgwn set forth with an armed escort to peruse his iniquitous and underhanded plans. Lined up against one wall were those retainers of Arturius that remained firm and resolute against the usurper. And as Maelgwn looked on it wasn't long before all lay dead at his feet through broadsword and arrow. Maelgwn chuckled heartily, "Now where is the handmaiden with Arturius's brats . . ." he called to the captain in charge of the slaughter, "Bring them to me at once!" he shouted. His thoughts were to seize the pair of them, kill the boy and take the young girl hostage, well, a ward, in order to legitimize his protection of Arturius's land and castle, for had not some unscrupulous villain now laid rest his men so that the only surviving child was under threat and needed his protection . . . And, it were a shame the youngest brother had met with an unfortunate accident, 'not yet, but he would', forcing the court of Arturius to welcome his mentorship of lands, castle and the young wench. The handmaiden though, seemed much too bright and informed about him to let live. She too would have to meet an unfortunate end. *'It was a shame because she was rather comely,'* thought Maelgwn. *'Perhaps I could have my fun aforehand,'* he smiled in a most vicious manner . . .

As he sat on the throne of Arturius, the usurper became more and more impatient and screamed shrilly at his men to find the wench and her young charges. But as time went on the captain of Maelgwn's guard realized she had fled aforehand and was nere to be seen or found in Camelot. Maelgwn, finding this to be the case flew into a terrible rage at having thus been deprived of the comfit she would provide in his bed and the pleasure of sending young Arturius to join his brother. And as for the baby, if she did not please him to live he would have fed her to his dogs. With these thoughts Maelgwn fumed and kicked the lowly dogs, both human and animal, around him . . .

Gwyneth kicked her heels in the steed's flanks underneath her, urging it on and entreating the young boy behind to do the same. They had fled in the night for she was well aware what was afoot in Camelot, and from an earthen embankment below the wooden surrounding palisade walls she and the small boy at her side had seen Maelgwn turf the young king over in the torch and firelight that kept darkness from entering Camelot. This had been enough for her and she had made to leave the walls and brave the darkness without instead of falling foul to Maelgwn's fetid odorous scheming. She would take her young charges to Myrddin in the hills and vales of Wales, for surely he would know what to do . . . It would be a perilous journey but she had no choice, to stay would probably mean death or worse for them. She had taken gold aplenty from Guinevere's hiding place. For a dead woman had no need of such things and before long Maelgwn would no doubt cast his bloody hands out to it. And, while Maelgwn searched high and low for them their steeds kept a steady pace toward safety and the welcoming arms of Myrddin. Only once did bandits try to take what was not theirs, only to taste the blade of Arturius. When at last they reached their destination Myrddin was nowhere to be seen and Gwyneth sat down on her haunches and cried and cried. She had been strong thus far for her charges but now, their last hope had evaporated leaving naught to hold on to . . . Arturius the younger put his arm around her shoulder and tried hard to sway her fears, for was he not Arturius's son. When at last the tears stopped falling down her cheeks Gwyneth cast about her, the cave had not been inhabited for a long time, there were no signs of combat or foul play, so Gwyneth got up and started to array their new lodgings and make them more comfortable. For it were not right that the son and daughter of a great Breton chieftain and king should live like vagabonds. Myrddin's cave was large and penetrated the hillside it was a part of. A waterfall and stream were but a short walk from it and berries and nuts littered the ground about. Myrddin had also planted herbs and mint on the hillside. In a little alcove off the main cave was his kitchen that boasted all the things they might need to cook and prepare food, even a fireplace and cauldron that only needed wood to warm hearts and stomachs. All that was needed was a rabbit for the pot . . . And thus they lived, happy in themselves to be out of the wicked clutches of the evil Maelgwn . . . But it were a chance meeting in years to come that would change all this . . .

The years passed and young Gwendolyn, once a baby, had now begun to show signs of womanhood. And even though still a young teen she was the splitting image of Guinevere, her mother. Through the years the fame of Arturius and Guinevere burned bright in the hearts of the peasant folk and tales were sung by bards around fires at day's end, but the Angles and Saxons cared not, underhanded deals were signed in blood, the blood of the farmers and peasant folk of Briton. Those who had stood beside Arturius were now either dead or scattered across the land of the Bretons. Camelot was now ruled by a puppet of Maelgwn, and though older, he was as evil as ever, for the years had taught him naught . . . In the land of the Scotti there was still hope in the form of an elderly bearded man, and as he saw his reflection in a highland pond he noticed other images as well, that of the heir to Arturius's throne, of battles yet to come, and, the reflection of one he had held dear and close to his heart, of a young girl who looked like her mother . . .

While Arturius the younger was out hunting one day
Gwyneth and Gwendolyn rode forth on their horses to a market
town to collect supplies for the winter months to come. Summer
days were busy, for foodstuffs, warm coverings and wood had
to be collected and stored in the cave, since it were not good to
suffer the cold heartless winter of Wales without being properly
prepared. Gwyneth had been taught the way of the bow by her
father as a youngster and the way of the sword by the knights of
King Arturius's court. But time had begun to tell on her and the
constant worry if they were to be found out pressed heavily on
her shoulders. Forays into the countryside as far as Avalon and
within sight of Camelot had painted a dismal picture of the land
once free of Saxon and Angles. All that were left now were tales
of greatness and nothing more. The halcyon days of Arturius
and his knights and the fabled Camelot were gone, and in its
place stood a vileness perpetuated by the squabbling kings and
chieftains of Briton. The blood of Arturius flowed within both
Arturius the younger and Gwendolyn, but would it be enough?
*'Have all I done been for naught,'* Gwyneth wondered, *'have all the
deprivations and hiding in the hills and vales of Wales just given evil
a chance to rule the land about?'* Gwyneth had sacrificed her life
for the two young charges she had kept safe, she had thought
of them as family and of Gwendolyn as her own daughter and
Gwendolyn thought of her as her only mother for had she not
suckled at the woman's breast as a babe. Gwyneth's own child
had died of fever just before Gwendolyn was born and her
husband, one of Arturius's knights, had died in that fateful
battle whence Arturius was mortally wounded. So now, these
two youngsters were her only family and she cared naught for
other males lest they prove to be unworthy compared to her
stout brave husband who had perished by the sword. Besides,
should a stranger find out the true nature of her and her two
youngsters what fate would befall them? So, they had remained
hidden all these years in the hope that the fates would smile
upon them and provide direction and good fortune, and maybe,

just maybe, allow them to retake what was rightfully theirs–
Camelot–But this was but a dream Gwyneth held on to in the
face of suffering . . .

With their horses tethered and being looked after by a stable
lad Gwyneth and Gwendolyn walked leisurely through the
market place. Gwyneth refused to let Gwendolyn walk about in
rags and clothed her well. Her hooded cape flowed gracefully
as she walked beside Gwyneth and everyone around surmised
nothing ere that they were mother and daughter. Gwendolyn
caught sight of an attractive cape clasp broach and entreated
Gwyneth to purchase it for her as well as thick material for
another cape and material for a new dress. What loving mother
could refuse the pleading eyes of such a pretty daughter and so
the deal was done and paid . . . But the eyes of a spy can never
rest and so it was with Maelgwn's paid men. He had never once
let up on scouring the land, just in case the brats of Arturius
survived. And it was just this chance sighting that brought his
men on horseback into the marketplace, for was not the face
of Gwendolyn the splitting image of Guinevere, and was not
Guinevere the most famous and beloved face in all Briton. It
was chance also that the spy in question had seen Guinevere,
when living, in Camelot, for Maelgwn had spies everywhere. The
spies were paid men who were privy to Maelgwn's innermost
desires and wonts, prepared to sacrifice all that was holy for all
that was vile. And because of this Gwendolyn was taken by force
after a fierce battle provided for by Gwyneth who would have
sacrificed her life for the young girl, Gwendolyn. And as she
lay on the ground with a bleeding head wound Maelgwn's men
made off with a screaming Gwendolyn till at last one of the vile
men knocked her unconscious for wont of peace of mind and
ear . . . A last glimpse of the still form of Gwyneth was the last
Gwendolyn saw before her eyes closed . . .

Darkness had begun to drape the hills and vales of Wales
as a worried Arturius the younger sat outside the cave. Just as
he had decided to go and look for them two horses appeared

in the distance in the shadowy stillness of night lit by nothing more than a waning Moon. Rushing over to them he noted only one figure lay crouched over the neck of the lead horse, and the other, it had no rider at all . . .

Arturius the younger took care of Gwyneth's injuries the best he could and applied those ancient herbs and remedies such as were used in times of old. During the weeks that followed he had made many trips to the marketplace and the stronghold of Maelgwn, pretending to be a lowly scullery lad delivering food. He had learnt that Gwendolyn was being held in a tower with bolted door guarded by a huge behemoth with tattoos adorning his arms. But, he was merely a man, and a man could be killed by sword or arrow, so reasoned Arturius the younger. Maelgwn had intended on taking Gwendolyn as a bride but Gwendolyn had refused his advances and pushed him away whenever he sought her. She was not as powerful as Maelgwn but her temper and fighting ability were not to be scoffed at. She was taught how to defend herself and others by Gwyneth who had herself once been taught by the knights of Arturius, the foremost and fiercest in battle, the art of war, by the bravest and most noblest of men in all Briton . . . Rebuffing an insistent Maelgwn yet again the daughter of Arturius would ere throw herself from the window were it not barred. She had obtained a knife for food and would slit his throat in the blink of an eye if he did not back off. Gwendolyn had but one confidant in the castle, the present and incumbent wife of Maelgwn who cared naught for his advances to the young girl and sought to constrain it, whether that ultimately meant poisoning the young girl to get rid of her or seeing her off the castle grounds and lands under the dominion of Maelgwn had not been decided yet. She cared not for the girl even though she pretended to, for she was as wicked as Maelgwn and wont to get her own way in whatever manner she could. At meal times in the great hall Gwendolyn would be careful of the food and wine she drank. At other times she was shackled like some dog and forced to sit on the ground at the lord's feet and forced to gnaw on the bones thrown to the dogs like an animal as a punishment. She longed for the day her shackles could be wrapped around the throat of her captor and tightened so all she would hear was his gasping for breath as the life eked out of him. And as time went by he became more insistent as to his amorous advances and had it not been for his wife's interventions he would have taken her by force already . . .

As the young girl was shackled at Maelgwn's feet a scullery boy knelt down to hand her a piece of meat and some potatoes. The face the boy wore was that of her brother Arturius the younger. Gwendolyn masked her inner feelings and grabbed at the food hungrily, A swipe of Maelgwn's hand knocked the food away causing it to mix with the hay upon the earthen floor, "Now you may eat it . . ." he laughed.

Gwendolyn picked up the pieces and hungrily ate what she could before being dragged away to her prison in the tower . . . The young boy's eyes followed her. Hatred and anger boiled inside his body but he quelled the flames and served the dishes as he was bade . . . Arturius the younger stayed long in the castle of his enemies but could find no way to secure the release of his sister, until one day, when Maelgwn was tired of his wife's insistent naggings and the pain and rebuffs of the young girl no longer interested him, he decided to offer her up as a prize in a sword contest, for the girl now wore tattered rags and her hair was unkempt for she had no place to bathe and keep herself clean. She was now little more than a vagabond from the gutters . . . Rumors abounded that she was of noble birth but none, except a privy few, knew who she really was . . . Because of her state few entered the competition open to all. Maelgwn had many mistresses but these bothered the wife of Maelgwn naught, for she was only concerned with getting rid of Gwendolyn, and if she fell into the hands of murderers and thieves it would be a fitting end to the young girl who was her competition in the eyes of Maelgwn . . .

At Myrddin's cave Gwyneth slowly regained her strength when one day a familiar shape presented itself at the entrance to the cave. Myrddin strode in with a stout man behind him, one that held a bow made from Welsh oak, and on his back he had a quiver full of steel tipped arrows. "How are you my niece . . ." said Myrddin, "It has been a long time . . ."

On the day of the competition, in a field outside the castle near the forest, the scullery lad who had his eyes upon the young lass did well, a little too well for Maelgwn, so he threw in some of his best fighting men to trounce the youngster. All to no avail, for the scullery lad bested them too with a sword that shone strong and bright in his strong hands. Even the tattooed behemoth that had stood guard outside Gwendolyn's prison in the castle was also bested, for his strength proved naught against the cunning and guile and swordsmanship of the young scullery lad. So in the end the boy won and claimed his prize. As the pair left the arena Maelgwn sensed he was being tricked. He wondered who the boy really was, and as his eyes flicked from the forms of Gwendolyn and the scullery lad, he realized too late who he was, the boy of Arturius, the heir to Camelot. Horses had been waiting for the pair outside the arena and as Arturius the younger and Gwendolyn, free from her shackles at last, mounted them, a great cry escaped Maelgwn's lips, "SEIZE THEM!" At that the brother and sister kicked away those that sought to detain them further and gave steel to those who brandished weapons. And from the forest a rain of arrows fell about those pursuing them causing them to fall dead on the earth beneath their feet . . .

In the forest Myrddin stood aside his niece Gwyneth, and aside them were Welsh archers, the few who had remained loyal to Arturius, with bow in hand and arrows knocked . . .

It was a sad day whence Arturius and Gwendolyn set sail for the land of the Scotti with Myrddin. And Gwyneth's eyes watered when the last sight of its sail disappeared, but she knew their time together had come to an end and she must find life anew in the arms of another, they were older now and soon they would need her no more . . . *But one day, one day, they would be back to claim what was theirs*, hoped Gwyneth . . . Even if it were but an old woman named Gwyneth who loved them with all her heart . . . The words of Myrddin had pained her much, "Their future lies on a different path to yours Gwyneth, one day they or their descendants will be called upon to rid our land of evil. When, I cannot say, for that time is hidden from me. Much I can see, but much I cannot . . . You must now live your life as they will of theirs . . ." They were words of wisdom, she knew, but they were words that pained her heart for she wished ever to be with them . . .

* * *

Between 1870 and 1890 my father's father had no training per say and learnt life the hard way, teaching himself what he needed to know to survive. While he was training to become a welder with The Great Eastern Railway, which later became the London North Eastern Railway, he met my grandmother at a fairground. Grandfather would go to circuses and fairgrounds to battle it out in the ring with bare fists just to make money to survive. He travelled all over England and was really good at slugging it out with the other contestants or chosen champion; he didn't really have much of a choice at that time. The family had struggled through a tough period when fortunes had been lost rather than made. When he retired he was given a walking stick with a gold band around it and a bowler hat, which in those days was the mark of the landed gentry. Grandfather came to stay with us for a while and it was during that time that he took Jim and I to a circus, it was the first time we'd been to one and we were really excited. As we walked around looking at the elephants, lions, camels and other wild creatures, grandfather told us many of his circus adventures and the fights he had had, knocking down big men twice the size of himself in David vs. Goliath battles. My grandfather had three children with my Welsh grandmother, Uncle Jack, Uncle Ken and Uncle Edward. My father's and Uncle Albert's mother was Ellen Peters who died in 1910. Dad took me to see Jack when I was still very young while he was running a confectionary business. He gave me a beautiful boat which I launched into the sea at the beach nearby. That was the last I saw of it as the waves and tide took it away from the seashore. I ran up and down the beach willing for it to return to no avail. All I could do was watch the wooden yacht with the red sail disappear into the waves of the North Sea, not realizing that my future would also see me sailing again and again into that same big wide sea and the ocean beyond it, facing terrible storms and an enemy that would hide beneath the waves . . . Uncle Jack became the Mayor of Lowerstoft not long afterwards. When we visited Uncle Ken he was, like my father, working for the LNER as an office manager. He was very bright and articulate, but very quiet. Dad and I went to see him often but I only met his son once and we never saw his wife.

\* \* \*

The Tale of the Knights Templar: There were two brothers, John and Mark, knights both, born of noble blood. In years past they had joined the Knights Templar to be of service to God, helping the safe passage of supplicants to Jerusalem. They had experienced many privations and suffered much in the service of our Lord, fighting the Moslem masses in the Holy Land and keeping thieves and villeins from the throats of those that sought to make pilgrimage to the Christ's place of birth and the walled city of Jerusalem. In many battles had they fought to make passage safe, pushing the Mameluke masses back for the sake of our Lord. They had witnessed many vile acts committed by both sides and had become disenchanted with what was seen to be a just cause. In castles high in hot Biblical lands they had repelled Mameluke hordes with sword and spear, with friends and comrades dying around them. Beloved brothers were they whose skulls were crushed by enemies vile in an attempt to stop them rising from the grave to smite down their killers. The Templar vows they had held not wishing to bring the wrath of God down upon themselves and the Rule of the Templars they had kept to the letter. They had remained abstinent and allowed their beards to grow and had not washed for what had seemed many years. In a castle strong in a green forested land awaited their father eager for news of his two sons strong and stout, riding solid steeds birthed on the very soil he stood. If it were not for his other children he would have long wept for their absence . . .

The fortified cites of Marqab, Tripoli, Acres and Tyre fell to the Mamelukes. At first the sultan Kala'un had led the Egyptian army but after his death on November 11th, 1290, on his way to Acre, his son, al-Ashraf, swore to continue the assault on the Christians in the Holy Land and kill them all. The Templar Grand Master Beaujeu had warned of the coming onslaught but no one had listened to him, preferring instead to hide their heads in the sand. They comforted themselves in the thought that the Moslems were eager to continue trade and make use of the banking facilities the Templars offered to Christian and Moslem alike. The Mamelukes had other ideas though; they intended to strike down the Christians, men, women and children without mercy, destroying any chance of them returning by striping down their giant stone defensive edifices brick by brick, and throwing them out of the Holy Land for good. When Tripoli's towers and a section of the wall had fallen Kala'un had ordered his men in, and as the battle continued Venetian and Genoese ships left carrying the wealthy and those in power, including the marshals of the Templars and the Hospitallers with Prince Amalric of Cyprus and the countess Lucia of Tripoli. The Knights Templar and Hospitallers defended the castle and the remaining Christians to a man. Every male in the castle was put to the sword by Kala'un's Mamelukes.

The surviving women and children were bound together and marched off to the slave markets. After this Kala'un declared a truce that was as empty as a discarded flagon of ale. He then ordered his Syrian army to move to the coast of Palestine and the Egyptian army to march to Acre. The sultan wanted Acre and offered to let its inhabitants leave peacefully if a ransom of one gold ducat per person was given. The leaders of Acre scoffed at the offer and sent envoys to the sultan. These were taken to the sultan's dungeon and murdered. The defenders of Acre boasted a fighting force of fifteen thousand men; the new sultan had a force of one hundred and fifty thousand men. It was not long before Acre fell when the sultan's engineers undermined the defensive walls bringing them down. And as the men, women and children were slaughtered inside the city the harbor filled with distraught citizens seeking to escape. Boats sank with the weight of people trying to leave. A Templar by the name of Roger Flor sold places aboard a Templar galley for the jewel cases noblewomen held. The city was in rout. In the end only a fortified Templar building remained as a thorn in the sultan's side. For the Templars preferred to defend the women and children of Acre with their lives rather than fleeing in their galleys as had so many others. The sly sultan offered a truce allowing the Templars and their charges to withdraw but no sooner had one hundred Mamelukes and an emir entered the building they began assaulting its survivors. The Templars cut them down for their disgusting behavior unable to stand by and watch. The sly sultan then offered an apology and invited the Templar marshal and his officers to be his guests. That night, as they approached the sultan's tent they were attacked and beheaded. This subterfuge gave the sultan's engineers time to undermine the fortified walls. In the end no Christian was left alive within Acre . . . This pattern was repeated with Sidon falling and then Beirut and Haifa, and the monasteries on Mount Carmel torched and the monks slaughtered, the small garrison in a castle at Athlit, a few miles from Haifa, withdrew, and the Templar castle at Tortosa was abandoned, for against the whole of the Egyptian army their sacrifice would have been a worthless gesture. So they boarded their galleys and just sailed away . . . The Templars stayed on at their castle on Ruad, two miles across the sea from Tortosa, but since there was no water on the small island and everything had to be brought in by galleys, they withdrew and left it, since it was more trouble than it was worth . . . The Holy Land was now lost to the sultan and his Moslem Mamelukes . . . *For, in their eyes, Christian and Jew were now unbelievers, dogs, deserving of nothing more than death itself* . . . But, in years past Moslems would protect the lives of Jews, Christians and Sabaens alike, for they spoke of them as being *'Those of the Book'* and they referred to them as brothers and kindred spirits . . . *At that time they shared a love of the one true God whom they all worshipped in peace and harmony . . .*

The Knights Templar were a monastic order of knights, knights that had chosen to follow the Rule, which was embodied in three basic vows, the first of chastity, the second obedience and the third of poverty. They were beholden to no one except the Pope and divided into three classes. The first of which were the full brothers, and were the fighting arm of the Templars, these were freemen of noble birth; the mantle worn by them was white with an eight pointed cross on it, this signified purity of thought and deed. The second class, who were termed sergeants, and drawn from a free bourgeoisie, wore a black or dark brown mantle with the red cross on it. They acted as squires, men-at-arms, grooms, stewards, sentries and so forth. Thirdly were the clerics who were literate scribes, they served mass, kept records and were clean shaven, unlike the knights who left their beards to grow and kept their hair short. Their mantle was green with a red Templar cross on it. The Templar flag was vertical with one block of black to represent the world of sin they had left behind and another block of pure white representing the pure life of the Knights Templar. The banner was called 'Beau Séant' which was also the battle cry of the Templars and meant 'Be noble!' and 'Be glorious!' For the Templars were expected to fight to the last man. They were not permitted to retreat unless ordered to by the field commander. Even if the opposing force was innumerable the Rule had to be obeyed and most Templars expected to die in battle, for the knights of the order never retreated and never surrendered, for no ransom would ever be paid for a Knight Templar because the order forbade the use of funds for this purpose. Surrender would mean summary execution if a Knight Templar were to be captured . . . The Templar Rule was subject to the Grand Master and could be changed or ignored, depending on the exigencies of the time. The Templars were permitted two meals a day and could also eat meat because of the strenuous nature of their work. The order, itself, held over nine thousand manors over Europe, and a large number of mills and markets which they derived funds from, let alone their banking facilities, and loot and other sources, including dowries from knights and gifts from wealthy benefactors. With all this amassed wealth the Templars were able to afford their own galleys, but along with this abundance of material goods there were those who were jealous of the Order and its possessions, wanting to take control of them . . .

Thrown out of the Holy Land by the Mamelukes the Knights Templar set up base in Cyprus along with the Knights Hospitallers after King Henry reluctantly gave them permission to do so. He wished to control the military might of the Templars but the Grand Master de Molay refused, eventually the matter was put to the Pope and the decision reached was that the Knights Templar in Cyprus remained an independent body apart from King Henry's men. The entire debacle in the Holy Land would not have occurred had those in charge of the cities listened to the Templars, for they had foreseen through their own intelligence gathering what was about to occur and could have taken steps to avoid it . . . Jacques de Molay had been a Knights Templar since the age of twenty one in 1265, he was elected Grand Master after Tibald Gaudin had died, and now at forty eight he was in charge of the order that now had no reason for its existence. Jacques de Molay was a strong disciplinarian and reinforced the Rule with strict control to ensure the Knights Templar remained orthodox. He even outlawed literacy and the owning of books for the Templars. He still had control of thousands of agricultural manors all over Europe, the markets and mills, and the Templar banking operations, but because they now had no foothold in the Holy Land donations and gifts started to dry up. He pushed Pope Boniface VIII for a new crusade which eventually led to the Pope calling for a meeting in Paris to discuss his plans to integrate both the Knights of the Hospital of St. John of Jerusalem and the Knights of the Temple of Solomon. The new order would be called the Knights of Jerusalem with a single leader known as the *Rex Bellator*, or *War King*. This order would control the vast sums of assets and money of both organizations for supposedly a new crusade to take back the Holy Land. King Phillip opposed this for he owed large amounts of money to the Knights Templar and he had his eyes on the valuable assets they owned in France where the bulk of their property and assets were. He devised a plan to rid himself of his debts and acquire their possessions. Jacques de Molay had no clue as to the subterfuge and trickery King Phillip of France and his co-conspirator, Guillaume de Nogaret, had put into place, even going so far as to plant spies in various commanderies of the Templars. De Nogaret had gained infamy by engineering the kidnapping of Pope Boniface VIII after his father and mother had been burned at the stake as Albigensian heretics. No deed was too low for him as he pursued his course of revenge and enrichment. While de Molay outlined his plans to the Papacy Phillip and his partner in crime, de Nogaret, planted two spies in Toulouse, one was a former Knight Templar who had been expelled from the order and was out for revenge and money. Both had been condemned to death and confessed to each other. The former Templar filled his confessions with lies about the Knights Templar and untruths about rights and initiations. The spies were subsequently released and rewarded and the information passed on to the King. The operation entailed the capture and jailing of fifteen thousand Templars in France which was to be done simultaneously and in secret. The plan was the same as the one that de Nogaret had used against the Jews in France on July the 22nd in 1306. He and Phillip had incarcerated and exiled all the Jews in France and seized all their property and monies. All Jewish chattel was auctioned off by the state and all debts owed by King Phillip and France to Jews were cancelled. Any sums to be paid to the Jews of France were confiscated by the Exchequer of France, leaving French Jews penniless. Now these same tactics would be used against the Knights Templar so he could enrich himself and continue his war against England, for he had no wish to take part in any new crusades to retake the Holy Land. The Templars were aware something was afoot and one knight was even commended on leaving the order because a catastrophe was about to befall the Templars. Jacques de Molay, secure in his belief that only the Pope could countermand him on this earthly plane of existence, was lulled into a false sense of security, for wealth, position and the force of men-at-arms under his control had inured him to any possible danger to the Knights Templar. And so, while de Molay acted as a pall-bearer at the funeral of Princess Catherine, King Phillip's sister in law, the plan was set in motion . . . At the appointed hour seneschals all around France opened their sealed and secret orders . . . On Friday, October 13th 1307, fifteen thousand sets of chains were clasped around the hands and feet of every single Templar in France. The following day de Nogaret announced his fallacious claims about the Templars to the citizens of France to get popular support for his and Phillip's iniquitous behavior. Pope Clement V had approved an investigation of the Templars but not the mass arrest and torture of them. Phillip returned that he had merely been assisting the pope. The pope stood firm and ordered an immediate end of hostilities against the Templars and that they should be released. To this Phillip launched a propaganda campaign against Clement V charging him with leniency toward the so-called heretics, and wanting to gain Templar wealth for himself. Phillip, with an army behind him surrounded the papal city and threatened to kill all those within and burn it to the ground if the pope refused to relent. In the end the pope gave in to Phillip and declared the charges against them to be true and ordered the arrest and torture of all Templars in monarchies aligned to Christendom . . . On the first day of their arrest many died while being tortured by priests of the Inquisition. The agony-death borderline was taken to the limit in the quest for incriminating evidence, including the use of hot irons, disembowelment, the rack, thumbscrews and mediaeval confinement, including throwing recalcitrant prisoners into an *oubliette* where waste from the prisoners was collected. Templars were even roasted alive to force confessions from them, even having their legs burnt off, with the victims wishing only to die to stop the torture. With a heinous array of instruments a confession was sure to be rung from even the most pious of individuals. With such wicked, evil actions on the part of Phillip, de Nogaret and Clement V, it is no wonder that the Templars of Briton fled into hiding to prevent the same persecution being heaped upon them. De Molay and Brother de Charney were tortured, they confessed, then recanted their confessions publicly, de Molay confessed, "I must declare the Order is innocent. Its purity and saintliness are beyond question . . ." This was an embarrassment to Phillip and the church for they were immediately taken off the platform to be burned alive . . . As de Molay and de Charney were roasted they proclaimed their innocence vehemently, with de Molay bringing down the wrath of God by cursing both Phillip, his family, and the pope . . . Clement V died the following month and Phillip in November of that year . . . In England arrests of the Templars began at the behest of Clement V who even sent torturers to Edward II for the express purpose of wringing confessions from the English knights. In Scotland Robert Bruce had no interest in arresting the Templars for he had his own problems to attend to, especially the thought of an English army crossing the Tweed to trounce the Scots . . . And, it is against this background that our story takes place . . .

The journey from the Holy Land had been long and hard for John and Mark, for they, along with many of their brethren and those that had fought with them, were returning warily to their homes in Briton. For having faced the Moslem hordes the survivors now faced an even greater peril, that of King Phillip of France and Pope Clement V, who, having conspired against the Knights Templar and seizing its assets now wanted every Templar imprisoned, tortured and killed. Phillip's lust for treasure had been consummate, for he had rallied his wicked forces against the Jews and now it was the Templar's turn. It were a terrible thing indeed and not good that a man, a holy knight, should be under threat of sword continually and eventually perish by torture, having the flesh burnt off his body, having his bones broken, being disemboweled and hung, having served his God with so much passion and fortitude . . . This was an evil thing indeed to do to the men of the Knights Templar. The Templar galley had set sail and rowed out from Cyprus at the first indication things would not go well for them should they remain. The word of what had transpired in France and the order from Pope Clement V to imprison and torture all Knights Templars had propelled the Knights Templar in Cyprus to action. They had stockpiled food and water in their galleys and gathered together a small fortune in jewels and gold ducats. Moslem merchants were used to sell any chattel owned by the Templar Order to avoid suspicion. The Templars only refuge would be under Edward in Briton, for word had come from the Temple in London that safety could be sought there . . . It had been a hazardous journey indeed avoiding the spies of France and the Friars of the Inquisition. They had anchored in out of the way places and sought sustenance and water. They had given

France and its dominions a wide berth and kept to the African coastline as much as they could. They had sailed around Spain with but one stop to resupply with water, fruit and meat. They had money; plenty of it, for it was no good to leave it in Cyprus where it was sure to be taken. No, they had chosen correctly for the agents of Phillip and Clement were after them, and if caught the only succor they could hope for was a swift and painless death. But even that was unlikely, it was more likely they would have received a roasting and then a burning at the stake screaming for mercy or calling down the Holy wrath of God upon their persecutors. John shook his head as thoughts of what could have happened filled his head. Both he and his brother Mark wore their white mantles with the red eight pointed cross emblazoned upon them proudly. They had done their duty for both God and the Templar order. They had not shied away at any order that could have meant their deaths. For many years past they had vowed to each other when young they would make their father proud and follow in the footsteps of the crusaders who had freed the Holy Land from the unrighteous and given it into the hands of the God fearing Christians. They had held this belief close to their hearts and when faced with those self same Moslems who had been spoken badly of by the priests of the Catholic faith, they realized we are all believers in some form or another, and that it is man himself who seeks the demon in others. Their exposure to the Moslems gave them another perspective than the one they had believed in from the time they were but babes. They had learnt that in many respects the Moslem culture had much to offer, that their understanding of medicine was by far superior to the witch doctors of Christianity. That cleanliness was next to Godliness, that what was pursued as the truth and word of God was not necessarily true, for they had seen much evil and greed in the halls of supposed holy ones, and this had made them question the veracity of the Holy Church. But they believed in what they were doing, even if all others failed in keeping the word of God they had determined to do their utmost to protect it and hold it close to their chests. Unfortunately the lies and iniquities of others in holy places and kingship had now tainted their beliefs even more. They had done their duty in the Holy Land and had not spared the sword to those who had taken up arms against them. They had never used them against women and children of any faith, for that indeed, were a foul thing to do in the eyes of God and would lead to everlasting damnation. Let those heathens do evil, but those of the Templar Brotherhood do that which is good in the eyes of God. Let them be the upstanding ones without an evil stain upon their white mantles. Mark breathed in the the salty air, John stood next to him as the pair looked into the distance and the heavy rollers hitting their port beam. The seas were becoming rougher and all aboard hoped and prayed that they would make it home to Briton. But if they did not, well, it would be a fate much preferable to the Inquisition, that was to be sure . . . Amongst their hastily assembled crew were scribes and priests of the Order, and squires, men-at-arms who tended their horses and kept their armor and swords bright and free from rust. Also aboard was a Moslem merchant who they had saved in Acre from the Roman Christians who had savagely sought the blood of his kind; and a French Jewish family who had sought refuge from persecution from both secular and priestly powers in Europe, for, penniless, they hungered for a better life somewhere in the known world . . . The Rule those Templars aboard the galley had kept, but now there was no Rule, no Order, and no Knights of the Temple of Solomon. There would be no new crusade, which was clear in John's mind, for with the wealth of the Knights Templar grabbed and dispersed into the coffers of King Phillip of France and his agents' pockets, no one could even begin to finance such an undertaking. Besides, it was the Templars who had been pushing for a new crusade, no one else. For the Teutonic Knights concentrated their efforts and had taken control of Prussia and the Knights Hospitallers had sought out Malta as their domain. But de Molay had ignored all of this and misguidedly stuck to the dream of retaking what had been lost to the Mamelukes. But all that had now vanished with the painful cries of Jacques de Molay and de Charney as they had been unjustly burned at the stake, their only real crimes being that of arrogance and a failure to see what was happening around them. Jacques had entered Paris in pomp and ceremony, taking residence in the Templar castle instead of arriving incognito and going to the Papal residence immediately, ignoring the pope's commands. This had indirectly led to all that had later transpired. With jurisprudence what occurred may have been averted had de Molay taken heed of the signs all around him and had he been a masterful tactician in courtly manipulation. If he had, maybe the Templars would have still existed. What they should have done was take by force their own island in the Mediterranean. Somewhere safe they could defend and keep their wealth, or at least a portion of it . . . This could have been their saving grace . . . But that was all chaff in the wind now, for no safeguards had been taken to prevent the impending doom of the Templar Order . . . Many had known of it but none dared to question the Grand Master . . .

Both John and Mark looked forward to returning home and seeing their parents and siblings again. They looked forward to the green lushness of the land of their birth, the tall trees and rolling hills and mountains of Wales and Scotland . . . But above this thought they wondered what the reception of their ship would be. Edward was at war with Phillip and he had no love of him that was for sure, hopefully the persecution would not be as bad as the rest of Europe . . . And then there was Robert Bruce and the land of the Scots. He had no love of Edward and the orders of Clement V . . . Would it be possible to find sanctuary there . . . *Only time would tell* . . .

The southern English coastline was spotted during the night and it was decided that they would plot a course for a little fishing village whence an old Templar was to be found to ascertain what the reception would be if they continued to

the Thames River and London itself. For it had been decided
in Cyprus that the galleys of the Templars would rendezvous
there and head for the Temple for further instructions. John
and Mark checked their horses and those of others, for they
could not bear to leave them in Cyprus having served their
masters well. They were well trained and tested in battle, and
the horses would kick and bite those around them if need be.
They had much armor as a warhorse was wont to wear. In the
hot climes of the Holy Land John had nearly lost his to lack
of water. The Jewish family was already up and at the rails.
They had family in London and hoped it would be possible
to land there. Mohammed, the Moslem merchant was also at
the rails, having nere seen Briton before and wondering what
his reception would be. He viewed the Christians aboard as
brothers for he was not like the Mamelukes who had ravaged
the Holy Land, he wished just to continue his trade in peace and
harmony, but the sultans of Egypt had destroyed his business
with the Christians and he resented them for that. He had no
love of them and saw in the men around him brothers and
kindred spirits and not unbelievers, they were different yes, but
they held firm their belief in God . . . Mohammed had much in
the way of eastern goods to trade, for he had brought his entire
stock with him and once sold would return and hopefully come
back with more spices, silken cloth and the like. At one time
he had been a man-of-arms, but now that he was older he just
wished to live in peace and make an honorable living, wherever
it may take him. Even for John and Mark the future looked dim,
could they continue as knights? It seemed doubtful, unless they
travelled to the land of the Scots. Neither looked forward to
that cold and rain soaked land, but where else could they go, to
the Far East, to the land of the Vikings, back to the Holy Land
and the welcome arms of the new sultan who would have their
heads stuck on posts outside some dusty city's walls, no . . . The
only recourse for both French and English Knight Templars was
Briton, for t'was a dark day indeed when Phillip had launched

his underhanded campaign against the Knight Templar Order. John wondered whether he and his brother could stay at their ancestral castle . . . this was in the lap of the gods and King Edward . . .

It did not take long for the pilot to steer a course for the little village and before morning in the early hours they had found it. They had to be very careful as they rowed their small boat to shore for England was at war with France and it would have been a tragedy to be seen as a French raider. As the small boat was dragged ashore a voice in the darkness called out, "Are ye Englishmen?"

John held up his head and took a grip on the long sword hanging by his side, he called back, "Of course, who else would we be. We are knights returning home to our families . . . Show yourself voice in the darkness . . ."

A small man with a pole axe stepped out from behind some bushes. "I see by your garb who ye are Templar. I too once served the Order, ye are welcome home . . . May God be with you . . . Do ye have Frenchmen aboard your galley?"

"Yes," replied John, "But they are Frenchmen no more, their once king has declared war upon them and vowed to roast them alive. They seek sanctuary in our fair isles . . ."

"All is well then, ye may be about your business, but know this the Pope has wont of ye blood so be careful who thou speakest to . . ." noted the guard with the pole axe, shying slightly at the sight of the Moslem in their midst.

"Aye, we shall . . ." stated Mark as he walked up the stony beach, "We shall leave these men in your good care whilst we seek the one we came to find."

With that John and Mark, with Mohammed following, headed to the village to seek the aid of a man whom they knew they could trust . . . Trudging up the dusty street it were not long before a certain door was found and John tapped on it lightly.

An elderly man opened the door but a fraction, his sleep fogged eyes opened wide, "Who be that at such an early hour?"

"It is one of your brothers Samuel, a brother who has travelled long from the Holy Land looking for a safe place to rest his weary head . . ." spoke Mark with a broad grin upon his face.

"Yes, you old dog, open up your door so we may proceed in out of the chill of your cold and inhospitable land . . ." chuckled John.

Samuel scanned the dark faces without his cottage intently, "Is it really you Mark and John, my brothers that have come to my humble abode . . ."

"Of course it is, who else would awake their own teacher at such an ungodly hour to warn him of an attack, Samuel . . ." said Mark.

Throwing open the door and shaking the proffered hands of John and Mark he then griped both in a bear hug and then said, "Long thought I that both of you were dead, I never dreamed that one day I would see either of you again. I had thought if the Mamelukes had not cleaved off your heads the King of France would have put you on the rack and then had his torturers eke out some sort of false confession from your lips before disemboweling you for words of mirth at the very least, let alone being a Templar . . ."

"Luck was fortunate for us good Samuel," spake John.

Samuel looked at the figure behind them, his face turned pale for his eyes were not that good anymore, "And who is that dark figure lurking behind you?"

"Do you not recognize him Samuel, it is Mohammed your old friend, the one whom you spoke so highly of in Acre many years back, he has come with us to make his fortune in selling silken cloth and other things from the Holy Land and the east.

"Is it true, that you are indeed Mohammed, my old friend?" spake Samuel.

"Of course it is you old mountain goat, whom else would it be darkening your doorstep with these men at this hour . . ." answered a laughing Mohammed.

"Then come in, lest there be spies of France and the Pope gadding about in the hope of securing some bloodstained reward," entreated the old man. With that the door closed behind the men going inside and it were not long before old Samuel offered them hot beverages of mint tea and hard cakes to slake both hunger and thirst . . .

The reunion could not last forever for the tide waited for no man and the galley would do naught but raise suspicion to the spies of King Phillip and Pope Clement. Samuel advised them to remove their mantles and that the Templar galley should have its flags and banners taken down to be replaced by one of England and the ships that plied back and forth for war against Phillip. He withdrew a standard from a locker that he had kept safe for such an eventuality should it come, being a man of great forethought in battle and providing water and supplies for the Knights Templar in the Holy Land. He was a man of great strategy and in some ways had seen the growing lust of Phillip when he was in France. Never did he trust the man. But who was he to advise a Grand Master . . . Samuel gave them the name of a Templar, a merchant now in London, who could sell the galley for a fair price, since all Templar chattel was confiscated and t'would be no good were it to fall into the Hospitallers' hands . . .

When they left all three vowed to come and see him again. Unseen by Samuel, John had left a present for him, a box with the Templar cross on it, and inside the box were many gold ducats and precious jewels. For they had all taken vows of poverty, but the old man needed more, of that John could see . . . Just before they left he whispered in the old man's ear, "I have left a small gift of appreciation for your sacrifice Samuel, hide it well . . ." with those words the three left and headed back in the twilight to the rocky beach . . .

The galley slipped up the Thames and took dock unnoticed by all because of the standards and flag it bore. The horses were taken ashore and led to a nearby stable to be cared for. Mohammed's goods were also taken ashore and placed in a storehouse for which the owner was paid handsomely. The Jewish family disembarked and left to find appropriate lodgings and extended family, which in London, would have been a difficult task indeed were it not for the Rabbis and places of worship, for there they would find both brothers and sisters of the faith . . . They had need of a country to call home and Briton seemed to be the safest at the moment, in France they were unwelcome and in Germany the hands of many were covered in the blood of those who kept the ancient Mosaic Laws . . .

John and Mark, being the leaders in their expedition had a brief meeting with a shadowy figure which led them to an unassuming dwelling in Cheapside that night. Rain and a chilled wind kept most of the inhabitants indoors where it was warm. The pair pulled their hooded cloaks tightly around them as they carefully avoided the human detritus that flowed in the open sewers. A man motioned them from a darkened alcove to follow him. The circuitous path he took left them completely lost in this warren of lost souls, and before long he led them to a dwelling secluded from all and sundry. The door opened and the men filed in going up a flight of stairs to a chamber filled with many hooded men such as they themselves . . . An hour later the men left in small groups and disappeared into the dark rain filled night.

As John and Mark neared the docks John spoke of what they had heard, "Things seem not well for us, do they, Mark?"

"If you speakest of that dog Phillip destroying what God has built, then yes, I agree . . ." said Mark somberly.

"We were lucky to have escaped with our lives, for even now in Cyprus things go badly for the Order," noted John.

"I wonder how long before this satanic persecution of Phillip will spread its evil rot even to these green lands," added Mark.

"We will have to make haste then, for I wish to see father and mother before we ourselves disappear never to be seen again . . ." spake John, shaking his head from side to side, "I would hate them to think ill of us or the Templar Order . . ."

"Indeed . . ." whispered Mark with the same dark melancholy that pervaded John's spirit.

As they passed a tavern a tremendous shout rang out, "Get him!" A familiar figure bounded out the doorway and bumped into them, it was Mohammed, bleeding from the lip and bruised on the eye. "Save me fair knights, for the men inside wish to do me, a poor merchant and your friend, harm, and take the tradable goods that are mine . . ."

A large man rushed out the low doorway and nearly bumped his head on the lintel. Behind him were many weasel faced ingrates wishing to do the Moslem trader mischief. "And what do we 'ave 'ere, more lambs to the slaughter?" shouted the burly thief.

"We are lambs to no one's slaughter my good man . . ." piped in Mark, his hand on the hilt of his sword under his cloak. "Oh, so ye be wantin' a fight, do ye?"

"Nothing of the sort, we wish to carry on our chosen path with no harm to us or this man chased from yonder establishment," said John in a calming manner.

"Unfortunately we can't allow that, this man has sold us all his cloth and goods for a fair price, one gold coin . . ." hissed the burly man.

"That is a lie, you offered to leave the flesh on my bones should I hand over everything I own," said Mohammed with contempt.

"If that be your final word we are in disagreement then," snorted the burly man pulling out a long wicked looking knife, as did the others behind him.

Two swords flashed bright in the darkness and ended pressing against the throat of the burly would be thief. "If I were you I would think twice before you ere think of committing yon dagger to anything save its sheath . . ." put John to the man. The man gulped and gradually returned the blade to its leather. Turning, the men behind him returned to the tavern, however, before the big brute entered he turned and snarled, "You should not have become involved for ye are dead men now . . ."

John and Mark, with Mohammed following, slipped carefully down narrow streets keeping an eye out for any untoward movement. "I think maybe you should come home with us, Mohammed, London, it seems, does not agree with you . . ." smiled John.

"Nor I with it," said Mohammed with a touch of remorse . . .

The following day two knights rode their horses slightly ahead of the two carriages behind them. And behind them were two knights formerly of the Templar order mounted on two war horses that had also seen the hot sands and dusty rocks of the Holy Land. Mark chuckled, "Had you told me that someday I would be protecting the life and goods of a Moslem merchant in Briton en route to the castle of our forefathers, I would have laughed heartily . . ."

"As would I brother, as would I . . ." added John.

In a forest not too far from London the thieves that had nearly tasted Templar steel lay in wait, hoping to take what was not theirs. A log barred the progress of the carts and the small entourage of Templars, their men-at-arms, the two cart men and the merchant. At once, the cry of "Beau Séant!" was sung by the men high atop their battle steeds as men of ill-repute fell upon them in droves with weapons of steel. Shod hooves kicked out and sharp biting teeth found the soft flesh of those wishing to do the noble knights harm. Templar steel, hardened in battle, cleaved skull and body alike in a bloodletting frenzy that shocked the assailants, for they had never seen the like of the Templars in battle, where there was never a thought of surrender nor backing down to a foe, for forward they pushed smiting hither and thither until no foe remained on the field of battle, just the heaving perspiring flanks of horses and the sound of snorting escaping from the mouths of these self-same steeds . . . The battle had been swift and the enemy lay on the ground about them . . . "We had best continue on our way lest there be more of them," panted John as his horse wheeled about in circles searching for any foe that might remain alive.

"Agreed!" chorused the knights in unison. And so they proceeded, but more wary now, for the woods, once pleasant and calm, seemed full of thieves and vagabonds intent on the deaths of those who accompanied the merchant and his goods . . .

They stopped not for the night but pushed on wanting to be as far away from London as possible, just in case the fiends responsible for the attack decided to come back in force . . . At the first decent tavern they felt was defensible they stopped to take rest and sustenance. The Templar Order was filled with men inured to hardship and toughened in battle, and even their horses worried not for water and food but could travel vast distances with metal encased men atop them. The group posted watch outside the tavern and all kept a wary eye out as they tended horses and went about their business . . .

It was early in the morning when a shrill cry rent the mist without the tavern, "To arms men!" shouted the watch. Having slept in mail with swords still strapped on the Templars were greeted by more of the vagabonds they had bested two days before. But, as on that day, Templar steel prevailed and the blood of thieves was yet spilled again on English soil, such was the welcome the knights received at the hands of those wont to steal what was not theirs, thinking that the Moslem should give up his goods for this was their country. Not so, thought the knights who defended both him and his belongings with the swords that had most recently defended Acre in the Holy Land and cut down many a Mameluke that had run amok in its streets once fair and good, having been turned into a slaughterhouse with the blood of Christians . . . John and Mark had been amongst the few who had survived for they had but fully expected to die at the bloody hands of the sultan but were instructed to defend a galley with their lives for it contained both wealth and important persons from the city . . . This was their lot then, to forever regret not facing the Egyptian

Sultan's men in a last bloodletting with their own life's blood soaking into the sands where prophets once strode. They had then survived while others had not . . . This stopped them not cleaving steel into the bodies of their attackers, for they leapt into battle full of vigor and righteous anger . . .

When the last sword drank the blood of the vanquished the tavern keeper sent them on their way, not wishing for more trouble, as it was, how would he explain what had transpired in the dead of night . . . Packing quickly and girding themselves, the knights left with goods and merchant intact and no worse for the fight undertaken . . .

The merchant swore he would not stop until he was safely in the abode of the brothers' ancestral castle. The two brothers were wont to agree with him, for the country of Briton seemed full of louts and vagabond thieves out for their blood . . .

In the castle of their forefathers a father and mother greeted their long lost sons with fervor and gladness beyond comprehension, for they were sure never would they see them again. The brothers' father's heart beat out a quickened and welcome beat when he caught glimpse of them riding across the moat bridge. His men-at-arms were shocked to see them still alive, for all thought with the fall of the Holy Land they had perished in the battles against the Mamelukes . . . A fair banquet was held that night, a banquet of gratitude to one most high, the God of the Christian faith. Even so, Mohammed, was not left out and even he was welcomed warmly by all and sundry who attended. The affair was kept in secret though, for all knew the edict from Clement the fifth and how he persecuted all those who accepted the Templar Rule . . .

Many days later it was decided they should head north to the land of the Scots where Clement the fifth's edict held as much water as a rotted leather water bladder. There they would find life in the hills and vales, and possibly work, instead of enchainment and torture should it be found that they were at home in the stone battlements of their forefathers. With much sadness from all the party left with promises to return one day if it were possible, for who knew what devilment Phillip and Clement would brew next . . . As the tears of their mother and sisters disappeared behind them and the rutted track toward Scotland stretched before them Mohammed spoke part in mirth and part in all seriousness, "I have need of two strong men such as you to protect me from your countrymen, whilst thou serve me as truly as you have served your Order?"

John, Mark and the others in their party laughed, then John turned to the Moslem in the cart aside his horse and cheerily voiced, "To be a slave under yon Moslem yoke, verily ye jest good friend Mohammed?"

Mohammed looked shyly at him, "Then be it as my business partners then, how wouldst that suit ye?" Mark slowed his steed to fall back to his brother. "It could go well my brother," said Mark mirthfully. "Aye, that it might, but we had better change our ancestral name for they will ere be searching for our Templar blood, how is the name le Chapman for you, brother Mark? It is a fitting name if we are to be merchants with yon rascal . . ." John said nodding in Mohammed's direction. "Aye, it will be fitting. Let it be so then . . ." finished Mark to the conversation. Kicking his heels into his steed Mark let his big horse canter forward, turning he called back, "Most decidedly fitting, for the names of our past will be searched for high and low in the entire Christian world . . ."

\* \* \*

Willy Noakes and I decided to join the Sea Scouts since they sounded more interesting than the normal land based scouts, and I always wondered what it would be like on the high seas going to far and distant exotic lands. I would regularly take a walk to the Thames and the docks watching ships coming in and going out. The captain of the Sea Scouts was an interesting man in his mid-thirties who had a wealth of experience at sea.

Joining the Sea Scouts was really exciting; we learnt rope work and how to tie knots, how to steer a ship and use a compass. How currents moved around the British Isles, the oceans and seas surrounding it, how this large body of water had shaped the island we lived on and the seabed underneath. One of our outings was to the docks to see the big ships up close. Our captain really made sure we got the most out of each and every little adventure, making sure the learning experience was imprinted upon our young minds. On one trip we went to Walton on Naze. It had a river very near the entrance to the sea. The tidal plain stretched out about two miles and we were told that under no circumstances were we to venture out there since the sands were far too treacherous, for when the tide comes in it could cut you off from the shore in a matter of minutes. Even though we were warned it looked safe enough and was very enticing for a young boy. We didn't realize how the water swirled and eddied making islands out of the sand with deceptively fast currents running between them. You could get cut off from the shore very easily and in all probability drown. Well, like a fool, and me being the leader of our pack in our part of the camp, I took the boys away for a jaunt on the sands stretching tantalizingly before us. Luckily the captain saw us and started shouting for us to come in as the tide was coming in. It was just as well he spotted us for by the time we reached solid sand we were wading up to our knees in fast flowing water. When we got back to the camp I was called before the captain and read the riot act. The following morning, he explained, I would be sent home in disgrace for my behavior. With my tail between my legs I headed back to the boys and told them what had happened, they were all shocked. They made up their minds that if I had to go they would follow me home. This time the captain was shocked after he was informed that if I had to go the whole lot of them would pack it in as well, he didn't realize how popular I was. He changed his mind and told me I could stay. After that we all had a good time even though it was raining nearly every day. I even received a leadership rating of which I was really proud of . . .

\* \* \*

The Tale of Captain de Croix: Once upon a time in the emerald Isles, in the 16th Century, there lived a beautiful young girl called Elizabeth O'Sullivan, her flaxen hair and pale complexion were admired by all in County Cork where she lived with her parents, in a manor house surrounded by lands as far as the eyes could see. She had the most wonderful dolls to play with, for her father travelled far and wide to exotic lands to collect them for her. Elizabeth's favorite doll was *Betsy*, for wherever Elizabeth went *Betsy* was sure to be with her. The manor and its estates were admired far and wide and coveted by many. One person in particular had his greedy eyes set upon owning both the manor and the lands surrounding it, an English lord who was put in charge of the area in which they were situated. He concocted a story, an untruth, in which Elizabeth's father had stolen cattle from him and that he had committed treason against their English over-lords. The English lord also coveted Elizabeth's mother and determined to get the manor, the land and her. Elizabeth's father was arrested one stormy fateful night and tied to a stake in front of a firing squad. His lands and home and contents were confiscated and given to the aggrieved lord for damages, and now he would face the muskets of the soldiers. As the rain cascaded down upon them Elizabeth and her mother broke free from the soldiers holding them and shielded both father and husband. As the soldiers were preparing to shoot the peasants of Cork surrounded the manor and the soldiers with pitchforks and torches threatening to kill them if they touched their beloved fellow countryman. The leader of the rabble said, "You have his house, his belongings, his land and all on it so leave him with his life . . . If you do not spare him we will fight and throw you off the Emerald Isles!" Sensing both he and his men were outnumbered the lord relented and let them go free with their lives. They were now penniless beggars in their own land. Even the ship that Elizabeth's father owned had been seized. But the worse thing of all for poor Elizabeth was that *Betsy*, her favorite doll, was upstairs in her room and she was not even given leave to fetch her for they were chased off the estate with but the clothes on their backs. In the pouring cold rain the family left, and cold and shivering came upon a deserted cottage, a croft, on the coast of County Cork away from the prying eyes of all . . . Because Elizabeth's father had been fair and kind to all those under him the folk of Cork left eggs, chickens and pigs and clothes for them outside the door so that they would not starve to death. The clothes were naught but tatty rags for under the heel of oppression from the English that was all the folk of the area could afford to give, for they themselves were now treated as nothing more than penniless vagabonds and serfs enslaved to the land they ploughed and cared for. They now lived under the yolk of enforced labor and had become nothing but mere slaves to the English lord who had stolen the land away from the O'Sullivan family . . . From a vantage point on the coast, high on a bluff, Elizabeth's father could see the comings and goings of the ship he had once owned and this made him very sad, so sad in fact that he became ill from his heartache. He was now a broken man and wherever he went for work or to conduct some sort of business the merchants would whisper and point at him. He was now shunned by those he had once made wealthy, people he had once thought were his friends. The only ones that would talk to him were the downtrodden folk and there was little they could do to alleviate his woes. Wherever he went the English would prod him along with their bayonets or even give him the taste of the wooden stocks . . . It was because of this maltreatment that he died shamed and beaten by all save the good folk of the land he had once owned . . . Elizabeth's mother died shortly thereafter, heartbroken with her husband's death . . . Elizabeth was now alone, bereft of the two people she most cared for in the world. She had not even *Betsy* to share her angst with . . . Elizabeth was soon forgotten by all and the eggs and chickens stopped coming, forcing her to scavenge for herself with the three pigs she had raised from birth. A stray cat adopted Elizabeth and became her best friend along with the few chickens and ducks from whom she collected eggs from. Her life from before soon became a distant memory . . .

The years passed by and Elizabeth started to blossom. She was growing into a very beautiful young woman. She now had sheep from which she would collect the wool to make sweaters and warm clothing from, these she would trade in the village nearest her for dresses and other things to make her life a little less miserable. From the bees in the woods surrounding her croft she would collect honey and raspberries and nettles and mint for tea. She took nuts and ground tubers from the forest from whence she had planted them away from prying eyes. Her friends were the trees and animals and birds of the woods, for she never harmed one of them. When she found a trap set up by the villagers or townsfolk she would destroy it much to the annoyance and chagrin of those laying them. Those in the village were jealous of her beauty so she would put mud on her face and clothes to make herself less attractive when she went there to sell her meager goods. Elizabeth much preferred the company of the animals of the woods for they did not hurt her with untruths and wickedness . . .

One night a terrible storm tossed the sea like an angry god driving a wooden galleon towards the shore and the rocks. Elizabeth watched from her vantage point on a bluff as the men aboard her managed to steer the ship into her favorite secluded cove shielded by the woods from the shore and rocky outcrops from the waves lashing the coastline of Cork. Unbeknownst to Elizabeth the ship belonged to Captain de Croix, a Spanish sea captain, who had just survived the destruction of the Spanish Armada and been blown off course onto the fair emerald isles they now found themselves on the coastline of. After anchoring the ship to make sure she would not ground herself, Captain de Croix and some of his men set out in a wooden rowing boat and headed ashore to find out where they had landed. Captain de Croix and his men followed a small path leading up the rocky sides of the cove to the cottage whence he knocked politely on the door. Seeing his handsome and non-threatening visage through a crack in the wall Elizabeth stood quietly inside wondering whether she should open the door. Captain de Croix knocked then said quietly in English, "Please open, we have travelled far and wish to know only where we are . . ."

His voice was calm and welcoming so Elizabeth opened the door and stood looking at the tall distinguished man in front of her. The captain smiled, "We mean no harm, we just wish to know what land is this?"

"It is Ireland and the county of Cork . . ." replied Elizabeth. Captain de Croix smiled warmly at her. She looked intently at the man, "And from whence do you come?" she asked.

"My men and I come from Spain, I am in command of the ship in yonder cove . . . we were forced to make landfall by the storm . . ." responded the captain.

Captain de Croix was not old at all and his responses were very cultured as he came from a well to do family in his home country . . . With this first introduction both were smitten with each other and Captain de Croix made sure, under pain of death, that his men would not harm her or take her livestock, for he wished to court her, and maybe, just maybe, take her to his family lands and seat in Spain should he ere return, for sailing in the rough seas around the English and Irish coasts was a dangerous thing to do in a wooden galleon . . .

The secret cove became the captain's favorite refuge and port of call when he was not raiding the English ships of their precious cargo and selling it to those in the emerald isles, for, he had no wish to travel too far away from his love, Elizabeth . . . In truth Captain de Croix was not a pirate for Spain was at war with England so any ship sailing the English flag was fair game. The English, however, viewed things differently and labeled him a pirate and put a price on his head. A large sum in fact . . . Captain de Croix showered Elizabeth with gifts from many lands but the poor girl had nowhere to show them off, for if she did the English lord's soldiers would take interest in her and no doubt arrest the poor girl. Elizabeth dreamt of a day to come when she would be free of the shackles and constraints binding her to this perilous place and the overlords in soldiers garb who held in their hands the life and death of every person under their subjection. Every night before she slept she would visit the graves of her parents and pray things would someday change for her. In the village Elizabeth was called the little patchwork girl for she would always wear her old patched skirts and dresses, not daring to wear the finery Captain de Croix had given her. One day Elizabeth put on one of the dresses and went for a walk in the woods to gather nuts and berries. While she was collecting them two girls from the village were spying on her, one of them said, "Isn't that *Patchwork?*"

"Why yes, it is, I wonder where she got that dress from?" replied the other girl.

"Well, why don't we follow her and find out, I'd like a dress like that too . . ." continued the oldest of the pair. So, with malice aforethought they shadowed Elizabeth through the woods to her cottage . . .

At the manor house where Elizabeth once lived they had decided upon a masque to celebrate one of the English lord's daughters coming of age. Sumptuous food arrived by the cartload as the peasants starved, fine material by the bolt had been turned into dresses for the lord's four ugly daughters. In truth they could have been attractive but by their very nature they had turned themselves, just like their father, into ugly excuses of the pride of English aristocracy . . . The manor house was being turned into a veritable wonderland for the well to do guests who were due to make their arrival at the masque the following

day. Since Captain de Croix traded the goods he obtained in
Ireland, he too was given an invitation to attend, since those
in power knew naught of his piratical activities and thought he
was just a merchant from Spain along with other ships which
had escaped the destruction of the Spanish Armada. Captain
de Croix pleaded with Elizabeth to come with him not knowing
that her family had once owned the manor. Eventually Elizabeth
relented, and since it was a masque her identity would not be
revealed. Captain de Croix brought her a beautiful gown for her
to wear on the following night and so, when the time came, he
met her a little way away on a road that clipped the forest that
hid her croft from view. It was well known throughout Ireland
of the licentious behavior of the Spaniards, but de Croix was
different, he always treated Elizabeth with the utmost respect
and courteous behavior, he was of course madly in love with her
and did not want to disrespect that love by crude actions . . .
As the carriage headed for the manor Captain de Croix gave
Elizabeth a mask to put on when they arrived. Elizabeth was
happy about it for she did not know what kind of reception they
would give her. She was ill at ease for she was not one to mix
with others and spent most of her time alone with her animals
and cat, or, with Captain de Croix when he called to visit. The
captain always behaved like an officer and a gentleman and
nary a thing was said other than he had good intentions toward
all womenfolk and especially Elizabeth; above all he was a man
of principle and good breeding . . . Stepping into the grand hall
was overwhelming to Elizabeth and it brought back so many
memories it was hard for her to keep her composure. Elizabeth
had been taught to dance many years past by an instructor
and it did not take long for her to get into the swing of things
after a few awkward missteps and bumping into others on the
ballroom floor. The lord's daughters were entranced by the
tall dark and handsome Spanish captain and wondered what
trollop had entranced him so. They determined to find out
who she was. Elizabeth went to the balcony with the captain for

some fresh air. As the captain fetched some refreshments for them Elizabeth saw the staircase she had used as a child and wondered what her room was like now. Elizabeth decided to go take a little peek even though she was somewhat frightened. Creeping up the staircase she kept glancing back furtively just in case someone should see her. When she got to the top she turned wistfully wondering should she continue, then, gulping in trepidation she sucked in her breath and made her way to her old room . . .

One of the lord's daughters had decided to lie down and rest for a while, for as she put it, *her corset was too tight* . . . She headed to her room following the same stairs Elizabeth had climbed up. The lord's daughter headed to her room, the same one Elizabeth had when she was a child.

When the lord's daughter opened the door she screamed, for inside Elizabeth had found her doll *Betsy* resting on pillows she had once slept on adorning her old bed. Elizabeth was now holding her doll *Betsy* to her chest. The scream frightened Elizabeth and as she rushed past the daughter her mask was pulled from her face. As she ran down the stairs the daughter thought she recognized her from a large portrait painted by one of Italy's finest painters that adorned the wall running up next to the curving staircase. It dawned on the lord's daughter who she was. She screamed shrilly bringing soldiers to the fore with swords drawn. Captain de Croix drew the sword at his side and defended Elizabeth, his lady love, to the best of his ability. And with Elizabeth still clutching *Betsy* to her chest the pair retreated outside and managed to gain respite and the carriage. The carriage man was one of de Croix's crew members so he was not shy at all to pull out a hidden cutlass and defend his liege. With musket balls tearing holes in the darkness around the carriage de Croix and his lady love made their escape into the night . . .

In the following weeks the English lord had his men search far and wide for Elizabeth O'Sullivan, the heir to the manor and its estates, for he was frightened that the true nature of his seizure would be revealed one day and that he himself could face the law in this respect . . . For worry to the wicked is a most troublesome thing . . . For he had thought the family all dead by now . . .

In search of the doll he turned both houses and villages of the surrounding area inside out and sought the Spanish merchant who had brought her, to question him, under lock and key in one of his dungeons or hanging in a cage therein, for to the lord torture was just as normal as you or I drinking a cup of mint or nettle tea. For he was truly a nasty man by temperament and cared not for God nor the afterlife . . . His wicked demeanor intensified after the search of the surrounding area proved fruitless . . . And the spoilt rich ugly brat that portrayed itself as the lord's daughter kept screaming, "Where is my doll and why isn't the trollop that took her hanging on the gibbet on the road outside the manor . . ." For she was incensed 'her' doll had been taken from her room by the girl whose property it once was. That aside, the lord was more worried that his false accusations would be unearthed for the new judge of the area had no liking of him or the manner in which he had acquired his wealth and property. For what proof had he before other than hearsay and the barrel of a musket. To the wicked and evil lord, it was imperative that he find Elizabeth . . . But the villagers around the manor had no clue as to the identity of *Patchwork*, the young girl with mud on her face and clothes . . .

Captain de Croix, not realizing the depths to which the pretender who had taken Elizabeth's father's place would stoop, had taken to sea during this time conducting business as any self respecting pirate or freebooter would, sending a shot over the bow of any English merchantman heading to the Indies or returning from it with their cargo holds full of booty ready for the taking. Captain de Croix was not a man to take a life unnecessarily so he took what he could and left the vessel intact, and, as courteous as ever would always present his hat when leaving a vessel and thank them for their hospitality and the goods they had given as he swung back to his ship, for de Croix was, first and foremost, a gentleman above all else and did not suffer the maltreatment of any, no matter how lowly in life their station was . . . For he believed wholeheartedly in the Lord our God and of the Christ, and as his name would suggest, *of the cross* . . .

During this time Elizabeth stayed out of sight and out of the minds of the village folk, for who would ere suspect a patchwork quilted muddy girl of being the beautiful woman in the arms of the dashing Captain de Croix attending a masque of all things, for did not *Patchwork* live in a croft in the woods far from everyone . . . Around the woods was a barrier of thorns and nettles which deterred people from entering them, except for the two girls who continued spying on *Patchwork* in the hopes she would leave the cottage unattended . . .

While Elizabeth was in the market one day soldiers came overturning things and irritating the vendors on the lame chance they could find the missing doll and the girl who took it. When Elizabeth returned home she found her croft in a mess, the two girls had come and taken her fine clothes with them. Elizabeth turned ashen, and she went immediately to the hiding place in which she had secreted *Betsy* under the floorboards. Fortunately the girls had not found her and Elizabeth breathed a sigh of relief as she held her most prized possession to her heaving tremulous bosom . . . At night the pair of them would keep each other company as old friends are wont to do, for *Betsy* loved Elizabeth as much as Elizabeth loved her . . .

One market day the two gadding girls put on the dresses they had stolen from the croft and waltzed around in them showing off. Unfortunately one of the gowns was the exact same one that had been worn by Elizabeth at the masque. This was also noted by the captain of the guard who had seen them . . . The two girls were taken screaming out of the market to the manor where they were thrown into a dungeon. With the threat of a hot iron loosening their tongues the proverbial cat was out of the bag and they told from whence the fine gowns had come, *the croft of Patchwork* . . .

That evening when Captain de Croix called upon his lady love she was nowhere in sight, everything was turned upside down and strewn hither and thither. Outside hoof marks were imprinted in the soft soil and marks of heeled booted feet belonging to many men. Captain de Croix followed them until he came to an old vagabond on the roadside who told him what had transpired. Forthwith the captain called his men to his side and they proposed a rescue party to save poor Elizabeth. Armed to the teeth they headed for the village to secure her release.

At the village in the center of the marketplace stood a high pile of logs with a stake in the center, and, tied to this stake was poor Elizabeth, now charged with being a witch for want of the company of a cat . . . and, a black one at that . . . Villagers stood in attendance as did the household of the manor and the four ugly daughters . . . As the lord's men lit the pyre the crowd parted like a wave as Captain de Croix and his men strode boldly to the fore. Brandishing swords and cutlasses he and his men forged forward desperately seeking to save the fair maiden as the flames licked ever higher to the skirts of poor Elizabeth . . . Swords flashed and struck one another in the firelight and muskets spoke horrendously of death's sonata as Elizabeth was rescued from a fiery death at the hands of the wicked usurpers of her father's estate and lands. Captain de Croix held the usurpers at bay and was the last to leave the field of battle, and, as he left the village bade them all goodnight and tipped his hat as he was wont to do . . . thanking them all for their hospitality and fairness of blade . . . And so, with nary a scratch to mar his fine clothes he left to melt into the darkness . . . Incensed, the lord put together a party to take revenge upon the Spaniards who had trounced them so soundly . . . but, by the time they had reached Elizabeth's croft they were nowhere to be seen . . .

The following morning Elizabeth stood on the deck of Captain de Croix's galleon looking at the sunrise. Clasped in one arm was *Betsy* and sitting on the wooden deck comfortably was a cat, Elizabeth's cat. Captain de Croix sidled up next to her and clasped a hand, he said, "Do not fear Elizabeth, we shall go to my home and be married, for I shall nere let you down, on my honor. And someday we shall return to the fair emerald isles to reclaim what was once yours . . ." Elizabeth held on tightly to him and whispered, "I will love you forever . . ."

Captain de Croix looked deeply into Elizabeth's eyes, "Aye, and I will love you for all eternity."

Unnoticed by all, *Betsy*, Elizabeth's doll, bore a smile on her China face that could have endeared a million hearts, for she had been reunited with her true owner at last, and the true love that was spoken of by many but found by only a few had found her mistress after years of suffering and loneliness . . . A thought flashed within her, *'Maybe there is justice in this wicked world after all . . .'*

\* \* \*

My bicycle was an important part of my life when I was young, I had found the frame on a rubbish dump and took it home to clean and repair it. By the time I and my father had finished with it, it was like a brand new bike. My best friend at Loxford Primary school wasn't able to afford one so I ventured onto the open roads around Ilford on my lonesome. I cycled to Barking on the Thames River then north to Cambridge, then on to Newmarket to see the horses in training. My next trip was to Caxton where the old A10 road led up to East Anglia, Norfolk and beyond. Caxton Gibbet was a well known cross roads with the hangman's gibbet still standing. It wasn't too long ago that on that same gibbet highwaymen were still being strung up by the neck, the last to be hung there died in 1920. The highwaymen were strung up and then left to rot atoning for their misdeeds. A hotel by the same name stands in mute testimony nearby. I would always laugh to myself when I thought of the highwaymen on their fast steeds galloping on the exact same road I was cycling on only ten years and a bit past. My cycle took me up to North Wales and to a little inn not far from Portmadoc. The innkeeper told me that in North Wales and most other parts of this little mountainous kingdom the police force was literally non-existent up to 1932. He told me the story of a travelling salesman carrying bolts of cloth on a donkey. The salesman was from Manchester and stayed in the inn one night in 1925. After a pint of beer he went to bed. At 2:00 am in the morning a tap on the door woke him, it was the innkeeper come to warn him that two men came in after the salesman had gone to his room, and talking in very hushed tones they planned to rob the salesman and kill him if necessary. The innkeeper had sharp ears and heard everything that had been said. He implored the salesman to leave post haste and not worry about payment for the room. With nary a word the salesman packed quickly went to the stable, saddled and cinched his horse, and repacked the donkey for a quick getaway. Down the dark and misty road he headed for Portmadoc with all the speed he could muster from his tired animals. Seeing a bridge with a stream running under it he decided to hide there. Leading his horse and donkey down to the stream's edge he found a patch of grass under the very old stonework and tethered his animals to a bush completely out of sight from above. It was still cold so he wrapped his blanket around him and waited. Not two hours later the sound of horses' hooves could be heard galloping his way then thundering over the bridge above. Peeking out of the bushes he spied the two highwaymen the inn keep had spoke of. A short while later the salesman packed his bedroll on his horse and set back the way he had come until he came to a quiet road off the beaten track that headed back toward the inn. Taking it he eventually reached the inn unharmed whence the inn keep allowed him to stay another night without charge. At that time

North Wales was still not safe unless you knew exactly where you were . . .

*They would see him here, they would see him there, they would see him everywhere . . .* On my bicycle at a young age I covered the whole length and breadth of all England, Cornwall and Wales, from Londinium to Hadrian's Wall, from Land's End to Mount Snowdon and the waters of the Irish Sea. At two to five years of age I was constantly wandering about, picking up cats or dogs and taking them home. On the other hand, because of my effervescent nature, I was always being invited into other people's homes to play with their pets and have tea, bread and jam, biscuits and cake. Jimmy would always be telling my mum that I was at number 60, or number 70, or number 101, or, in fact at a shop playing with the resident mouse catcher or canine companion. My mother would continually say to her friends, "Oh Stanley, he is always going off to someone's house. I have a job just to look for him–"

Jimmy would always find me on my way home carrying an odd assortment of dogs, cats and birds. Mum would say, "Take it back, Stanley–" or, "Now where on Earth did you find that? Alright, let's take it home shall we–"

When we arrived at Becontree Avenue I was around three years of age and very curious about where we were and would go up and down the tram lines then to the railway lines on the other side of Chadwell Heath railway station. Goodmayes was on the way back to Ilford – Manor Park – Leytonstone and Stratford. We were number 352 and roughly in the center of Becontree Avenue. One morning I walked all the way to Goodmayes and Hitherfield Road, a dual carriageway. I carried on up Hitherfield until I got to the railway bridge at Chadwell railway station. I stood there for hours watching the steam locomotives barreling out of the tunnel followed by plumes of smoke heading for Romford or Raleigh. Some of the drivers would see me and blow the engine's whistle. That really made me happy as I thought maybe he knew my father. While I was walking back home on my little legs a policeman came up to me and said, "Where are you going?"

I replied, "To see my daddy–"

"Do you know where you are?" asked the policeman.

With my head hanging down bashfully I shook my head from side to side. The policeman took me by the hand and we marched off to the police station. When I got there the other policemen started giving me cakes, biscuits and tea. They kept me there until my mother came about an hour later, she said, "Stanley, where have you been, we've been looking all over for you."

A couple of weeks later I did the same thing again, this time I looked out for a policeman and said, "I want to go home–"

The policeman answered, "Where do you live?"

I replied, "I don't know–"

He took me to the same police station. The same officer I'd met on the road before was at the desk, "Hello Stanley," he greeted. I sat down thinking I'd get the same treatment with cakes, tea and biscuits. Instead the officer just smiled, laughed and said to the officer, "He knows his way home–" No cakes, no biscuits and no tea . . .

My mother always said, *I had the true spirit of a wandering Irishman . . .*"

\* \* \*

The Tales of Chapman the Explorer, Thomas Reinolds and Chapman the Hunter: In 1607 an English ship, the Consent, was becalmed along the southern coast of Africa and the Pilot managed to find safe harbor in Hout Bay. Lt. John Chapman was the first to sight the hill and it was he that skillfully piloted the ship to safety. The Peak under which the ship anchored was named *Chapman's Chance*, after him. After anchoring the galleon the captain of the ship sent Lt. John Chapman ashore to find provisions and fresh water. Over the years the name stuck, but *Chance* was eventually replaced by *Peak* . . .

John Chapman's ship eventually left the barren coast devoid of man and headed back to London, England, with its mission of exploration and accumulation of tradable goods to the Far East complete . . .

Thomas Reinolds, my 8th Great Grandfather on Grandma Maria's side, stood on the bow of an ancient sailing ship watching the mid-Atlantic waters pass underneath. The year, circa 1625. He preferred topside to below decks where it was stuffy and there were too many people for his liking crammed into a small space. The weather had been fair, thank goodness, and no storms had sprung up unannounced. Even so the waves in the Atlantic were not to be scoffed. There was a constant head sea which caused the boards of the ship to creak and groan as if the ship were a living thing. Thomas was looking forward to the freedom the New World would give him, and he yearned for the wilds it promised waiting for men of the old world to till it. It offered opportunity for stout strong men and even latitude when it came to one's religious beliefs. '*Yes, there were Indians to contend with, but surely reason would mollify them,*' he thought. A large wave struck the bow of the ship sending cold sea spray over him. Thomas wiped the spray from his face and smiled, was this not the adventure he sought, and the promise of land and potential wealth lying ahead in front of him in that far off land called America? True, it was far from his family and the place he had called home, but, if needs be he could return, though he doubted it, for what future, if any, would be in store for him in olde England. No, he would face the trials and tribulations of the New World and be the man his father had wanted him to be, and should Indians attack him and his family, well, they would taste his righteous wrath, for no man had stood against a Reinolds in anger and fared well . . . And as the wooden ship with tall masts filled with canvas sail cut through those cold briny waters, Virginia and the Isle of Wight beckoned them to her virgin shores, a wild land waiting to be tamed . . .

The years passed quickly for Thomas Reinolds, time had marched on with incredible speed, his family had grown and he still bent his back at any task needing to be done. The New World had been kind to him in many respects, he had a sense of self that only those exposed to constant danger inherited. He was a man borne of a wild land now, and as the screams of Indians rent the darkness around him he gritted his teeth, he had emptied his musket into the chest of a Powhatan with a hatchet running at him. He had swung the smooth bore's wooden butt into the head of another and stopped a third with what remained of it. Time now was not on his side, there were just too many of them. He threw what remained of the shattered musket at the approaching horde and withdrew his knife and axe from his waistband . . . The dark wilds of Virginia in the Americas closed around Thomas and for each drop of his blood spilt the savages around him paid dearly . . . Thomas Reinolds was not the sort of man to sell his life cheaply . . . and the price that was paid for his soul proved to be much for the Powhatan raiding party, for Thomas Reinolds the Powhatan blood staining the keen edge of his hunting knife and the keen edge of his axe was still not enough, no, no amount would ever be . . .

In the 1800's when James Chapman was but a boy in England his father said to him, "Be a giant amongst men, an eagle that soars and a lion that roars . . ."

These words James took to heart are the words that sent him to Southern Africa in search of fame and fortune, for he wished to hunt the biggest of all beasts and the bounty they carried . . . their valuable ivory tusks. James Chapman set sail from London on board a sailing ship yearning for an adventurous life filled with the prospect of returning home with his coffers full of gold and precious things. What he did not realize was that the precious things he yearned for were but pale in comparison to his life changing exploits and his experiences in a wild untamed land in Southern Africa. The name Africa actually originated with the ancient Romans and means *'place of the Afri'*, the *Afri* being an indigenous North African tribe at the time the Romans were expanding their empire . . . When James left Britain few people had seen the magnificent African elephant in the wild; fewer still had survived encounters with this beast. And yet, there were far more dangerous things he would have to deal with, lions for instance, and savages armed with spears, assegais and shields; these were amongst the most treacherous of all creatures found in Africa. But his troubles didn't end there, snakes that threatened to end his life within an hour, and mosquitoes, those winged insects of death that brought to those bitten, fever and sweats unlike anything else a white man had experienced, turning Africa into *the white man's grave* . . . When James reached Cape Town he travelled north to the fabled lands of the Ivory kings. In Europe ivory was sought after for piano keys and decoration, it was a highly prized commodity. He thus sought out the pachyderm that gave rise to it in vast quantity in the bush, forests and plains of Africa, especially Southern Africa where the white man had gained a foothold. In the great forests of Central Africa it was difficult to track and find elephants, besides, the size of the forest elephant was smaller than those of the plains. Also, disease ravaged those who dared walk under the giant boughs and branches of the rain forest, and the indigenous populations were mainly cannibals. So, with that in mind he headed for the wild lands adjacent to those the Bechuanas, Damaras and Ovambo peoples inhabited. The lands he traversed were full of lions and vultures and scarce ever had they seen a white man. On his first elephant hunt James and his men were accompanied by several Boers who wished to tag along and bag an elephant or two or three. Before long the tracks of a herd were picked up forcing one of James's servants up a tree to ascertain where they were. The poor man got a shock when he spied a giant herd with a massive male with huge tusks not one mile in distance from where they were. Since some of the Boers had gone in another direction looking for the elephants, men were dispatched to fetch them. James was impatient though, and after ten minutes of waiting next to his wagon he jumped on his horse and headed for them accompanied by twelve men. Shortly, a herd of about two hundred elephants came into view with the huge male about four feet higher than the others which consisted of females and adolescent males. The men, unused to hunting elephants, dashed to the side of the column about sixty yards away and poured round after round into it with little noticeable effect. James wanted the big bull elephant and proceeded to hunt it on horseback trying to hit it behind a front leg and get a round into its heart. A game of cat and mouse ensued with the hunter eventually becoming the hunted as the elephant's tusks sought to tear James apart and its giant feet threatened to trample him into the dust. On several occasions the tusks nearly ripped him to pieces until at last he was able to hide behind a tree waiting for the beast who eventually succumbed to the lead projectiles from his rifle . . .

Many times during his forays into the wilds of Africa James's quest for ivory nearly killed him. Once, while left with the ivory of an elephant, his men went to fetch his wagon with a full load of the precious tusks. During his long wait James felt the feverish grip of malaria render him near incapable of movement forcing him to crawl for water at a river just to slake his thirst as fever wracked his body before his wagon and men turned up . . . Crossing the Madenisana Desert his party nearly succumbed to the privations of water as they trekked for days in search of a water hole or depression with rainwater in. Their only casualties were an ox which died just before a waterhole was reached and one of the servants, a scoundrel and thief, who had taken a horse and all their water provisions and absconded . . .

Snakes were an ever present danger in the bush and could be found everywhere. One snake dropped from a tree into the wagon as James and his men were preparing to inspan. It took less than a second for everyone to jump out of the wagon. After building a hut for the night for protection against mosquitoes none of the men wished to fetch their blankets just in case they brought the snake with them. On another occasion a snake fell into the fire next to James causing him to jump up in fright. Snakes were even trod underfoot by James as he guided the wagon over rocks and bad tracks. An eight foot black mamba coiled around his leg trying to get purchase on the hunter as it struck out at his high leather boots with poison enriched fangs, causing James to jump twice to free himself from its clutches . . .

James made a good living for himself hunting the Ivory kings and even wrote a book about his travels and exploration of Southern Africa. Eventually he married and settled down returning to his native England . . . *Did he make his fortune . . . yes . . . but his wealth was more than material in nature for he had enriched his life with experiences no one else had dreamt of . . .* He had faced the giants of the African bush and the spears of angry tribesmen and survived . . . and, the bushvelt's most dangerous creature of all . . . *the mosquito . . .*

# CHAPTER 4

## Whispers of War

**W**e had a small Marconi television set at home in the front room of number one Meath Road in Ilford, Essex. The wooden casing held a marvelous advance in tube technology and only twelve months had passed since they were introduced into the market place. I marveled at pictures of the Mayo flying boat filmed in black and white, and the Mercury, a small seaplane on its back. It was the beginning of a new age and the successful takeoff of the Mercury off the back of the Mayo signified a great advance in experimental aviation and the modern aircraft being designed and built at the time. Cobbled streets were becoming a thing of the past as more and more roads were being covered in asphalt. As a young child the lamps in our road were powered by gas turned on and off by a lamp lighter man from the gas works. We had gas lamps on poles for street lighting all the time we were in Colegrave Road, but when we moved to Becontree Avenue the street lamps were electric. Gas street lamps and cobble stones were rapidly being replaced by electric power and asphalt . . . As always the October and November months carried with them a mist and fog that clung to London like a damp cloth. Log and coal fires turned the misty sky above into a dirty grey. Sometimes it was impossible to see no further than a yard in front of you, for the grey noxious fog was so thick, at times when I stretched my arm out while walking along the street I couldn't even see my hand. In the fog trains and buses would be late as they tentatively worked their way through it, accidents were common. Walking to school or work I would traverse the sidewalk at a snail's pace for it was easy to make a misstep and twist an ankle or step into the road and be run down by horses towing carriages or even an automobile, which weren't that common. As gas became more common for heating coal and wood fires went out of fashion . . . Gradually the London smog lifted as the Clean Air Act came into force and the trappings of modernity changed the face of London forever . . .

\* \* \*

Sitting at the docks and watching the ships: From the age of ten I made my way to the River Thames. I would sit for hours watching the ships come and go at the docks near the Blackwall tunnel which was my favorite spot. There were so many different types from so many distant and far off lands. Each ship had its country's flag and I was always eager to talk to the seamen who manned them. Most of those men couldn't speak English though and I struggled with hand signals to make them understand me . . .

When I visited the docks I would walk through the Blackwall tunnel under the Thames. The attendant looking after it would always complain vociferously that it was not a playground and that I shouldn't walk through it again. I paid no attention to him. One day I rode through it on my bicycle and he refused to let me get out on the other side. That was the last time I cycled through. I ended up having to dodge the man on my future trips to my fantasy land. He could never understand why I wanted to go there. While sitting on the docks and watching the ships I would close my eyes and say to myself, "One day I will go where these ships are going, sailing out of London to far distant lands having adventures like a modern day Sinbad the sailor . . ."

My mother would always be looking for me when I left the house to the docks. She would ask Jimmy and Ernie, "Where's Stanley, have you seen him?" They would shake their heads from side to side. At the docks I would listen to the old sailors regaling their tales of adventure and what it was like to man the big sailed craft in their younger years. I was always drifting off to new, and to me, unexplored places. I would give an ear to the elderly folk and listen attentively to their stories of bygone years, of life as it was in *ye olde England, Wales, Scotland and Ireland.*

The *Hippodrome* cinema at Barking was about two miles away from the docks. So after my mental flights of fancy I would head there taking note of the cinema advertizing to see if there was a film I would like. If there was a western I would make a beeline to the cinema. If you were under fourteen you couldn't go into the cinema unaccompanied so I would join the queue and ask if someone could take me in. The patrons were always willing to help me so I never missed a movie I hankered after. On my way back I would stop at Barking Park which backed onto the road in Ilford near Richmond Road. This was my shortcut home after playing on gymnastic frames, swings and attacking the children's fortress. Loxford Central School wasn't too far away on the opposite side of Richmond Road. It was all very convenient for a young lad; the park even had a small pool, a ball park and miniature golf. For the children of the area it was a veritable cornucopia of delights . . . keeping them occupied for hours and hours . . .

\* \* \*

One summer month: During the summer months we would travel to Leiston and Saxmundham in Suffolk, which was quite close to Lowestoft where Uncle Jack had a general store, and it was he that gave me the model sailboat years before. It didn't take us long to reach Leiston by rail from London and it was 11:30 am when we left the station and walked down the short road toward my Uncle Edward's house. It was the same house father had lived in as a boy. There were about six houses on both sides of the road and in short order we reached the house and my mother knocked on the door. My uncle's wife answered and we were greeted by our two cousins, two sisters. Their mother explained that my uncle was on shift work and would be home a little later. I always looked forward to our trips to Leiston because in London I never got to see the sea and smell the briny air blowing down from the north. I loved watching big waves crashing against the shore. I wanted to go to the shingle beach with my cousins but mother said, "Watch Teddy and make sure he doesn't go out the back gate . . ." I stood looking at the big apple tree and the cherry tree nearby, and thought, *All this way and I don't even get to go to the beach . . .*'I was a little upset, so after pondering the chicken coop and the green house for a while I decided to make a break for it. Teddy was now playing with the girls so I carefully made my way down the path to the back gate and slipped through without anyone seeing me. The meadow behind the house was rather wide and it took me five minutes of slogging through tall thick wet grass to get across. I stood on top of a rise looking down at the shingle beach below me, the waves weren't too high but the shingle beach was rather steep and the tide was coming in. It all looked far too dangerous though to take a paddle in. I had tasted the salty sea breeze and seen the sea, my work done I headed back to the house . . . Our day out wasn't a total loss however, there were plenty of blackberry bushes around the house and inside my aunt always had plenty of jars packed full of blackberry jam. Tea, scones, cream and blackberry jam . . . *what could be better* . . . It was on one of these family outings with mother and my younger brothers to St. Paul's cathedral that she mentioned Christopher Wren, the architect, was an ancestor of ours. Our family certainly had a design and artistic flair, and I had no doubt she believed what she had said, so I suppose somewhere along our line blood must have mingled . . .

\* \* \*

My father: As a profession the railway engine driver was highly respected and thought of as a very responsible person indeed. To the engine drivers, even though the job could be dirty, a clean presentable engine and a clean railway uniform were paramount. My father was always well presented and scrupulously clean, time to him meant everything, the railways worked because of their unsurpassed time-keeping. Dad always wore his W.H. Smith pocket watch with long Roman numerals on a long chain hanging from his right waistcoat pocket to his left where he kept his round silver pocket watch. No one, but no one was allowed to touch it. Every seven days father would wind it up. His watch always kept perfect time, and every now and again he would pull it out of his pocket and check it, it was a good habit for a railway engine driver. Trains had to leave and arrive right on time. We always wondered what dad would bring home in the way of railway spoils, a brace of pheasants, duck, partridge or rabbits. The steam from the locos thundering down the line would disorient the birds forcing a collision with the steel horses. Father would stop to retrieve the spoils and at night bring them home to be de-feathered or skinned and prepared for the pot or the roasting pan.

Most engine drivers were given allotments on railway land by the London North Eastern Railways; dad's was about forty by thirty yards in dimension. He loved rearing his rabbits and chickens there. The chickens provided meat and eggs, and the rabbits a tasty meat treat for our family. Dad was a very fast walker and had been a champion runner for Essex in his younger days. He had started as a cleaner on the railways and progressed to fireman then engine driver. He rose through the ranks quickly and became the youngest ever steam locomotive driver in Britain. Jimmy, my older brother, was following in dad's footsteps and had become a cleaner for the LNER on his way to a fireman's position then engine driver. We had so many members of our family on the railways you could have called us a *railway family*, what with my grandfather and uncle as well.

Dad loved growing flowers on his allotment, that and vegetables like cabbage, cauliflower, pumpkin, potatoes, carrots and anything else he could grow that would supplement our family's meals. He would take his sons along to the plot on Sunday morning; I was one of his little helpers from the age of six, though sometimes I was more of a nuisance than a green fingered assistant to him. The other locomotive engineers passing would always toot their whistles and wave at us as they trundled down the steel tracks riding their solid iron leviathans. Every weekend mum would expect dad to bring something home to roast for Sunday dinner. My father worked hard for the railways and at day's end he would put his feet up and relax letting mum take care of the boys. If we were naughty he would threaten to take off his thick leather belt. Mum would say, "Wait till your father gets home . . ." Dad never had reason to chastise us physically though, we always resolved our brotherly differences amicably in the end.

Dad's father was about 5'8", he was fair of complexion with a long handlebar moustache. He had a distinct air of confidence about him even though he wasn't a man of letters. He always looked smart in his navy blue suit and white shirt, he reminded me of a real gentleman. One time, after having just retired, he was sitting in our living room reading a newspaper, trouble was he had it upside down, I said, "Granddad, the newspaper is upside down!" He chuckled and laughed then quickly turned it over. My brothers and I would sit enraptured for hours as he regaled tales of his life and his bare-fisted boxing matches. He was a master of his craft in the railways and I could see he missed it. Dad had steadily moved up in his career, he had progressed from the shunting yard which was about one by one mile in dimension to driving passenger trains while we were growing up. As one flower opens its petals another starts to dry and shrivel up . . . *it's a terrible shame* . . .

\* \* \*

Building coaches at Stratford: I was fourteen years old when I arrived at Stratford coachworks with my father just after New Year's Day at the beginning of 1938. I was very excited at the prospect of not only learning a trade but also of earning a salary, even if it was only ten shillings per week. The manager of the coachworks knew my father well; since he was a much respected engine driver working for the London North Eastern Railway, and my Uncle Kenneth also commanded a great deal of respect as an office manager working for them. Even my grandfather who had just retired from his profession as a boiler maker commanded an equal amount of respect from the senior management of the LNER. So I suppose it was right that I followed in the footsteps of my grandfather, father and uncle and also start a career with the LNER. Even Ernie, my older brother, had started his working career with them and was near to finishing up his apprenticeship and getting certification as a fully qualified railway engineer. My father was very proud to have his sons following in his footsteps, so much so that he bought me a Mr. J. Cobbs tool chest with a full complement of handmade tools. Dad paid £5 for it, which at the time was a king's ransom . . . When I joined the team of apprentices, who were all older than me, it wasn't long before I realized something was up, namely my initiation into LNER. Dad hadn't said anything about it, I guess he was too preoccupied, for at the time he was busy delivering huge quantities of food to the London docks destined to be dumped into the English Channel . . . all so food prices could be kept inflated even though there was a depression on and many people couldn't even afford a loaf of bread. Unemployment reached its highest levels between the years 1936 to 1937. And as the fat cats relaxed in their private clubs feasting and gorging themselves on the suffering of others, many Londoners starved . . .

My initiation started when all the lads gathered around me, and it wasn't long afterward that I was dancing across the tops of the luxury Pullman coaches as naked as a Jay bird covered in brown rust proofing paint doing a Highland Fling. Below me all the boys and men laughed their heads off. When I asked dad about the initiation that night he just smiled and said, "Everyone goes through it . . ."

Being an apprentice coachbuilder at the time was a very honorable profession which was highly regarded with classes and studies covering all aspects of rolling stock including the Pullman luxury coaches, high speed semi-luxury coaches that took passengers on long routes north, east, south and west of London. The coaches of 1916 to 1938 were some of the most beautiful rolling stock ever made . . . My apprenticeship as a coachbuilder was no cakewalk and was broad based and covered every aspect in the construction and assembly of coaches. At night I attended a drafting school getting instruction on design engineering to boost my future career in engine, coach and truck design. I had always loved drawing and designing things and the technical school gave me the enthusiasm and drive to learn something I was really gifted at. One of the things the technical school impressed upon us was employing the *critical path method* combined with *time and motions method* which was the latest thing. For a big project this was an invaluable lesson and something that could be applied to more than just drafting. *Now, at fourteen, my life was going somewhere and I was looking forward to the future, I would make something of myself that my parents would be proud of* . . .

*The future looked bright for our family* . . . We were on the up and up, we had a much bigger house, new furniture, peace and harmony . . . little did we know of what was in store brewing on the other side of the English channel . . . Times were good even after the depression of the early thirties, though on occasion we heard Hitler was on the march again in Europe. The news reels would be full of German health programs proudly displaying fit German boys and girls all with blonde hair doing physical jerks and taking part in social welfare programs. Underpinning this was their penchant for saluting Hitler and shouting, "Heil Hitler! Heil Hitler!" The pot was on the boil in Europe. Summer was approaching and mum was planning our holiday, first to Blackpool, then Bournemouth, and finally Scarborough. Dad had applied for his railway worker's privilege tickets for the whole family and we were looking forward to our holiday . . . Mum, well, she was looking forward to the time she could afford a new piano to replace her old one. As for Hitler, no one expected his rise to power to be so rapid . . .

* * *

My days as a coachbuilder for London North Eastern Railway: My apprenticeship would be five years long with the LNERLY filled with workshops and night school, including art, concept drawing and draftsmanship. Our instructors were all very impressed with my drawings and drafting and thought I would become a good candidate for the drawing office. I also spent a good portion of my time assisting with the maintenance of the railway coaches. I was very passionate about the Pullman coaches; they were all handmade with beautiful wood carving work. I would become inspired running my fingers over the polished wood paneling. Their kitchens and dinning coaches were fitted out for the rich and famous. These coaches traveled to far off places being transported to Europe on train ferry ships. They went from London to Dover then over the channel to Paris in France. From there Europe was an open book to them. The Pullman coaches had everything a passenger required, nothing was lacking in creature comforts. Pullman was a household name with their livery being basic black with gold trimming lines and roofs of white, they looked very stylish. The interiors of the coaches were incredibly luxuriant and I loved working in them, I would visualize myself as a passenger travelling around the world in them . . .

* * *

Chamberlain going to Germany to see Hitler: I first heard about Hitler and Germany around 1932 to 1935. I was still young so the constant arrogant ramblings on of a small Germanic dictator didn't interest me much. Hitler's speeches and the actions they prompted gradually built up over a long period. It was hard to take him seriously. That was, until he stormed into the Rhineland in 1936. Marshal Foch said after the Treaty of Versailles, "This is not peace; it is an Armistice for twenty years . . ." How right he was, for it was only a matter of time that would see Europe embroiled in war once more, for the burdens placed upon Germany had crushed a once mighty country; its colonies had been seized, its weapons taken, it was separated from the countries surrounding it by a demilitarized zone and a severe depression between 1931 – 1932 had seen its currency weaken and become worthless which had eroded the very fabric of German society. All it needed was a charismatic leader with a cause to inflame the hearts and fan the flames of the ordinary German citizen to be at odds with the world extant from her borders once again . . .

Hitler's Nazi Party gained the majority in the Reichstag during the depression and in 1933 Hitler became the Chancellor of Germany. He quickly discarded the Treaty of Versailles and began his march for world domination. In March of 1938 he took Austria, in September he grabbed Sudetenland. Storming across his borders he then occupied Bohemia and Maravia during March of the following year. Not satisfied, and emboldened by the lack of action from the rest of Europe and Britain he annexed Memel. On August the 23rd in 1939 he signed

a non-aggression pact with Russia. On the 1st of September 1939
he invaded Poland. The Polish borders were like porous cheese
and the Polish military might consisted of old First World War
field guns and horse cavalry. The Polish cavalry charged the
German guns and tanks bravely. They didn't stand a chance.
They were slaughtered to a man. They held the fighting tactics
of the 18th and 19th centuries close to their hearts, things such
as honor, bravery and sacrifice. The Germans could not have
cared less. These men full of misplaced pride and dignity fell
like flies to the Prussians, and along with them died an era of
military style and tradition and combat tactics . . .

During this time the British government with Chamberlain
at its head had taken too long before realizing the threat that
Hitler posed to the stability of Europe and the entire world. By
the time they started to take Hitler seriously and sent envoys to
stem the tide of German military persecution, it was too late, the
damage had already been done; the rest of Europe had ignored
or downplayed the gradual rebuilding of the German military
to its detriment, they had been outfoxed by Hitler and failed to
see where he and his brown shirted confederates were heading.
The world at that time was still mired in the 19th century and
the previous war Germany had lost. The Treaty of Versailles had
taken much from Germany, its currency was valueless and it
had paid dearly for its warring ways. Hitler exploited this fact in
forming his new party. Gradually Hitler put into play a strategic
game removing or having assassinated any who stood in his way
to the position he coveted, that of becoming the Führer, the
master of the master race . . . Their mantra, and part of their
national anthem was *Deutschland uber alles*, 'Germany over all'.
Hitler's book *Mein Kampf,* started while he was incarcerated, laid
out his strategies and his hatred of the Jews. To succeed he had
to demonize one section of the German citizenry, playing one
against another and using this as a lever to mobilize and create
an up-swell of popularity for himself and the National Socialist
Party he led. The added benefit was that he could seize both

property and money from the dispossessed Jews to further swell his military coffers and take revenge on those who had stood against Germany in the 1914-1918 war. He would prove to the world that the Aryans were the master race and that they would take control of the entire world by force to create a *Thousand Year Reich*. Hitler had no intention of backing down; he was just playing for time to put his plans into operation, he treated Chamberlain like a fly being tempted into a spider's web, a web of Hitler's creation with him being the master manipulator and spider.

\* \* \*

One glorious summer before the storm: Summer was now here with warm bright blue azure skies and fluffy white clouds. Willy Noakes and I had purchased an old tent and planned to go to Epping Forest which was much larger than Hainalt Forest. When we arrived Bluebell flowers littered the forest floor by the millions. The camp site we chose wasn't too far from the camping site toilets, a café, a fruit market selling dew fresh strawberries and apples very cheaply, and other amenities. A warm azure blue English summer sky spread out above us as we lay on our backs looking up at the clouds, we hadn't a care in the world . . . Willy and I were still members of the Ilford Sea Scouts going on camping trips to Wales, Shell Bay, Walton on Naze and other places. The Sea Scouts always had events we would take part in, and we learnt a lot about seamanship and how to handle a boat . . .

On the streets of London trams were becoming a thing of the past as trolley buses replaced them. There was talk of pulling up the tram lines to use as scrap metal because of the looming threat of war in the future. My rides on the top deck at the front of the trams were becoming few and far between as more and more trams were decommissioned. There were suggestions of London's citizenry wearing gas masks if we went to war with Germany and that air raid shelters would have to be dug . . . On London's streets the horse and cart was also being replaced by the motorcar. Things were changing; modernity and a new metropolis were slowly creeping in. Dad entered a raffle for a car, first prize was an Austin 7, he paid £10 to enter it and three days later he won! Dad didn't want the car so he put it back in the raffle and promptly won the car again plus the £1000 the organizers promised him for putting it back in the raffle. After that mum said it was destined to be his so he should like it and lump it. Mum got the £1000 to spend on upgrading the house, school uniforms and clothing for her children, and a little bit to spoil dad and herself, and me, well, I got much coveted camping gear . . .

\* \* \*

Everything was just peachy: My father loved animals and especially horses. When he was growing up a farmer in Leiston gave him the opportunity to lead his plough horses to turn up his fields. Life was much as it had always been from the early 1800s. People were friendly and helpful and working on a farm was invigorating with the aroma of apple blossoms on the trees and the scent from other fruit bearing bushes saturating the air around. Everything was organic, vegetables were fresh and untainted. Cabbage, corn, cauliflower, marrows, turnips and carrots filled row after row of tilled naturally fertilized fields. After a day's hard work in the fields everyone was invited to a barn dance on the farm, they even had a jester come clown all dressed up for the occasion . . . Life was simple, simple was nice . . . But the Great War had brought terrible hardships to the slums of London where the Irish had lived and died. Even though they faced awful circumstances beyond their control the Irish were still able to laugh and sing never letting anyone put them down, and woe betides those that did, for they soon felt the slings and arrows of the Irish if they treated an Irishman badly . . . Mother sang like an angel and played the piano like a concert pianist from Crystal Palace, she was self taught and couldn't read a note of music but she could listen to a tune or song on the radio then sit down and play it, singing the words as well. From a young age she was determined to have her own piano, her ability was natural and her hands always fluttered over the keys, she had an innate and inborn talent that had been with her since birth . . . She was Irish, what more can I say . . . She had two loves in her life, my father and her Granville piano which she had saved and saved for . . .

Dad never forgot *Dolly*, his horse in the Great War, the wound to his wrist was a permanent reminder of his time in France, my father never cried out in pain but I would every now and again catch a glimmer of the pain etched on his face as he suffered from his wrist. The doctors had nearly amputated it, he was lucky to have it at all. When he joined the railways people were so surprised he could hack it, they never expected him to have the use of his digits or the hand itself. Through all the pain dad had proved them wrong . . . and those that worked with him were really quite astonished . . . for Dad never gave up.

Father's love of animals extended to the common and garden cat as well, once when I was young I picked up a cat by the neck only to be reprimanded by my father. He then showed me the correct way to hold and cradle a cat so it wouldn't get hurt by folding your arms and letting the cat sit against you while you stroked its back . . . He would say, "The cat has feelings too you know, so be gentle with it. They put their trust in us so you have to be deserving of it . . ." Those words of wisdom stayed with me . . . Father could see into the souls of those around us, he could feel any animal's mental presence . . .

\* \* \*

A merciless dictatorship: In 1938 Nazi power had reached its zenith in Germany, all life was at its mercy and those in power had lost all sense of humanity as a small boy wandered, limping across the border from Germany to Holland. The little boy, barely three and a half years of age, had been beaten and whipped by the enemy of humankind, a wicked merciless enemy that preyed on the weak and powerless, an enemy which had nothing but wickedness and evil beating within its breast. A coal black shadow representing itself in human form and led by one whose insanity expressed itself in the persecution and suffering of others. Hitler . . . The little boy, with tears in his eyes, walked away from Germany with a sorrow in his heart words could not begin to describe or express. Truuss Wijsmuller, a social worker, was driving down the deserted and wooded road when she caught sight of him. Stopping, she asked, "What happened?" The little boy turned to her and replied nearly incoherently, "They killed my papa and mama. I saw it . . ."

Truuss took the young boy to hospital and returned to the border and found five young child fugitives escaping the carnage and hatred that the Nazis had meted out upon those of Jewish origin. On that day she determined to do everything she could to save these little ones from an evil that had started to spread its darkness over Europe and beyond . . .

* * *

Internment of the Jews: The ill treatment of Jews by the Germans and the shipping of them to concentration camps and death camps was not common knowledge. Even those in the cattle trucks and death camps were not aware of what was in store for them. The Nazis gradually and surreptitiously stepped up their anti-Semitic campaign, first of all banning them from certain occupations and training, to stopping them from owning land and property, to seizing bank accounts and other assets. Then the pogrom against them reached a climax in what was called *Krystal Nacht,* Jews were now thought of as sub-human, their shops and businesses were trashed and destroyed.

Glass littered the streets in Germany hence the term *Krystal Nacht*. Jews were rounded up and forced into ghettos bereft of belongings and money, forced into submission by an evil personified by Hitler himself . . . If there was news about what was happening I didn't hear it, I don't think many people knew about it, and if they did they were in utter disbelief . . . The murderous actions of the Nazis were well hidden, any news footage or photographs of these atrocities would have been acquired through the spilling of journalistic blood . . . Any information gathered by British Intelligence operatives would have fingered the spies in question putting them at risk. British politicians were focused on the survival of both Britain and her empire, she had her back against the Atlantic and she was in serious trouble . . . The way in which the Nazis had orchestrated their takeover of Europe made acquiring such information an impossibility . . . Those that experienced it were either already dead or on their way to being another victim of Nazi hatred and evil . . . *It was nothing for them to pull out a Luger from its holster and shoot someone of Semitic origin* . . . The true horror of what was happening was hidden from the world . . . Travelling to Austria Truuss Wijsmuller managed to get 600 Jewish children released into her care and transported to Holland after an interview with Adolf Eichmann, who supervised anti-Jewish activity there. Truuss, and those that worked with her, saved 10,000 children, taking them by train from Germany, Austria and Czechoslovakia, then on to England . . . and as the dreaded jackboots neared Amsterdam Truuss rounded up buses and filled them with Jewish children from a municipal orphanage and got them and other Jews aboard a ship about to steam from Ijmuiden to England . . . No one was left behind . . .

\* \* \*

Britain declares war against Germany for invading Poland:
Chamberlain came back from Germany with the declaration of,
"There will be no war in our time with Germany . . ."

Newspapers were not that common in the 1930s, and we
listened to our Ultra radiogram with a microphone, loudspeakers
and gramophone with apt interest for the most up to date
news on the whispers of war. Mum was very proud of our Ultra
radiogram and our Granville upright piano, "One step up from
the Joneses," she would say. Mum loved nothing more than to
play her piano and had the innate ability to listen to a tune and
recreate it on the ivory and ebony keys under her fingertips.
On our Marconi television set, which had a rectangular screen
the size of a saucepan lid built into a wood cabinet, I would
always see Chamberlain coming out of No: 10 Downing Street
on his way to see Hitler, he was tall, slim with dark hair and a
big moustache, he wore a bowler hat and carried a walking stick,
he was a very religious man. The BBC was the first to broadcast
the Mayo Sunderland flying boat launch the Mercury seaplane
in piggy back fashion from off its back. We watched orchestras
filmed at Crystal palace and the like. Then Germany waltzed
into Poland in a Blitzkrieg using its mechanized might to crush
any resistance. Britain didn't have much choice but to declare
war, it had a defense agreement with France so if either was
invaded the other would come to its rescue. It would not be
long before France would be invaded. Two days after Germany
invaded Poland on the 3rd of September 1939 the newspaper
headlines stated, 'BRITAIN DECLARES WAR!'

After its invasion of Poland, France and Britain would be
among the next countries to face the Germanic hordes and
the steel nailed boots of the Nazis . . . I had been walking to
the train station in the morning and *War Declared* was on the
lips of every person I encountered. As the day progressed and
I focused on my work as an apprentice coachbuilder the news
didn't really worry me, but as time went by I began to fully
realize what a serious predicament we were in . . . I had just got

home from work when my father walked in, he just shook his head and said, "Not again . . ." Dad was on shift work, he would wash up have his meal and go to bed. He didn't say much else about it . . .

* * *

The war build up – the machinery of preparation: Chamberlain was ill-equipped to wage war against Germany, he was a man of peace, what Britain needed was a warrior to lead her into the dark times ahead . . . onto the political scene strode a man that fitted that role to perfection–Churchill, a cigar smoking Man O' War if ever there was one . . . Churchill seemed to slide into the role of Prime Minister without any fuss or hullaballoo. He had inhabited a political wilderness not un-like Moses, and when called to lead his people, he was ready, willing and able. He was a rock to which the whole of Britain anchored itself. The call-up of all men between the ages of 18 and 45 years started. Those of Jewish decent were not allowed to fight, but many joined up regardless. It would not be the first time those of Semitic origin had taken on a different guise to survive in Europe. Women of all ages joined the forces and the land army to cultivate food for the long campaign ahead. The Italians living in London with businesses, even ice cream manufacturers, were picked up and interred on the Isle of Mann. I commented to my father about going there to visit an Italian shop owner I had befriended, and Mum said, "You have to go by sea to get there." Dad said, "Don't worry, I'll take you by train and ferry and we'll stay with a friend of mine from the Royal Field Artillery in Douglas . . ." As the war began to shred our lives into a thousand little pieces thoughts of my friend ceased, replaced by thoughts of survival . . .

It wasn't long before the Royal Air Force mobilized its squadrons to defend Britain on grass strips on the eastern seaboard; its fighter capability consisted mostly of Hurricanes.

Churchill and Roosevelt met in the Atlantic on the battleship HMS Prince of Wales to hammer out a deal between the United States and Britain in August of 1941. It would involve the exchange of land under the control of Britain for supplies, armaments, weapons of war, oil, food and other goods to secure Britain's survival and enable it to face Germany and Hitler head on. A card which Churchill had had printed and was signed by the two leaders bore a verse from Longfellow which Roosevelt had sent to him in his own hand during the dark days of the Blitz, it read:

Sail on, O Ship of State!

Sail on, O Union, . . . strong and great!

Humanity with all its fears,

With all the hopes of . . . . . . . future years,

Is hanging breathless on thy fate!

Roosevelt knew the Germans would not stop once they had defeated Britain and her dominions, and next on their list of conquests would have been the United States of America . . . If it had been up to Roosevelt he would have declared war on Germany that very day but he knew such an action would have been unpopular on the home front. What he could do was supply Britain with the materials to defend itself . . . *It had not taken Roosevelt long to realize that eventually American blood would be spilt in Europe once again* . . . and, on December the seventh of 1941 when the Japanese bombed Pearl Harbor his fears became a reality. The war in Europe had now blossomed to encompass the entire world . . . In the Pacific theatre the Japanese had already attacked China and were on their way to Malaya and Singapore with the intention of marching across Borneo in an effort to wrest control of Australia and New Zealand and every island in the Pacific, let alone Burma and India . . .

\* \* \*

With the invasion of Denmark and Norway in April of 1940 followed up by the attack and seizure of France and the Low Countries in May of 1940 Italy joined the Axis powers formally in June of 1940, especially once the German victory over France was assured. After this it didn't take long for the conquest and land hungry Italians led by Mussolini to make the jump to North Africa. So while Hitler attacked the Balkans the Italians invaded Egypt in September 1940 then advanced to Greece in October of that year. In these same months the Battle of Britain raged over the English countryside in blue summer skies. At the same time Hitler was planning Operation Sea lion, an invasion of Britain across the channel by a huge force of landing craft carrying German tanks and soldiers of the Third Reich. Realizing what was about to take place British air and sea forces made a determined effort to scuttle Hitler's plans by destroying the assembled landing craft. Thwarted, Hitler then changed his plans and attacked Russia instead. The Italians, meanwhile, were kicked out of Greece and mired down with General Wavell in Egypt. As a leader Wavell proved very effective against the Italians and between December 1940 and February of 1941 he led his force successfully against them in both Libya and Ethiopia. Until, that is, Rommel came on to the North African scene. He recaptured Cyrenaica in April of 1941 and turned the tide against the British forces . . . Britain was now in serious trouble . . . In that same month Hitler invaded Yugoslavia and took Greece back for the Axis powers. After this success they attacked and overran Crete . . . The next on their list of conquests was Malta, a strategically important island in the Mediterranean . . .

# CHAPTER 5

## The Blitz

**W**hen war was declared most people were advised on the installation of air raid shelters in their back gardens. My father had the parts delivered quickly and the council started excavating trenches in Meath Road so we could drop the galvanized sheeting in. The assembly of the Anderson Shelter required a deep wide ditch to be dug then the galvanized sides were dropped in with the curved sheeting making a roof bolted to the sides. It took a couple of days to get one finished and we did our best to make ours as comfortable as possible. It would provide shelter from bomb blasts and falling masonry but a direct hit would certainly kill the occupants. To make them even more effective soil could be piled on the sides and even the roof if the shelter was deep enough. Two days after our shelter was built food rationing started. Sugar and many other items now became very scarce and difficult to get hold of. Most factories producing food related products had to shut down. There were no ingredients to make sweets and other things. Essential items now had to be shipped in from other countries. Protected convoys had to bring in raw materials and other products. All types of ships, including old freighters whose steel was destined for the scrap-yard were brought off the mudflats and put into use again. The old ships were not seaworthy and were urgently fitted out and repaired for the Atlantic convoy work that lay ahead of them. All the time the German navy increased its stranglehold on Britain, trying to stop any ships from leaving and any ships getting into British harbors with their much needed raw materials, food and manufactured goods. The Germans used any and all means to bring Britain to its knees and force the British people to capitulate and surrender to them. The Kriegsmarine used submarines, Man O' War ships, cruisers, battleships, destroyers and whatever else they had in their inventory. British and Allied ships also came under attack from the skies; the large Condor would search the seas for the convoys while Junkers 88s and Stuka dive bombers would wreak havoc upon them. Back in Britain the Women's Land Army started helping farmers as their male farm workers were conscripted into the armed services . . .

* * *

Sending Ted and Alf off to Wales: It wasn't long after war was declared that all children under fourteen had to be evacuated. My two younger brothers were completely ignorant about what was about to happen to the world around them. I guess mummy wanted to shield them from the harsh realities of life, the coming war, even more so. They couldn't understand why everyone had to carry a gasmask and it was hard emotionally to make them realize what could happen. One day mum dressed them up in their Sunday best and said, "You're going to have a nice holiday in Wales, so don't be sad . . ." I was older and knew exactly why they were going. There were thousands upon thousands of children from London and other large cities being evacuated. We didn't even know where they would be going, other than it would be somewhere in Wales. It was going to split our family up, I didn't like it one bit, I loved my brothers, especially the two younger ones. I would now be on my own as Jimmy was in the army and Ernie in the navy. My world seemed to be fragmenting into little pieces. It really tore me apart. Siblings fight like cats and dogs, but in the end we would all make it up to each other with no hard feelings. Mum would say, "You, Jimmy! You, Ernie! You, Stanley! What have you done now!"

Cries of, "Mummy, Jimmy slapped me!" would burst from my small lips when I was young. Mum would say, "When I get hold of Jimmy I'm going to give him a good one too!"

Of course she never did. Her boys were the most precious things in her life. Our rampaging rambunctious ways were just growing pains and she knew that. She knew that we would grow out of it someday and be the best of buddies in the end . . . I began to miss our petty little wars and spats . . . I started to feel very lonely without them around . . . Distance had started to strain our bonds of fellowship and our brotherly love was fast disappearing because of the war . . .

Mum and I walked to Ilford train station with them and put them on board a coach bound for Wales. Alfie started to weep so I knelt down telling him we'd visit them, after all, it was only a holiday so he shouldn't cry . . . Mum was a bit teary when the train pulled away, watching it slowly fade into the distance. We only left the platform when the last coach disappeared round a bend. Walking home without them was soul destroying for mum. Later that night when dad arrived home he had tears in his eyes, the thought of Ted and Alfie leaving weighed heavily on the Chapman household of number 1 Meath Road, Essex . . .

\* \* \*

Going to the cinema with Willy Noakes: Willy and I decided to go to the Regal cinema in Ilford High Street to see the 2 o'clock matinee. We had been sitting in our comfortable seats for some twenty minutes when just before the movie was about to start an announcement came on over the speaker system from management that the air raid warning siren had just come on. They informed us that those people who would like to leave may do so but that they would also continue to show the movie. This was the first time ever the sirens had sounded in London. Willy looked at me, I looked at him. We were both sixteen at the time, we shrugged our shoulders, I said, "No point in wasting our tickets, we may as well stay, I don't fancy spending the time in a shelter . . ." Willy agreed, it was as though we had not a care in the world. We sat and watched the movie as bombs dropped on the streets and buildings of London without. Every now and then it sounded as though someone had dumped kitchen utensils on the roof above us. The muffled noise of explosions sounded all around us as we sat and laughed at the comedy. One time an extra heavy load of cutlery dropped on the roof above, again we both shrugged and I added, "I wonder which idiot dropped the dishes that time . . ." Willy grinned and laughed heartily. So there we sat, watching our movie all the way through until the end. Because the show was repeated the same announcement came over the intercom again. Will and I decided to leave. Getting outside I saw everyone looking up at the sky and the barrage balloons above us. When we turned the corner from the entrance we had the shock of our young lives for everywhere shrapnel and empty shells littered the street. Meath Road wasn't very far from the cinema. I looked south in the direction of home and saw a huge cloud of smoke forming over Barking docks on the River Thames. The rubber dump had caught alight. I thought of my brother Jimmy who had been called up immediately since he was in the Territorial Army. He was now in Barking at the docks operating one of the big anti-aircraft guns with his unit. Will and I started running towards home. I was fast because like my father I was also a good runner. I never entered competitions and won like him but I was pretty quick on my feet. When I arrived home my mother said, "Where on earth have you been, Stanley?"

I replied nonchalantly, "Oh, just to the Regal to see a movie . . ."

"Well, why didn't you come home when the air raid siren went off?" she asked.

I answered, "I didn't think it was all that serious, but Will and I saw a lot of smoke coming from Barking docks, I'd like to go over and see if Jim's alright?"

Mum agreed and so off Willy and I went to Barking to see Jim ... There was little if none TV and radio coverage of the war in 1939, what we knew of it and the damage caused by the falling bombs was either first hand or from conversations with other people, letters and maybe the cinema news reels. Willy came half way to the docks then headed home. Another half hour and I was in the dockyard area. I crossed under the Thames via the Blackwell tunnel. It was a pedestrian only tunnel which we use to run through until they posted guards at the entrance. I now had to look for Jim's anti-aircraft gun battery. Jim wasn't so happy to see me when I eventually found him; maybe because they'd been very busy fending off German bombers or the fact that I'd risked my life coming over just after the air raid. Or, possibly because they didn't know when the next air raid would come and he'd rather I was at home with mum, I don't know. I looked over the gun he'd been using then said goodbye. Jim waved hastily and got back to work preparing the gun for the next wave of bombers. The walk home took longer than I thought ... *That was the day the bombing started in earnest* ...

\* \* \*

The bakery and the bombs: I popped in to Willy's house to see him but his mother said, "Willy's gone to the bakery shop . . ." Willy worked part time at the baker's so I thought I may as well go see him. Sure enough he was still there and he invited me down to the basement where specialty cakes were made. Since the basement was deep below the store they used it as an air raid shelter as well. It was comfortable down there so I thought I'd stay awhile to give William some company. However while I was waiting for him to finish up the air raid sirens started to wail. As the bombs started to drop the baker gave Will and I a plate of donuts which we merrily chewed on. The *all clear* came and went then the air raid siren came on again. I wondered what to do and decided I'd better go home because mum would be worried. Our house in Meath Road was about a mile away. I figured I'd get home before the German bombers got to us. They took about ten minutes to cross the English Channel once the sirens went off and they started dropping bombs on London. By the time I got home they were flying low over Ilford and I sprinted down Meath Road. I dashed through the front door and out the back of our house to the shelter. I managed to get there just before they started to drop their loads. Mother was furious with me. She was on her own with the cat on her lap; she said crossly, "Where the hell have you been?" Before I managed to answer a bomb whistled over our heads, it made a horrible rushing sound like someone had turned on a tap full, and at the same time it made a whirring sound. There was a horrible thud then silence . . . When a bomb drops you automatically begin to crouch forward the closer it gets, your head going towards your knees. I found out later that the bomb had landed near to the *gasometers*, large tanks filled with gas. Most houses used gas for cooking and heating and this was where it was stored. They were around fifty feet in height and twenty yards in diameter . . . Mum and I waited tensely for the bomb to go off but it never did . . . *The silence was eerie . . .*

\* \* \*

The gasometers: The following day I scouted around looking for the bomb that had zipped over our heads so closely. The ARP had located it and the *Bomb Disposal Unit* was trying to deactivate it near the *gasometers*. It was a very large bomb and they thought it had a delayed action fuse. During my scouting around I noticed there wasn't too much damage and the ARP told me there seemed to have only been three drops in Ilford. The large bomb had buried itself about three feet into the soft ground about two hundred yards from the tanks. You could see the fin sticking out of the soil. As I arrived the *Bomb Clearance Squad* also arrived and taped the area off. I had never seen a bomb that big before. They told me to move away, the farther the better. If the bomb blew up it would have damaged the *gasometers* and probably caused them to explode. The damage this would have wrought could have destroyed an area with at least a half to a quarter mile radius around the tanks, taking out Ilford Lane, shops, offices and houses, and killing a large number of London's citizenry. The following afternoon the siren went off again. The Germans were coming back. I had been to work at the LNERLY coachworks and thought it would be nice to take a stroll down Ilford High Road with a friend of mine from the Sea Scouts. We were just about to go home when the sirens went off and the anti-aircraft guns let rip at the incoming Luftwaffe bombers overhead. They didn't seem very worried about the barrage balloons for, instead of avoiding them, their gunners opened fire downing as many as they could. Our relaxing day window shopping had ended leaving us to bolt home and find a comfy spot in our Anderson Shelters for the night . . .

* * *

The Heinkel 1-11: The whining undulating scream of the air raid siren filled the air around me in the shunting yards of the Stratford engineering works and marshalling yard. I had set off during my lunch break from the coach repair shop to see my father who was working as a locomotive driver. The canteen was subsidized and I had picked up some extra sandwiches to share with him. Dad would always tell me when he would be back and I knew exactly where he would be, so, off I went, barrage balloons littering the leaden grey sky above me. Yes, the war was on but I had no fear of the bombs or the Germans, just the air raid siren that was more ominous than the whistling bombs and explosions . . . As I was crossing the railway lines toward a concrete covered shelter an even more ominous sound filled the air around me, the throbbing undulating sound of a twin engine German aircraft coming directly towards me. I turned round and saw the plexi-glass cockpit of a Heinkel 1-11 with a machine gun sticking out of the nose and a turret on its underbelly bearing down on me. I ran as fast as I could toward the shelter leaping over the steel railway lines all around me, I turned once more to see if the Heinkel was still behind and I could see the large black crosses on the underside of the wings, its belly painted a grey blue and fuselage in a mottled dark green. The nose gun and belly gun seemed to explode with flashes of light and the ground about me erupted in small bursts as shells slapped into the earth and pinged off the railway lines sending sparks showering all over the place. I threw myself to the ground. My packet of sandwiches ended up ripped to shreds by German lead and splattered all over the place. I prayed that the shells would miss me . . . The Heinkel flew overhead between the wires of the barrage balloons as I lifted my head, seeing clearly the black crosses on its sides and the swastika on its tail, *Yes, the war had really begun and I seemed to be the target for every bloodthirsty Nazi with a machine gun . . .* I picked myself up, shook my fist at the offending aircraft, then stood watching the disappearing Heinkel for a few seconds until it vanished pulling into the clouds just above me. The whistling sound of bombs falling from above and their dull explosive thuds in the distance spurred me to action, forcing the weakness out of my legs and catapulting me toward safety, if you could call it that, as nowhere, not even a bomb shelter would be safe if a bomb landed on top of you . . . I had already lost my sandwiches and had no intention of losing my life as well . . . *Stanley's sandwiches – 0, Germans – 1* . . . When I eventually got to the bomb shelter everyone crowded around me asking if I was alright, some of them had seen the German bomber and bullets smacking into the ground all around me and thought I was a dead man. They started to check me for holes, but I assured them I was fine, no damage to mind, body or soul . . . *for I reckoned I had an angel looking after me* . . .

\* \* \*

Lord Haw Haw and our Ultra radiogram: Many times after work I would turn on our radiogram at home and Lord Haw Haw would be broadcasting. He spoke in perfect English with an aristocratic lilt to his words. He would say things like, "Our Third Reich will march into London and pay a visit to your king. Our healthy National Socialistic youth will assist those in all walks of life. We have many ways in which to assist our friends, as we have done all over the world . . . Heil Hitler . . ." He did this year in and year out . . . Was anyone actually fooled by his propaganda, maybe a few weak minded individuals, but in our family, not one . . .

\* \* \*

Joining the ARP: Having walked the streets of Ilford I was shocked at the condition of the houses, some had no doors, windows or even roofs, huge chunks of brickwork had been ripped out and were lying in gardens and on the road, in other places the buildings had been totally reduced to piles of rubble. The place looked like a rubble strewn building site. I decided then and there the best thing to do would be to join the ARP. At least I could do something and not feel so helpless when the bombs started to fall. I could do my part at staving off these aggressive Nazis. My Sea Scout training and the fact that I was a section leader made me a little more adaptable than the average Londoner to the bombing by the Luftwaffe. The ARP office was near the railway station in a small office with *'ARP Headquarters'* painted on the window. It was about a mile away from our house through rubble strewn streets. When I got there most of the staff had gone on duty. I was only 16 years old and had been told you had to be 18 years or older to join. I didn't let that stop me. I marched into the office and said, "I've come to join . . . I want to be an air raid precautions officer. The man behind the desk in front of me didn't ask my age and I was glad of that. They needed more help to patrol the streets of London and save it from burning to the ground. He pushed some papers in front of me and said, "Sign these . . ." I did, and now I was officially an ARP member. I had been doing what I could already and had an ARP helmet and gas mask with shoulder bag. I also had a first aid kit as these were required in the Sea Scouts for all section leaders. Since I was still working as a coachbuilder apprentice I had to rush home at day's end to carry out my duties, checking streets, buildings, shops and houses for bombs, damage and injured people . . . *But now, officially, I was part of the war effort . . .*

* * *

Aunt Mary and Uncle Percy O'Sullivan being bombed: As the bombing increased there were many times that I couldn't get a bus or train to work. Since I was now a member of the ARP I was told that the bombing had been very heavy over east London. I decided I'd better go check to see whether my Aunt Mary and her family, in Bow, were alright. At least I could then tell mum, who worried about her extended family, everything was okay . . . Mum was also very close to her sister, Mary. I hopped on the tram train and went as far as I could with it. The bombing had cracked up the rails in sections and rubble covered the road in others. I started walking and on my way the air raid siren went off. I sped up and then started running as I heard the whistle of bombs as they fell from the Luftwaffe bombers in the grey sky above me. I had just reached Bow Bridge and tried to get to the other side. The whistling of bombs was right above me so I threw myself to the ground. I couldn't do anything else, there was no cover and I didn't know where the shelters were in this part of town. Not that it would have helped at that moment, the bombs were now nearly on top of me . . . A full load of Jerry goodwill dropped around me and the blast rocked the buildings nearby shattering windows and blowing the tiles off them. As soon as the mortar falling around me hit the road I got up and ran as fast as I could, Aunt Mary was only a little distance away and I had a terrible feeling that the flats they lived in had been near the epicenter of the blast . . . As I rounded the corner into Sugar House Lane where Aunt Mary lived I was shocked to see that half the block of flats they lived in had collapsed. Aunt Mary and Uncle Percy had had a flat on the fourth floor. I just couldn't believe my eyes. I looked around and saw my Uncle Percy lying on the street not far from me. He was bloody, torn and shredded with his legs blown off and obviously dead, the ARP in Bow and a medic were already on the scene, I tried to go over to him but was told there was nothing anyone but God could do for him. Uncle Percy had been blown clean out of their fourth floor flat. If the blast hadn't killed him the fall from that great height surely would have. As he lay there in the middle of the road dying he had called out for help, he had been in great agony and had writhed on the ground where he lay, ripped apart by the blast, and his legs had been blown off. He pleaded while in great pain and agony for someone, anyone, to help stop his suffering . . . and then, he stopped moving, he lay still in death in the blink of an eye, before the medics could give him morphine to ease the pain. My uncle died before anyone could do anything else. I turned away and saw the steps leading up were still somewhat intact. From under a stairway slab I could see my Aunt Mary and my young Cousin Marie trying to extricate themselves from under a landing slab with the help of the local ARP and some policemen using jacks. I joined in to help but was shocked to see my beautiful little cousin's nose had been blown off and Aunt Mary had taken nearly the full weight of the slab on her body trying to shield Marie as the building fell to pieces around her. She was so firmly wedged under the slab it was very difficult to pull her out; she was in shock and felt every movement pressing against her broken bones. We pulled Marie out but Aunt Mary took some time to extricate. I looked around but couldn't see where Doreen or Violet were, I found out that they had been split up on the way to the shelter, they had made it at least and were safe. It took about ten minutes for the ambulance to come. It didn't even bother to turn on its siren, if it indeed had one. The carnage in London at the time was just too great for such theatrics . . . I helped put Aunt Mary into the ambulance and held her hand; she was in a bad way. Tears started to well up and moisten my eyes, I said, "Don't worry Aunt Mary, they'll take good care of you . . ." my aunt just looked at me and didn't say a thing. She was in a terrible state of shock. As we took Marie to the ambulance she held out her hand and held onto mine tightly, she was frightened and didn't want to let go of it. She was having difficulty breathing and the medic had pulled up a sheet to cover her face leaving only her eyes showing. Quavering, I looked down at her, "Uncle Stan loves you . . . you'll be alright, just stay strong . . ." Why I said that I don't know, I was a year and a bit older than her. She was small for her age and looked so forlorn, like a little injured bird. My heart went out to her; it pained me to see what had happened. And as my cousin Marie and Aunt Mary were taken away in the same ambulance I stood silently near to Uncle Percy standing in testament and giving a final silent solemn prayer for his soul . . . There had sometimes been friction between mum and Uncle Percy who was the jealous type. One day mother had taken him to task for mistreating her sister and decked him, mum was consoling Aunt Mary in the living room when Uncle Percy came in, but all that was in the past now . . . *with only tears replacing any ill-feelings of those times . . . Hatred coursed through my veins and I vowed to make the Nazis pay . . .*

* * *

The way home: I felt a sudden urge to go to Bow Church where mum and dad had married. I wanted to have some stable influence in my life and to know it was still standing. It meant so much to our family. It was our place of worship. Half the buildings around me had been destroyed as I worked my way through the debris. The church was still intact when I reached it. I said another prayer for Uncle Percy, my aunt and cousin, and then left for the ARP station, I was late. As I walked away in the direction of home, or what was left of it at least, a million thoughts flooded my mind. I thought of my family, of Jimmy in the army and Ernest in the navy, of my two younger brothers evacuated to Wales, of my aunt and uncle and my cousins, of my father and my mother. I wondered how we were all going to survive this vicious German onslaught and would there be anything left of my London when they were finished with it. I wept silently inside not wishing anyone to see the tears welling up from within. My hands shook a little after seeing what the bombs had done to my aunt and uncle and my cousin. I shuddered to think what an even greater tragedy it would have been had not my other cousins reached the shelter or been evacuated. The Germans and their bombs didn't care who they killed. They were impartial. Good, bad, they didn't care. I was pleased I had joined the ARP and had put my Sea Scout training to good use; it took the edge off what was happening around me. The first real bombings I experienced had been bad; they had targeted commercial factories, the docks and a tire storage depot. Back then I had felt like a child blown this and that way by an unconscionable evil wind, but now I had a sense of purpose, and in my own small way I could now help. It took the inhabitants of London three days of bombing to realize *this was war* with all the ugly potential that it encompassed. People only then started to look for shelter with an eye toward self preservation. They saw the London Underground rail system as an extension of their survival kitbag and box of tricks to save them from the falling bombs. It was an ideal place away from the exploding German ordinance and the havoc wrought upon the world above. As a member of the ARP we also patrolled the underground. At times I would go down at about 5:30 pm and start my patrol, already people had started to queue hoping to get a safe spot away from the bombs. By 7:30 pm the place was packed, people were huddled together like rabbits in a hole, no-one cared about the London that had been, it didn't exist now, personal boundaries had disappeared and the only thing on the minds of the frightened faces around me was that of surviving another night. Much of the underground had come to a halt because people would rather risk electrocution on the rails than the falling bombs outside. It was safer down here than in most public shelters. Families would huddle together and would stay longer than the night if need be to secure their spot . . . As I patrolled through my section I tried to keep a semblance of a smile on my face to allay the fears of those around me, I tried to be as stoic and steadfast as I could even though my insides were churning about like a rough sea in a wild storm. I tried as hard as I could to hold back the tears for my family and poor old Uncle Percy . . . A lone tear rolled down one of my cheeks and I wiped it away quickly before anyone could see it . . . *No, it would do no good for the crowds around to see me cry, no good whatsoever . . .*

* * *

Going to work on the train: Many times while I was going to work or heading home the air raid sirens would go off and the train I was on would stop under a bridge until the bombers had passed or the all-clear sounded; sometimes there were no trains or buses at all and I would have to walk to work. It was very hard on me. I would at times get to work late because of the bombing. The Germans wouldn't even let me rest there either, the sirens would go off and we would all head to the nearest shelter. When I eventually got home I would change into my ARP gear and start my rounds. The bombers didn't give us a break and life became very disjointed. Sometimes I could get home and sometimes I couldn't. I spent many a night under a bridge curled up in dad's big railway overcoat because that was the only cover I could find when the sirens sounded . . . those nights were damp and wet at times . . . I would shiver in the cold as the bombs dropped with only an empty stomach and explosions as company . . . I was lucky though, for like Uncle Percy the Pearly Gates were open to so many unfortunate souls . . .

\* \* \*

Mum moving to Buntingford: The German bombs had blown out some of our windows and the house was looking a little worse for wear as night after night the Luftwaffe continued to shower us with their explosive gifts. My mother wasn't happy at all. The bombs had already claimed one member of our extended family and ripped apart her sister's life, nearly killing her and her children. Dad had found a house in Buntingford, a two up and two down plus a scullery, it wasn't really big enough for us but property outside London was at a premium. Dad had met the owner, a Mr. Jack Poulton, while he was driving trains up and down to the terminus. Mr. Poulton owned quite a bit of property and farms in the area around Buntingford and was happy to help. Mum had some of the furniture moved to Buntingford and we shifted what we could into the cellar beneath the house. She didn't want to really move but it was just getting too dangerous for her to remain and the bombs were telling on her, she wanted a break from the continual night raids and our cold Anderson Shelter in the back garden . . .

\* \* \*

50 Shilling Tailors: The ARP headquarters and shelter were on the other side of Ilford Railway Station, too far to walk from our house if the sirens went off. There was a large shop called 50 Shilling Tailor's on the corner of Ilford High Street

and the road that crossed the railway line not more than a mile and a half from home. The entrance to the shelter was around the side of the shop near the railway bridge. It was around eight in the evening and we had suffered a whole night of bombing the previous day. I had spent those dark hours in the Anderson Shelter at the bottom of our garden. The raining bombs had stopped me going anywhere, by the time the air raid sirens went off the bombing followed shortly after. Anderson shelters were basically a hole dug into the ground with a curved corrugated steel roof. It would shield you from bomb blasts and falling debris but not a direct hit. I'm not so sure about bombs landing nearby but if you didn't have a deep shelter or access to the underground it was better than nothing. They had saved many lives in London. They were damp and cold and had no creature comfits but kept you alive. I thought tonight I'd like to be somewhere warmish and comfortable and be able to shut my eyes for a few hours because the shelter under 50 Shilling Tailor's had been built deep beneath it. I hadn't had a wink of sleep the night before; I had sat shivering in one corner of the shelter rubbing the sides of my arms and hoping that the bombs wouldn't kill me. The droning of the bombers above and the constant explosions had worn me down. I was the only one at home since mum was now living in Buntingford in our little cottage. The siren went off and I grabbed my coat, tin hat and gas mask bag. I walked quickly towards the tailor's shop and was nearly there by the time I heard the first wave of bombers approaching. I was about twenty feet away from the entrance when I turned to look at the bombers lit up by searchlights from the anti-aircraft guns. I became mesmerized by something new in the darkened sky, a parachute with a cylinder flattened at both ends hanging beneath. It was the first time I'd seen one even though we had been briefed at our ARP meetings. I stood there rooted to the spot just watching the cylinder gently floating down to the streets of London, a gift to its inhabitants by a generous Germanic overlord in the form of a dark haired, moustache wearing, dictator. Landmines had a barometric pressure detonator so when it reached its desired height above ground it would blow up. They were much more effective than the normal bombs since the pressure wave would cause more damage. It was about thirty feet above the houses on the other side of the bridge. The next moment I was sitting with my legs splayed apart and dazed at the bottom of the two flights of stairs leading to the shelter of 50 Shilling Tailors, I was covered in dust and fragments of masonry with people staring at me in the strangest manner possible. My helmet, which had been firmly affixed to my head, was lying next to me minus its strap, my gas mask bag twisted around my back. I hadn't seen the mine explode nor felt anything, I hadn't the faintest clue as to how I'd ended up where I did. I just picked myself up and dusted my coat then found a comfy corner in the shelter to doze as the bombs exploded above us . . .

After the all clear siren had heralded in the early morning rays of the sun I stood up stiffly and yawned, it had been another night of heavy bombing but at least I had got some sleep. Climbing up the steps to the world without I reached the top and the havoc wreaked by our German cousins. Looking through the smoke over to where I had seen the landmine floating to earth I noted that most of the houses had had their roofs blown clean off by the blast. I started walking over the bridge in the direction of the houses that were now empty shells; one of my duties was to report on the damage done to infrastructure and buildings . . . *It seemed pointless but what else could I do . . .*

* * *

Going to Wales to see my brothers: Visiting mum in Buntingford over a weekend I told her I'd got a *Privilege ticket* from dad to go to Wales to see Teddy and Alfie, the ticket would take me to Swindon and then on to my destination, Caerwent in Monmouthshire, South Wales. She wished me a safe journey as I headed back to London and the bombing. I had managed to get two day's leave for my trip and boarded the train at Euston station and settled into my seat. The steady 'clackety-clack' of the bogies over the rails was comforting, it was nice leaving London and the stench of burning buildings and the smell of fear behind me. The scent was all-pervading and was reflected in the eyes of so many. The German's had said they would blow us all to bits; cowering in an Anderson shelter at the bottom of a garden as explosions rent the smoke filled blackness without and the dull thuds and rumbling earth beneath our feet vibrating from a chorus of Germanic origin, I had started to believe they would. Around me the other passengers stared vacantly in front of them, looking at nothing in particular. No-one said a word. It was nearing the end of summer and going into autumn, scattered clouds filled the sky above. And, lucky for us, no German bombers soared in that blue azure expanse, for now they were seriously strafing trains or dropping bombs on them. The solemn look on the faces around me reminded me of a funeral and I was glad to get off the train at Bristol. As I stood on the platform my mind tried hard to comprehend the madness around me, how one country had ruined our lives and taken our loved ones away, either to Wales, foreign theatres of war, or . . . away in death . . . Half an hour later I was on the move again as the train duly took me to Swindon where I was told I would have to go on to Cardiff then to Monmouth on an electric train. From there I would have to walk to Caerwent anyway. It would take a whole day of travel to do it this way so I thought I may as well walk to Caerwent from Swindon.

I steeled myself for the long walk ahead of me, some 35 miles, and, with my father's peaked cap and long railway coat I set off into the countryside. Some five miles and a few blisters later a truck carrying cattle drove up. The driver slowed down and stopped next to me. Leaning out the window he asked, "Where to sonny boy?" I smiled and replied, "Caerwent . . ." He looked down at me and pushed his cap higher up his forehead, "Well, I'm goin' down some ten miles to a farm, it'll take some weight off yer' feet . . ." He pushed the door open and I jumped in thankfully. We talked about rationing and I told him my brothers had been evacuated. "Well, sorry ta' hear 'bout that, but it's fer the best seein' yer' from London an all . . ." said the driver. Before he dropped me off he gave directions and told me which roads I should take. Standing on the road he waved at me cheerily and turned down a rutted track towards a farm. The road looked long and uncompromising in front of me. Sighing, I took a deep breath and carried on trudging in the direction of the cottage, only another twenty miles to go. After some miles of plodding a horse and cart carrying bales of hay drew up beside me. The farmer said in a welcoming voice, "Hop on, you look all but done in . . ." He asked me where I was from and where I was going to. "I'm from London on my way to see my brothers who were evacuated . . ." I replied. "Wish I could take you all the way my boy, but I have to deliver the hay," noted the farmer. We talked about the war and how it was affecting our lives. "I shouldn't think it'll last more'n a year, mark you, we licked them in the first war so I would 'spect your brothers will be home soon . . ." he expressed in a West Country lilt. "I sure hope so . . . I hate the bombs and what they've done to London." I said, shaking my head in disgust. "Aye, with all the rationing there's nothing in the shops and many businesses have closed their doors because they have no materials to make things with . . ." he added. I looked up at the sky above and thought how quiet it was, a far cry from the devastation of my home, where I lived, where I played as a child, yes, a far cry away, a different time and place . . . Maybe the war would end in a year, I didn't know, all that had happened since had changed me, hurt me, Uncle Percy dying in the street with his legs blown off, Aunt Mary trapped under the slab, my cousin Marie losing her nose, and the others, what about the others, there were just so many of them, the dead and dying . . . their faces would be forever ingrained on my mind and haunt me for an eternity . . . Another nine miles passed under the cart before the farmer pulled up and headed for a farm not too far distant. I waved goodbye and he waved back. The long road stretched out in front of me and I started to walk again . . .

I was hot and tired by the time I reached a little country pub. Being under age I ordered a lemonade shandy and sat outside on a bench and sipped my drink, thinking . . . for the war had followed me, engulfed me in its tendrils not wishing me to forget it like a jealous lover, wrapping around my conscious self like a fog, stifling me, suffocating me . . . I continued walking and eventually came to a bridge and saw houses on the other side. Enquiring at one of them the lady told me I wasn't far, just a little further for she knew the lady my brothers were staying with. Following her directions I couldn't believe my eyes as two figures ran toward me, Teddy and Alfie! Their faces bore wide grins as they embraced me joyously . . . Their brother had come!

The middle aged Welsh lady who spoke little English entreated me to stay, and of that I was so thankful, for the journey had been long and I dreaded the thought of having to leave before nightfall and walking in the dark . . .

We spent a glorious afternoon together and I took photos of them with my Kodak Brownie camera outside the cottage. None of us were happy about being split up but what could we do? What would have happened had a bomb hit our house, like it had so many others? What then? Teddy asked, "When are we going home?" I lied to make them happy, to see a smile on their young faces, "The war will be over soon, not to worry, and we'll all be back home . . ." I kept saying to them, "Enjoy your holiday . . . maybe I should come here and stay with you?" I sincerely wanted to, to be away from the death and destruction, the devastation of what once had been a proud city, now littered and strewn with rubble and the dead, smoke from burning buildings stinging my eyes, those once innocent eyes that had now seen far too much of the horrid wicked deeds man could do to man . . . Teddy and Alfie both piped in, "No, you can't stay with us, the lady would be cross!" I smiled, thinking only of the now and let the future be damned. I wanted these memories of my younger brothers to be happy, joyous ones I could dwell on while sitting and waiting for a bomb to drop on me ending my time on earth . . .

The following day my heart was torn in two as I saw the sadness in my bothers' eyes, a yearning for me to stay with them . . . but I had no choice but to leave. As I waved goodbye I could see in their eyes how sad they were; I walked up the road to a bus stop where the lady had told me to wait, the bus would take me directly to the station. With my last glimpse of my brothers, a thought crossed my mind, a dark hurtful thought, *'Would I ever see them again?'*

This time I caught the electric train to Cardiff and then caught another train to Swindon, and then home . . . The train was half an hour late because we stopped under a bridge, for German bombers flew overhead. I went straight to the railway works to meet dad. He told me that he would be moving to Bishop Stortford as they had lost some drivers already because of the bombs and had no desire to lose any more. The die had been cast . . . I would be all alone in Meath Road. On the upside mum was so happy to hear that her two babies, as she put it, were perfectly safe, well and happy. When I arrived at Buntingford Aunt Mary was there with Marie, Doreen and Violet. I was glad she and my cousins were out of London. It was also a constant worry to mum after their building had been blown up while they were still in it. Aunt Mary's body was covered in bruises and her injuries were on the mend. Marie had had reconstructive surgery and bird's cartilage implanted into her nose cavity to build it up. I didn't have a bed available to me in Buntingford, but I was happy, happy that my aunt and cousins were now safe from the falling German bombs and that now at least they could have some relief from the pain and suffering they had experienced . . .

\* \* \*

The lady who refused to leave her house: During the air raids the Germans would also drop *fire grenades*, small phosphorus incendiary bombs that would ignite and cause a tremendous amount of damage. We would go around checking on houses and kick them out like footballs if we saw any. One of our many duties was to locate any unexploded bombs and warn the *Bomb Disposal Unit.* Of course looking after the inhabitants of London was our major concern and making sure people heeded the air raid sirens and took to the shelters . . . On one particular evening when the air raid sirens went off we were checking the streets and houses I saw a middle aged lady standing at the door to her house looking up at the searchlights. She seemed mesmerized by the lights and the sounds of German bombers coming towards us. As the bombs started to drop I tried to convince her to get into her shelter at the bottom of her garden, "Why aren't you in your shelter? You'll be safer there . . ." I said. She stuttered out something unintelligible. She seemed shell shocked. I tried my best to move her but she refused to budge. The bombs started dropping around us in earnest sending bits of building in all directions. Two incendiary devices dropped through her roof . . . I kicked them out the front door. "See, if I'd been in the shelter they would have burnt my house down," she said. "Yes," I agreed, "but let's go down to the shelter were you'll be a lot safer." As I ushered her to the shelter I said, "Don't worry, I'll stay with you until the bombs stop . . ." She nodded her head thankfully. I sat with her until she fell asleep. She was still shocked and I put a blanket that was in the shelter over her shoulders to warm her. I stayed awake next to her while bombs dropped around us and it was early morning when I left her, most of the bombers had dropped their loads and only intermittent explosions now rocked London. As I headed home the *all clear* siren sang out wail-fully. I was now very tired at having been up the whole night. I walked the rubble strewn streets with the *all clear* siren playing its merry tune. When I got home I washed and got dressed for work. As I walked out the front door I grabbed my father's big black overcoat and peaked cap . . . *it was just another day in war torn London* . . .

\* \* \*

The Lucky and the Dead: The first bombing of London was a shock to everyone, me included, we didn't really think it was going to happen, but when the Luftwaffe arrived en masse the siren for that day never let up, from morning till late at night; Hitler wanted to make his point, and we, the residents of London suffered . . . We got use to the sirens blaring out their woeful tones in the morning at 6:00 am, then again at around midday, then again at 11:00 pm at night, or before, depending on how nasty the Germans were that day. People died, thousands of them . . . Initially the bombing was sporadic then the Germans started targeting certain areas. They made a mess of the docks from Barking to the Tower of London. Lord Haw Haw came on over the radio and said, "We do not want to bomb Buckingham Palace because our glorious leader Hitler will make his triumphant march through London and take up residence at the Palace and use it as an office for the Third Reich . . ."

Many old historical buildings were hit though, some badly damaged, some destroyed totally. When the order came to wear gasmasks during heavy bombing people really started to fear what was going on, the stiff upper lip of the British started to quiver, and for some it was just too much to bear, like the lady I tried to get into the shelter when she was frozen to the spot looking up at the searchlights and bombers overhead. Some people refused to get into the shelter not because of mental incapacity but because they feared unscrupulous individuals looting their houses. It is not a nice thing to say but certain police officers became quite wealthy robbing houses that had been bombed or had been left vacant . . . On many occasions we came across people so badly injured we just held onto their hands as they said their last and final farewell, shattered souls leaving a shattered London, all ended because of a small dark haired, moustache wearing man in Germany wanting to rule the world. Willy Noakes and I gave them as much comfort as we could in the bombed out ruins of their homes, others lying still in the street gasping for breath, still others crying because they knew death was near, their last breath drawing nearer with each passing moment. When I remember these poor souls tears well up from the depths of my being crying out to all humanity, *'Why?'* We came across souls with bodies torn asunder; we picked up the pieces and respectfully put them in one place to be taken away. Willy was a smoker, me, never, he would offer a cigarette to shivering souls close to life's end. We would wrap them in our overcoats trying to make them as warm as possible, they would say to us, "I knew you would come . . ." We would comfort them while we waited for the Red Cross, offering those that could a sip of tea from the flasks we carried . . . Some, unable to speak, as their life force ebbed would pass into the unknown with eyes still open . . . we would close their eyes for them . . . It was incredibly heart wrenching to see these poor people die . . . The pain we saw, the hope we witnessed fading, the loves and lives of so many ending in a flash, the dreams we saw ending in the common grave of mankind . . . *none of it was right . . . only a demon would do this to another human being or creature . . .* At times the only equipment we had available to dig the injured out from under rubble was our bare hands, and even though cut and bleeding from the debris Willy Noakes and I dug and dug until the poor souls buried underneath were freed . . . some dead, some still alive . . .

At day's end when Willy and I headed home for some rest and a chance to shut our eyes the guns would still be firing, hot shells would be dropping from the sky and shrapnel from ack-ack guns would fall by the bucket load. We would take shelter in doorways or wherever else we could. Passing by blown out doors and windows we saw many incendiary devices ready to detonate and add to the carnage that was London, homes that were now burnt out shells, streets full of acrid smoke, shattered lives and the dying and the dead . . . into those houses we would stride, and kick out those offensive gifts of violent Nazi death . . . *They had destroyed our lives leaving our loved ones dead and dying in the streets of London and I prayed for the time when the favor would be returned . . .*

* * *

Spitfires' reign over London: Initially Hurricanes were the only fighters of choice to the Royal Air Force but this gradually changed and the Spitfire became more visible in the skies above Britain. During one air battle I saw a Spitfire chasing a Luftwaffe bomber; it fired short bursts and sent it plummeting towards the ground. The Spitfire followed it making sure it never reared its ugly head again. After it had finished with that one it headed back into the fray weaving in and out of the enemy aircraft above our heads trying to break up their formations and bring down more . . .

I did my best in our neighborhood and offered to assist people in mending roofs that had been damaged or blown off during the raids. I now felt, young as I was, that I had to do something more to fend off these attacks. It was neither funny nor amusing now; the initial disregard and contempt of Hitler as a dancing baboon had dissipated. I was a member of the ARP but I wanted to be more actively involved in fighting the Nazis who were intent on killing and destroying everything I loved and cared about. They had already killed Uncle Percy O'Sullivan, seriously injured my cousin Marie and nearly ended Aunt Mary's life, I wanted them to pay for it . . .

* * *

Uncle Dan's gift: One Saturday during a lull in the bombing I popped in to see how Uncle Dan was. He asked how mum and dad were and how I was. Did I have enough food and clothes, was there anything I needed. "How are you surviving with the bombing," he asked. "Just managing," I answered. My clothes had taken a hammering, and there wasn't always water to wash them if the mains had been hit. "Mum's in Buntingford now," I added, "Would you like her address?" He wrote it down then said, "Look in the safe, I've put something in there for you."

I did as he asked and my jaw dropped, inside it was full of five, ten and twenty pound notes. "Take some, whatever you like, it'll help you with what you need . . ."

I was quite shocked and only took £20 in one pound notes. Uncle Dan laughed, "You're just like your mother, I knew you wouldn't take much . . ." He reached in and pulled out a wad full of notes and said, "Here's £150 go buy some new clothes and whatever else you need . . ." I really needed clothes and shoes, mine had started to look shabby as the war over English skies and the bombs had taken their toll on me and mine. When I left I visited our local Jewish tailor the first opportunity I got, he kitted me out with everything I needed, shirts, shoes, socks, a suit and pants. Trouble was there was nowhere safe to put them . . . not even our home in Meath Road . . . It didn't take long for them to disappear with no one permanently at the house . . .

* * *

Thurgoods and building Mosquito main-planes: I had volunteered for service in the Royal Navy but somewhere along the line they had lost my papers. They said not to worry as they were sure to locate them. The bombing in London was bad and I looked forward to a time when I could relax a bit. My father said I should move to the cottage in Buntingford in preparation to join the senior service. It was getting more and more difficult to get to Stratford Works where I was an apprentice coachbuilder, and besides, I wanted to do more for the war effort. I was sleeping on the floor in Ilford since most of the furniture was now in Buntingford. Going to work was becoming just too burdensome, what with the trains having to stop, the buses running infrequently and the tram lines being torn up by the bombs . . . Artisans were needed at Ware to assemble the main-planes for the all wood Mosquito fighter bombers. I made an appointment with the manager and arrived at ten in the morning. He immediately took me on as a junior assemblyman as they were in dire need of people with my experience. They were so desperate to have me they arranged to have my big heavy rosewood tool chest picked up at the coachworks that very day and asked me if I could start tomorrow. The following day I duly arrived and found my tool chest waiting for me. A supervisor sat with me for about an hour showing me the basics of assembling the Mosquito main-plane and said, "Carry on . . ." Within two days of my arrival he told me he was very impressed with my work and was glad to have me on board as there was a shortage of skilled men. I couldn't bear to tell him I had already volunteered for the navy and was waiting for my papers to be processed and my eighteenth birthday to come along. I would be sorry to leave the ARP when I eventually joined the navy, I had made a lot of good friends there and many a time they would give me a meal at night during the bombing of London. Working at Ware gave me the opportunity at times to sleep in Buntingford where I would share a small bed with my cousin Marie, who, with my Aunt Mary and her other children had come to get away from the bombing. Marie's reconstructed nose looked a lot better and Aunt Mary's injuries had all healed but the bruises kept coming out. She had been so badly crushed under the slab they would do this for a long time afterward. Mum, having worked in London tending to those brought back injured from France during the First World War nursed her back to health. Dad was kept so busy on the railways he had scant time to even come home; he eventually had to get accommodation in Bishops Stortford where he had been stationed by the railways. When I visited mum in our new home she and I would sit outside and watch the search-lights over London and the anti-aircraft guns let rip at the German bombers. It was just like a massive fireworks display. *When I was at home in Buntingford I thanked God I was still alive and in one piece after all that had happened to me . . .*

While working at Thurgoods and building the low-flying Mosquito light attack-bombers at Ware my life at times became even more disjointed, sometimes my home would be in Buntingford and sometimes at our house in London, since we still had lots of things stored in the cellar and mum and dad didn't want it to be stolen. One particular day started out normal in Buntingford as I ran to catch the train as usual, since my ARP duties and work really tired me out and I had great difficulty rising once my head hit the pillow; I was burning the candle at both ends. The conductor knew I would be late and would hold the train up just for me, yelling, "Come on, Stanley! Hurry up!" On the train people commented, "You look old enough to join up so why aren't you in the forces?" There was a lot of pressure from everyone I met and there were also posters plastered on every wall proclaiming in big bold letters with a Sergeant Major pointing his finger straight out, "WE NEED YOU!" My work at Thurgoods excited me, for I was now building aircraft even while I was still an apprentice, to me this was a big step up from railway carriages. At lunchtime I sometimes popped into Hertford town center, which was not too far away, to peruse the shop windows just to bring some sort of peace to my mind and normality into my life and escape from the carnage before I went back to London. The bombing, at times, was so severe it could drive a sane man mad and leave him shivering uncontrollably in the gutter. I had seen it so many times; some people just couldn't take it, it wasn't their fault, for the blame rested squarely on the shoulders of the Germans . . . While I was in a bookstore devouring the contents of an interesting book a man came in after propping his bicycle up on the wall outside, he was wearing a tweed coat, plus fours with long socks tucked underneath and a brown felt fedora on his head. He smiled at me and said, "I can see you love reading . . ."

I replied, "Yes, Sir . . ."

"Are you at school or are you working?" he continued.

I then told him about Thurgoods and the Mosquito bombers and the fact that I would be receiving my call-up papers in the near future and that I vacillated between London and Buntingford. We carried on chatting about the war and life in Britain and the war effort, then he added, "You must come and have afternoon tea with me before you leave and we can chat some more . . ." he shook my hand and continued, "Do you know where I live?"

I replied, "No . . ."

He then wrote down his address on a piece of paper proffered by the shop clerk and handed it to me, "Just ask anyone in the village where my house is . . ." With that he left the shop picked his bicycle up off the wall and rode off. The shop clerk looked at me, and noted, "Do you know who you were talking to?"

"No . . ." I answered.

The clerk gave me a wry look, "That was George Bernard Shaw, the writer . . ."

I laughed and shook my head and made a mental note to schedule time to visit him. It was not to be for a while though since there were just so many things happening to me all at once. George Bernard Shaw was a great promoter of the literary arts and a very wealthy man, his ethos was, 'Every child should know how to read and write!' I was told he always gave a signed copy of one of his books to anyone who visited him . . . I kept the note with his address on it in my wallet, but the war took even that as I scrambled over the bombed out smoking ruins of a house one weekend with Willy trying to save some poor unfortunate souls trapped inside while German bombs fell all around us . . . My wallet slipped out of my pocket never to be seen again . . .

Not long after I had some free time at the factory in Ware one day so I hopped on a bus and headed to the village he'd written down on the note. Since I didn't have his address I asked the first person I met and was readily given directions to his small farm. I walked down the country lane until I reached his property, and after I knocked on the door his housekeeper answered and explained he was away and wouldn't be back for quite some time. I left with my tail between my legs as I was looking forward to seeing him again. One of my aspirations in life was to write a book and to have George Bernard Shaw as my mentor, *it would have been a dream come true . . .*

# CHAPTER 6

## Call of Duty

Everybody had left the house, my brother Jim had already shipped out to Africa and the Middle East with the Eighth Army, mummy had gone to stay in Buntingford in our cottage there, Ted and Alfred had been evacuated twelve months before to Monmouth, Ernie was on his ship HMS Arethusa as a chief petty officer, and Dad, well, he was on shift work with not a minute to spare and stationed at Bishops Stortford where he stayed in a room out of London and away from the constant bombing. I never had much of a chance to sleep at home what with the bombs falling at night, my work as a coachbuilder and the building of Mosquito main planes, the wooden wings of that beautiful machine was an essential service and because of that I didn't have to go on active service. I spent my off time grabbing some sleep on subway platforms, on the escalators leading down to the subway tunnels, in shelters and even under bridges. Not that we could get any sleep, I would just close my eyes and curl up into a ball wearing my warm railway overcoat. The best place was a tube station, but they were always packed full of people, the Anderson shelters were just too damp and too small and not particularly comfortable.

I opened the front door and picked up the mail lying on the wooden floor. Mummy had asked me to check the house and see if the remaining furniture, and, for that matter, the house was still okay. I could see from the outside that some of the windows were broken, but, other than that, the house looked in good shape. I saw a buff envelope addressed to me and opened it, I knew they were my call-up papers. I chuckled, *for even with all the bombing the post was still being delivered . . .*

I was really tired from the previous night's ARP duty as the last of the *all clear* sirens had wailed their notes into the gray English skies above me as I trudged down the bombed out war torn streets. The Nazis had been busy that night, a little too busy for my liking as bomb after bomb had rained down on us destroying anything and everything that got in the way of their high explosive. I hadn't had a wink's sleep all night. I was home alone as I made for my favorite comfy chair in the living room. A few blocks away from our house Aunt Mavis had had a nicely furnished two story tenement house. My auntie had been home when the first bomb had hit the roof tumbled through and exploded. Aunt Mavis was lucky; she had ended up under the stairwell and was trapped until she could be rescued. Her husband hadn't fared as well, there wasn't much left of him after the bomb had detonated. The streets I had grown up on, had played games on with my friends, had kissed my first little girlfriend at age nine had disappeared under piles of masonry, broken wood and shattered tiles. And . . . and the blood of the innocent . . . There were no little girls playing *Hopscotch, Skip to My Lou, or, Ring-a-Ring o' Roses, a pocket full of posies, atishoo, atishoo, we all fall down.* No, there was none of that and few children in all of London since most had all been evacuated to Wales and other such places far away from the falling German bombs. No, all we did was await the sounds of the sirens heralding the imminent arrival of more German bombers with bomb bays full of death and destruction. England had suffered before from the black death, but which was worse, the plague or death dealing bombs, I didn't know, but in the future there would be no children singing the praises of Herr

Hitler as in the song *Ring-a-Ring o' Roses*, we would soak up the punches of the thousand year Reich until we were in a position to strike back.

Hitler was bent on destroying London and all its inhabitants. He had swept across Europe in a blitzkrieg of unstoppable mechanized machinery full of so much destructive power countries had fallen like dominoes under his jackbooted fiends. And now, it was our turn, we would either succumb to the onslaught or rise like a phoenix from the ashes of London to smite our foe down where they belonged, in the eternal fiery grave of Gehenna where they would be tortured for an eternity.

The buff envelope addressed to Stanley William Chapman from the War Department contained what I expected–*a call to service.*

But my face turned ashen, oh no, not the army, this was decidedly not on, there was no way this side of hell I was going to be one of those poorly attired trench slobs in an itchy green uniform, no offense to my dad and the others, but my dream had always been the navy and to become one of those smartly dressed sailors I would catch a glimpse of every now and then on shore leave. How I was going to get out of this I hadn't the faintest. On reflection I should have signed up with the Royal Naval Volunteer Reserve (RNVR), for with all my experience in the Sea Scouts I would have become a midshipman with immediate effect . . .

I left Ilford and arrived by train in Romford, Essex the following day to sort things out. Walking into the call-up office I sought out the biggest and meanest looking sergeant major I could find, politely I said, "Excuse me, Sir, but I'm not going into the army, there must be some mistake in my call-up papers . . ."

He looked at me quizzically for a second or two, then, replied haughtily, "We make those decisions young man, not you."

I looked him straight in the eyes and stated, "Well, I'm not going in the army!"

"And why not?" queried the sergeant major.

"My brother is in the navy–" I stated resolutely, neither budging an inch nor backing down from the over-bearing figure standing in front of me.

He looked at me and took a step back, "Well, er, um, then you'd better go home until you're called up for the navy . . ."

I guess no-one had ever done that before and the office boys couldn't believe their ears, even the new recruits all lined up like pins in a bowling alley looked at me disbelievingly. I turned and left the way I had come with my chin held high and my shoulders square, *I would become a navy man and no-one would stop me, not even the sergeant major . . .*

Of course I had neglected to tell him I also had a brother in the army, Jim, but they didn't need to know that. I had my pride and I wasn't going to be pushed around by anyone, either by the sergeant major or the whole blamed army for that matter . . .

\* \* \*

It was another two weeks before I was called up to report to HMS Ganges and an all expenses paid holiday to Shotley in Suffolk. I had had my hair cut before I had left London *just in case*. I wanted to look smart before I arrived; I wanted to at least look like a navy man from the very beginning. My service number was PJX 408402, and it was a number that became etched so deeply into my conscious mind that I would never forget it.

The trip down by train was uneventful; the station was crowded with soldiers and other service personnel, either on their way to postings, leave or the just enlisted. The instructor who took down my details and ushered me into the life I would lead for the duration of the war was a decent fellow. Next on my things-to-do-list was to line up for a haircut. The barber seemed to be a decent sort as he kept asking how the boys would like their hair cut. Some of them made a real fuss, complaining, "I don't want my hair cut at all!" To those dissenters he gave the

roughest of treatment. One young lad, full of pride with his
bush of curly red hair, standing in the queue in front of me, sat
down in the chair when it was his turn. The barber asked, "How
would you like your hair cut?"

"I don't want it cut at all, just a few snips here and there if
you don't mind and leave it long . . ." he replied.

The barber looked at him curiously then smiled. That
was the worst thing the poor schmuck could have said. The
barber picked up his shears, eyed them for a second then ran
them all the way from the back of the new recruit's head to the
front. Red curly hair dropped to the floor in piles. The boy was
so distraught he started to cry rivulets. After the barber was
finished he patted the now bald plate and said, "Done! Next
please . . ."

Two other new recruits were in front of me before it was my
turn. When I eventually sat down he asked me, "So how would
you like your hair done?"

I had cottoned on by this time and said, "Oh, just do anything
you like."

He gave me a really smart short back and sides and sprayed
on a sweet smelling spritz which made me feel like a million
pounds in sterling.

The following day after a good night's rest we headed to
the outfitters and got kitted out with uniforms, shoes, boots,
socks, underwear and everything else we would need for the
foreseeable future. Next we were given a trade test for which I
was thankful I failed, it would have meant becoming a shipwright
petty officer and a posting to a big ship where I would have been
one of the many peas in the pod.

Everything at Ganges was very strict and in the parlance of
the day, *very pusser!* The code of conduct was, "Yes, Sir, yes, Sir!"
Three bags full, Sir, up to you . . ." or, as we use to rephrase it,
"Up yours too, Sir!" I was posted to a seaman's group in Hawk
division; there were about thirty to forty of us all in the same
barrack. Some of the men had difficulty adjusting to life in the

navy and some were just plain obnoxious, one in particular had been to a good school and kept ribbing me about how superior he was. One morning he made a really dirty remark about my parentage. It made my blood boil and was all I could take from him and his rubbish, I said, "Come here and repeat that . . ." He came up to me and being a little taller thought he could bully me and reached out to grab my arm and twist it behind my back. I was too quick for him and grabbed his throat then threw him to the ground, but not before I'd smacked his head on the steel bunk bed behind him a few times and let loose a flurry of punches to both head and body. The fracas was stopped when one of the boys shouted, "Stan, stop it! Number three's coming!"

In the past HMS Ganges was a boys training ship and its instructors knew how to deal with the unruly behavior of errant youngsters. You had to run everywhere and said, "Sir," to everyone on the ship. I flew over two bunks to get to mine and landed with a creak of springs just as number three entered our barracks. I lay there with my hands clasped behind my head trying to look as calm and unfazed as possible. The churlish lad I'd collared looked rather sheepish and high-tailed it to the toilets. Number three cast his eyes about, he knew there was something going on, and you could see it in his eyes. He pivoted and left as smartly as he had entered grunting slightly with a shake of his head. I breathed a sigh of relief; I'd dodged a big bullet . . .

Later in the day I had the misfortune to run into the same lad. He and his friend had decided to tackle me on the parade ground and make me pay for defending myself and my family's honor. The parade ground was a 300 x 300 feet square. The lads cowardly crept up on me from behind with the intent of giving me a real thrashing. Sensing something was wrong I ducked at the same moment they launched their attack. They both flew over my back and ended sprawled in front of me on the concrete. One of them had broken his kneecap and the other had had his pride shattered and gained a few bruises for his trouble. The fight had been short and sweet but not unnoticed by one of the instructors. The young fellow who had been harassing me ended up in hospital then kicked out of the navy. They had no desire to cultivate bullies and an unruly element in the superior service . . . His partner in assault was shipped out immediately and ended up on guard duty for the rest of his naval career and the duration of the war.

How they ended up sailing over my back is anyone's guess, but, my mother always said, "Stan tells you things long before they happen . . ." Elizabeth O'Sullivan-Chapman knew many things and she knew her son had a gift, a gift I would be thankful for on many occasions. After that episode everyone at HMS Ganges started respecting me and what I said.

That afternoon the swimming instructor informed us to be at the pool by 0600 hours the following day. I thought, '*Great, we can do a bit of swimming and relax a bit,*' gee, was I wrong!

We formed up and were given white canvas duck suits. When dry they were barely sufferable, but when immersed in water they became unbearably heavy. The wet canvas seemed to soak up every ounce of water it came in contact with. As we lined up in single file around the pool I wondered, '*What now?*' Around the pool lay several boat hooks, these were longer than a broom with a hook on one end and were used when lowering life boats over the side of a ship when letting them down from davits. Woe betides any seaman who let a life boat hit the side of a ship, for if he did the punishment would be severe.

A barked order, "Line up at the edge of the pool!" was given, then, "All men who cannot swim, take one step back from the edge!" The next order, "Those by the edge jump into the pool!"

While we were treading water in the lead weighted duck suits the instructors started to attack the non-swimmers with the boat hooks driving them into the pool like a sorry bunch of lemmings being driven toward a cliff edge. I couldn't stop myself from laughing at the sight and the poor suckers facing the boat hooks. I thought, '*Oh gosh, the poor buggers are going to drown!'* They were then shoved into the pool unceremoniously. Of course they didn't drown for the instructors hauled the poor blighters out by the scruff of their duck suit collars by the boat hooks like half-drowned rats. After that escapade we all received certificates of competency in swimming. After all that the white duck suits became our wear all item with heavy military boots and a .303 Lee Enfield rifle. We were then marched to the assault course, which at Ganges is on the coast. Marching into the sea at the instructors orders we wheeled about and attacked the coastline like badly formed Vikings up an embankment of sand and tumbled down on the other side into a wide ditch with water in it, then climbed up the facing embankment. Some distance away there were gun emplacements which we had to take. Halfway to them we sat down and had lunch, I guessed the 'Germans' were taking their well earned lunch break as well, since; *stomping on the heads of the innocent takes it out of you.* After our tea break we were ordered to clean our rifles in readiness for our assault on the guns facing us. We had to traverse a barbed wire section in which crawling, diving over and getting tangled up in it was all part of the fun. If at all possible we were ordered to, "Take those guns!" I managed to get over the wire entanglement in one piece with only a few scratches and charged the guns screaming my heart out . . . If there had been actual Germans manning the guns and firing live ammunition at us it was doubtful I would have survived but my instructors were impressed with my efforts.

Each time you passed a course section you were issued a competence certificate, if not; you would get the boot and get transferred to the army. Many of the washouts cried their hearts out when that happened. I always gave it my best and passed all the courses with flying colors. The courses were basics, defense, rifle handling, armament knowledge, seamanship, assault and rifle drill. I passed them all with 100 out of 100.

* * *

Four weeks later I was transferred to HMS Victory at Portsmouth and when I arrived I met other men all awaiting transfer to ships or shore stations. While waiting I was sent to Whale Island for gunnery practice on Oerlicons, Bren guns and pretty much everything else the navy had on hand to shoot Germans. I really enjoyed myself and turned into a crack shot at whatever I tried my hand at. After two weeks of gunnery I returned to Portsmouth and was introduced to a strange fellow, a boffin of sorts, his name was Watson Watt. I didn't give him or our meeting much thought. I was given a two week pass so I headed home to my mother at our cottage in Buntingford, the house in Ilford, Essex was just too prone to bombing. It had been difficult initially for mother to get a cottage as everyone in London was determined to get out so accommodation outside was at a premium, but dad had sorted that out. Teddy and Alfie, as evacuees, were still in Wales far away from the falling bombs and German machine guns. I had a surprise when I got to Buntingford as dad was home when I arrived and they were so proud that I'd passed muster. Rationing was in full force but we had a little party with what we had. The two weeks flew by and it felt as though I'd just arrived when it was time to leave.

Within 24 hours of returning to Portsmouth and HMS Victory shore station most of the men I had been barracked with were given various postings and had left to join their ships. I wondered why I was the only one left. I was called in to see the commanding officer of the station. *'Oh shucks,'* I wondered what transgression I'd committed and what my punishment was going to be. I started to perspire while waiting outside his office. One of the other officers, a lieutenant, came up to me, "Follow me," he ordered sternly.

*'Oh boy, I've really had it now,'* I thought, *'Are they going to give me the boot?'*

Two more officers walked in behind me. I was told to take a seat. One of the officers sitting quietly to one side said, "You have been selected for a secret operation," he slid some papers across the desk in front of me, "You have to sign these, they are a written oath of secrecy." The station commander added, "You will be on trial for four weeks at a secret destination after which you shall be evaluated."

I breathed a sigh of relief, at least I wasn't going to be keel-hauled and then drawn and quartered. I was marched off to fetch my kit with one of the officers, after which he accompanied me directly to the railway station and handed me a ticket to Liverpool. "You are to report to this officer," he said, handing me a slip of paper, "they will be waiting for you at the station."

He stayed with me until the train arrived and saw me on board, only leaving once I was seated and the train had pulled away. As the train made its way to Liverpool, the steam from the locomotive settled over the countryside and the carriages in great puffy plumes, my mind raced, *'Surely not submarines?'* I wondered, *'I hate subs . . .'* I pondered what fate had in store for me.

The train slipped unnoticed into Liverpool by everyone including the Germans, which pleased me no-end after all the bombs dropping around me and flying over my head. After two days of hanging around I was given a ticket to the docks and a ship going to the Isle of Mann. If there were any quislings about or German spies they wouldn't have a clue as to where I was going and what my mission would be, I sure didn't . . .

The sea was exceptionally rough as the *Isle of Sark* crashed through the high waves. Nearly all the passengers were gripping the rails and greeting Neptune heartily. I joined them in his praise. When we arrived at Douglas on the Isle of Mann I couldn't wait to get ashore. Down on the wharf two officers were waiting and escorted myself and ten others to sea front hotels.

Once ensconced in our lodgings we were briefed as to our duties and the training we would undertake.

One of the officers said to us, "The work is highly secret and you are to reveal it to no-one, not here, on your ship if you get a posting, or to anyone, either in England or overseas. Do I make myself clear?"

We all replied, "Yes, Sir!" Whatever work we would be doing it was highly secretive and very important to the war effort, this was made very clear to us.

After our brief the training started in earnest and we were marched up to a castle. It had been commandeered by the navy and fitted out with *Radio Direction Finding* equipment, all very hush-hush. The course lasted three weeks with our daily routine starting at 0800 hours in the castle. At 1200 hours lunch was served then another four hours training on the 271PQ radar set (RDF system). The set was being continually improved by its inventors and designers. It was totally British in design and something no-one else in the world had. Its inventor being none other than the famed Watson Watt, the boffin fellow I had met at Portsmouth.

At the end of our course I received yet another competency certificate as a Radar Technical Operator and got a lightning flash and one chevron in gold wire to put on my uniform. We left the Isle of Mann after passing our course and headed for our postings, me to a Flower Class Corvette at Birkenhead which was being refitted. The corvette was being given better guns, RDF equipment and other armament to be used against submarines in the Atlantic.

I arrived at the dock kit bag in hand and stood by the side of the Sweetbriar, she looked a terrible mess, unpainted and patchy, spots of rust, dirt and grease everywhere, ropes and wires curling around her decks with nowhere in particular to go. I mouthed the words, "Oh God, this is the ship I'm going to war in!" I walked up the gangplank and was met by the coxswain. I introduced myself and told him that I had just been posted to the ship. He was bewildered and had no clue what the *special* equipment was or what it did, and I wasn't about to tell him. It took me only a few minutes to realize it wasn't a regular pucker naval vessel; it was too cramped with armament and men to be so.

My accommodation was pretty pathetic but I didn't complain, I was a newbie and no-one would listen anyway. The crew looked like a rough lot, but I just grinned and took everything in my stride. Food was cooked aboard in a small galley, it was hot and that was all that mattered. It took another two weeks before the RDF system was fitted. The captain impressed upon me for the need of secrecy for the radar system I was in charge of and that I was not to reveal it to anyone aboard. "The Germans must not get wind of its existence," stated the captain very seriously.

Of course the men onboard the Sweetbriar approached me, all wanting to know what was going on, but I refused to answer any of their questions.

After hanging about the boat doing nothing of importance new orders came for me sending me to Scotland for one week to HMS Pollock, a coal burning destroyer. I was given a ticket and took the train to Glasgow where I was met by an officer who took me by car to the port about forty five miles away on the River Clyde where I joined the ship for more training. I was to report the altitude, position and direction of Beaufort twin engine fighter bombers attacking HMS Argus up the River Clyde. The Argus was a very old aircraft carrier built just after the First World War upon which the Beauforts would unleash their cargo of dummy torpedoes.

Going ashore to the Isle of Arran for some rest and relaxation was always an adventure, for every time we chugged across in a smoke-stacked ferry boat about 20 feet in length we had to climb down a rope ladder on the Pollock with basking sharks thrashing about in the water below. I don't know if any of the crew had the misfortune to lose their grip on the ladder and go swimming with the fishes but I for one was determined not to do so.

We were so busy that my one week went by in a flash and I was sent back to my ship along with the rest of the inductees back to theirs. When I got back I was greeted by two officers I hadn't seen before, First Lieutenant Tom Brocus (RNVR), a New Zealander, and Second Lieutenant Alf Cole (RNVR), also from New Zealand. They were very casual types so unlike Sub-Lieutenant Lunn (RN) who had been onboard when I had left for Scotland. I immediately got on well with them. My contact with the rest of the crew was limited to just Burton, our radar technician, White and the ASDIC operator, Bill Sears.

*During the war I kept our ship away from danger and made sure we knew where our enemy was and any ordinance fired at us. I was indispensible at keeping the ship, and our convoy, safe from harm; the crew's lives depended on me knowing the difference between a discarded lifebelt, a piece of flotsam, a periscope or a torpedo. A few years later after the war I met Bill Sears, he had opened a butcher's shop in Bedford, he hardly had the time of day for me, when we were aboard the Sweetbriar he would always laugh and find something to make a joke out of, but that had all faded now . . .*

New Zealanders and Aussies, in general, are not stuffed shirt types, very much like the Irish which is why I got on so well with Tom Brocus. I went on a stem to stern inspection of the ship with Tom. As we navigated our way over ropes and cables Tom said, "We'll be doing our first mission shortly taking forty ships across the Atlantic. It is imperative for the war effort they have a safe journey, and it's up to you to make it so . . ."

A few days later we were under steam toward Loch Ewe. And as we left the harbor I stood on the bridge with the officers full of pride and a sense of duty as the dock hands bade us farewell . . .

# CHAPTER 7

## HMS Sweetbriar, K209

HMS Sweetbriar was a Flower Class Corvette, she had already suffered a great deal in battles past being hammered by the huge Atlantic rollers, protecting the convoys taken under her wing and keeping enemy subs at bay. The Flower Class Corvettes had gained distinction due to their maneuverability and speed which topped around sixteen knots. Even though they were slightly slower than the U-Boats their small size gave them an advantage in combat and dodging torpedoes. For their size they packed a wallop with depth charges on racks on the stern and hedgehog depth charges which were fired remotely. Lewis guns were mounted on the bridge and engine room roof and 20mm Oerlikon cannons mounted on the bridge, and depending on the theatre of operations up to six spread on top the engine room roof. The boats were called Flower Class because the Royal Navy gave them flower names. The Canadians named theirs after the cities of Canada.

The displacement of our boat, depending on refits and weaponry, was about 950 tonnes with a length of 62 meters and beam of 10 meters. The earlier boats were powered by reciprocating piston steam engines, later boats were powered by diesel oil. Our boat was fitted with both ASDIC and RDF, which, at the time, was cutting edge technology and highly secret.

The 100mm gun stayed on the foredeck through 41' to 45' with some of the machine guns replaced with a two pound pom-pom gun. Imagine sitting everyday on seventy depth charges and a hedgehog forward throwing bomb launcher with 12 to 24 depth bombs, that's what we had to contend with, we were a floating arsenal. One torpedo amidships would turn life into death and blow the ship into little pieces with all the sub destroying explosives we had on board.

The corvettes crisscrossed the Atlantic Ocean to turn the tide of the war in the Atlantic, and ultimately it was these dedicated little boats that turned the war away from disaster and allowed precious wartime supplies to get from America to Britain. True, not all ships could be saved from the onslaught of the Kriegsmarine and their U-Boats, but, without the Flower Class Corvettes to protect the convoys the wolf packs would have had them for breakfast, lunch and supper.

The High Frequency Radio Detection Finder, or Huff-Duff, as it was called really turned the tide against our jackbooted, foot stomping foe, as did my type 271 with which I could distinguish between a life belt and periscope appearing and disappearing in the rough waters of the Atlantic in zero visibility.

The Flower Class Corvettes had originally been designed for inshore patrol and harbor defense against subs, but with its exceptional range the boats were deployed in the convoy escort role. An added benefit was the fact that because of their size they could be supported by any small dockyard or naval station anywhere in the world. The corvettes were admired for their flexibility and long range in combat and when it came to repairs and refitting. Because there was less likelihood of the Atlantic convoys encountering German fighter bombers our armament was focused on our anti-submarine role but vessels assigned to the Mediterranean Sea had their anti-aircraft weaponry beefed up.

When the Sweetbriar had undergone her refit just before I joined her she had had her bow lengthened and modified making her more capable of handling the rough seas of the Atlantic. It had given the bow a squarer more forceful look. The mast had been shifted back to accommodate her cheese, a new radar hut and the cutting edge technology it contained. Even her pom-pom guns where updated. Eventually this facelift even included her paint scheme; it was changed to a more uniform grey in a move by the navy away from the splinter pattern with tones of blue used from the beginning of the war. This also brought it into line with US Navy ships which used a plain grey, making it easier to identify allied ships and differentiate them from the Germans. We had IFF (Identification Friend Foe) but by standardizing the US, Canadian and Royal Navy ships' paint schemes the combined admiralties forged not only closer psychological links but created a more unified fighting force. However, there was no cut and dry rule and in the heat of battle it was providential for ships to be visibly different from our enemy.

\* \* \*

*'Pusser'* was a naval term for strict and applied to those serving on big ships or naval land based stations such as HMS Victory, HMS Ganges and other shore based stations. When Royal Navy *'pusser'* types came on board for seamanship training, usually sub-lieutenants, the crew and officers would give them hell. Particularly Tom and Alf who were wavy navy Royal Naval Volunteer Reserves, and being New Zealanders they had no patience for pretentiousness of any sort, not being fond of the class system that still existed in Britain at the time.

The Sweet 'B' belonged to B2 Group which had two destroyers, the Hesperus and Vesper, and four corvettes, the Sweetbriar (K209), Poppy (K213), Clematis (K36) and Campanula (K18). It also had one ocean going tug, and even as small as she was she could still pull any large transport ship with ease. Lieutenant Nicholas Monsarrat served aboard the Campanula first during his time with the Royal Navy. We didn't have much of a chance to rub shoulders as the ships in B2 Group were always berthed far apart when we reached our destination, for not only could we have been sitting ducks for Jerry torpedoes if together, but they would also know about the return convoy giving the wolf packs a chance to surround us on our journey homeward. At the time I didn't realize our common experiences would be immortalized in his books, and that the Sweetbriar featured so prominently even though under a different name . . .

* * *

When I boarded the Sweet 'B' the coxswain wanted to show his authority, he didn't realize I was not an ordinary seaman. He liked pushing people about. I was a skilled radar operator with the radar operator flash on my shoulder and a chevron beneath it. I was never in the mood to be toyed with, even if I was a newbie to the crew. The buffer, a petty officer, was a rough looking sort with big square shoulders and a look that made most men wet their pants, he took no nonsense from anyone. After our first meeting I had little to do with either of them, most of the time I was on the bridge, the wheelhouse below or in my radar hut, except for meals and catching some shuteye. My second and final brush with the coxswain had been on a jetty when we were docked for several days. My set was down and since I had no shore leave I was helping them straighten out a half inch cable that had been curled up tightly. It was straightened up alongside the ship on the jetty to get the kinks out. The coxswain started to whistle at me and wave his arms about, so I did exactly the same to him. He came up to me and said, "I'm going to put you on a charge–"

I ended up in front of the captain and explained to him, "I am not a dog to be treated such, the coxswain should have given his orders in proper naval terms and in a clear precise manner–"

My argument fell on deaf ears and my punishment was seven days number 11, cleaning toilets for seven days five times a day. I mumbled, "Bugger–" as I closed the captain's door behind me.

The captain was a lieutenant commander who spent most of his time in his cabin. When he did pitch up on the bridge he reminded me of an empty whiskey glass. Some captains of corvettes didn't stay very long, at least that seemed to be the case on our boat. It was a hard posting if you didn't have the stomach for it and I'm sure it frightened the hell out of many of the crew. On one memorable trip we ended up in the center of a terrible storm, the decks were awash with seawater, gigantic waves three times the height of our ship hammered us and I thought for sure our old tub was on a one way trip to the ocean bed. I had been on the bridge looking at the waves coming at us for some time before my relief came. I was glad I could get some respite from the lashing waves and cold sea spray. I started my way down to our small canteen gripping hold of the railings as best as I could, all the while keeping an eye on the waves so I wouldn't be swept overboard – when all of a sudden I caught a glimpse of something flailing about in the waist which was totally flooded with water, "Oh my God, Williams!" I hissed. He was in danger of being washed over the gunnels as the ship pitched up and down in the storm. I held on as best as I could and worked my way over to him holding on to any piece of the ship I could. Just as I got to the waist, and also nearly waist deep in sea water, the stern heaved upwards washing the seaman to me–I thrust out a hand to grab his collar and pulled with all my might towards me! He was a dead weight and seemed immobile by then. I didn't know how long he'd been in the water, but I hauled him in like a 500 pound marlin. We got to the hatch leading below and I just pushed him in and threw myself down the stairs just as another huge wave struck the ship nearly rolling it over. Williams, it seems, had had his false teeth knocked out by a wave and then tried to retrieve them, the wave had washed his false teeth overboard and he had nearly followed them. If

I hadn't left the bridge at that exact moment he would have followed them to *Davy Jones's Locker.* For some time after he had only his gums to chew his food . . .

We had 83 crewmembers on board the Sweet 'B' and conversation was limited to basic greetings and orders. Every man on her had a position and duty to fill. Unless you had a specific duty to fill in a particular area of the ship you stayed where you were assigned. Only on inspection when I accompanied our first officer, Tom, did I go aft or to the engine room. Initially my emergency Action Station was to fire depth charges if needed, though I was a damned good shot with a rifle, the Oerlikons and pretty much anything else one could fire projectiles with. During my gunnery training at Whale Island I achieved the highest possible marks and I enjoyed letting loose with the .303 Lee Enfield . . . When the weather had died down a bit I had to show one of the new crewmembers where the potato locker was located in the stern. We started behind a round down as the waves pummeled us and every time we moved toward the locker we would duck down behind something seemingly solid that would give us protection from the waves. I had timed it to perfection thus far until we were nearly there, I said, "On two!" We lifted our heads duly and got smacked straight in the kisser by a big wave . . . the one thing I learnt from this is that waves are not always predictable . . .

Our First Officer Tom Brocus was a really swell fellow, and we had got on famously from the time I joined the Sweetbriar. He knew the ship from stem to stern. He and Alf Cole were two of the finest officers you could ever wish to serve your country with. They instilled confidence in you through fine seamanship and cool qualities under fire and in very precarious situations where only those calm enough to make correct combat decisions would survive. Sub-Lieutenant Lunn was a fine fellow but he never spoke much, he kept to himself and hardly interacted with the other officers, he had come to the ship straight from Admiralty Headquarters. Alf was studious and more concerned with the administration of running the ship, he always treated me with the utmost respect and I admired that and the way he handled the crew. Other than the crew on the bridge I spent little if no time talking to anyone else, other than the two cooks, and that was more to do with the quality of the food than anything else. Food was always a sore point. In the wheelhouse Tom, Alf, Sub-Lieutenant Lunn and I would pour over charts and plot our course. Being in the wheelhouse I was also able to take over the Sweet 'B's helm on quite a few occasions. At one time the weather was rough, it was in the dead of night, and the helmsman had started dropping off to sleep while at the wheel, I took over keeping the ship on its heading. The waves were throwing the ship all over the place and it was with some difficulty I kept the ship within five degrees on either side of our course. Cole came into the wheelhouse with Brocus and smiled, "Chapman's at the wheel again–" Tom and Alf both laughed. I loved the ship and would take any opportunity to avail myself of another skill set and learn more about what it takes to run a corvette. At one time they needed someone in the crow's nest with binoculars to spot periscopes, I zipped up even though the ship was rolling from side to side . . . Being up the mast in inclement weather is an experience all by itself . . .

Finding a spot to sling a naval issue hammock or space on a locker was always difficult in a corvette. Sometimes you could grab a shower and oft times not which would require a rub down with a bowl of soapy water and a face cloth.

On board we had several ASDIC ratings, Bill Sears, 'Bomb-head' Burton, Kenny Feck and 'Willy' Hill. Ken was a chain smoker, which didn't go down too well with the officers. I hated the smell so I was none too friendly with him. Our radar mechanic was David 'Whitey' White. And then there was Whitehead. He was a bit of a bully and liked to push his weight around on the ship. His nickname was 'Tanky' because he was in charge of the meat-locker. The men nicknamed me 'Gus' because of my dark curly hair, which I really hated. It was short for Gustav because they said I looked Russian. I begged to differ but the nickname stuck anyway. But then I guess most of the men had tag raps which they didn't necessarily like. We called Burton 'Bomb-head' because he had a large head. There was 'Taffy' in the engine room, he was Welsh hence his nickname. Then there was Seaman Paddy Black, he loved the girls and he always had a different dame on his arm every night we were in port. Ten days in one port would equate to ten different broads. Here's the thing though, on so many occasions I overheard them say to him, "When are you shipping out, Paddy?" I always wondered in his inebriated state did he ever let slip vital information on where we were headed, what we were doing and when we were coming back . . .

Our 4.5 inch cannon on the foc'sle was manned by the engineer and loaded by two of the engine room men. The shells were really quite heavy to manhandle into position. It could pack a punch even though it was old. The pom-pom amidships was a more useful piece of hardware; it fired rapidly and could revolve in a complete circle. It fired twenty rounds a minute and packed one hell of a wallop. It was ever ready for subs and aircraft–a very flexible and useful piece of weaponry . . .

We had plenty of .303 rifles on board but they were heavy to use when the ship was going up and down and sideways all at the same time. They proved very useful for detonating mines in the Irish Sea that had broken free from their moorings; the mines had been laid in a pattern that made it exceptionally difficult for German submarines to operate there . . .

\* \* \*

It was not long after I boarded K209 that we received new orders to prepare for a convoy. We had three days to get the ship prepped and ready for a return trip across the Atlantic. The Germans, of course, would provide their normal cabaret with other amusements planned for us; Hitler and his cronies the clowns in this charade. All painting, cleaning and oiling had to be done doubly quick. Our guns were thoroughly checked over and any other maintenance was expedited. Food supplies, mostly of the canned variety, were loaded down below. Large lumps of salted pork, potatoes and other perishables were stowed away in food lockers. I prepped my radar unit with David White, the mechanic and co-operator, making sure everything was in order. To familiarize myself with the rest of the crew we met in the mess with the ASDIC (Anti-Submarine Direction Instrumental Controllers) technicians and some of the other ratings. When it came to food the consensus had always been self catering, meaning we would receive an allowance of ten shillings a week to purchase rations which were then prepared by us then given to the cook for cooking. On my first attempt I made a pudding with flour, eggs, bacon and tinned peas. I called it a *'Bacon and Peas Pudding'*. It actually turned out very tasty and our sub-lieutenant mentioned it in the ship's newspaper, the gen was, *'Chapman's steamed bacon and peas pudding, guaranteed heavy enough to sink you!'* He made a joke about it but he was the first one to ask for an extra helping . . . Radar technicians and officers were always treated with respect on the ship and we were always being asked about what we did and information about our new fangled machine. We were under strict orders not to reveal anything to anyone except the commanding officer of our ship and the 2IC; the system was classified Top Secret. I managed to acquire a locker unit for sleeping and eating on, space was tight and it was up to the crew to allocate their own personal and down time space. The mess was forward up in the bow next to the anchor cable locker. The locker had a three and a half foot high sealed access door, which like all of them, was very heavy. The anchor locker was used for storing perishables like bananas purchased in the semi-tropics like the Mediterranean. When the Sweetbriar got to Gibraltar they would be purchased green for the trip back and by the time we arrived in port in Britain they would be yellow. The noise of the anchor chain rattling in rough weather could be very tiresome, especially if you were trying to get some kip. When I made my famous *'Chapman's bacon and peas pudding'* I would empty out a can of bacon and slice it up then mix the peas with it. The flour I mixed with some powdered egg and water. In this batter mix I added the bacon and peas then tied it up in a mutton cloth and gave it to our cook. There was a lot of laughter all round but when it came back after being in the pot and I sliced it up between myself, the ASDIC fellows and David White there wasn't even one crumb left. If the food allowance wasn't spent on food it came back added on our wages. This prompted the crew to cadge meals from the big ships we were tied up next to and also gave rise to an interest in fishing whenever possible. One time we spotted what we thought was a German sub on the ASDIC sonar system and depth charged it. It turned out to be a large school of fish and needless to say we had fish for breakfast, fish for lunch and fish for supper cooked in every conceivable manner possible for the duration of the mission. We were issued with huge slabs of chocolate two inches thick, but since sugar was rationed it had nothing to sweeten it. You would count yourself lucky if you had half a teaspoon of sugar to put in your tea; when ashore one or two teaspoons of sugar in your cup of char would truly taste disgusting . . .

On the trip through the Irish Sea heading to Loch Ewe the radar set was closed down and I became so sea sick I sat under the pom-poms amidships. I lived on toast and coffee, I couldn't keep anything else down. This brief acclimatization period lasted until we reached the Loch and gave my body time to adjust to sea conditions, I counted myself fortunate the set was down until we met up with the rest of B2 Group and started rounding up struggling old ships just north of Ireland and Scotland preparing the convoy for the tough task ahead.

Two days out into the Atlantic we followed instructions from the commanding officer of B2 Group. The Hesperus and Vesper were leading while the Poppy and Campanula followed on the port side of the convoy. The Sweet 'B' and Clematis took the starboard quadrant. We all followed a zigzag course two miles from the nearest transporter. If a warning was given we were to close up on the nearest transport ship. The distance between the Clematis behind us was about five miles. The Vesper maintained a five mile separation in front also. The convoy moved as fast as the slowest ship which was about ten knots. To keep up with it while we proceeded on our zigzag course we had to maintain a speed of at least fourteen knots. We knew there were subs in the area because of the tremendous explosions heard from the other side of the convoy. We didn't know who had been sunk because of radio silence, we were also not supposed to stop and pick up survivors because we would be a sitting duck for any tin-fish launched from a Jerry submarine. Nor could we go off pattern and desert our ships in search of survivors. We stuck to our allotted course and heading and kept watch either through binoculars, the ASDIC system or our radar. Because of the curvature of the Earth the only visual reference of the ships in our convoy were their masts, barely visible on the horizon. The wolf packs seemed fully informed as to the size and course of our convoy, hungrily circling us like ravenous beasts in a forest. Since there was only the Clematis and the Sweet 'B' on the starboard side we had our work cut out, determined not to let one Jerry sub through we remained vigilant day in and day out. The weather report indicated rough seas, a cold wind and hail. I didn't mind it, rather that than some Jerry captain laughing at us as we sank beneath the waves. Night had fallen and so had the temperature, I was going on duty so I climbed up to the bridge. Alf Cole was already up there with a pair of binoculars glued to his face. "I'm bloody cold," noted Alf, shivering. "Would you like a cup of cocoa before I go on duty?" I asked. "Yes, please!" replied Alf. I didn't bother asking David, I knew he'd be glad to get down below and have some shuteye. It wasn't long before I climbed back up to the bridge with a big mug of steaming hot cocoa for Alf, he accepted it gratefully, warming his hands around the mug and taking little sips of the South American nectar as the Sweet 'B's bow cut a steady swathe through the dark cold briny depths. It was hard to make out anything in the pitch black ocean and the pitch black sky above, both dark stygian hues melted into each other. The constant splashing of foamy sea thrown up from the bow was eerie in this all encompassing black nothingness. In a way I was pleased, both with the weather and the cold, anything in fact that would make life hard for the submarine crews would be welcome to me. To fire the torpedoes they preferred to surface because of accuracy, *'The rougher the better,'* I thought, *'well, not too rough . . .'*

After four hours on duty David's eyes were red and sore, he rubbed them absentmindedly when I opened the hatch and entered. He could hardly keep his eyes open. The radar screen of the 271PQ was round and about the size of a large cooking pot with a thin green line rotating around the center of it. On my right was the PPI, the Plan Position Indicator, and the IFF set, Indication Friend Foe. The IFF set sent out a strong pulse every twelve seconds. If the ship or aircraft was friendly their IFF set would make my line jump up. Every time I sat down in front of my set I knew both ship and crew members relied on me to keep them safe from attack. For four and a half hours that screen was mine and I made damned sure nothing, but nothing, escaped my attention, our lives depended on it and so did the poor souls of the merchant marine transport ships we were escorting. This gave me the strength to carry on day in and day out for the three solid weeks it took us to reach Canada. The weather was rough, high seas, hail and sleet. When it broke I couldn't believe it, a sunny day at last, *'Hoorah!'* It didn't last though, for in short order the seas became even rougher. There was always a calm sea before a storm and birds never flew westward, only eastward. On our return journeys I nearly always saw two or three birds dropping down from the sky in mid Atlantic and landing on the Sweetbriar's deck to rest up a little. They would stay for half a day then off they would go soaring into the heavens above, unconcerned about the petty wars we humans wage, just happy to avail themselves of a firm vessel on which to lie up for a while . . .

The long hauls our ships and those of the merchant marine took may have been overlooked in the battle-roll honors, but, without our sacrifices Britain would have crumbled and been reduced to ashes under falling German bombs and rockets. Our voyages were kept very secret, any loss of cargo was damaging to the war effort, every item sent from the US and Canada was vital to stop our jackbooted foe striding across the channel and invading our homeland. I never saw any ships of B2 Group near the Sweetbriar's berth at Gladstone dock in Liverpool. This was a deliberate strategy on the part of the Admiralty to secure information on the movements of the convoys. The rationing of foodstuffs wasn't nice, there wasn't much of anything but bread in the shops, but if not for the lives freely given by the men of the Royal Navy and Merchant Marine, the war would have been lost very quickly and Britain would have succumbed to the Nazi war machine. . .

\* \* \*

Our Course Next to the Convoy: At times the commanding officer (CO) of B2 Group and other senior personnel would come aboard for inspection; this also gave them time to discuss pertinent points concerning the convoy and its smooth running. It was no mean feat herding the forty-some ships across the hazardous submarine infested waters of the Atlantic. Since the convoy always moved at the speed of the slowest ship and our zigzag course took us out and back we had to contend with one minute of roll to the starboard side then another minute of roll to the portside. At the same time the ship would encounter first a beam sea then a head sea, pitching the deck up and down uncomfortably. This, combined with sea-sick matelots transferred directly from shore based training ships, was a

recipe for a toilet disaster. At the best of times the bathroom
facilities on board were poor, at their worst, they were awful . . .
The color of a matelot for the first third of our journey was
green . . . But then, even the best of us had had an off day, for
me it was throwing up on the deck outside the captain's cabin, a
serious offense. I was on the bridge and feeling a tad rough when
I couldn't constrain myself any longer. It looked pretty terrible
and there would have been hell to pay if anyone had seen it.
Lucky for me a large wave swamped the decks and spirited it
away leaving the deck spotless, and me, out of trouble . . .

* * *

The Aircraft Carrier: A new addition to convoy protection
was an aircraft carrier converted from cargo vessels that once
transported wheat. The superstructure was removed and a flat top
was built over the decking. After the First World War the flattops
were just that, flattops, but as time progressed so did the design
until an island with the bridge, a viewing and operational deck
and smokestack graced it. The Swordfish biplane that operated
from the carrier could not only drop a torpedo if necessary but
could drop bombs and was an excellent observation platform
for spotting subs. We were moving westward to Canada and were
four days out from Liverpool when our zigzag course brought us
to within a mile of the carrier. It wasn't long before a Swordfish
took off from the deck to do some aerial observation work. The
aircraft had made several circuits on his patrol before coming in
close to the Sweet 'B' and taking some photos of her. Standing
on the bridge I could see the pilot and his observer clearly and
waved at them. The observer picked up his large camera and
took some photos of me waving. Before peeling off the pair
smiled and both of them gave me a thumb up sign which I
returned. They did another two circuits waiting for the rolling
deck to stabilize before attempting to land. Both the carrier
and the Sweet 'B' were running a beam sea with a slight roll.

The Swordfish touched down on the deck landing perfectly, but when halfway down the deck the carrier rolled to port sharply. The Swordfish slid off the deck and landed upside down in the drink. The distance from the deck to the ocean below was considerable–There were no survivors–both pilot and observer were killed instantly–Signals flashed from ship to ship but there was nothing we could do as the aircraft had submerged below ocean rollers never to be seen again . . . Death came quickly to any unwary soul on convoy work . . . it wasn't just the Germans but unforeseen circumstance, a stupid mistake or just plain bad luck . . .

* * *

The Queen Mary: We were on our way to Canada and the US running with an ever present beam sea when just after 1200 hours I picked up a vessel on my PPI (Plan Position Indicator) screen about forty five miles from our position. The vessel was large enough to report its position and heading to the bridge. The IFF (Identification Friend Foe) echo showed it was a friendly. It was on a course similar to ours but the speed was far greater, it was steaming along at thirty knots. We were only doing fourteen knots on our zigzag pattern, which equated to the speed of our convoy's slowest vessel. This speed would ensure no ship would be left behind. On the bridge we thought it was a cruiser or battleship but were informed it was the Queen Mary. Her length was 1,018 feet with a tonnage of 73,000. She had four engines that powered four huge screws, providing 200,000 horse power, which equated to 100 ultra modern British express locomotives like the A4 my father drove. They had taken great pains to get her design perfect in the four years leading up to late 1930 when her keel was laid. She had the strength to withstand even the most abnormal conditions possible in Atlantic waters. Her design made her near impervious to fire and sinking from accidental collision due to a liberal amount of bulkheads and a double hull which made her practically unsinkable. RMS Queen Mary was a true super-ship. Her travelling refinements were second to none, the main restaurant and dining saloon rose three tiers to a height of 30 feet, with a breadth of 118 feet and a length of 160 feet. The main lounge was 100 feet long and 70 feet wide and 26 feet high, this salon could be used as a lounge, theatre and even a cinema. She was launched on Wednesday the 26th of September 1934 in Clydeside. Oil burning and with a capacity for 5000 passengers she was built and designed to be supported amid-ships by the crest of a wave, withstanding the worse the seas and oceans could throw at her and much more. And in the event that the ship had to be evacuated all her boats were on gravity davits with only one man needed to operate the electric winch. Each boat could be lowered in 60 seconds.

She plied the Atlantic carrying vital war materials from the US and evacuees from Britain in less than seven days. The captain, Brocus, Cole, Lunn and I stood on the bridge and waved as she passed close by us in her oatmeal livery, she was massive compared to our ship and even bigger than the transport ships we were escorting. She cut through the waves effortlessly on our portside heading west with the heavy unrelenting sea pressing onto her starboard beam causing her to list to port. A rare sight to behold indeed as she vanished into the mist on the horizon . . .

\* \* \*

The Tanky Whitehead incident: There is always lot of jostling on board any ship in the navy to see who's who in the pecking order, especially on a small boat like ours. There were men who would do their best to make life a misery, in stark contrast stood the dockies. When we sailed the men at the dockyard would always come and see us off, saluting and waving goodbye knowing full well that we might not return and this would be the last they would see of us. At times the convoys would take such a hammering that few ships would make it back to port. On one perilous journey after being at sea for nearly five weeks we entered the harbor to an almighty cheering and hearty clapping of hands. They had all been told we had been sunk with two other merchant ships. It was on that trip that Tanky Whitehead and I had our battle. He was called Tanky because he was in charge of the meat locker on board the boat. I never knew why but Tanky had had a grudge on me since I had set foot aboard. On the day of our battle he was washing cutlery after we had messed and I was on my way topside. As I passed him he picked up a handful of knives and forks and threw them straight at my face. I yelled, "Get up on top now!" pointing to the foc'sle. He turned and raced up the stairs to the top deck. I was close behind him seeing as there was room for only one man at a time. As I reached the top and started to pull myself out of the rounded top hatch he swung around and punched me full in the face. "You lousy dirty rat!" I screamed, returning the favor and laying into him with everything I had. My vision had blurred and all I saw was a red mist through angry eyes. I punched him repeatedly, my mind had switched off and I was in a murderous blacked out rage I couldn't control. The next moment I opened my eyes and I was standing over him pummeling his bloody red face. My left hand was gripping his collar and my right hand was balled into a fist ready to strike and hammer him into submission. He was pleading, begging me to stop. I looked down at his mashed face and swallowed hard, I could get court marshaled for this. I inhaled sharply and let him be, my fist was shaking because of the adrenalin pumping through my veins, and it was still held poised above his face as I released my grip on his collar. Turning, I left the way I had come and went back down to the mess. Sitting down I held my head in my hands, *'Oh hell, I've really had it now . . .'* I thought. I felt the side of my mouth, it was slightly swollen, my teeth were fine and I had a little cut on the inside of my lip. I decided I'd better go to the sickbay and get it checked out . . .

While sitting in the passage outside sickbay the coxswain came up to me and patted me on the shoulder, "Are you ok?" he said.

"Yes, fine . . ." I answered.

He walked away with a smile playing on his lips. I sat there twiddling my thumbs for some time before the door opened and out came Tanky Whitehead. His face was like a balloon all blown up. His eyes were just tiny little slits, his lips cut to shreds and his nose was mashed into what was left of his face. He walked past me with nary a glimmer of recognition. I stood up as the medic bade me enter. The time of my hazing had ended and from then on I received both the respect of the men and Tanky.

* * *

The boxing match: During our convoy work en route to deliver empty ships that would be resupplied in the United States with food, oil, raw materials and other items needed for the war effort, we would hug the American and Canadian coasts. By doing this we had the added advantage of their air surveillance and coastal defense weaponry. Even this was not foolproof though; a Canadian corvette not far from us and closer to the Canadian coastline was blasted to hell and back by a torpedo from a German submarine. There were no survivors; the tin-fish amidships detonated every piece of high explosive on board, instantly killing her crew and sending her straight to the bottom of the Atlantic.

We were about three hundred miles from the coast with our convoy when a message was received from the Hesperus; one of their crew was a professional boxer and they had decided to have a boxing tournament when we arrived at St. John's port in Newfoundland to boost the morale of B2 Group's compliment of sailors. I was instructed that I would fight a man named McIntyre from Glasgow. There was no, *'Would you be interested in boxing a fellow from the Hesperus that just happens to be a professional?'*

No, it was an order and that was that. The news had got around that I had pummeled and beaten a man much bigger than myself with only a slight swelling on my bottom lip whilst he, on the other hand, had such a swollen face he could hardly open his eyes and had trouble speaking through swollen lips twice their normal size. I was now the man to fight McIntyre for three long rounds. The entire crew was keen for me to crucify McIntyre, so how could I refuse. I had never fought in a ring before, never wore boxing gloves, never even hit a punching bag, and never had a chance to get away from my 271PQ set or the bridge of our corvette to do any training, not that I could have done anything. The corvette is small compared to a destroyer, hardly a pleasure cruiser with space to run and shadow box, besides we were surrounded by Kreigsmarine wolf packs and my mind was on making sure our ship and those in our convoy were safe.

When our ship entered St. John's port we were bombarded by copies of the local newspaper proudly exclaiming how I had challenged McIntyre to a fight and that I would whip him senseless with my hands behind my back. The news could only have come from the Hesperus and I greeted it with a smile. Our crew were constantly patting me on the back and saying, "Just do what you did to Tanky, you nearly killed him, do the same to McIntyre!"

We had two days in port before the match so I managed to train a little. When I was about fourteen years old my father and grandfather started to show me the rudiments of boxing, the stance, keeping your arms up to protect your face and use them as a shield to protect chest and lower abdomen.

On the night of the fight I was taken to the hall where the fight was to take place. I entered the changing rooms half expecting to see McIntyre. He was nowhere to be seen. After waiting for three other matches to finish the time came for me to step into the ring. Burton and Sears from our ship got me ready and were in my corner as I climbed through the ropes.

Opposite me stood this pugnacious looking stocky fellow a
couple of inches shorter than me. His nose was squat and ridged
on the top as though it had been broken more than once, he
shrugged his shoulders and jabbed into empty air to warm up
his shoulders and arms. He had just enough time to move his
head round in circles before the bell rang. I verily jumped out
of my corner and went in for the attack, jabbing with my right
and feinting with my left. I pummeled his head with a flurry
of punches that caught him off guard. All I could think of was
knocking him down. I caught him time and time again in the
face and head but when he came in and got through my guard
he punched me in the chest and stomach trying to catch me
under the ribs. His jabs were taking a toll on me and sucking the
air from my lungs catching me under the diaphragm and solar
plexus. I had used his face as my personal punching bag and
beaten it to a bloody pulp, even breaking his already flattened
nose in the process. He was bleeding profusely from his mouth.
The bell rang for us to go back to our corners. I sat down and
felt fine. I thought, *'I've beaten this guy, there can't be much left of him
now . . .'* How wrong I was, his blows to my chest and heart had
been telling on me, sapping my strength, breaking me down
little by little. When the bell rang for the third and final round
I got up without the spring in my step of the first round, like
a fool I had focused on hitting his head and protecting mine
without protecting my core. *Buck fever.* I had acted like a rookie.
I knew I was beat, even though there wasn't a mark on my face
or even a bruised lip. Three minutes into the third round I sank
to my knees, out of breath because of the pummeling to my
diaphragm and out of luck. The match was over . . .

There were many reports and arguments about who had
really won, I was confined to my radar hut and the bridge
keeping a keen lookout for subs most of the time, and, on a
corvette there was hardly room to wriggle a finger . . . No one
criticized me and most sympathized my valiant attempts to
uphold the honor of our ship . . .

Many of the crew came up to me afterwards and said, "You really did well Stan. To think you were fighting a professional boxer and you nearly won. Why don't you take up boxing as a career when the war's over?"

I replied, "No, not for me–" My pride had been stung. The officers looked on at me with renewed admiration, stating, "It's such a pity Stan, you had him beaten in the third round . . ."

Even McIntyre was impressed as he told the sailors of the Hesperus, "Don't take Chapman lightly. He could become a champion boxer if he took it up seriously and trained properly. He would be a professional to be feared . . ."

Later I received news that McIntyre was only a second or two from quitting and throwing in the towel, he had had enough and the cuts above his eyes and blood dripping into them were obscuring his vision . . .

*In the end there was one thing I was proud of during the boxing match, that I had defended the honor of the HMS Sweetbriar with dignity and fortitude to the best of my ability . . .*

\* \* \*

Submarine duty: We had been back at Birkenhead for some time when the skipper called everyone on deck at 0930 hours in the morning. Tom Brocus had informed me we would be shipping out shortly on another convoy mission but the navy required twenty volunteers for submarine duty. My name, as a radar officer, was on the list of volunteers that the captain read out to the crew, "You have all volunteered for submarine duty and will be leaving the ship for training . . ."

I quickly stood to attention and clipped my heels together and said loudly and firmly, "No, Sir!"

The assembled crew was a little startled at my response; a few surreptitious looks were cast my way. No one had dared do that before. All the men were dismissed, except me. I stood on the quarter deck firm in my conviction and unwilling to bend whatsoever. Then the captain came up to me looking me squarely in the eyes about two inches in distance away. I saluted him smartly careful not to clip his face in so doing. Behind him was Lieutenant Tom Brocus who was studying me intently. "Why are you refusing submarine training and duty, Chapman?" said the captain with a hint of menace in his voice.

I looked at him in the eyes and could smell his breakfast on his breath and a hint of whiskey underneath it, I answered, "During the bombing of London in the Blitz, Sir, I was a member of the ARP and we would have to look for survivors in bombed out tunnels that nearly buried us alive while the Germans continued to bombard us from above. At one time we narrowly escaped by digging ourselves out with our hands. To tell the truth, Sir, it was harrowing to say the least, trapped underground as it were . . . One tube station we were in was bombed out and I was underground near the entrance when the bomb exploded, I nearly died then and there, Sir, left me gasping for my breath in the choking dust, Sir. Since then I really have no taste for tunnels and such-like, Sir. Besides, I love the Sweetbriar too much to leave her, Sir . . ."

The captain smiled at me then looked at Tom Brocus, "No one will ever let him go for submarine training, he's already done enough and had too many bad experiences in the ARP . . ."

Tom nodded, then the captain turned back to me, "Alright, Chapman, dismissed . . ."

# CHAPTER 8

## The Cruel Sea?

**W**ho was crueler, the sea or the Germans? Imagine being in a sea aflame, the burning oil sticking to frozen bodies around you, black smoke and searing flames licking your face and hands, peeling the very flesh off them. The hot flames searing your lungs every time you inhaled trying to stay alive but one minute more. The thick black oily smoke making you cough and filling your lungs every time you tried to fill them with life giving air as you watch what remained of your ship, now a shapeless mass of steel, slipping beneath the waves . . . Murderous mariners on a German submarine opening fire on a life boat as crewmen scrambled aboard it trying to save themselves and the lives of their shipmates from the burning oil around them . . . Their blood mixing with the black oil their transport ship was carrying . . . their bodies slowly sinking below the cold waters of the Atlantic . . . Others, still alive and overlooked by the Jerry gunners shiver, their bodies cold beyond belief. Shivers that turn into rocking, uncontrollable spasms wracking their frozen bodies, their faces contorted as they lose all feeling in their legs and then arms . . . Eventually even the pain of burnt flesh is felt no more as minds become numb and are inured to the pain and suffering they are experiencing, then finally, unconsciousness creeps in, no pain for evermore, just a final thought of slipping under the waves, under the surface, never to be seen or heard of again . . .

And the sea, that unforgiving sea, and the cold, hail filled, North Atlantic winds that had no conscious thought or direction, nor did the mighty freezing waves and storms we encountered, they treated both friend and foe alike with the same disdain . . . killing you in seconds should you dare transgress and trespass on the domain of Neptune . . .

\* \* \*

We were taking on provisions for yet another convoy mission across the Atlantic. We would meet the rest of B2 Group out at sea. Both the US and Royal Navies had leant a valuable lesson at Pearl Harbor, never have your ducks berthed all at the same port. The Pacific Fleet had taken a severe hammering at Pearl by the Japanese and the lessons this had imparted upon naval operations had been taken to heart. Having the group's ships at various ports had a twofold effect, for not only was it more difficult for the Germans to launch a bombing raid that would take out more than one ship, but also there were German spies everywhere, having ships all over the show would make it more difficult to plot ship movements. *'WALLS HAVE EARS!'* and *'LOOSE LIPS SINK SHIPS!'* these weren't just catchy lines issued by the Admiralty; spying was an ever present danger, for if the enemy got wind that a convoy was preparing to ship out, the wolf packs would be waiting. We were always very aware of what we said in bars and on shore leave, for one unintentional slip could mean lives lost, ours and those on other ships in the convoy. Supplies for the ship included topping up our armory with shells, bullets, depth charges, hedge hogs and everything else we needed for an Atlantic brawl with the Nazi forces. Food, mostly of the canned variety, rum, tea, potatoes and the like also had to be loaded and packed away for the voyage. The ship itself was thoroughly inspected making sure every part of it was water tight and correct in every detail. There was always a great deal of suspense and mental preparation for the journey, it would always put us on edge when we received news that a corvette or transport ship had been sunk, we never became inured to the suffering and demise of our fellow sailors, their pain was our pain. We knew that but for time and circumstance, it could have been us. There was a tremendous amount of camaraderie between sailors that shared the same danger, and respect for those protecting the convoys, ships coming in would give us a respectful hoot of their ship's horn as we left for a mission. Dockers would salute as we left our berth heading for the dark wild waters far beyond Britain's coastline.

When at last we did slip away from our berth in harbor the dockyard workers would look at us with concern, *would they come back?* Our thoughts were much the same. Being a mixture of both excitement and dread though, we would mask our faces with a sickly grin or a half smile. We gave the dock hands a friendly wave goodbye and they reciprocated. Once out at sea and busy our thoughts of dread dissipated and we got on with the work at hand. Up to about two miles out the sea would be calm but after that point it would become progressively choppy. By the time we reached the North Atlantic past Ireland we usually encountered high waves and strong winds. Compared to the transport ships we were tiny. Many times when we reached Newfoundland and went ashore the crewmen from the transports would greet us, saying, "Where were you, we didn't see you at all on the trip over?"

What they didn't realize was that our zigzag course took us away from the convoy then back to it stopping submarines entering the convoy and sinking them. It was a strategy that worked well, but in the course of a war nothing is foolproof…and, if the waves were high it was near impossible to see us bobbing up and down in those seas like a cork.

About 200 miles off the coast of Newfoundland is an area of sea that is as calm and flat as a pancake, some ten by twenty

miles of it, as far as the eye can see . . . I have never seen so
many fish in one spot. The downside to this was that we weren't
allowed to stop and do some fishing. It was an uncanny section
of ocean that was never rough whether we were coming in with
a convoy or going out with one, and however inclement the
weather was around it . . .

\* \* \*

Another day, another convoy: Generally the Irish Sea is
always a little choppy with short sharp waves but the Atlantic
has a long rise wave heading due east. They are mainly head
seas which throw up a lot of salt water spray over the foc'sle.
My radar office on the bridge had its advantages not least of
which was the high vantage point it afforded and the fresh sea
air. Being high up meant I wasn't covered in sea spray all the
time . . . The convoy had just cleared Scotland when I began
picking up signals of enemy aircraft and began reporting to
the bridge, "Radar–Bridge. Echoes bearing east 10 degrees
north. Speed 300 knots. Enemy aircraft. Rats." There was no
indication friend or foe signal from them, the usual blip every
twelve seconds. Rats indicated they were bombers. The bridge
returned, "Bridge–Radar. Have got course. Over." I gave the
range and their closure rate; the enemy bombers were now
increasing speed.

"Bridge–Radar. Prepare for Action Stations!"

I replied, "Aye, aye, Sir!"

The ship's siren to Action Stations sounded as I bolted out
the hatch to the Oelikon gun on the bridge, my new action
station, seeing as I was one of the best gunners on board. I was
already at the gun when my loader sprang onto the bridge and
started to load the gun in short order. I could plainly hear the
bombers then caught a glimpse of them flying very low, about
300 ft off the deck. They were twin engine aircraft carrying
what looked like torpedoes. Other ships in the convoy started

to open fire and I joined in. There was the reassuring and steady *'Thump, Thump, Thump!'* from my Oerlikon as I tracked one of the bombers in my sights, my tracers lighting up the sky on every twelfth round. The German bombers flew past us on a run aiming for the transport ships. They had targeted two in particular. Gunfire from the Campanula hit one Ju-88 and smoke started to billow from its tail section. It changed its course dipping its nose and headed straight for the bridge of a transport ship. The Junkers hit the bridge nose on and exploded into a million pieces throwing up a huge fireball that seemed to engulf the ship. More aircraft were inbound; I counted six as I continued to fire keeping my loader busy. As my gun kept up a steady stream of gunfire there was a flash of light and a searing pain in my eye, but my attention was riveted on the bombers, whatever it was would have to wait. Two of the aircraft veered off with smoke billowing from their engines. The men of the Sweetbriar had no intention of letting these raiders through! Another Jerry plane was hit badly by our fire and burst into flames while yet another, with a stream of smoke trailing, dived into the sea. One man bailed out while the rest of the crew was trapped inside. The anti-aircraft fire from our escort group was very accurate sending two Junkers bolting and into a steep climb banking and heading east. B2 Group was then ordered to lay a smoke screen, which proved very effective. The German aircraft vanished, their attack was over. Standing at my Oerlikon and tracking the departing bombers in its gun-sight I whispered, "Thank God for that!"

I quickly went back to the radar hut and got back to work, there were U-Boats about and we needed to know where they were. I picked up signals from the periscopes of two submarines. Tom, our first officer, always complimented me on my ability to pick out anything on the 271PQ . . . *Fun for the day was over as I took a deep breath and focused on the screen in front of me . . .* my eye had now started to smart, I would need to go down to sick-bay as soon as I could get a relief to take over, I didn't know what had cut it, possibly a piece of shrapnel?

\* \* \*

Walking the plank: Whenever we received replacements there would always be at least one thief amongst them, but we had our own way of dealing with any transgressor to the sanctity of ship and possessions, quite simply, we would make them walk the plank . . . If things started to go missing it didn't take the crew long to narrow the suspects down and the bosun would step in and, while not exactly strapping the fellow in irons and heaving him overboard, we gave him the shock of his life. Any thief would be surrounded by our motley crew with boat hooks in hand and be escorted to the waist of the ship where a short plank was rigged. The miscreant, wearing a life belt, was prodded towards the lip. The thought of being cast overboard into unrelenting rollers and freezing cold seas with nothing but the fishes to keep you company made many a man pee his pants. A friendly shove would send the thief over into the drink; whereupon the miscreant was hauled out quickly with the boathooks . . . There wasn't much chance of the fellow drowning for we made sure there were plenty of lifebelts available to be thrown in just in case . . . After this experience the fellow was hauled in front of Tom who would give him a thorough ear bashing. Characters like this were described as unfit for duty on small ships and given the heave-ho when we got back to port, ending up unceremoniously walking with kitbag over shoulder down the gangplank to the jetty never to be seen or heard of again . . . *Thank goodness* . . .

\* \* \*

The USS Iowa: On one trip we arrived in Argentia after taking the convoy to Canada. Argentia had been given in trade to the United States government for one hundred years by

Churchill for forty US destroyers. St. John's port couldn't handle our B2 Group of two destroyers, four corvettes and an ocean going tug hence heading on to Argentia and docking there, even so the docks weren't long enough for our ships and we ended up tied to the USS Iowa. The Sweetbriar being only some 60 plus yards in length was dwarfed by the huge battleship. To get to the dock we had to walk across a gangplank into the Iowa then through the lower decks of the ship to reach the jetty. On my first trip across I met an African American seaman with a polishing machine and asked him what he normally did, "Ah polish da floors," he responded. Then I asked him what he did at 'Battle Stations', he again replied, "Ah polish da floors . . ." I just didn't believe it, we started to chat and he took me to their mess deck. I couldn't believe my eyes, while we were subsisting on meager powdered rations with a limited food palette they were feasting on humongous steaks as thick as my wrist with all the trimmings. He asked if I'd like something to eat which I replied gleefully with a big, "Yes–" I couldn't believe my luck, and they even had an ice cream machine. After stuffing myself to the brim and finishing my meal off with a jumbo sized bowl of ice cream I headed to the jetty, boy was I impressed . . .

During the course of our layover I became friendly with two of the Iowa's crew and they invited me for a tour of the ship. I was impressed with the lack of red tape and the friendliness of all the crew, from deckhands to high ranking officers. One of the officers, a commander, told me that if you were a radar officer on board the Iowa you would receive a commission immediately to the rank of lieutenant. Even though red tape on board the Iowa was sparse there was not a hint of unprofessionalism, every man knew exactly what he had to do and completed their assigned tasks expertly. US Navy equipment was by far superior to the Royal Navy's, Britain had been caught napping since WWI and hadn't really upgraded her ships and planes, sure the designs were there but the money wasn't. It had taken a tremendous amount of persuading by Watson Watt to get the backing of the British government to develop the radar system with its directional finding capabilities. On this the Germans had lagged behind thank goodness, mainly in part to the arrogance of their leaders. Germanic pigheadedness I praised. The US government had also turned down attempts by two of its naval officers to investigate the effects of radio waves and their ability to detect objects from afar. They had been testing sensitive equipment when they noticed a return echo from a ship as it passed in front of them heading out to sea . . . To me the guns on the Iowa seemed to dwarf and outdate the British guns. The commander I had befriended winked and said, "Maybe you should join the US Navy, a man of your qualifications would be snapped up by the recruiters back home–"

On my way through the ship one of the crew members I had befriended took me aside conspiratorially and said, "Look, the commander's just about given his blessing and I could give you decent accommodation on board, why don't you jump ship and head to Boston, I'll give you the name of a navy recruiter buddy of mine, he'd jump at the chance to have you and you'd be a lieutenant within six months–"

We went up on deck while I seriously considered his offer, it was tempting, very tempting. And then I thought of Tom Brocus and Alf Cole, two upstanding wavy navy officers, and the crew of the Sweet 'B'. I thought of the ship herself and how she would be defenseless without an operational radar officer on board. I thought about how I had been recommended for a commission to the Admiralty and how they had refused it taking no notice of the glowing reports from the Sweet 'B's' captain, Tom, Alf and Lunn, and all because my mother was Irish, because of that I was in half a mind to leave. *But no, I couldn't just leave her . . . I stayed. For the officers I respected, the crew that I both loved and hated, and the Sweet 'B' herself . . .* As I headed back to our ship I felt like kicking myself, steaks aplenty, ice cream by the gallon, decent benefits and a good salary that would put my ten shillings a week to shame, plus a launderette, and a commission, what more could you ask for, oh, and decent quarters . . . I smiled and kept on walking . . .

A bear hug in Placentia: We stayed to replenish our food supplies and await another convoy assembling outside Argentia giving us a few days to while away and prepare ourselves for the trip back. So the crew was given shore leave of nine hours a day from 1300 hours to 2200 hours at night. I figured it would be nice to pop through to Placentia, about ten miles from Argentia. There was only one train a day threading through the thick green fir forest. The train left at 1200 hours with two coaches and a mail caboose. Burton, our ASDIC operator, wanted to come as well and get a taste of the wilderness. We had just missed the train so we decided to walk, *'After all, ten miles isn't all that far,'* I thought . . .

The road running next to the railroad was way too rough to walk on so we switched to the rail track. After about three miles of trudging Burton said, "Hey, there's someone else walking behind us through the woods."

"Are you sure?" I asked, stopping and listening to the forest around us. "Maybe it's just your imagination," I said as I bit my tongue and exuded an air of bravado.

Burton gave me a wry look. We carried on walking. Burton said worriedly, "Now they're fighting–"

I stopped again to listen, "Yes, I suppose so–" I replied, distinctly hearing noises from the trees around us. We carried on walking. After a while I became conscious of heavy breathing behind me. "Burton," I said, "Surely you're not out of breath already?"

"It's not me–" he said tremulously. "Then who is it?" I queried.

"Maybe hunters in the forest or someone," ventured Burton peering around into the verdant green growth.

We carried on walking and the heavy breathing followed us, our pace quickened to that of a jog. The heavy breathing still continued to dog us. Turning, I caught sight of a big lumbering bear coming out of the forest onto the railway tracks. Burton turned, gasped, and started to sprint. I put on speed and outpaced my comrade in arms. Burton called to me with much fear in his voice, "Hey, don't leave me here!"

We weren't on the ship so I figured it was every man for himself–

I ran all the way to Placentia with Burton and the bear on my heels. Maybe not so much the bear because he gave up the ghost and probably figured he could find something to eat that wasn't so fleet-footed. We ran straight to the first bar we could find and stood outside catching our breath for a few seconds. An old man smoking a pipe and sitting on a rocking chair outside looked at us incredulously. "You aint' bin walkin' through dem woods have ya?" he drawled.

We nodded affirmatively as we tried to get some air into our lungs. I coughed and heaved the exertion out of my chest.

"Dem woods is fulla' bears and wolves, by golly!" he stated incredulously.

"We know now," I said with one last cough and a deep lungful of air.

With that we went into the bar and ordered a pint of beer each. The locals didn't believe we had come by foot and not by train, they all chorused, "You're lucky, if you weren't nobody would have seen head nor tail o' you ever. People in them thar woods jest disappear . . ."

We had had enough of walking and the bears for one day and figured it was best to take the train back. Two hours later we were in one of two coaches being pulled toward Argentia by a big black Wild West steam locomotive with a cow catcher on the front puffing out steam and smoke. I looked out the window at the trees as we chugged past, thankful that we were heading back to the ship with a full complement of arms and legs . . .

* * *

Returning from convoy duty: We had completed three trips across the Atlantic and back; escorting empty ships over to the United States and then fully laden ships back to besieged Blighty, our little island off the west coast of Europe which was surrounded by the might of the German navy and air force. B2 Group, which was made up of six naval vessels, was off the coast of Ireland sailing line abreast of each other in formation. Poppy, a corvette, was farthest out, then the Vesper, a destroyer, the Hesperus, also a destroyer, the Clematis, a corvette, and then the Campanula, also a corvette. Last but not least and closest to the shore, was the Sweetbriar. The commanding officer of B2 Group was on the Hesperus. The commander gave the drill order to increase speed then a command to alter course by five degrees to starboard. This order put us perilously close to shore. We were only about 150 yards away from the coastline. On my scope grass filled up the screen. A grating and grinding sound from beneath the ship sent me flying from the radar hut to the bridge. I could see a car driving along the coast road next to us with its headlights on. The sound of scrapping on the Sweetbriar's hull increased as she lurched to port then righted herself.

She had struck the rocks below ripping off our ASDIC dome. We had come so close to tearing a large hole in her hull that would have sent the Sweet 'B' to *Davy Jones's Locker . . .*

Lucky for us the only damage was our ASDIC dome. The decision from command was quick, *"Leave B2 Group and head for Belfast to the dry dock there –"* the instructions were carried out forthwith and we duly set course for Belfast in Northern Ireland. It was late at night when we struck the rocks and it took us only 6 hours to reach our destination, arriving in the early hours of the morning. It was the first time I'd been there and as we steamed into the bay my eyes went wide with admiration, the bay truly was a beautiful sight to behold. We cruised into the bay and on towards the dry dock. Reaching it we slowly slid in, it was far bigger than our ship and much later I was told that it was the same dock the Titanic had been built in. We were all given 72 hour passes outside the dockyard so I thought I'd take advantage of the situation and have a bit of fun. I went to a dance and met a nice girl by the name of Jean Black. After the dance I escorted her home and met her parents and brother, also named Stan, they all insisted I stay the night at their house, and there being nowhere else to go other than back to the ship, I was happy to acquiesce.

Her brother was the same height as me and even looked very similar; the biggest difference between us was his North Ireland accent. Jean's father was working at the docks where the repairs were being made to the Sweet 'B'. They had no TV unlike our family so while I was there I slept on the sofa and escorted Jean to another dance and the cinema. Jean had to go to Dublin in Southern Ireland to visit a relative so I thought it would be nice to take her down there since I'd never been to Dublin and we would return the same day. I borrowed some of Stan's clothes, his big overcoat and identity document. The photo on it even resembled me. An identity document was required going over the border at the Dundalk border post. I was now to all intent and purpose Stanley Black with a tweed jacket, grey slacks and brown shoes. The trip to Dundalk was uneventful but as the train pulled into the station I stuck my head out the window and looked at the station platform, I gulped, it was full of Red Caps–I started to perspire and got very hot under the collar. I fidgeted with the identity document in my pocket and felt very uncomfortable. *'Maybe this wasn't such a good idea after all . . .'* I thought again, *'I could get thrown in the brig real quick if things went wrong . . .'*

There was a footbridge over the railway tracks to the other side of the platform. I bade Jean adieu and sauntered over the bridge, trying to act as normal as possible. I couldn't wait to get back to her parents house and change into my uniform as soon as possible. Jean got back that night and in the morning at 0700 hours after a decent breakfast I said farewell and thanks to the family. I headed back to our ship as quickly as I could. I strode down the main street past the shops and was about to cross a bridge to get to the docks on the opposite side when a policeman ran up to me yelling for me to hit the ground. I duly did as he requested and enquired why when he got next to me, also sprawling on the hard pavement. "There's shooting on the other side," he panted. "Anyone walking over the bridge will be shot!"

He was very friendly towards me and said, "If you ever come back to Belfast, give me a call–"

He wrote down his number on his notepad then gave me the slip. He glanced over then all around, seeing it was all clear he sprang up and motioned me to follow him. By the time we crossed the bridge the shooting had moved further down the street and river bank. I shook his hand and thanked him. Breathing a sigh of relief I put as much distance between myself and the gunfire. I was really glad when I reached the gates to the dry dock, and even happier when I set foot aboard the Sweet 'B'. I was aboard less than fifteen minutes when one of the crew came up to me and said, "The captain wants to see you in his cabin–"

I wondered what an earth for, were they going to transfer me? I had no intention of going to another ship, way to *pusser* for me. *I felt at home in our old tub, this is where I wanted to stay.* I knocked on the door of the captain's cabin. "Come in–" intoned the captain.

I quietly opened the door and went in, the captain was seated at his desk and Lieutenant Tom Brocus was sitting opposite him, very quiet and subdued. I thought, *'Uh, oh, what's happening now?'* So many things popped into my head. The captain looked at me, "Where were you going on the day you boarded the train for Dublin?"

I answered, "I was taking Jean, my girlfriend, as far as I could, Sir, to Dundalk, Sir, she had to visit a sick relative in Dublin, Sir–" I tried to sound as apologetic as I could.

The captain nodded, "Alright Chapman, you can go now–"

Did the captain believe me, probably not, but that was the last I heard of the Dundalk incident, *thankfully* . . .

* * *

After the ASDIC dome incident we headed back to Liverpool where we had a brief break before we replenished the ship's supplies once more then were off on another convoy in short order. We picked up the convoy and were about sixty miles off the coast of Ireland heading to Canada when a storm started brewing. We had to slow down to ten knots to keep the convoy together as the strong wind started to whip up whitecaps and large waves on our westward course. We only managed another twenty miles before the storm vented its full fury upon us. The whitecaps, once large waves, had turned to mountainous roiling rollers, giant waves smashing into us with such force as to even push the steel superstructure back. One second you would see the grey rain filled sky and the next a huge mountain sized wave bearing down on us. The Sweet 'B's engine worked harder and harder just to keep her position. The waves were three times and more the height of our corvette from the bottom of her hull to the utmost tip of her mast . . . Our small ship would reach the crest of a wave with the bow at a 45 degree angle and then plummet down the other side of the wave. As the bow smashed downward the stern would lift clean out of the water into thin air with the screws spinning away causing the ship to judder and shake. Then the next wave would come and it would happen all over again with sickening regularity . . . I wondered how the hull could take such a hammering . . . and, if you didn't get use to the motion, you would fall over in short order . . .

My radar showed the outcrops of rocks on Ireland's coastline, they had stayed exactly where they were for the past eight hours. Signals from the commander of B2 Group on the Hesperus were, "JUST STAY ON COURSE." And that is just what we did . . .

Sometime later we received a signal that some of the forty ships had headed south, rather risking the German subs than risk having their hulls cleaved in two or rolled over and dashed to pieces by the gigantic waves. We were a fraction of the size of the transport ships but there was no question about us going anywhere but tackling these monstrous behemoths . . . In the end I had to shut down my radar set because all I could get on it was grass, the waves seemed to be getting bigger and more ferocious with each passing moment . . . I had been stuck in the freezing cold radar hut just behind the bridge for hours when I decided enough was enough and I'd have a go at getting to the mess for a cup of something hot. My relief had never come, neither had anyone bearing a cup of hot cocoa, not that I expected it with these waves. I opened the hatch only to be greeted by a monster wave staring me in the face and threatening to come crashing down on me. I closed the hatch quickly just in time. I felt the ship rising and decided to make a bolt for it through the rain and slashing waters of the Atlantic. I slammed the hatch shut and gripped the railing tightly as I slipped down the stairs. The first hatch I got to on the heaving deck was locked and so was the second, they had closed all watertight doors. As huge waves hammered my freezing body I clambered up the wet stairs awash with Atlantic water, I swore as a huge wave bore down on me, I braced myself and just managed to wedge myself into stairs and railings to stop being washed overboard. There were two officers all the time on the bridge. It was Tom Brocus's and Lunn's turn on watch and I wondered how they were faring. I had a flask of two day old soup in the radar hut and managed to stay upright while I passed on two mugs to them which they gratefully accepted. The storm kept hammering us for another sixteen hours before it abated. After all that time I still had Ireland firmly fixed on the screen before me. If ever there was a perfect storm, that would have been it . . .

\* \* \*

On returning from the convoy to Canada and Newfoundland
we were heading into the mouth of the Mersey toward Albert
docks when our anti-submarine detection system picked up
what appeared to be a submarine lying on the bottom. The
echo return was very convincing. We alerted the Port Authority
of Mersey and they followed up on our report. Eventually they
retrieved the complete undercarriage and part of the wing
structure of a Dornier bomber out of the mud after depth
charging the hell out of whatever was lying on the bottom . . .
It could even have been the Dornier I had seen hit and losing
altitude as I rushed to the bomb shelter one day while I was
trying to get back to our ship . . . Liverpool and the docks was
a favorite target for the Germans. Even when I had finished
my gunnery course at Whale Island and then transferred to
Liverpool the city had came under intensive attack forcing me
to run for my life to the nearest shelter while bombs dropped
around me. I was pleased our anti-aircraft guns gave them what
for and had brought down four of them. One even burst into
flames above me and dived straight down into the mouth of the
Mersey . . . *Was that the one they had found . . . maybe,* I shrugged,
*there had been so many . . .*

\* \* \*

Roll of Honor: Many corvettes were sunk during the war,
either by mines, torpedoes, aerial attack or bombardment and
ramming. The Abelia (K184) was torpedoed and damaged on
the 9th of January 1944; The Arbutus (K86) was torpedoed
and sunk on the 5th of February 1942; The Asphodel (K56)
was torpedoed and sunk on the 10th of March 1944 by U-575
or U-572 while escorting convoys SL-150 and MKS-41. Of its
complement of sailors 92 crew were killed, there were only 5
survivors rescued by HMS Clover (K134); The Auricula (K12)
was mined on the 6th of May 1942 in Courrier Bay, Madagascar;
The Bluebell (K80) was torpedoed and sunk on 17th February

1945 by U-711 off the Kols Inlet; The Bryony (K192) was bombed and sunk on the 15th of April 1941; The Erica (K50) was mined and sunk on the 9th of February 1943 while escorting a convoy in the Mediterranean. Its entire crew was rescued by HMS Southern Maid; The Fleur de Lys (K122) was torpedoed and sunk by U-206 off Gibraltar. There were only three survivors; The Gardenia (K99) was rammed and sunk on the 9th of November 1942; The Gladiolus (K34) was torpedoed and sunk on the 17th of October 1941 by U-558 while escorting a convoy south of Iceland. All hands were lost; The Godetia (K72) was rammed and sunk on the 6th of September 1940; and this is just a sample of Royal Navy corvettes sunk or lost in combat during the war . . .

And the ships of the Merchant Navy, what about them, let alone the corvettes of the US, Dutch, French and Canadian Navies, how many lives were lost as brave men sank beneath the waves, their ships rent and torn asunder by German torpedoes? The Sweetbriar led a charmed existence, the crew was thankful of that. But you are only as lucky as the dedication of the brave men under you and the officers in charge, for were it not for skilful maneuvering and correct decisions she would have sunk under the waves on so many occasions. On one convoy the Sweetbriar had been such a thorn to the U-Boats they had targeted us for destruction and fired ten torpedoes at us in the space of two minutes . . . The U-Boat crews were tough . . . but the men of the Sweetbriar, well, they were tougher . . .

\* \* \*

There were operations involving the Sweetbriar that will forever be shrouded in mystery and a veil of secrecy, for everyone aboard her signed documents that they would remain so. All I can say is that the Sweet 'B' was a regular participant in clandestine operations and that we did our duty . . . Fifth Columnists could be found around every corner of the British

Isles, the Nazis were busy producing Allied currency by the millions and their spies travelled far and wide distributing it. The French Resistance did their part in dismantling the German war machine on French soil and at times its members were captured and tortured revealing the names of British agents and French Resistance fighters alike . . . German agents made their way to Ireland and Britain by U-Boats and it was up to the Royal Navy and ships like the Sweetbriar to stop them. The Sweetbriar took part in operations off the French coastline to rescue members of the French Resistance and retrieve British spies. One rescue mission of two women and seven men of the resistance involved the Sweetbriar, MTBs and commandos. Other operations included being involved in intelligence gathering missions along the French coastline in preparation for the Allied invasion of Europe, inserting Allied spies and operatives into France, and stopping German spies from infiltrating Britain . . . At times German guests were brought on board by British commandos for questioning after being captured by the French Resistance . . .

* * *

The U-Boat prisoners: We were headed west toward Newfoundland yet again. It was a grey day as normal; the Sun seemed to desert us during the war and especially in the North Atlantic latitudes. There was little wind and the Sweet 'B' cruised along at 12 knots. Another normal sailing day for us on the bridge, Tom was wearing his normal dark blue pants and white shirt with a soft peaked cap and was standing next to Alf with binoculars around his neck. I was more relaxed and comfortable in my blue jeans and pale blue shirt when seated in front of my radar equipment. I had just finished four plus hours on the 271PQ and stepped out of the radar hut on the bridge. Tom called me over with a hint of urgency in his voice. "I've just received a signal from the CO that a ship was sunk and the surviving crew members were ordered through a loudspeaker into one lifeboat by the captain of the U-Boat that torpedoed it. He machine-gunned the other lifeboats then said to the survivors, 'I'm going to sink your boat because you have no chance of survival out here!' He then ordered the boat sunk and the crewmembers killed. They riddled the boat and men with gunfire and then submerged . . ." I looked at Tom aghast, it was a disgusting and treacherous thing to do. Tom continued, "What they didn't reckon on were two survivors who had clung to the back of the lifeboat in the water because the boat was too full. They survived. After the sub left they inflated their jackets and clung together . . . They were in the water for an hour before one of our corvettes picked them up on radar. They thought it was a sub, altered course, and went to investigate. They spotted the men clinging to each other in the water. They pulled them out and the men told their story . . ." I was seething mad at this, I couldn't believe anyone could do something like that. Tom shook his head, "They were transferred to the Hesperus and made a full report to the CO . . ." If it wasn't bad enough that we were out here due to our enemy's wish to crush Britain into submission like the rest of Europe, now we had to contend with acts like this, it was incredulous that anyone could stoop so low. It only hardened my resolve against our foe . . . and what would we do if the roles were reversed, if we came across German mariners in a similar situation? I pondered over this silently. In the end I didn't have long to wait . . .

As our convoy plowed through stiff waves I picked up signals of what appeared to be a periscope. We stayed our course all the while monitoring the blip on my radar screen until we were ordered by the convoy's CO to investigate it. Duly we headed in the direction of the blip and low and behold, what was thought to be a U-Boat turned out to be three German submariners in an inflatable dingy who had survived a depth charging by one of our corvettes. We pulled alongside and lowered a lifebelt pulling them up one at a time. Their demeanor and attire were different to our sailors. At first they were thankful to be out of the ocean but also a little worried we would treat them as they would have treated us. Surliness soon surfaced as they were placed under guard in the petty officers' rest room in the aft of the ship and it was evident we weren't going to throw them overboard and use them for target practice. Instead we gave them all warm blankets, a cup of tea and bread . . . The CO wanted a chat with them so the Hesperus pulled alongside as we continued to steam ahead. They fired a line across and we hauled the cables across then set up the cradle to transfer the prisoners . . . As the last of the prisoners left the Sweet 'B', Tom said wryly, "And that is the difference between the German Navy and the Royal Navy . . . We don't shoot prisoners or mariners in distress!" No we didn't, not even after all the Nazis had done to London, murdering so many innocent civilians in the high rise buildings they had targeted for maximum casualties and destruction. How they had stormed through Europe and carted off millions of Jews to concentration camps to be starved and gassed to death . . . No, even after all this we behaved like decent human beings even if the other side didn't . . . Later that night as I sat at the mess table the scuttlebutt aboard buzzed of a string of skeletons, found by another corvette, roped together still wearing their lifebelts and floating in the Atlantic like a grisly carnival sideshow . . .

* * *

A prayer in a storm: The wild ocean around us could be cruel at times and the thought of a prayer in your time of need when there was no ship beneath your feet and you were sinking into the cold briny depths was always on your mind. The stormy seas, high winds and even higher waves seemed straight from hell. The spray lashing one's face turning to splinters of ice on the bridge when it was your turn to stand watch with only another officer next to you in the dead of night. The crew safely tucked away in bunks, hammocks or on top of a locker somewhere below decks was cold succor to you as you stood freezing with glasses stuck to your face, your hands cold and frozen in wool gloves. *'It is now midnight and I have another full four and a half hours before another officer comes to relieve me of my duty.'* The waves seeming to be the height of sky-scrapers are intent on crushing us beneath their feet and just don't stop coming at us. I pull the sou'wester down to try and cover more of my face, it doesn't work. My duffel coat is warm inside but my face is frozen. I say to myself, *'Will we get over this one, or the next one?'* it seems impossible but we do it anyway. I stand rooted to the spot staring into the ocean around us, forever vigilant and watching, waiting, for under those wild seas is our enemy prepared to strike when we are at our least watchful, when we will be at their mercy. We know they are out there, lurking, but the radar cannot operate in such high seas and is on standby. It doesn't seem possible that our small ship can stay afloat on the high seas when the waves are as enormous as these, but we do. Our corvette rides out the storm but makes no headway; all we can do is head into the wind at a steady 10-12 knots to stop the ship from turning and being rolled over by one of these gigantic waves from hell . . .

# CHAPTER 9

## An Atlantic Convoy

At the time few people in the Royal Navy realized the importance of Radio Direction Finding. Even the officers aboard the Sweet 'B' had no idea how important this technology was to their survival and that of the ships under their watch. The cheese-like little tower affixed firmly to the rear of the bridge on top of the radar hut would become the eyes of the ship, able to see what no mortal man could. In fog, in roiling sea, in darkness, in driving torrential rain and sleet and snow, whatever the condition and distance, the ship had a god's eye view of everything around it. My 271PQ set had a range of around forty miles in every direction, but the beam continued past the horizon and the curvature of the Earth so we were able to locate aircraft up to around sixty miles away depending on the altitude the aircraft was flying at. The communication between officers and watch on the bridge and the RDF operator would go:

"Radar–Bridge. Ship bearing 10 degrees. Speed 12 knots. Course NNE. Distance 5 miles."

"Bridge–Radar. Give friend foe identification."

This banter would continue 24 hours a day and every day we were at sea, there was no let up, unless of course the seas were so heavy and the waves so high all I could get on my screen was grass rendering the set unusable, at times like these we would shut it down. Initially the 271PQ had a six inch diameter screen with a revolving green fluorescent line rotating around its center point. No matter which way you pointed the aerial three hundred feet around the ship in any direction showed grass due to its metal construction. An object would create a return radio echo which we would report, "Echo bearing 45 degrees." By plotting we could then give its speed and course and determine whether it was an aircraft or a ship, or, even something smaller like the periscope of a submarine mounted on its conning tower. After several months we had another piece of equipment added to our technical arsenal, the Plan Position Indicator (PPI). It was just like a chart to us and made our work easier. The PPI was very advanced and enabled us to define coastal areas, and, the course and speed of aircraft . . . The next piece of equipment to bolster our intelligence gathering armament was the Indication Friend or Foe, the IFF set on other ships and aircraft would send a return ping or echo jump every 12 seconds indicating whether the approaching aircraft or ship was indeed one of ours. The Germans tried very hard to get their hands on the frequency of the IFF set and our equipment, but they never did . . .

As time went by the other officers on board the Sweet 'B' realized how important I was and the training I had received at HMS Valkyrie on the Isle of Man. Without Radio Direction Finding the Sweet 'B' would have been sunk many times over, either by torpedo, ramming or collision and attack from aircraft. The ships under our protection would also have been at far greater risk, many had been dragged off the mud banks and due for the wrecker's yard, they were slow and ill-equipped and the only thing that stood between them and a Nazi torpedo and a trip to the bottom of the ocean was us, and corvettes like ours. One ship full of supplies being sunk had a tremendous impact on Britain's continued ability to wage war on its heinous and disrespectful foe. In my compact office with the 271PQ set on the left, the PPI in front of me and the IFF on my right

I could pick up the periscope of a Jerry sub at great distance
and the Sweet 'B' would be off like a shot to engage the devils.
Sometimes I wondered whether the German sub skippers
would scream, "Ach no, die Sweetbriar! Dive! Dive! Dive!" The
Germans sure had a healthy respect of us, that's for sure . . . Tom
Brocus, Alf Cole and the captain were just itching to ram one
of the buggers and rip its conning tower off . . . all they needed
was its coordinates from me and the world would have been
one sardine-can less . . . It wasn't too long before Tom had his
chance, we had heard about two U-Boats being caught out by a
corvette travelling due west across the Atlantic. They were dead
in the water transferring weaponry across. Against the corvette
they came out second best. Our first contact was by radar, I
picked up two blips which I was positive were two surfaced
U-Boats. Our First Officer Tom Brocus ordered the Sweetbriar
to alter course so within ten minutes we were heading due north
at a speed of sixteen knots. It was misty and the sky was a leaden
grey, but there within our sights were two U-Boats with very
visible conning towers and some of their crew busy pulling in
one of their collapsible rubber dingys. The sea was rough which
gave us little chance of scoring a direct hit with our 4.5 inch
cannon on the foc'sle. We were closing in quite rapidly when
Tom gave the order, "Close all hatches, we're going to ram one
of the bastards!"

Their sterns were presented toward us as we barreled down
on them. Tom ordered an attack on the portside sub as we bore
down between them. They had no time to load and fire at us
with their deck guns since the subs would have to make a turn
and by the time they'd done that we would have cleaved them
in two. Well, at least one of them. Our paravanes were deployed
so if any torpedoes were launched we would have a sporting
chance. We heeled to port and prepared to ram one U-Boat,
the starboard side sub was crash diving in an attempt to fire a
torpedo. As the Sweet 'B' thundered down on the one U-Boat
at attack speed the other had managed to turn about and fire a

torpedo at us which had latched onto the sound of our screws. The captain of the U-Boat in front of us finally ordered his gun crews into the sub and gave the order to dive after realizing they were in a bad position to fire on us. The hatch on the conning tower closed as water cascaded over her bows. A torpedo passed on our starboard side as the bow of the Sweet 'B' scrapped the top of the U-Boat's conning tower. We keeled about and stayed on top of the sub and dropped a depth charge pattern. With the charges set on a deep setting we fired four off the port side and four off the starboard side and dropped four off the stern rails . . . Wreckage began to surface as we circled trying to get the position of the subs on our sonar ASDIC system. It looked a certainty that one U-Boat had been sunk and that the other one had escaped the wrath of the Sweetbriar. We made a report: "ONE SUBMARINE BELIEVED TO BE SUNK OR HEAVILY DAMAGED STOP NO SURVIVORS."

Our captain, a stiff upper lip Royal Navy three ringer woke up from his alcohol induced slumber. The motion of the ship had undoubtedly dumped him from his bunk. He scrambled up to the bridge with the aroma of gin and whisky following him. He gave Tom a lecture on what he should have done. Vehemently questioning why he had not been notified. This, after telling his orderly, "Do not waken me, otherwise I will lay a charge on you . . ."

Whenever the captain gave that instruction the orderly would inform Tom Brocus, who, for obvious reasons, tried to keep well clear of the captain at all costs. This particular captain of the Sweet 'B' Tom didn't get on well with. The penalty for incurring his wrath would be a report straight to the Admiralty and probably ending up being transferred elsewhere. The Sweetbriar had a total of five captains sent straight from the Admiralty to serve on the K209. They experienced what the Atlantic could dish out a-plenty to a small ship like the Sweet 'B'. It was not for the faint hearted . . . Most captains didn't like small ships which did without the creature comforts of the larger ones, wardrooms, big kitchens, cocktails and lavish food and surroundings. We had little or no space available on a corvette. Some of the orderlies were treated like waiters or worse . . . The rest of the trip passed without another incident on our side of the convoy, the other side was a different story however, for deep in the blackness of night as I stood on the bridge with Tom keeping watch we would hear explosions as torpedoes found their targets . . . we could do nothing to help any survivors though, we had our orders and that was that . . .

\* \* \*

The marriage that sunk: We hove to on our anchor and were lying off Holyhead about half a mile from the jetty with waves lapping languidly at the steel sides of the Sweet 'B's hull. We were awaiting further orders from the Admiralty. It was about 1800 hours and I was on watch on the bridge. Down below on the deck I could hear two seamen talking in hushed voices about their wives and their marriages. The conversation was broken because the wind would whip sentences and words away as it blew over the deck. I couldn't see their faces as they had their backs toward me looking at the jetty in the distance. One of them whispered, "I have to go home, I think my wife's messing around with some other bloke and she's pregnant as well . . ."

"You know what I would do, I'd swim over to the jetty then catch a train and head home . . ." replied the other seaman.

"I'm not a very good swimmer . . ." answered the heartbroken man. "All you have to do is just float with the tide and it'll take you to the beach on the other side . . ." said the man's friend.

I couldn't believe my ears, surely not, he'd be court-martialed for sure if he jumped ship. While I continued my scan around the ship I heard, "Just blow it up with your mouth!" I didn't think anyone could be stupid enough to try and swim to the jetty as the tide was fast flowing and you could end up being whipped out to sea in a shot. The next second I heard a splash. I leaned over and saw only one seaman now leaning over the gunnels. I hadn't seen anyone slip over the side and the remaining seaman didn't look perturbed in the least. I wondered whether the other seaman had changed his mind and gone below. There was no sense in raising the alarm and causing trouble . . . The following morning I heard the coxswain talking about a seaman who had gone missing. I said nothing. I didn't want to get involved. Later I heard he had been arrested at home with his wife. It had done him no good jumping ship and now his problems would be far worse . . .

\* \* \*

A new convoy: It was after this incident that our next convoy was being organized. Once again we would be fighting North Atlantic seas to deliver ships bound for Canada to be resupplied with items for Britain's survival enabling us to continue waging war against our common enemy, the Germans. We had been repainted and the ship was as clean as a new whistle. The Mersey looked like thick mud and silt with a little water added. We had sailed from Birkenhead docks and the naval shipyard there for two days of sea trials. The rolling deck had taken a little getting used to after my time ashore. I felt queasy with sea sickness for the first few hours but after that I got my sea legs back pronto and felt as fresh as a daisy. After the trials we headed for Gladstone docks. My radar hut looked like a new pin and I was proud to get inside and check all the equipment. Once we docked at Gladstone trucks arrived and supplies started being offloaded. It wasn't long before our armaments arrived for the trip as well. We got well stocked so I knew the next voyage was going to be a long one. Liverpool had been bombed the previous night, but the damage hadn't been too serious. It was business as usual for the Germans . . .

\* \* \*

Day one: We were called to our stations on the ship and I reported, "All okay, Sir–" my set was working perfectly, "all in order and correct, Sir . . ." I ended off. As we left Gladstone dock I stood on the bridge next to the radar hut. Dockies were waving goodbye to us as we slipped away from our berth, they knew we would soon be facing constant attacks by a gauntlet of submarines and enemy aircraft . . . and . . . the sea itself. Many ships never returned from convoy duty, the men at the docks were well aware of this fact; they had seen it time and time again. Even the surrounding ships sounded their ship's horns in salute knowing we would once again be braving heaving roiling Atlantic seas and submarines intent on sinking us . . . At 1200 hours it became quite chilly as we sailed along the North Wales coastline about twenty miles offshore. One always had the feeling, *will I ever return?* We changed course from due west to due north taking us past the Isle of Man. It meant we were not coming back for anything, for me it meant the point of no return. I noticed the skipper had received the dark brown leather bag. It contained the voyage's instructions from the Admiralty at the Liver buildings in Liverpool, all very hush-hush. The bag was not to be opened until approximately one hundred miles from point of departure. The sea was becoming choppier and I felt a bit squeamish. After a good greeting with Neptune I knew I would be alright. Some fellows never got over it and usually had to be transferred to a big ship. Me, however, I thrilled at being on the Sweet 'B', it was small in comparison to other ships and had no real hierarchy, strictness and authority like them. To impose such harshness on the crew of a small ship would have been disastrous. After five and a half hours we sailed past the Isle of Man. I could see Douglas Castle, where I did my training, through the binoculars from the bridge. The waves were getting higher as we passed the Northern Ireland coastline. Between Scotland on our starboard side and Ireland on the port side the waves increased in size dramatically. They were now crashing over the bow of the Sweet 'B'. With each passing hour the temperature was dropping. I thanked God I had my duffel coat on, a warm pair of dark navy blue wool gloves and my rubber sea boots. Wild guesses flitted from mouth to mouth around the ship about our destination; the skipper announced through the petty officers that we were to pick up a convoy off the coast of Scotland at noon the following day. The joke of the day was, "Now's the time to get off the ship!"

As darkness fell around us we had reports of two submarines off the Scottish coast. We were now at Action Stations for the whole night. Sailing up the Irish Sea we had a head sea but once we sailed into the Atlantic proper we had quite a roll with a port beam sea running. At that point I really had to adjust to my sea legs and walk slower. My stomach didn't really appreciate it.

In the middle of the night a pitch black stygian darkness enveloped us in its cloak-like folds. My radar took control of the ship and guided us after this, especially since Loch Ewe sits beyond a rocky entrance. The sharp green line in front of me kept me awake. When we entered the loch the ship stopped rolling, no Atlantic rollers or roiling seas in here. *Now, perhaps, I could get some sleep . . .*

\* \* \*

Day two: My next watch in the radar hut would begin at 12 midnight. It would be a long night as the convoy headed toward Iceland. Two destroyers took position at the front of the convoy and two corvettes on its port side and two on the starboard side. The corvettes made a zigzag pattern on either side of the convoy. Today we hardly ever saw the other ships of B2 Group. I did pick them all up on my radar set though. Our course was now due west. Our zigzag courses through the ocean rollers twisted and turned when you would least expect it. The weather was relatively calm today. I am off watch on radar at the moment and prefer to stay on the bridge. A Sunderland flying boat arrived and flew a search pattern around the convoy. Its purpose is submarine surveillance. Tom, our first lieutenant, has been informed it will be around for approximately four hours due to the limits of its fuel load. The mess deck up forward is full of smoking men. I cannot stand it; the smoke makes me cough and gets up my nose. I'd rather stay on watch on the bridge instead of going down below. I'll stay here until they go on their watch or they go to sleep. Over forty men sleep up in the forward mess deck. They are not there all at once luckily. Every half hour the ship rolls as it changes its course, it gives me twinges in my stomach. First a head sea then a North West, then a South West, however, it is the best way to combat submarines.

* * *

Day three: We received a report that a small German battle fleet had left Norway the previous day. It was heading toward Iceland. I wondered whether they knew about our convoy and if we were its target. I scanned the screen in front of me, diligently reporting every object and echo. I could even pick up discarded life belts, flotsam, periscopes, and all the works. Anything that's out there I'll know what it is. Tom noted once, "Chapman certainly stays on the ball and awake when he's on watch . . . you'll never find him sleeping or taking it easy . . ."

Bottom line is, we are here to protect the merchant convoy and our ships at all costs . . . Since the temperature has dropped I have donned my duffel coat, Wellington's and balaclava. We are taking the northern route to Canada, the USA and Newfoundland. Our next port of call may be St. John's but more likely Canada. The skipper and Tom have apparently had reports of submarines ahead of us, three or four. They behave like wolves ready to pounce on the convoy when a weakness is spotted. A German observation aircraft was picked up on radar about an hour ago by the Clematis . . .

I finished my watch period on radar after four hours and decided to sling my hammock up in the port passage. The air was fresh there and I could grab some kip. It was also warmer. The radar hut is a no-smoking area, thank God . . . After my next watch on radar I joined the watch on the bridge with a pair of binoculars. I perched myself next to the radar hut and chatted to Tom, our 2IC. Another Sunderland flying boat of the Fleet Air Arm flew low over us, he signaled, "BON VOYAGE STOP GO WELL." The pilot waved at us, he is now at the limit of his patrol. Before leaving us he signaled, "A SUB IS AHEAD OF THE CONVOY STOP POSITION NORTH WEST AHEAD OF YOU STOP DISTANCE APPROXIMATELY 18 MILES STOP OVER AND OUT." Tom looked at me and said, "How's that for service, Chapman."

Laughing, I answered, "Tell him to stop off and have a cup of tea . . ."

White came out of the radar hut and said, "I need to visit the head. Cover for me, Stan." He looked a bit seasick. We seldom if ever complain about anything. I went in but told White to bring me some chocolate, ours is a big slab of unsweetened stuff. We had no sugar because of the rationing . . . During my training I wanted to be the best radar officer I could be. I wanted to be exceptional at what I did on the ship that I would be assigned to. When I first set foot on the Sweet 'B' she didn't look like much but I intended to achieve the best results possible with the equipment at hand and give the officers on the bridge a very correct report of anything I spotted on the 271PQ. I would be their eyes at all times. It was no joke that I could pick up the periscope of any submarine within range of my set. When on patrol and looking for ships to sink the subs acted just like wolves stalking their prey, they would scan the horizon through the periscope raised to its highest position. Spotting prey they would lower their periscope down slowly and move forward toward any unsuspecting ship. This happened about every two minutes until they were sure of launching a tin-fish that would strike home. It was like looking for a needle in a haystack but I started to master it, the periscope blip looked like the sharp end of a pencil pressing upwards through a sheet of paper then gradually pulling back down through it. The tiny blip on my screen would become stronger then slowly disappear. I would plot this position then keep up my scan. Sure enough in two minutes the tiny blip would appear again and I would plot the sub's course. Normal flotsam would just be blown or thrown about by the waves and wallow about with no particular course or setting . . . on the other hand, the submarines had a specific course . . .

I would report this to the bridge and they would always view my reports with incredulity. Nobody had ever heard of a radar officer picking up a periscope on his 271PQ in the wild Atlantic waters. But, I was always right. Eagle-eyed 'Gus' strikes again . . . With this technique I could plot the submarine's speed, heading and its current position. Bill Spears was good on the sonar and reported picking up a sub on the sea bed, just lying there. It was too deep to waste our depth charges on so we left it. No doubt its captain wanted the convoy to pass then hitch on behind it. *I kept a lookout for it but didn't pick up anything on my scope . . .*

* * *

Day four: The seas today are very rough. It is very cold and windy. Big waves come at us from the west throwing sea spray right over the ship. White and I are on the starboard wing of the bridge. The subs have gone; they cannot operate in such rough seas. They go deep to avoid the turbulent currents. I went down to the mess to get hot chocolate for the officer of the watch, Sub-Lieutenant Lunn. He is quite close lipped, doesn't say much, I don't think he relishes another trip across the Atlantic. I understand he even requested a transfer to another ship, a bigger one. He doesn't like the way the Sweet 'B' rolls and shakes in stiff weather. To get down below from the bridge I grab the rails of the ladder and just slide down them chop-chop. When I got to the mess the cook offered me some soup. He gave me a

Billy can, a loaf of bread and some spoons, much more useful up on the bridge than an open mug that will soon be over-running with sea water from the spray. The waves are even bigger now. The spray is like a shower being switched on and off. *'Uh-oh, there's another big one,'* I thought as I ducked down behind the canvas protecting the bridge. It hit the bow and sent a massive amount of water up in the air just as I stood up. Got a load of it straight in the kisser, the cold water took my breath away. I let rip with all the swear words I could think of. It makes me realize how small our ship is next to these waves . . .

* * *

Day five: The waves were calmer today, a report came in that one submarine was sunk north of our course. During the Sweet 'B's time at Birkenhead an officer instructed the men to paint anything that does not move. We had to be careful not to lean on or touch anything just in case it was still wet. While everything was being painted two matelots were painting the side of the ship and forgot to fasten one of the ropes, the plank they were standing on dumped both of them into the water way below. I was standing on the dock when they did their *Buster Keaton* moves trying to stay on it. I had to laugh, couldn't hold it in. Luckily for us they didn't touch the bridge . . .

If the weather is very rough all we can get to eat are boiled potatoes from the engine room, or, maybe, a can of corned beef. We also have some hard dry biscuits but they have no taste whatsoever. The storm eventually died down. I went down to the wheelhouse and saw the helmsman was dog tired from battling the waves and being up most of the night. I suggested to him I take over for a bit. He handed me the wheel and said, "Keep within 5 degrees each way, it'll keep you on the required course . . ."

First Lieutenant Tom Brocus joined us in the wheelhouse to study our position on the charts. He laid them out on the table.

After spotting for the helmsman I joined him at the back of the wheelhouse. We discussed our course, he noted how difficult it was to keep it and was thankful we had such a capable man at the helm . . .

We deployed our PVs, or paravanes, in normal parlance. I had spotted the periscope of a sub following us, trailing us like a wolf in a thick forest of waves. The call to Action Stations came over the speaker system and we relayed this to the other ships in our escort group. Any submarine spotted and located within five miles of the convoy would elicit an Action Stations alert for any possible attacks on the convoy. The paravanes were launched from the stern of our ship and looked like stubby torpedoes with fins. They were attached to the ship by stout wires and because of the shape of the fins they would be forced far away from the Sweet 'B's steel hull by the water. The screws of the paravanes made a noise similar to a ship and would draw any torpedo toward it and away from us. I carried on plotting the sub's course and kept up a running commentary to the bridge. I know the sub's captain could see us clearly through his periscope and the subtle course changes Tom Brocus ordered. The sub's captain must have been shocked because not too long afterward the periscope went down and disappeared altogether.

* * *

Day six: Today we had to top up our fuel-oil and thank God it wasn't my job. When refueling at sea the ships have to move slowly, but even so every now and again a large wave would break over the bow of the Sweet 'B'. The oil tanker is about four times the size of our corvette. We came up on the stern of the tanker and they dropped a line attached to a float which we picked up with grappling hooks. We fastened the rope to our winch then began the process of pulling in a heavier rope and then a thick wire cable would be strung between the two ships. Every time the tanker went into a trough we would be going up the wave with the wire tightening. The noise of this alerted the wireman who would slacken off if it got tight to stop the wire from snapping. If it did the whiplashing wire would kill anyone in its path. Even up on the bridge Tom, Alf, the others and I wouldn't have been immune from its whip-like action. This happened once, and lucky for the men they all jumped high enough to avoid it . . . The fuel-oil pipe was then winched aboard and the process of refueling began. In heavy weather this was seamanship at its best. Everyone on the foc'sle and on deck was ready to duck or jump if the cable did break.

\* \* \*

Day seven: At times during convoy work and our escort duties it is necessary to transfer mail, supplies or crew members to one ship or another, today we have a very sick crew member. We don't have a ship's doctor but we do have our first aid attendant. He does what he can but our sick-bay is small and rudimentary at best and ill-equipped at worse. We had to transfer the seaman to the commanding officer of B2 Group's ship the Hesperus, since they have a full time doctor and decently sized and kitted out sick-bay which is more like a hospital. The sea was a little choppy to say the least and it was a tad difficult to get the Sweet 'B' and Hesperus within 50 yards and less of each other. We launched a small line at first which was anchored to the Hesperus. This enabled us to get a thicker and heavier line across. We then used grapple hooks and chains with a platform slung underneath to winch the poor fellow over to the Hesperus. The man was really ill and my thoughts and prayers were with him as he bounced up and down as the waves hammered our ships. It is hard to run alongside each other in rough seas and inclement weather. I was pleased when he got across safely.

\* \* \*

Day eight: Today was a quiet day, the sun had come out. A bird flew onto the ship and settled on a pom-pom barrel. Amazing how a small bird can fly across the Atlantic. Normally the birds will sit for no longer than three to four hours then fly off again . . . My watch begins shortly. The handover is duly recorded. I study the green line in front of me like my life depends on it, which, it does, me and the rest of the souls onboard . . .

* * *

Day nine: I have got into a comfortable position in the radar hut in front of my equipment after having had a good rest and now I'm ready for action. Our mail from Britain was sent by air to Canada and is now on its way to us onboard a destroyer that left Canada not too long ago. Letters are few and far between and I hope there is something for me in the mail sack. I have not heard anything from home or my brothers for three months now. The weather is fair with a cold wind blowing from Canada and Newfoundland. I was hoping we would dock in Canada but now it seems we'll head for St. John's. Two days ago a Canadian corvette was sunk by a German submarine so I guess it's a security issue. The area we are in now was a shooting alley last year. The loss of transport ships was near disastrous to Britain and many an allied sailor lost their lives in these waters. I make sure nothing slips past me and keep my eyes glued to the screen and my rotating green line . . .

* * *

Day ten: It is a clear day today and one of the destroyers traded with Churchill for the one hundred year lease of Argentia to the USA has just been spotted. It has four long and narrow funnels and is long and narrow. Looks a bit like a long cigar. It's old but does the trick. I bet it rolls worse than our tub. It's coming alongside us now so we can sling a cradle from ship to ship. The mail-bag looks big! I hope there's a letter in it for me . . .

* * *

Day eleven: Approaching the calmer waters of the Atlantic. It is so calm there it reminds me of a vast smooth mill-pond. It is teeming with fish so it must be the Grand Banks or around them. The depth of the Banks varies from 50 to 300ft and because of the converging Gulf Stream and Arctic currents the disturbed sediment makes it a perfect breeding ground for fish. I have just been informed we will not be heading for St. John's port but to Argentia and the new US Naval Base there. I wonder whether we can pick up things to trade back in Britain. Silk stockings are selling at a premium in the British Isles. I don't smoke so any cigarettes that come my way I trade for something more palatable. Something sweet often or not . . . Even naval blankets find themselves for sale on the black-market in Britain. Everything has a price because of rationing, there is simply not enough to go around, plus, naval pay isn't the best, it is difficult for married men to get enough back to their families let alone a single man . . . I hear that even silk from stolen or traded parachutes is being made into underwear . . . Then there are the stories of trucks, filled with sailors and surrounded by customs at the docks, disgorging packets of cigarettes onto the ground for free passage . . . I am so used to having tea without sugar now, it tastes funny when I put half a teaspoon in . . . But, there is plenty of toothpaste . . .

* * *

Day twelve: It's Sunday and I am looking forward to our pork meal which we always have for Sunday lunch. The cook always does a beautiful job of it. We provide the vegetables and usually a tin of fruit, like peaches. What our meal turns out to be depends on who is cooking and what he wants to prepare.

Salted pork was a mainstay for Royal Navy sailors during World
War One. Rum issue is always a happy time for the crew. Below
the rank of petty officer the measure is two parts water to one of
rum issued at 1000 hours during the morning of each day. Petty
officers and above receive a tot of rum neat, while many of the
crew keep their rum in a bottle for a special occasion. The rum
has the consistency of treacle and the happier members of the
crew would sing an old sea shanty while consuming their nectar:

*"Fifteen men on a dead man's chest,*
*Yo ho ho, and a bottle of rum,*
*Drink to the devil and he'll drink to the rest,*
*Yo ho ho, and a bottle of rum . . ."*

\* \* \*

Day thirteen: Today the captain ordered a dummy run with
our depth charges to keep the men on their toes. Our position
is somewhere near Iceland in the North Atlantic. I was on the
bridge when a pattern of charges was dropped. Two from the
stern, two from the portside and two from the starboard side of
the Sweet 'B'. There was a malfunction in the depth setting of
one of the charges and an underwater explosion a few feet from
the surface blew a plume of water up close to the stern. Needless
to say the force of the explosion heaved the stern up right out of
the water. We sustained a bit of damage and some of the plates
will have to be welded and riveted. It was a very close call . . .

\* \* \*

Day fourteen: The skipper ordered a lifeboat drill today.
Because of the lack of space onboard the Sweet 'B' lifeboat
drills and manning the lifeboats is not as easy as it seems,
especially when the sea is heaving the deck all over the place,
The lifeboats are very heavy and difficult to put over the side.
In an emergency I think the life rafts are an easier option.

It's easier to get them overboard and clamber on to them. I think the lifeboats would turn turtle in most of the seas we've encountered. The biggest drawback with the lifeboat was that of losing your life trying to launch it. Many of them would hang suspended from a ship hanging on one rope or wire, broken and unseaworthy. It took time to lower a lifeboat from a davit. Imagine doing this as your ship rocked with explosions and was thick with the smoke from burning oil, plus the deck would be at an angle. A Carley raft could be manhandled over the side quickly so you wouldn't be sucked under as the ship went down. On the occasions we picked up men from the ocean more often than not they were on Carley rafts, but, in truth, if you could get to a lifeboat your chances of survival were better because they were easier to see and would keep you from being soaked in the cold Atlantic waters . . . Picking up survivors on the high seas was a very dangerous operation. Our hearts went out to these oil soaked men in the cold water having just witnessed the burning remains of their ships sinking beneath the waves, their livelihood and belongings disappearing for good. But for us to stop our engines meant we were sitting ducks with our number on every U-Boat commander's lips . . .

* * *

Day fifteen: We are not too far now from Canada. We were all surprised to see a Canadian Navy Catalina flying boat, a PBY-4, with the spotting and machine gun bubbles on either side of the fuselage behind the wing. The Catalina signaled command onboard the Hesperus and we were told they were checking the sea lane for any sign of submarines near our convoy. I was surprised at seeing her patrolling so far from land. She must have long range fuel tanks fitted. After the 'Cat' had gone and pronounced no submarines in the area we were given the command for a smoke screen drill for possible air attacks when we returned to Britain. The smoke screen drill went well and covered us for several hours.

\* \* \*

Day sixteen: On board the Sweet 'B' one day seems to melt into another and you lose all concept of time. The mission of getting the convoy safely across the Atlantic, and ourselves, is the only thing on my mind. I spend most of my time in the radar hut at the back of the bridge or up front on the bridge with a pair of binoculars staring out into the limitless ocean around us. The weather has been favorable today, a bit cold but not bad otherwise. No massive swells throwing heaps of spray over the bridge. So far this convoy has had reasonable weather, well, compared to what we have experienced in the past. Some of the storms we have encountered I shudder at the thought. Our old ship has sailed through horrendous storms with hundred foot waves, waves that could turn a brave man's heart to jelly . . . Each trip across the Atlantic is different. One day we could be facing a gamut of torpedoes from a wolf pack and the next icy mountainous waves that wish to send us to the bottom of the ocean. Most of the men are wearing jeans, denim or checkered shirts. They are more comfortable than our regular uniforms. The dress code on the Sweet 'B' is more relaxed when we are out of port, comfort is more important for the job we are tasked with, my preference is jeans and pale blue denim shirt . . . however, there is no place for tardiness on board, even with a relaxed dress code one always has to be presentable, smart and neat . . .

\* \* \*

Day seventeen: Normal ship routine today, on-watch, off-watch in the radar hut, a spell of watch outside on the bridge, grab some kip, grab some food, grab a mug-full of soup or hot chocolate. No submarines and weather fair. Two ships have left today on their way to New York or further south . . .

\* \* \*

Day eighteen: The convoy is breaking up, ships are preparing to leave, and some are going to Canadian ports and others to the States. Our journey is more or less over; our destination is Argentia in Newfoundland that is official. I like it there, St. John's is a bit too scruffy for my liking . . .

\* \* \*

Day nineteen: We are now docking in Argentia. Because of a big US Navy battle cruiser called the Iowa taking up literally the whole jetty, we are tying up alongside her. The Sweetbriar looks like a rowing boat up alongside. We have to pass through the port passage to get dockside. The ship has everything we don't, an ice-cream parlor, washing machines and massive deck space. After the cramped quarters of the Sweet 'B' and the cluttered decks it is like a breath of fresh air to be aboard the battleship. I can breathe again. I feel like I could stay on the Iowa forever . . . She is a home away from home . . .

\* \* \*

A brief respite: The weather is clear and temperate in Argentia, being the middle of the year. Spent some time with the officers and crew of the Iowa, got invited to the canteen where I sampled the best steaks ever. Burton and I decided to head for Placentia about ten miles through the forest. We missed the train out so we decided to walk . . . but that is another story . . . we barely got back to the Sweet 'B' in one piece . . . Everyone on board the Iowa was very friendly, especially after having seen the cramped conditions we have to work in. Both officers and men aboard the Iowa have been very generous to the crew of the Sweet 'B'. They are busy picking up stores at the moment for the trip back. The mail has arrived, I got a letter from Mum, boy was I pleased, news at last!

\* \* \*

The long journey homeward: After being in Argentia for a few days it is now time to move out into the Atlantic and pick up another convoy for the trip back. We are back in the Atlantic and the captain has ordered an Action Stations drill. It is a reminder of what we should expect on our journey homeward. It is a necessary drill especially because the German subs will be waiting for us. They monitored us on the way over and tried to break into the defensive curtain around the convoy, and we can be as sure as hell they will do their level best to sink as many ships as possible on our way back . . .

\* \* \*

Picking up a convoy for the trip back: The weather is fine at the moment and we know that a stern sea homeward bound is going to give us a twist and roll for around eighteen days or more. Twenty ships are already lining up astern of us and twenty more are still to come. We have to wait for them. Every now and then we do dummy attack runs on anything suspicious and just to keep the men on their toes. The worse thing we could do is nothing and let some Nazi U-Boat take out a ship. It wasn't but a few days ago a Canadian corvette was sunk in these very waters so we cannot take a chance on letting anything slip through. The crew members of the Sweetbriar are like live wires ready for action at any moment. This waiting game is dangerous . . .

\* \* \*

On the way: The other ships have now joined us and we have now moved into position around the convoy. We have travelled roughly 120 miles eastward. So far no there are casualties. There are two Catalinas from the Canadian Fleet Air Arm patrolling around us and eastward of our position. It is comforting to know they are out there; every crewmember aboard every ship in the convoy appreciates it. Birds on their way to war torn Europe and the British Isles are setting down on our ship to rest for awhile. We put out a little water and crumbs for them to eat. A lifeboat with surviving crew members from a torpedoed ship was picked up. It had eleven men aboard, the ship's captain, however, was missing . . .

\* \* \*

A very fishy story: On our way home we were three days out from Newfoundland when Bill spotted a sub with the ASDIC. Tom ordered a depth charge run and we went in for the kill. Bill Sears had a solid reading and was one hundred percent certain it was a submarine.

We dropped the depth charges and up it came . . . when the focus of our charges surfaced we couldn't believe our eyes, thousands and thousands of . . . *Fish!*

What Bill Sears had thought to be a submarine turned out to be a very large school of fish . . . Tom and Alf ordered the boats to be lowered and sent out a fishing party to collect as much as they could; the boats were filled to the brim and after that for the rest of the journey home we had fish for breakfast, fish for lunch, fish for dinner, and with our tea instead of biscuits, you guessed it . . . Fish!

\* \* \*

The journey home and explosions of ships being torpedoed in the distance: Many times while I stood on the bridge under a clear night sky with the deck of the Sweetbriar rolling underfoot I felt as if history was repeating itself. I always had a sense of *Déjà vou* when at sea, especially when I looked at the stars above. Maybe I had inherited it from Captain de Croix, I don't know, but I always felt calm and serene even under the absolute worse conditions we faced, the sea was in my blood and bones and I craved for it like a mariner of old. It is tricky, I will grant it that, it changes from day to day and hour to hour, ready to cast off its millpond-like persona to that of a raging wild bull in the form of gigantic hundred foot waves threatening to smash any interlopers to pieces . . . The sea is a treacherous mistress and it takes a special man to tame her . . . As a boy I studied astronomy, in my Sea Scout training I excelled, at the helm of the Sweet 'B' I felt at home and at ease, *could I be the master and commander of my own ship, most assuredly* . . . The sea though always had to be treated with respect. The kindness she displays one day could be withdrawn on the following one. Our depth charges were the U-Boats' graveyard, they caused the subs to implode and the hull to collapse in upon itself. A direct hit from both sides crumples the hull and stops any egress from the conning tower, leaving the crew the only option but to slide out the torpedo tubes. A pattern of six depth charges dropped off the stern of our corvette onto a U-Boat could be devastating . . . One of the ruses they would try was to fire detritus and trash from their torpedo tubes to fool us into thinking they had been sunk, most captains were aware of this ruse though . . . During the cold dark nights on the bridge with Lunn, Alf or Tom I heard explosions in the darkness from far to our left or way in front. We were never informed what had happened. Was it a submarine attacking us? Only those involved would know, since the convoy is spread out far and wide. We hardly, as-per-normal, saw any of the other ships in B2 Group or in fact the merchant ships under our protection, except on radar of course . . .

* * *

The storm: We had had two reports of five U-Boats around Iceland, in the end they claimed one transporter, and there were no survivors. After five days of nice weather we had a storm warning and had to batten down all hatches. The wind started gradually at first then quickly wound its way up to 90 miles per hour and above. All hell broke loose upon us and the waves that bore down on us were enormous. As I stood up on the bridge I couldn't believe the size of them, some of them were twice the bloody height of the ship. I figured it was too rough to go below and even getting down would be fraught with danger so I stayed up top. At least up here I could see the blighters coming at us instead of down below where it was a bit claustrophobic with the worried faces of the crew to contend with. Up on the bridge I was free, albeit lashed by wind, freezing driving rain and sea spray by the truck load, but at least I could be of use to the ship instead of cowering below waiting for us to be overturned by some monstrous freak of nature wave. Up top with me, facing these waves, were the skipper, Tom, Alf and Lunn, though not all at once, there was always the chance of one or two of us being washed overboard and never seen again. Some of the transporters started to leave the convoy heading down south, in their words, "Better to risk being sunk or damaged by a U-Boat than the certainty of being broken apart and dashed to pieces or rolled over and sunk by these humongous walls of water . . ." As I stood there being slashed by the driving rain contemplating the next wall of water rising in front of us, and while I clung to a railing with the deck of the bridge rolling this way and then that way, my thoughts were of those brave seamen in the tug behind us somewhere . . . how did they fare in such conditions?

We were spotted by an enemy aircraft but the weather was way too bad for an aerial attack or from one by U-Boats. It was pointless keeping the 271PQ on or in fact the IFF and PPI. We kept them closed down for two nights and three days . . . After the storm broke we had a devil of a time locating all the ships in the convoy. Some of the ships had no idea where they were, they had no guidance systems or radar, just a compass and sextant. We were nearly out of fuel and had to get hooked up quickly, I prayed that the waves would calm down even more since oiling at sea is difficult at the best of times, at its worse, well, I'd rather not think of that, in bad weather it is a nigh impossible task. If we had no fuel oil for the engines and they stopped we would be doomed for sure, one of these large waves would have taken us straight to the bottom of the Atlantic. The one thought that crossed my mind on quite a few occasions while the storm had raged around us was, *'Will we even get home?'* But our luck was in and the waves calmed a bit allowing us to be hooked up to the tanker. As the storm abated the ship was given a thorough inspection, all gear, all clothing, radar equipment, ammunition and depth charges, spares, you name it. We even had a full dress rehearsal and inspection. Next on the list was to test fire all the guns aboard. At day's end the whole ship was squared away for the arrival of the commander of the escort group. We fired a line across to the Hesperus and in short order a ship to ship conveyance sling was set up and the CO with a group of four officers from B2 Group's other ships came aboard. The ship was like a new pin when they stepped on deck, courtesy of the Atlantic, which had scoured it spotless.

* * *

Spotting the Irish coastline: The Atlantic waters were not too bad today, just a little choppy and rough. We are not so far from home now and the Sweetbriar's crewmembers are all looking forward to some shore leave. We are still afloat and managed to fend off any interloping U-Boats. I think the U-Boat captains all think the Sweetbriar has a secret weapon onboard since every time they rear their ugly heads by way of periscope we are on to them in a shot. The Sweet 'B's secret weapon has a codename: Stanley, or 'Gus' as the men prefer to call him . . .

I have sighted the coastline of Scotland on the radar and our convoy is starting to breakup. We will be heading to our berth at Gladstone docks. The captain is eager to get home and ordered full speed ahead as the convoy is now officially disbanded. Maybe our speed is a little too fast for the sea conditions; we have a high beam sea on our starboard side. We spotted a Liberty ship about fifty miles off the Scottish coastline from another convoy; it had been broken in half. It was still afloat and there was no life seen aboard her. The Liberty ships are built in the United States; they are massive transport ships welded together for ease of construction. In the Atlantic this construction process could well prove hazardous. The sea can get wild out there. It is never the same. I would rather go to sea in a ship that is both welded and riveted . . .

We are half-way between the broken Liberty ship and the Isle of Man. The Sweet 'B' nearly rolled over because of our speed and the high beam sea. She was well known for being a bit top heavy because of her armaments. One heavy beam wave hit us and we rolled 45 degrees to port. I always wondered what I would do if she turned upside down. Luckily she slowly came back upright. I breathed a sigh of relief. Holyhead was off the portside and Tom ordered half ahead, well, at least until we passed the Isle of Man . . .

Our voyage continued until we had the Mersey in sight, thank goodness, we made it . . . *Home at last!*

* * *

Back home: When the transporters reached the British Isles essentials such as food, weapons of war, parts for aircraft, tanks, guns and other materials would be distributed, some of it to Russia, our ally against the Nazis. I smiled when we had passed the Isle of Man. The sun was coming up heralding a new day as I stood on the bridge. A Sunderland flying boat passed overhead and rocked its wings from side to side in salute. We passed a large transporter that had just left the convoy. She was low in the water as the waterline was way below where it normally would have been, some three yards; she had a full load onboard and looked almost as though she were sinking. She gave us a big long hoot of her ship's horn thanking us for her safe passage. We gave her a naval salute with our siren type horn, a high pitched blow of "Beep – Beep!" and then a very low horn blast. It was, we hoped, a good signal for her safe voyage to port . . . When we reached the Mersey only a few boats were cruising up and down, and every soul on every one of those little boats gave us a warm and hearty wave signaling our return, they knew we had braved icy mountainous Atlantic waters and German torpedoes to bring back the convoy and Britain's lifeblood . . .

When we at last arrived at our berth we received a tumultuous clapping and cheering from the dockies, there wasn't a dry eye amongst the lot of them, so many of them had lost good friends on corvettes sunk by the Germans and the word had got around we had been lost at sea, sunk by a torpedo . . . The weather at home was dull and grey as I cleaned and pressed my uniform, polished my shoes and prepared myself. Leave would be seven days and then I would have to be back on the ship. *'Oh well, at least it's something,'* I thought as I packed the gifts I had bought for the family . . .

* * *

Stepping onto the quay: I did not realize for several months how careful of my tongue I had to be. Any questions asked by dock hands and other querulous parties on the quayside or a public house, if answered, could mean serious trouble for a convoy. A slipped word or two from a seaman could be carried far and wide. Information could quickly get to Dublin and the German Embassy there. It wasn't much trouble for the Germans to buy intelligence with a few bottles of whisky. Their spies were everywhere. Whenever I heard of a corvette being sunk I would wonder when it would be our turn . . . With my seven days leave I headed to Buntingford to see mum and dad. It could be a bit boring but maybe that was what I needed after being at sea. Unfortunately for me the general rule was that returning service personnel would be pressed into buying the rounds. I tried to keep my drinking to a minimum, one beer and one shandy, but the bars were always full of chaps expecting their free drinks. It could be quite expensive . . . I waited at the station until my train came and I climbed aboard heading home . . .

# CHAPTER 10

## Gibraltar and the Med via the Azores

**W**e left Gladstone docks one spring morning at approximately 1000 hours. The ubiquitous leather bag was opened by the skipper as we headed south past Wales toward Land's End. We were on our own as far as I could see on the 271PQ. The commander of B2 Group on the Hesperus and the rest of the ships would be heading straight to Gibraltar escorting a large battle cruiser while we had other orders. We would be going south so we had to change from our normal uniform of navy blue to that of the tropical whites. We would now be searching for enemy submarines down South in the Atlantic past the Azores toward Argentina. Reports had come in that German subs were operating quite freely in the south around Argentina and would also take the Cape Horn route to escape detection when travelling to Japan. Other spurious reports stated that the Germans even had a base in Antarctica. At any rate, the Admiralty had sent the Sweetbriar down South to do a spot of sub hunting. The actual reason was not as spurious as most of the crew thought. We were to be an advance scout ship searching for submarines and keeping them well away from our battle group, interdicting any that came our way. And if any U-Boats were foolish enough to chance a meeting with us, we would send them to the bottom of the Atlantic.

So we duly headed south. We kept well clear of the French coast on our way south to Lisbon, our first port of call . . . The weather was bright and sunny all the way down and the seas were calm. But even with the beautiful weather conditions we were experiencing there was an ever-present incoming rolling swell on our starboard side from the Atlantic through the Bay of Biscay. It was, to put it mildly, big . . . I wondered, *'If this is what it is like in calm balmy conditions what would it be like in a vicious storm?'* I shuddered at the thought . . .

We arrived at Lisbon on the following evening at around 2000 hours, standing on the bridge I marveled at Lisbon's lights, it looked like a fairy-land of delights. It was a veritable Christmas card scene near the middle of the year. We dropped our sea anchor about two miles out and relaxed for the night, well, so, so, for Lisbon was full of Germans, and even though Portugal was neutral there was always the possibility of enemy saboteurs trying to sink the ship. We had a watch on the foc'sle and one on the stern; I stood watch on the bridge with Lunn from 2000 hours to 2400 hours. The cruise down had been a busy one and a half days making sure no U-Boats got the scent of the convoy behind us. Since it was warm I slept on the upper deck, not the normal thing to do and definitely frowned upon but I didn't fancy it down below with the smell of smoke and stale body odor. Even the port passage where I hung my hammock was too hot. I laid my blanket out and fell asleep looking at the fairy lights in the distance, above me, strung out across the deep black sky were nature's party decorations, shining down on me and twinkling comfortingly. London, Liverpool and the rest of Britain had been blacked out for what seemed like an eternity. I had gotten so use to the stygian black of our homeland it was a shock to see lights during the dark of night . . .

By positioning ourselves off Lisbon we were in a perfect position to monitor the movement of German shipping and other nefarious underwater activities. Both radar and ASDIC were a hive of activity, and the Sweetbriar's gun crews were on high alert, just in case. Even though for all intents and purpose the onboard activity seemed calm and placid, we were, at a moment's notice, ready for action. Another reason for us lying off the Port of Lisbon was for the escort group to catch up a little. We had left some time before B2 Group had formed up on the giant cumbersome ship with her city smashing one ton shells . . . That night, as the Sweet 'B' slumbered, green phosphorus tinted waves lapped at its hull and continued shoreward with their crests turning the harbor into a greenery-filled forest carpet under a waning moon . . .

In 1795 an earthquake had wracked the city of Lisbon sending its inhabitants fleeing to the marble promenade running along its shoreline. As thousands of the city's populace watched in a panic stricken state from the security of the promenade as half the city tumbled into ruins and fire spread through the buildings, they were blissfully unaware of the terrible tragedy that was about to befall them. The waters of Lisbon harbor began to bubble and recede from the jetties and the promenade. Wooden galleons in the harbor started to flounder. A large roaring and thunderous noise reached the ears of those gathered in front of their crumbling city. A series of giant waves struck the promenade hurling people hither and thither, smashing them against marble and brick then sucked their lifeless bodies into the dark depths of the Bay of Biscay and the Atlantic beyond . . . The once proud wooden-masted ships were torn asunder and sent down to *Davy Jones's Locker* never to be seen again . . . I pondered over this tragedy as I stood on the bridge at 0700 hours the following morning with the Sweetbriar's engines throbbing to life. With our sea anchor up we headed seaward . . .

The weather was perfect, above us blue sunny skies and relatively calm warm seas, as we steamed toward Madeira. It didn't seem long before we reached and passed Madeira and headed to our next waypoint, the islands making up the Azores . . .

We had sailed one hundred miles past the islands of the Azores when we received new orders, we would now sail back in a circle and head to the Mediterranean. If we had carried on into the South Atlantic and headed for the coast of Argentina we would have had no access to refueling or resupply ships, and this would have posed a problem for us. If we had docked in Argentina our ship could be impounded. There was much sympathy for the Germans in Argentina and the risk for us would not be worth frightening or sinking the odd U-Boat. Besides, going down there was not what we had intended. When sailing anywhere the importance of logistics, fuel, oil, spare parts and food for example, is largely overlooked by those based on land, however it is an indispensible key to any operation which would pit us against the Germans who were able to exploit the sympathies of many South American governments. Argentina, especially, had a long wild coastline on which to drop off gold, currency, strategic goods and military personnel. The Germans had built up wealth for themselves by secreting stolen treasures and valuable items from all over Europe in case their war against us turned sour, which, at that moment it was. For, the tide was beginning to slowly turn against our cruel foe. I suppose there must have been some forward thinking Germans in high positions that felt the same way and had begun to hedge their bets . . . "HEAD FOR GIBRALTAR STOP AWAIT FURTHER ORDERS." This simple communiqué from the Admiralty was all it took to send us to Gibraltar. It would be a change from the cold rough waters of the North Atlantic which we accepted but never quite became accustomed to. We changed course and headed up towards the Pillars of Hercules.

* * *

When we arrived at Gibraltar the weather was clear, warm and sunny. We were all wearing our tropical whites and caps and were eager to see the *Rock* up close. At the docks, tied up, were the two halves of a big transporter ship that had been torpedoed. The ship had been split in half by a torpedo, but thanks to its water tight compartments it had stayed afloat. It had been in Gibraltar for some time and was a stark reminder that even though the weather was good and the seas calm, compared to the North Atlantic, this was still no safe harbor and sea to flit around unconcernedly about. The Italians and Germans operated mini-subs, both enclosed for the crew and ones you rode on that looked like torpedoes. If they got through the submarine nets they could cripple ships in the harbor either with tin-fish or magnetic limpet mines.

Within ten minutes of berthing the Sweet 'B' we were given shore leave to await our new assignment, that of escorting the battleship along the coast of North Africa with the rest of B2 Group. Even though this big ship was built in the First World War its big shells had the capability to flatten completely any city or fighting force it decided to unleash its guns on. Whether the ship fired no rounds and was just used as a deterrent to force the removal of Rommel out of Africa once and for all, or it unleashed the floodgates launching a torrent of shells upon her foes, the result would be the same, disarray and withdrawal–or death!

* * *

I headed ashore with Bill Sears, Burton and Hill. It was a one and a half mile hike from the docks to the town. We decided to head for the nearest bar which advertised a guitar playing trio, *The Three Amigos*. Hill was a band leader from South Hampton, tall with fair hair, and loved playing jokes at the crew's expense. Sear's was about my height and build and in a bar fight he could hold his own. We had no thought of getting into a fracas but today Hill was in one of his *May the Devil Take Me* moods. We sat down in the bar and were enjoying our beers when in walked a bunch of *pongoes*, our vernacular for army personnel. The beers that Hill had downed didn't help the situation. Army and navy men were well known for their rivalry, and we couldn't help it if they were mud-eaters . . . Hill started baying like a sheep which pissed off the *pongoes* no end. One of them really got cross and wanted to start a fight. I had no intention of becoming embroiled in it and even less to have to deal with the Shore Patrol or Red Caps and end up in front of the captain on a charge. We paid for our drinks hurriedly and had to drag Hill away from the angry *pongoes*. Gripping his shirt we tried our best to haul his bulky frame out the door but he held fast to it and kept making sheep noises, especially at the meanest, biggest and ugliest looking one of the lot. We traded a few punches in an effort to drag Hill away from them and out the door. We had to hang on to him as we headed down the street. He really wanted to fight the whole flock of them. Laughing, we walked to a Tombola hall, thinking we'd try our luck. I turned back more than once half expecting them to barrel out of the bar–but no one came out and nothing happened–that was the end of the *pongo* bashing incident . . .

Strutting down the road towards the Housey Housey Tombola hall we saw several apes, bigger even than a full grown baboon. One of the locals was feeding them with green bananas and nuts. "Where do they go in winter?" we asked. "They disappear, but I think there is a tunnel that links Tangiers to Gibraltar, it's only twenty miles away . . ." he replied, then noted, "There is a tunnel between the docks and the beaches on the other side of the *Rock*, so why not a tunnel from here to Africa–"

We nodded in agreement and went on to the Tombola. We found the Tombola room in a hotel with a bar, mainly because of the cries from the patrons. I bought a ticket and sat down. The man started calling out numbers, "Blue, blue number two–" Then he called out, "Clackety-clack number six pick up six–a knock at the door, number four–" This carried on for a while until all of a sudden I realized I had a line up, I couldn't talk because of the shock. I showed it to Bill and he said, "Shout line-up–Damn it!"

I managed to croak out, "Line-up . . ." through my hoarseness, my throat had clamped shut, I knew I was in line to make a lot of money. Some two hundred pounds–the first time I'd won anything . . . Bill turned out to be my lucky charm, for every time he accompanied me, I won!

After Tombola we toured Gibraltar, even going to the wire fence separating Gibraltar from Spain next to La Línea, which is just on the other side in Spanish territory. We took advantage of the bistros and local cafés everywhere we went. La Línea really was a quaint little town on the sea front, my kind of town! The lads and I wanted to walk over to the Mediterranean side of Gibraltar but we were warned that it was steep and dangerous to continue from where we were, they said rather go back down through the town and you'll get to a tunnel that leads to the beaches on the Mediterranean side of the *Rock*. We followed their directions and headed back down much to my relief, and it wasn't too long before we found the tunnel. Going through the tunnel from the docks we found it very big and spacious, it was even big enough for automobiles to pass through and more than big enough for pedestrians. Could there be a tunnel to Tangiers–*Quite possibly*–It took us about twenty five minutes to get to the other side and the beaches. It was much more relaxing than back in the town, there were just a few people on the beach, this was wartime of course and they were all dressed very somberly. Walking down the beach with the warm rays of the sun shining down on us from the heavens and with the beach-sand between our toes was exhilarating, especially after the freezing cold Atlantic waters and constant threat of attack by the Germans, it lulled us into a false sense of security. Life had become sane once more and I felt more alive than I had been in ages. Yes, I knew the war raged not far from where we were but the warm sun on my face had filled me with hope and the zest to continue fighting . . . With our batteries recharged

Bill Sears, 'Bomb-head' Burton, Hill and I made our way back to the ship with the setting sun in our faces and dancing pastel sunbeams turning the dockyard and ships into a work of art by one of the French impressionists . . .

That night as I stood on the bridge with Gibraltar cloaked in blackout darkness without, I cast my eyes toward La Línea on the Spanish coast, it was all lit up in the same manner as Lisbon, the war seemed not to affect it at all. Granted, some of the cafés, restaurants and other places of merriment in Gibraltar were decked from head to toe in their inner sanctums with little fairy lights while their patrons' caroused to the sounds of guitars and Spanish dancing, which filled the night air, and with beer and wine flowing freely, but we were still at war and the men fighting it needed to forget it, even if only for a little while . . . Gibraltar didn't really experience a cold winter, so in summer and winter most of the cafés stayed open from five in the afternoon all through the night. During the day patrons would sit comfortably in chairs under umbrellas at the front of the little bistros, though always observing their midday siesta . . .

At the docks I had enquired about the possibility of air attacks, I was told, "No, none, just attacks from saboteurs and that German supporters frequented the restaurants and cafés of Gibraltar . . ." The heavy Red Cap presence in Gib now began to all make sense. We had returned from our foray into Gibraltar at 2000 hours even though our liberty leave was up till 2200 hours. We had taken in the sights and sounds of the *Rock* and had much to discuss back on board. At the airport we had seen three Spitfires and two C-47s landing. The friendly locals had told us the Dakotas had brought in medical evacuees from Africa belonging to the 8th Army . . . Our boys fighting the Germans in the north of Africa needed a helping hand, hence the battleship to give them a bit of a nudge. At 2200 hours I was put on deck as night watch for saboteurs and given a Lanchester machine gun. On Whale Island I had become very accustomed to the Lanchester during our gunnery course so it felt like I was reacquainting myself with an old friend . . .

The Sweet 'B' lay in total darkness, we were still at war and the blackout rules reigned on our ship just as they did the rest of the ships in the harbor and on Gib. Other than the bistros of course, they partied like there was no tomorrow. I said to myself, *'No saboteur is going to take out the Sweetbriar . . .'* I would make sure no limpet mines were attached to our hull by Italian or German navy divers riding on their two-man torpedo subs, and that no-one would clamber aboard up the anchor chain in the dead of night. There were anti-submarine nets strung across the harbor entrance but you never could tell, when it came to war anything could happen . . .

I thought, *'If I see anyone suspicious I'll fire on them.'* Shoot first and ask questions afterwards. At around 2330 hours a Spanish looking man walked toward the Sweetbriar down the dock in the darkness with only the half moon above lighting his face. When he caught sight of me he turned sharply away and carried on towards a dockside warehouse. I kept my eyes on him and my finger on the trigger of my Lanchester machine gun. He climbed up a ladder onto the roof of one of the dockside buildings. This, to me, was a sure sign of a saboteur at work. I made up my mind to give him a few warning shots. I squeezed the trigger on the Lanchester and aimed in front of him and over the top of his head. A staccato burst erupted from the machine gun and sent a barrage of lead in his direction. Lead rounds pinged all over the place as the man retreated hastily down the ladder all the while screaming bloody murder in Spanish. As though someone had flicked on a light switch the whole of Gibraltar came alive and blazed with light. Two Spaniards arrived in short order and calmed the man down. It turned out that he was a night watchman on fire duty, hence his penchant for clambering over roofs. The duty officer of the watch on the Sweetbriar breathed a sigh of relief as he looked at me, "Thank God you didn't kill him . . ."

After that the lights of Gibraltar blackened and the crew of the Sweet 'B' went back to sleep, that is, everyone but me and the others on watch. I hit the hay and my hammock at 0300 hours the following morning to dream of sweet Spanish music and even sweeter Spanish dancers with long flowing skirts and castanets clacking between their fingers . . .

* * *

As the sun rose the Sweetbriar was once again at war preparing to depart from Gibraltar. At 0700 hours two officers were piped aboard. They were joining the Sweet 'B' to see some action. As I stood on the bridge, I pondered, *'This would be a nice place to live in and retire, if that is I live through the war.'* The Skipper gave the order, "Let go for'ard, let go aft . . ." With those orders the Sweetbriar slipped away from the dock she had been tied to and we were away. Everyone on board the Sweetbriar thought we would be heading westward in search of submarines as we left the port of Gibraltar. It was a warm sunny day as we slipped past the anti-submarine nets and headed seaward, but, to everyone's surprise we met B2 Group escorting a large battleship, HMS Centaur, steaming through the Straits of Gibraltar. Only a privileged few on board the Sweetbriar knew our real mission and why we were sent ahead. My shipmates couldn't believe it when they saw the Hesperus, Vesper, Poppy, Clematis and Campanula surrounding and leading a massive old battleship with its guns primed for action. This iron clad battleship was weighted down with concrete to make it more stable at sea. In reality the guns on board her needn't be fired, just one look at this ferocious elderly ship would send the Germans packing. She was an awesome beast to look at, as beautiful as an aged Spanish wine kept hidden in a cool cellar unbeknownst to all save a few. It had two large turrets both fore and aft, each one weighted with three fourteen inch guns. The commanding officer on board the Hesperus saluted us as we sailed up to her then gave us a position at the rear of the escort group. We transmitted as much information as we could of our scouting mission in the Atlantic and the journey to Gibraltar. The battleship with its escort group then headed for the coast of Africa and Algeria. We were well aware of the fierce fighting taking place between Allied forces and Rommel's forces, the Afrika Korps, in North Africa. We knew that the Germans were now retreating on all fronts from the advancing columns of Allied tanks and soldiers; we had heard this from several British soldiers in Gibraltar, that and the fact that many were being treated at the hospital on the *Rock* before being shipped home . . . As the warm blue waters parted before the Sweetbriar's bow I could see over fifty porpoises from my vantage point on the bridge, all swimming alongside the ship. They played blissfully unaware in both our bow and stern waves without a care in the world, delighting in the human presence our intrusion into their domain had presented them with. In all truthfulness I sincerely hoped we would not have to engage any U-Boats for these wonderful creatures would take the full brunt of any underwater explosions unleashed upon the Germans beneath the waves.

We were ten miles off the coast of Algeria when we heard the sounds of gun and shell fire. Not one or two shots mind you, but constant firing and shelling, Africa was definitely in a war with our treacherous foe. Overhead a German Blohm & Voss six-engine flying boat came toward us from the direction of the French coast. It circled around us at a distance reporting on the movement of our escort group. The Blohm & Voss made sure it kept out of the range of our anti-aircraft guns since the combined firepower of all our ships would have blown it into so many pieces all the King's horses and all the King's men certainly wouldn't have put it together again. It would have crashed in a fiery-ball of flame into the Mediterranean waters below it. The messages it was sending back to German High Command were quickly translated for us, the pilot reported that a huge battle fleet was steaming toward Alexandria. We knew by then that Rommel had started to withdraw the German forces from Egypt and with the hasty communications transmitted from the Blohm & Voss our arrival would hasten their departure. Just the threat of the battleship's big guns flattening Rommel's retreating forces was enough . . . *The Admiralty had seized the day without even firing a shot* . . . We sailed eastward toward Alexandria at sixteen knots for two days hugging the coastline at a distance of ten miles. All this time continuous reports from German aircraft were being sent to Germany and France of our movements and the troop movements of Allied forces in North Africa. The aircraft above came and went, reporting, "THE LARGE ATTACKING FORCE OF SHIPS WITH A BATTLESHIP IN THE GROUP IS CONTINUING TO ALEXANDRIA . . ." Eventually the last Blohm & Voss made its final report and vanished for good northwards in the direction of Italy's south coast. While looking up through my binoculars at the departing aircraft from the bridge I wondered whether the Germans knew that our signals section on board the Sweetbriar were listening in to their reports. At any rate the message had been clear to Rommel, "Get out of Africa!"

On the final night of our escort we handed the battleship over to two destroyers safe and sound. Her next port of call would be Malta to scare the hell out of the German's in Sicily. B2 Group now had new orders, "RETURN TO BRITAIN AS SOON AS POSSIBLE." We turned about and headed back to Gibraltar . . .

\* \* \*

Being in the navy I could keep abreast of what was happening on some of the other ships in the Royal Navy and was informed that the Arethusa, Ernie's ship, had been badly damaged by a torpedo. The light cruiser had suffered the explosive head stoically but many on board her were killed or injured. I had received a letter from mum that Jimmy was still in Africa fighting the forces of Rommel's Afrika Korps. It seemed so long ago that I had seen either of them. I had not seen Jimmy since he had shipped out to Africa, even Ernie, once he'd been called up had not been home to Meath Road, the German bombs had seen to that. He had done his seamanship training and had become a chief petty officer on the Arethusa. It was a life-time ago now when the war began. We had been a family once, and now, well, the war had finished that. Still, I couldn't complain, I was still alive and kicking. I found out much later that Ernie had had such a close call when the torpedo struck the Arethusa; he had just left the mess deck and closed a bulkhead door behind him when all hell broke loose. Everyone on the mess deck had been killed. He had cheated death by half a second. Many of those killed had been his close friends; he continued to be haunted by their deaths for a long time and suffered much because of it. Still, life goes on, we were still at war and wouldn't be able to rest until Hitler and his jackboot wearing fiends were well and truly kicked back to where they belonged . . .

\* \* \*

Sunny Mediterranean skies spread above us as the Sweetbriar cleaved the waters below, porpoises danced in the blue waters around the ship, *'This is the best cruise yet,'* I thought, while standing on the bridge soaking it all in and letting the warm rays of the sun warm my Atlantic chilled bones. As we headed back to Gibraltar the porpoises continued with us and at times jumping six feet out of the water. You would have thought we were on a pleasure cruise the way they were acting. I wondered idly whether they did this next to German ships, or did the Germans slaughter them as well . . .

On our way we picked up survivors from a Free French Navy ship that had been torpedoed by German U-Boats from Crete or Sicily. We did this quickly to avoid becoming another kill for the U-Boats. A German aircraft circled out of range of our guns as we searched for other survivors. There were none. After that we continued to port. Our passengers, who only spoke French, would be dropped off at Gibraltar for their own people to assist them . . .

As the Sweetbriar docked in Gibraltar we were told we would spend two days in port while the ship restocked on supplies and fuel for the journey home. The crew would have time to shop and while away a spot of shore leave in the cafés and restaurants. That suited me and the lads fine so off we went on our various forays and expeditions in search of presents and bananas to take back home to the family. When I arrived back at the ship for my watch duty I was informed that the captain had requested us to be in full uniform, our naval whites, for an inspection the following day at 1000 hours in the morning on the dockside. The ship was also to be inspected at six bells so the order of the day was everything had to be cleaned, polished and stowed away correctly. The captain had also invited other ships' officers to attend a luncheon before we sailed home.

The following day as we stood at attention on the dockside a ship's band from the harbor came to bid us farewell as did the Lord Mayor of Gibraltar and his entourage. The Lord Mayor was very impressed with our turn-out and said, "When the war is over you will all be most welcome in Gibraltar . . ." After that he added, "Your efforts in the war are most appreciated . . ." The entourage he had brought with him then brought forth a large amount of fruit for the crew of the Sweetbriar. After lunch the Lord Mayor and his entourage and a group of officers from neighboring ships in the harbor toured the Sweetbriar from stem to stern. They were even allowed to see our radar hut, which surprised me, but were not allowed to take photographs of any of the equipment inside as it was still on the secrets list. I had a nice chat with one of the guests who said he had heard a lot about the bombing of London and thanked God that Gibraltar had not been attacked. I suggested to him that because Spain was only a stone's throw away any bombing would have affected it also. The Spanish, no doubt, would not have been pleased had Germany bombed Gibraltar. The day had been a good one full of naval pomp and ceremony. Everyone aboard the Sweetbriar was treated with respect and dignity. On that day a good hearty time was had by all and the following morning we left Gibraltar for good, with my bananas safely tucked away in the anchor locker and the presents for my family in my kitbag . . . As we left the warm sunny waters of the Mediterranean and its porpoises far behind I wondered what the future had in store for the Sweetbriar and its crew of combat seasoned sailors . . . On that trip back we hit a storm which forced us to head for the south coast of Ireland and up its western seaboard to northern Ireland then back past the Isle of Man to the Mersey . . . *personally, I preferred the Mediterranean . . .*

# CHAPTER 11

## D-Day

Most naval men were admired for the work they did. The risks, the ships sunk during convoy missions and other operations, the turbulent oceans only too eager to suck a ship down into their depths and the Germans ever so eager to assist. The people of any port and those living in the coastal areas knew only too well the risks we faced, of the ships lost to storms and our enemies alike. Their appreciation was shown in a smile and a helping hand if needed; they did what they could to ease the strain we endured at sea. A naval uniform worn by the men and women of the Royal Navy drew out warmth seldom seen in the generally cool persona of the British people. I had met Bob Jordan, an electrician, while he was working on our radar system in Newcastle upon Tyne, and he said, "Why don't you come and have a holiday in Willington Quay, my wife Ethel and I would love to have you over if you're ever in the area?"

I gratefully accepted but wondered when and if ever I would have the chance. On arriving in Liverpool after another convoy to Canada we were given ten days leave. It was an opportunity I couldn't miss out on; the alternative was to stay on the ship while we were at port in Birkenhead and potter around Liverpool. I didn't fancy that and it had been a long time since I'd seen my family. I decided to take the train down to London then one to Buntingford where mum had relocated to during the Blitz. I'd stay a few days at home, and then hop on the train to London then visit Bob and Ethel up in Newcastle then go back to the ship. Foremost in my mind was a nice soft bed to kip on. Sleeping space was paramount on board the Sweet 'B' and a hard locker or hammock could never replace a comfy mattress and clean sheets on terra firma. It wasn't long before I was sitting comfortably on the train to Euston station in London. I had only bought a ticket to Newcastle and hoped there wouldn't be a problem. When I got there I told the ticket collector I had got on the wrong train, he said, "No problem, just hop over to Kings Cross and catch the train to Newcastle that's waiting on the platform."

Instead of the Newcastle train I took the one to Buntingford instead. When I arrived home I found mum in the back gardening, planting some vegetables. I dropped my kitbag to the ground and said, "Mum . . ."

Turning she tilted back her sun-hat and wiped her forehead. "Stanley!" she said in surprise. Standing she came over and gave me a big hug. Dad wasn't home he was still working and as busy as a beaver for London North Eastern Railways driving trains. The family was still split up, Ted and Alf were still in Wales, Ernie on his ship and Jim either in Egypt or Italy. Mum had taken to using my beautiful rosewood inlaid tool box as nesting space for her chickens, I shrugged my shoulders and let it be, what else could I do. I stayed three nights at home then figured I'd better be on my way to Newcastle. Mum had grown use to seeing me go; our family was now one of nomads in all corners of the globe. It was a necessary evil if our lives were ever again to see the semblance of normality. To me now the sounds of bombs whistling through the air and then exploding was normal, waves pounding our ship's hull threatening to tear her apart, was normal, German subs seeking us and ever so willing to launch a tin-fish at us was normal, people dying was now normal, Nazi atrocities were normal. We were living in a very twisted period of Earth's history where the norm was death and destruction on all fronts. Members of our family had been killed at home by falling German bombs, others in combat. There were no tears when I walked out the door, they had all dried up, Hitler and his not-so-merry-men had seen to that . . . Soon, I was in the train on my way to Newcastle hoping for some sun and fun to take my mind off the grim memories I held close to my heart now . . .

When I arrived at Newcastle I set off in search of Bob and it wasn't long before we were on an electric train bound for Willington Quay. Dinner and beers were served within two hours of our arrival. Ethel, Bob's wife, had invited a friend of hers, Mary, a young lady who had taken on the job of delivering milk in the area as her contribution to the war effort as part of the land army. She was a nice lass, not my type, but she had taken a fancy to me and I thought the honorable thing to do was to be a good companion and chaperone for her since Ethel had arranged some outings and a trip down to a small holiday town with a beach. It was nice to wake up again in a comfortable bed. Ethel went to town and even brought me a tray with my breakfast on it. I was really chuffed. When we got to the little holiday town later that day the weather had turned, it was a bit chilly and rain started to pour down, so instead of laying on a sandy beach and soaking in the sunshine we headed for the cinema and took in a Fred Astaire and Ginger Rogers movie. Mary was pleasant company but time flew and my leave was nearly up. I headed back to the ship in Liverpool, I felt refreshed and the memories of mountainous waves, freezing cold water, stinging windblown icicles, burning sinking ships and drowned oil drenched sailors had begun to fade away and sink into my subconscious . . .

\* \* \*

I climbed up the stairs and made my way up to the bridge fully expecting to be headed once again into the turbulent waters of the North Atlantic with the rest of B2 Group; we were meant to pick up a convoy on the 15 – 16th of May, instead Tom said we would be heading to the North Sea and then Newcastle for a refit. I smiled to myself, *'Maybe this time I would get my day sun-tanning on the beach outside Willington Quay . . .'* how wrong I was. Before we got into Newcastle we would be patrolling the North Sea. We passed the Isle of Man then the Clyde and then the far north of Scotland. We were now in the North Atlantic in very rough seas. Around us we saw huge whirlpools big enough to swallow a big fishing vessel or an old time wooden galleon. Many a vessel in that area had been sucked under to *Davy Jones's Locker* never to be seen again. The Sweet 'B' kept well clear of them as we headed towards Norway. My duties became frenetic because of the possibility of attacks from not only U-boats but Junkers 88's as well. I kept up a steady flow of reports, "Radar–Bridge . . . Radar–Bridge!" I didn't miss a thing, and calls to Action Stations were fast and furious . . . With our patrol finished we did our practice depth charge runs, letting rip patterns of six off the stern enough to awaken any slumbering shipmate aboard the Sweetbriar. All our guns were fired, keeping both guns and gun crews on form. After our drills we headed to the Tyne and our refit . . .

* * *

With the journey to Newcastle over it wasn't long before the ship was crawling with men working on her refit. Bob was working on the electrical system for our *Hedgehog's Chicago Piano* on the foc'sle on either side of the 4.5 inch gun and had been told to get a move on since we'd be shipping out shortly. They also serviced the Oerlicons on the bridge, one on the portside and one on the starboard side. We were now bristling with armaments once they'd finished. While he was busy checking the Oerlicons over, he said in a worried voice, "These guns were tested a few days ago, you must be going somewhere for big action . . ."

I replied, "I haven't heard anything yet, but I guess you're right . . ."

Later that day I met Tom up on the bridge. "I suppose you're wondering why we're packing extra guns and Hedgehogs," said Tom.

"The thought had crossed my mind," I answered, smiling.

"Well, we're not doing convoys now, we have to go to the river Thames . . ." he noted in grave tones. I knew well enough not to ask why, *loose lips sink ships* and German spies could be anywhere. It was best I didn't know yet. There would be plenty of time later. In fact I didn't much care where we went as long as I was on the Sweet 'B' with the men I respected and had grown fond of. As far as I was concerned this was my ship and no damned Jerry would harm her while I was on duty.

I stayed at Bob and Ethel's house while the ship was in dock but the mood had changed, at dinner Ethel was visibly worried. She reached across the table and squeezed my hand, "We hope you have a safe journey wherever you're going," she said in a warm protective voice. The day before Bob had told me they'd lost a close relative to German guns in Egypt. Receiving a *Killed in Action* letter would be a shock for anyone. I guess the prospect of losing someone else they had grown fond of was just too much for Ethel as I could hear sobs from their room in the dark of night as I lay on my bed in the guest room . . .

Once we had finished our refit and were on our way Bob and Ethel stood on the quayside watching as the Sweetbriar slipped away from her moorings. Ethel's eyes were misty and red as ships all around us hooted us farewell and good hunting, they seemed to know where we were headed. I stood on the bridge watching and returning the salutes from the dockhands and fitters and other naval personnel. It was a sad, moving and mournful farewell I had experienced. Tears filled my eyes as I stood at attention saluting. In my mind a *Jordy* song played over and over:-

*"Wer yer gannin tanight,*
*Wer yer gannin ma sweet,*
*Wer yer gannin, way aye,*
*Hum gan yam . . . I'm going home . . ."*

'I'm going home to the sea, where I belong, to the heat of battle and the stench of death, and if needs be my life's blood be spilt, then so be it, for that is where I belong, with the men I have fought with, served with and laughed with . . . Yes, that's where I belong . . . I'm going home!'

\* \* \*

The Sweetbriar was in her element once again as we forged through the waves close to the eastern seaboard of Britain, for we were now sailing toward the Thames. Our destination was now Sheerness where we would tie ho. I was on the bridge as normal, not in my radar hut but outside with a salty sea breeze caressing my cheeks and a pair of binoculars pressed against the hard bony surfaces around my eyes. If I wasn't glued to the radar screen I kept watch on the bridge. It was too hot and stuffy down below, and besides, as always, I preferred the company of the senior officers. I asked Tom, our 2IC, "What the hell are we going up the Thames for, are they disbanding B2 Group?"

"I can't tell you anything yet, Stan, but what I can say is that what we are about to take part in is one of the pivotal moments in this whole damned war . . ." replied our 2IC.

I left it at that, if he could have told me he would have. I whispered to myself in hushed tones, *'Well, dear old England, whatever it is we're up to we shan't let you down.'* I put my binoculars to my eyes once more since Burton was in the radar hut and I could have a little break. It turned into a beautiful morning and we were about eight sailing hours away from Newcastle and about 20 miles off the coast of England near the Wash in the North Sea. The sea looked comely and inviting as the skipper climbed onto the bridge. He chatted to Tom and Alf briefly then announced over the ship's intercom whether anyone would like to go for a swim. It wasn't long before the ship hove to and a sea-boat and life-boat were lowered and fifteen of our shipmates took advantage of the warm sun and cool sea. A *Jacob's ladder* was lowered off the ship but I decided not to go in, I'd much rather see what was below me if I had the choice.

I suppose the skipper wanted to give the men a little break to buoy their spirits before the real action started, the swim almost made me feel we were on a pleasure cruise and took my mind off whatever was to come . . .

* * *

The contrails of fighters and bombers alike crowded the azure sky above while the murky waters of the English Channel parted at our bow, foamy froth bubbling along the port and starboard sides of our boat. We were now on our final leg to the Thames. The refit had been extensive, extra weaponry and munitions and whatever else could be crammed into and on top of our Flower Class Corvette. On the mind of every soul aboard the Sweetbriar was one question, *'What on earth was it for, and what were we about to do?'* On the bridge we were put on alert for submarines and in particular the small two man subs that might slip by unnoticed. Our orders had been clear and concise as per normal when we reached Sheerness we would hove to and tie up to a buoy. As we headed up the Thames to our allotted position passing ships would hoot in respect, they knew something was up, hidden from us and further up the Thames it was hard to hide all the troop ships and men from prying eyes, the LCMs and LCTs, British, Canadian and American troops, their tanks and weapons. There were just so many of them. Men from all nations had gathered to finally push Hitler out of Europe and back to Germany where he belonged. There was a bubbling, almost palpable, common sense of purpose in the hearts and

sentiments of all those around us. You could almost reach out
and touch it. We still didn't realize what was about to happen but
I felt a sense of pride as I stood on the bridge proudly saluting
to those on other ships as they passed us by, their ship's horns
blaring out both a welcome and a heartfelt salutation. At that
moment I was filled with a sense of pride in both the uniform
that I wore and the fact that I represented a proud tradition of
Royal Navy seamen defending the British Isles from a wicked
and cruel foe, in my subconscious I knew that finally, it was now
our turn to strike back . . .

* * *

When we tied up next to the buoy the captain called us all
on deck. Standing in front of us he said, "You are now having
shore leave. It is now 1500 hours and the liberty boat will be
alongside our ship within one half hour. All crew going ashore
must return by 0700 hours in the morning . . ."

Burton, one of my closest friends on board, made some lame
joke about the lousy length of the liberty out the corner of his
mouth but soon changed his mind and jumped at the chance to get
ashore. He didn't fancy staying the night on the Sweet 'B' tied up a
half mile from the docks and the streets of London so tantalizingly
close by. Even if it was wartime and the sights and sounds of the city
had been dampened it was still better than being rocked to sleep
by a clanking anchor in the midst of a bunch of sweaty snoring
shipmates. We boarded the liberty boat with the majority of the
crew eager to taste the delights London had to offer. I thought all
this and the swimming was a bit of a doddle. *Best mission I've been
on,'* I thought. Burton was happy at the thought of a quiet beer. We
met up with other boys from the ship and went to a dance hall. It
was a welcome relief from being holed up in the radar hut and on
the bridge with binoculars looking out for Jerry subs. The dance
was a typical barn and farm affair with a live band, drums, piano,
accordion and guitar. Burton didn't like it and ended up consoling

himself by looking at the bottom of his beer mug time after time. I danced my sorry ass off with whomever would partner with me, there wasn't much chance of exercising on the Sweet 'B', deck space was limited and cluttered with the weapons of war. There were about thirty of us Royal Navy boys from various ships in the dance hall and a lot of wartime civilians. Dancing was good for being on a ship like the Sweet 'B', the ship rocked and rolled all the time because it was top heavy with the armaments she carried. If you weren't too good at balancing and took a fall on board you would definitely feel it the next day. I pretty much had to carry old Burton out of the hall he was so pissed, as we headed back to the ship he pleaded with me to find a nice bed and breakfast establishment. The drink was telling on me also, not the alcoholic beverages I had consumed but because the other boys and Burton had been tipping whiskey into my ginger beer shandy mug as a jest. I was so under the weather I thought every white line on the road was a hill and kept on stepping over them to avoid tripping. We found a guest house run by a pleasant middle aged lady who said, "Providing you don't make a noise and rumpus you can stay for five shillings each for the night . . ."

That was good and well for that was nearly all we had now after our evening's entertainment and dancing . . . Up the stairs we went to our room and a rough old bed with very clean sweet smelling sheets. It was hot for the beginning of June so I stripped off my uniform and slumped down on top of the sheets falling fast asleep. I think Burton was asleep by the time we got to the top of the stairs. He woke up in his inebriated state just long enough to remove his boots, lanyard and naval rig with Nelson's tie, and then started to snore. During the night I woke up and looked for the door to the toilet. I was still tipsy and stumbled around. I couldn't find it. I made my way back to the bedroom and fumbled around looking for a basin. I didn't see one but I spied Burton's boots and laughed to myself . . . It was 0600 hours when I woke old Burton up and said, "Time to go or we'll miss the boat." He was dragging his heels so I shunted him along, "C'mon now, we haven't all day, we'll be put on a charge if we don't get there on time . . ."

Burton slipped on his boots post haste, screaming, "Bloody hell!" he looked around aghast, "Someone's pissed in my boots!"

I tried to keep a straight face and not burst out in laughter. With a smile I chuckled, "I heard it rained last night . . ."

A second later I was out the door like a shot and running down the stairs with Burton after me mumbling unhappily. The woman stopped me briefly and said, "Wait, I haven't checked your room yet!"

I explained we had to get back to our ship and that we'd be back tomorrow then slipped out the front door. Burton had been accosted by the woman and wasn't so happy when he caught up with me as I strode quickly to the Thames and the liberty boat. "Hey, the old hag's taken all the rest of my money!"

I told him he'd spent most it on the beers the previous night except he was too drunk to remember. I gave him ten shillings anyway, especially since I'd taken liberty with his boots . . . enough said . . . this, at least, brightened the day up for him . . .

The boat was just leaving the jetty as we ran up. We had to jump for it and landed in a jumble amidst a bunch of half sober sailors. On board the Sweetbriar I reported to the bridge, "All present and correct, Sir . . ."

"Very well, Chapman," said our First Lieutenant Tom Brocus. He added curtly, "The captain wants to see the crew, now . . ." That was his way of saying something important was up . . .

* * *

When everyone was present and correct on the quarter deck, the captain ordered, "Everyone on the Sweetbriar has to write a letter home to their loved ones. The liberty boat will wait for one hour. So prepare them and get them on board before the hour is up, for in all probability the coming action will be hard on us . . ."

Standing on the deck with the other members of the crew we all knew we had a stiff battle ahead of us somewhere, I thought, *'They expect us to be in the thick of it with little or no chance of us seeing home again.'* After we had been dismissed I sat down on the quarter deck trying to write my letter to mummy and wondered how she would feel if I too disappeared under the waves as so many of our comrades had. My mind was in turmoil and it felt like I was writing a chapter of *War and Peace*. I kept screwing the pages up until at last I felt I'd said what I could, all the while I did so the thoughts of, *'This will be the last letter I ever write,'* crowded my mind :-

*Date and Place: NOT ALLOWED*
*Dear Mum,*

*Today we were told to write home. It doesn't seem as though we have much chance of returning from wherever we're going, so if anything does happen to me you'll know I've done my duty. I suppose you're busy doing your household chores. Have you played the piano recently? Have you heard from Jim or Ernie? I understand that the ship Arethusa was badly hit, is Ernie o.k.? Jim I heard is now in Italy. The Germans are on the run. Right now I can't tell you where we are going, not that I know for certain, I am not allowed to tell you where we are either.*

*I love you and dad. By the way, have you been to Wales yet to see Teddy and Alfie. Give them all my love. I must sign off now otherwise I'll miss the post. All my love and best wishes. Tell dad to get the car ready for me. I'll need it when I get home . . . o.k.*

*Love you, bye for now.*

*Your Ever Loving Son,*
*Naval speed, Stan, xxoo*

It would be another two days before we found out exactly where we were going and why . . .

* * *

On Monday the 5th of June 1944 at 0400 hours, "Action Stations!" was announced over the intercom, everybody was instantly alert and all drowsiness vanished as sailors tumbled out of hammocks or rolled off the top of lockers, pulling britches on and stuffing be-socked feet into boots, all the while on the run to their stations.

We left Sheerness and sailed up the River Thames. I couldn't believe my eyes as we headed up the river, troop carriers with thousands of troops lining the guard rails all waving and yelling at us. They knew we were there to protect them, our ship's horn let rip a few blasts in greeting. . . There was a huge troopship, a converted liner full of troops we were to escort, approaching us heading toward the English Channel. We turned around and sailed alongside it heading for the mouth of the Thames. The troops onboard leaned over the rails waved and saluted us as the big ship gave us two deep long blasts of its horn. Tom gave his signature horn blasts, "WHOOP! WHOOP! WHOOOOOOO . . ." In response to the men on the troopship every man on the upper decks and bridge of the Sweet 'B' returned their salutes. The Sweetbriar had pulled ahead of the troopship as we steamed through the Thames Estuary, the skipper then blew the ship's horn and whistle over the loud hailer. Everyone got a shock and it sent Whitey, our mechanic, scrambling up to the radar hatch. I was already on the bridge. He came up to me and said, "What the hell's going on, and what's all the fuss about?" he glanced astern and behind us at the troopship. "I wonder where they're going?"

"Same place we are, I guess, could be Gibraltar to support the 8th Army in Italy, or maybe France more likely . . ." I replied. I didn't have much chance to ponder over this for just then the captain ordered, "Action Stations!" I was closest to the radar hut so I flew through the hatch and switched on the three sets, reporting to the bridge, "Radar–Bridge. Echo bearing 15 degrees. Range 5 miles. Speed 12 knots–" I kept up a constant stream of information and because of this I knew we were now headed for France–and we would remain at Action Stations until the coming battle was over . . .

\* \* \*

I scratched my head, wondering, *'Where in France could we be heading?'* Not long after we were also joined by another huge troopship and a mass of landing craft before leaving the Thames Estuary. The two troopships steamed side by side with enough separation between them for the assault craft nestled in-between. Other vessels then appeared and formed up next to us in the course of the day, an MTB, some LCTs and TLCs. In the twilight of the gathering night sky of the 5th of June I saw a V-1 flying bomb overhead, then another and another. They flew overhead with their ominous *'Chug, Chug'* sound. We had been instructed not to fire on them, keep radio silence and be as quiet as possible as we headed toward France. They had said the air force would take care of them. Sure enough three Spitfires came diving down. One Doodlebug was blown up over the cliffs of Dover, one was turned around by a Spitfire by using its wingtip to gently nudge it back the way it had come, another was tipped gradually onto a south western course that would see it eventually running out of fuel and exploding harmlessly in the ocean. The final one was chased over Britain just past the white cliffs and was also shot down. The captain now confirmed our destination was France and that the invasion had begun and we would have the honor of being one of the first ships there. We were heading for Juno beach near the port of Caen. That night on the radio Vera Lynn sang her heart out to each and every one of us headed for France as *'There'll be Bluebirds over the White Cliffs of Dover'* played over and over again, it brought a smile to our lips and a warm feeling to our hearts . . . Another corvette joined our battle group with more landing craft carrying tanks, troops and cattle. I thought initially the cattle were for consumption then rationalized they could more likely be herded onto the beach to detonate the mines . . . *It would not have been the first time for an attacking force to use such tactics . . .*

\* \* \*

A great armada had left the shores of Great Britain to cross the English Channel with American, Canadian and British troops crammed into ships of all sizes and shapes, its destination, France . . . In the midst of this armada was a near insignificant Flower Class Corvette by the name Sweetbriar, she had sailed across the Atlantic braving icy seas and deadly German submarines, she was packed full of explosives, so much so that the slightest spark could send her to the bottom of the ocean in a blink of an eye with no survivors. But she was our ship, our home and we would not only protect her but also the thousands of men destined to shed their blood on the beaches of France, even if it meant sacrificing our own lives . . .

\* \* \*

D-Day, Tuesday the 6th of June 1944: The steady build-up of men and machines and the materiel of war had grown unabatedly in England, unbeknownst to the Nazi war-mongers in Germany and Europe. Intelligence had been gathered from every source possible by the Allied commanders and every effort had been made to lull the Germans into a false sense of security and misdirect them . . . All this effort had culminated in one day . . . The Longest Day . . . And on that early morning flight crews donned their flight gear and headed for ready rooms and then on to aircraft waiting silently on airstrips around East Anglia and other southerly counties of England. These metal beasts of war stood on hooves shod with rubber, their lances–.50 caliber machine guns and bombs, their hay–aviation fuel . . . it was time for Saint George to slay the dragon in France with gliders and aircraft that would disgorge their honorable men-of-war, and fighters and bombers to soften up ground forces . . . The tanks that had lined narrow country lanes around England had now disappeared, so had the servicemen and airmen from far off lands who now called England their second home. For many of them the dances they had enjoyed and drinks bandied about and spilt and drunk as others played darts and sang around pianos on dark cold nights, it would be the last time they felt the warmth of a feminine figure and tasted the white froth covering the top of a pint of The Banyers, or some other public house's, finest ale . . . And in the midst of this world gone mad the little town of Royston in Hertfordshire began to awake, a milkmaid delivered fresh farm milk, tea brewed on stoves of early risers and farmers stretched and yawned mobilizing themselves for the day ahead . . .

The engines of an aerial armada such as the world had never seen had belched and coughed into life, for an avenging force was on the move, a force that would ultimately lead to the destruction of Nazi Germany . . .

But life had been hard in Royston and the rest of Britain, for every city, town, village and hamlet had suffered the deprivation that the war had wrought upon her communities, as rationing had brought her citizens together and they shared what little they had and made do with what they had not, but now the *winds of war* were changing direction and the ill-wind which had continued to blow viciously over those green isles was about to be turned . . .

And in that small town of Royston, George Langridge, a member of the Royston Home Guard and ARP, and his wife Iris, arose before their two young children, David and Elizabeth. Iris put the kettle on the stove and prepared breakfast as George washed and shaved and dressed and prepared to go to work at the Farmers Manure Company he managed. For to increase the yields of farmers' crops this fertilizer was a sorely needed commodity and a vital part of the war effort. But they were still at war and the cellar of number 68 Orchard Road was fully prepared for the air raid sirens with food, water, beds, toys and books, and everything they would need should the Germans decide to make war on this little English country town . . . George went down the stairs with his square gold cufflinks, bought in Cambridge during WW1, dangling from one side of both sleeves. "Iris!" he called, "will you help me with these please?" Dutifully, Iris wiped her hands on her apron and went to the living room where George stood about to turn on the radio. He held one hand out and Iris threaded the gold link into the other side of the double cuff of his neat white pressed shirt . . .

Ernest Andrew Chapman, formerly of the Royal Field Artillery, stood on the driver's plate of his huge smoke belching iron-horse, he looked down at the darkened tracks afore him, then turned behind to look at the long train of munitions trucks behind. The early morning wind threatened to tug his cap off so he withdrew his head from the slipstream and looked at his gauges. He breathed uneasily for he knew that one German bomb would blow both him and his fireman, and the train, to smithereens . . . He glanced briefly at his silver pocket watch on a chain as they approached a small station, "On time!" he voiced loudly to his fireman. He reached up to blow the horn for the station master, an old friend of his, "Tooot! Tooot!" The station master stood on the small platform and waved as they passed . . . Next to Ernest his fireman was furiously shoveling black lumps of coal into the burner of the wartime black A4 . . . The long train disappeared down the tracks towards its destination. Night or day, rain or shine, the railways were forever on the move, transporting people, the soldiers, sailors and airmen of the armed forces, and moving foodstuffs and weapons of war, for this is also how a war is won as every man and woman sacrificed their dreams and wants for the greater good . . . And in the little village of Buntingford, Elizabeth Chapman, Ernest's wife, got out of bed and ambled down the stairs and headed for the kitchen. She filled up the kettle and put it on the stove and looked outside the window of her cottage at her little Victory Garden as the sights, sounds and tumult of a thousand and more Valkyries filled the skies up above . . . a whistling noise brought her out of her dream-like state as the kettle bubbled over with a rush of steam . . .

* * *

It was just before 0400 hours and a dark heavy mist still shrouded us in its womb-like midst. I was monitoring the coast very carefully and thought *'Surely they must have detected us by now?'* The troops were now being loaded onto the landing craft. There were so many of them it was impossible to count them; I just couldn't believe my eyes, both off and on my radar screen.

Our objective Juno beach was reached at 0400 hours and we were within shooting distance of the French coast. All around us silence reigned. The nearest French town was Caen, not that it mattered, this would be no stroll on the promenade or bathing in the cold sea under sunny skies, no French ice cream salesmen and no French girls wearing black berets carrying French loaves in baskets to welcome us with open arms. The only things that would now greet us would be German guns with projectiles manufactured in a country ruled by Nazis, barbed wire and anti-tank traps and booby traps all courtesy of Herr Hitler. All this and more was prepared for an Allied invasion force, its purpose, to spill blood, our blood . . .

I was glued to my screen making sure no German subs crept up on us unannounced when the first German shells were fired, their whistling awash with the sounds of small arms fire and that of the MG-41 which could fire 1200 rounds per minute, pretty much the same guns that had cut down so many British troops in the First World War, guns which my father and Uncle Albert had faced in the battle of Flanders and Verdun, and now I too would be facing that same foe, those same guns . . .

In the following minutes the hounds of hell broke loose, released by our jackbooted foes, their steel jacketed rounds striking the sides of our boat with such ferocity it belied imagination. Seaborne tanks were getting hammered and sank to the sandy bottom, their crews never to be seen again. The Sweetbriar was drawing heavy fire as it escorted its little friends and it sounded as if pails full of nuts and bolts were being hefted at us by a giant Germanic ogre, its strength that of a god, hell bent on us joining the poor souls in their sunken tanks. The battleship HMS Rodney wasn't in position yet as the first troops landed getting caught by mines attached to crossed breakwater beams and wires strung between them up to one hundred yards out into the sea, or leaping off the landing craft and dropping into deep water, not realizing that hidden under the murky depths was an undulating seabed, and then drowning as the weight of their equipment pulled them under. Every now and then a mine would explode on the beach and plumes of water would erupt in the sea around the Sweet 'B' and landing craft as the shore batteries let rip. German guns opened fire on the men as they ran up the beaches, many falling face forward onto the sand never to rise again . . . As dawn broke above us a thundering noise rent the blue azure sky apart as it rapidly filled with gliders and their airborne tractors. Some even towing three gliders at a time. Bombers paraded into the skies with fighters of every description belonging to the Allied Forces. It was packed so full it reminded me of Piccadilly Circus at rush hour . . . Landing craft were being hit and sinking around us and another ship down the line, a brand new Royal Dutch Navy vessel was hit. It exploded into a huge ball of fire sending shards of metal in all directions. When the smoke cleared nothing remained of it. There were no survivors of the all-Dutch crew . . . Was it a torpedo from a two-man sub or a shell fired from the

German shore batteries, no one would ever know . . . On that beautiful summer's morning hell hath no fury compared to that of the Germans who were as pissed as hell we had come to reclaim France back for the French people and kick them back to their own country . . . The German defensive lines were very tough, mines were attached to everything they could be, breakwater poles and the like, pillboxes and bunkers were everywhere and so was heavy artillery which started to bombard us with shells. The sky above erupted with anti-aircraft cannon sending Allied aircraft plummeting to the ground . . .

We were under strict orders not to stop for anyone or anything, we were not allowed to render assistance of any kind to another sinking vessel, we weren't even allowed to pick up casualties, we had to maintain our pattern and fulfill our duties to the letter whatever the cost. If we had stopped it would have meant the ship being at the mercy of German guns and mortars, or torpedoes from two-man subs. Losing was not an option, neither for us or the British and Canadian troops storming the beach in front of us. HMS Rodney had arrived and we were now marshaling barges around it to stop two-man Jerry subs from sinking it. All the while the radio played songs by Vera Lynn and *'Under the Lamp-Light'* by Marlene Dietrich. One ton shells started hammering the German positions from the Rodney. She had started her bombardment. The noise was deafening, just a thunderous roaring, as shell after shell exploded from her guns. A shell whistled past the bridge behind me and exploded just behind us. I said a little prayer to our maker as I kept up a steady stream of information to the bridge as German shells exploded around us, creating water spouts, as they tried to bracket us . . . The Rodney kept up her punishing regime of shells and never stopped to get her breath back, not even for one minute, she pulverized German positions. The Germans were no slouches either and their shore batteries and guns took a heavy toll on us shedding Allied blood by the buckets on the beach and venting their anger on ships and landing craft alike. As the Sweet 'B' made sure the Rodney was safe from a submarine attack she would at times find herself behind the Rodney which gave us a brief respite from the projectiles launched from German positions. The Sweet 'B's steel plates weren't as thick as the battleship's. All the same, the skipper ordered the helmsman to head as close as we could to the beach to protect the landing craft with our guns and the steel sides of our hull. It pained the captain to watch men die in front of him; he had had enough of seeing these small boats being pummeled by German cannon and being rent apart and sinking beneath the waves. He ordered the ship about and went in for the attack. Doing anything he could to save those brave men sacrificing their lives to take the beach-head. The Sweet 'B', eager for valor, would protect her little friends with her life's blood. It was at times like this that our ASDIC dome, Burton and Sears, were an indispensible part of the crew, for without them we would have run aground and been torn apart by cannon fire. We were a single fighting unit. The survival of both the ship and the men on board the Sweet 'B' required each and every one of us to perform our respective duties perfectly and in unison without letup. Even the lowliest of crew members was indispensible; all were a valued and important part of our battle for both survival and success against our enemy. . .

The smell of cordite hung heavily over the battle field, both on shore and over the sea surrounding the beaches . . . Blood flowed freely mixing with the waves and washing the beaches in its red hue . . . Under fire and under threat from our Germanic foe the Sweet 'B', its captain, Lt. Cdr. William Whitfield, its officers, Tom Brocus, Alf Cole, Lunn and every man aboard did their duty to the letter, never faltering, never wavering, not even for one second . . .

\* \* \*

Operation Overlord was a major pivotal point in the war against tyranny. The one major action that resulted in the Axis powers losing their grip on Europe. It forced them to be on the defensive instead of the offensive. Pressurizing them and causing them to lose balance. The Assault force consisted of some 4000 ships, both big and small, with an escort of 600 warships of the Allied navies. Its aerial assault was massive, 7000 fighters and fighter-bombers filled the skies above the beaches with 2,500 bombers tasked with softening up the German positions and forces, and innumerable gliders and paratroop aircraft. All this and 176,000 soldiers and their materiel, including specialized equipment to batter through beach obstacles, tanks, trucks, jeeps and everything else the combined American, British and Canadian forces would require ensuring the success of the operation. This huge combative force was threatened by bad weather at the beginning of June but cleared allowing Eisenhower to make the decision to attack on June 6th. But even with such great numerical numbers on their side the taking of Utah, Omaha, Gold, Juno and Sword beaches between Caen and Carenton was no easy task. The US 5th Corps were pinned down on the beach because they lacked equipment to deal with shore defenses and by midnight they had pushed forward to create a bridgehead of no more than one mile. Specialized armor that smashed through shore obstacles and detonated mines enabled British and Canadian troops to gain a good foothold of Gold, Juno and Sword beaches creating beach-heads to bring in more men and materiel . . . but all this relied on lives sacrificed and lost for the greater good, for on that day German guns, bullets, shells and mortar fire took the lives of many good men as they headed to the shore in landing craft and scrambled up the beaches . . . flew overhead . . . parachuted and glided in . . . defended the small seagoing landing vessels and pounded German positions . . . June 6th 1944 at 0630 hours, when the first soldiers made landfall on the beaches of France, was a day of bloodletting and sacrifice . . .

\* \* \*

By the following day the battle had pretty much been won and the beach-head had been taken for all intents and purposes, we continued on patrolling for two days until we were ordered to proceed to Portsmouth to pick up sixteen landing craft with 600 troops and equipment aboard. Then after delivering them safely we would leave Juno beach-head and proceed to Milford Haven where we would escort a mine inspection ship, the HMS Plover. After delivering the landing craft we turned about and headed into the mine swept channel toward Southampton. One hour away from our position at the beach-head a mist started creeping towards us. A very thick low sea mist enveloped us and wrapped its tendrils, cloak-like, around the ship. It had now become pea soup. I was now the eyes and ears of the Sweet 'B' . . . On my scope a blip appeared. I warned the bridge, "A large vessel approaching head on at approximately 15 knots. No indication of friend or foe!" It still came interminably on toward us with no response. The distance closed between it and the Sweet 'B' as I kept reporting its position. Our signalman on the bridge worked feverishly trying to contact the vessel and the captain picked up the loud hailer and called out in some very salty words, "What kind of bloody fools are you? The captain of your ship must be a complete and utter blithering idiot!" It was now very close and didn't alter its course one fraction of an inch, whoever the captain was he had made a terrible mistake and followed the wrong mine swept channel on their way to France. Tom ordered a 15 degree turn to starboard. Both our horns were blowing frantically as we tried to get a response from the idiots onboard the phantom ship . . . A huge bow loomed in front of us through the mist, it was a Chinese ship, a massive troop carrier, about to cleave us in two . . . It is the law of the sea that if two ships are approaching head on both must turn to starboard. The Chinese ship did nothing. The Sweet 'B' just managed to miss it and crested its bow wake. I looked up at the steel-plated sides of the huge vessel out of the hatch of the radar hut as it ran by us, *a troopship alright* . . . It had no radar . . . The captain ordered a change of course, he didn't want to risk another incident like that one. Our small corvette would be sent straight to the bottom and right into the hands of *Davy Jones* himself if a large troopship collided with us. We now headed for *Land's End* and the River Severn in South Wales . . . We had come so close to losing our lives in the heat of battle, even my radar hut had not been immune to German shells, one had punched through the steel plating near my head and exited through the steel on the other side, missing my head by an inch or two. It had then exploded leaving my ears ringing . . . *We had been fortunate not to have ended up scattered all over the ocean . . .*

# CHAPTER 12

## Victory at Last

The importance of protecting Britain and her shipping through the use of mines cannot be overlooked, and even the Germans were not averse to laying them outside a port or harbor for some unsuspecting ship to plough into. Corvettes like the Sweetbriar had multitudinous duties, not just escorting convoys and warships, protecting them from submarines and air attack, for the biggest advantage of the corvette was that it was highly flexible, well armed and equipped with the latest advances in radar and sonar technology. Though even with the advanced equipment we had we were not totally immune from mines, torpedoes, bombs and bullets. Every time we left harbor we were at risk . . . The Flower Class Corvettes had steel hulls that would attract a magnetic mine, some MTBs and minesweepers had wooden hulls that were suited to coastal waters were the mines were situated, but since the corvette plied the seven seas in rough deep water steel hulls were better suited. The mines were laid out in fields to protect the British coastline and areas of importance, especially shipping lanes and places such as ports and harbors. They were a deterrent to German submarines from attacking us on home ground, since we knew where the fields were and the Germans would have to find out for themselves. The mines were anchored to the seabed and held into place by chains. The mines had different lengths of chains which would enable the fields to present a veritable curtain of explosives to any submarine intending to penetrate them. And since they were magnetic and attracted to steel hulls the mine fields would be nigh impossible to traverse . . .

* * *

On the way to Milford Haven: The skipper, Tom and Alf set the Sweetbriar on a course for Milford Haven as per orders. We would now be escorting the Plover, a converted luxury yacht, on sea-mine inspection. I opened the hatch to the radar hut at 1600 hours after handing over to 'Whitey'. I stretched my arms and yawned; it had been a long day. The trip so far had been uneventful, especially after D-Day. I needed to sleep, and somewhere nice and quiet to relax and close my eyes. The past week had been very intense. We had been under constant threat all the time from subs, shore batteries and German aircraft. The operation had been a great success though and Allied forces now had a foothold on mainland Europe, and it was only a matter of time before the Germans were kicked out of France once and for all. I yawned again then nodded to Tom and Alf on the bridge before I made my way down the ladder to the mess. My position on the bridge and as a radar officer on board the Sweetbriar gave me access to a lot of operational information on ship movements and defensive strategies, and of course radar technology that was highly classified, even the frequency of our Identification Friend Foe equipment was of such high value to the Germans they would have sacrificed anything to get hold of it. The men on board knew I was privy to all sorts of intelligence and would always ask questions of me. As I headed for the mess two crew members asked what was going on and where were we going? I joked with them, "Well, there are twelve U-Boats in the area, so either they'll tin-fish us or we'll get them . . ."

They pushed the issue and asked what our next mission would be. I responded tongue in cheek, "We're heading for Milford Haven for three day's leave, so you can go home by train or stay with me and visit every pub and every dance hall we can find and meet some beautiful Welsh girls . . . That's our next mission . . . Just don't bring Paddy Black though . . ."

The men stood in the passage laughing as I ducked through another hatch to the mess for a mug of hot soup and a piece of bread as a chaser . . . I wondered whether I'd stay awake long enough to finish them off . . .

* * *

Getting to Milford Haven and a day's shore leave: There was no rest for the wicked and I felt drained the following morning as the Sweetbriar arrived in the estuary of the River Severn, as we steamed up it towards Milford Haven we passed several small fishing boats. The port at Milford Haven was very old; to me it appeared shabby in many respects. When at last we tied up at the jetty I noticed two tatty fishing boats tied up next to us. Compared to these relics the battle worn Sweetbriar looked like a new gold pin adorning some well-to-do's cape. The men were given shore leave almost immediately as the last stanchion was fastened. I quickly prepared myself with Burton standing over me impatiently pushing me to hurry up. He didn't want to waste even a second of our leave time. We scrambled ashore with the other men and sought out the nearest cinema, the movie didn't matter, anything to just have a break . . . As we rushed through town Burton slapped me on the back and said, "I thought we'd never see home again, 'Gus' . . ."

I smiled and replied, "The war's not over yet 'Bomb-head', the Jerries still have plenty of time to make our lives more miserable than they already are . . ." We both laughed as we spied a cinema not too far away, we strode over to it and chose a Fred Astaire and Ginger Rogers movie to watch, *something to laugh at and something to help us forget . . .*

* * *

The fisherman that fell into the sea: When we docked at Milford Haven we had a very shaky gangplank to the dockside which went up or down depending on whether the tide was in or out. The port was in blackout and the moon was hidden by clouds so one had to be careful navigating around the docks to find your ship. I was returning to the Sweetbriar after our shore leave. I had lost Burton in a dance hall somewhere along the way and as I threaded my way through the docks to our ship I heard cries for help. Rushing over to a large fishing vessel I saw a man struggling in the cold dark water between the boat and the jetty. I cast around and the only thing I could see was a ladder, grabbing it I managed to lower it down so the man could grab hold of it, which he duly did. He seemed a bit inebriated and had probably come from town after an alcohol fueled binge. It was coming up to 2200 hours and I was due to be back on the ship in a few minutes, being late was not an option but I wasn't going to let the poor man drown. As I held the ladder firmly I cast around for something to secure it to the jetty, as I did one of the dockyard hands came up and grabbed hold of the ladder, "You go back to your ship," he said, trying to take charge of the situation, "I've got everything under control . . ." He pulled the ladder away from me and jerked it upwards away from the drowning man. He then promptly dropped the ladder on the man's head sending him under the dark water. Another man from the docks jumped in and tried to get the man's head above water, he himself, then went under, he couldn't swim. I quickly went over to another trawler and found a life ring which I threw down. Man number two tried to grab hold of it but his flailing panicking fingers kept pushing it away. Both would be rescuer and the man he had tried to help disappeared under the black waters of the harbor . . . Should I have jumped in to save the first man, I didn't think so, he was so panicky there was a good chance he would have pulled me under as well . . . I headed back to our ship, I was due on watch shortly, I shook my head with disbelief, the whole thing had happened so quickly and I had had everything under control before that idiot pushed me aside because he knew best . . .

* * *

The mine laying vessel and escorting the Plover: As we steamed out of the Severn toward the Plover, which was a wooden vessel used to check on whether or not mines had broken loose from their moorings, a large vessel about four miles away passed in front of us. To me it looked like a cruiser or battleship it was so big. One of the other fellows on the bridge said it was the Manxman, a big mine-laying vessel. I wondered whether we would be checking on the new mines she would be laying. Mine-laying was highly skilled work, any mistake and the high explosive magnetic mines with detonator pins, called striking knobs, mounted on rods covering its round surface, would explode. Both the British and German navies used them to protect sensitive coastal areas . . . It wasn't long before we picked up the Plover and headed towards our inspection area. The mines were laid in fields across the Irish Channel and we were very careful to stay just outside the mined areas. We had the authority to detonate any free floating mines we came across. Any mistake on our part would have deadly consequences . . .

The weather in the Irish Channel is wont to be fickle, one day the weather could be atrocious and another as good as it gets on a fine English summer's day. Today the sea-gods had been kind to us and it was a beautiful day with hardly a breeze. Normally the Irish Sea is choppy at the best of times but today it was calm. The Plover moved ahead of us and was about two miles away cruising through a damned minefield, it was not my idea of fun, but at least the Plover had a wooden hull and the mines wouldn't be attracted to it, while we, on the other hand, we had a steel hull and any mine broken loose from her moorings would be attracted to us like a moth to a flame. But thank goodness we were operating just outside the minefield, still, that didn't negate the fact that one of those damned spiky round hunks of metal and explosive wouldn't be attracted to our steel hull and blow us to *Kingdom Come* and back, and besides, how far were we from the minefields or were we in the damned middle of them? I wondered. We received instructions from the Plover to be on the lookout for some mines that had broken loose she had spotted. It was now up to us to detonate them. Once the mines were armed the best way to deal with them was to hit the detonator plungers on the tips of their spikes. Of course you wouldn't want to go up to the blamed thing and do it since the explosion would shred you and the ship you were on into a million tiny pieces. Our tactic was to utilize the venerable Lee Enfield .303, and hit it with a bullet and not a stick, providing you were well away from it. Two of our gunners stood on either side of the bridge .303s in hand looking mean and nasty for the spiked suckers. I scanned the sea around us intently from my vantage point on the bridge and was the first one to spot a mine. Our rifleman on the port side let rip a whole clip without any success and I felt like saying to him, *'Give me the rifle you idiot, I'll get it with one shot'*, I didn't though and after he'd reloaded he struck the pin–The mine blew up with such a deafening roar it made me deaf for a couple of minutes afterwards–my ears continued to ring for another half hour. Not long afterward we spotted another. When it exploded it seemed even louder than the first one. We never saw another until late in the afternoon when the waves had got a lot choppier and it bobbed up and down so much so that our gunners just couldn't get bead on the spikes. Eventually the Plover detonated it sending a massive plume of water into the sky. The sea was becoming rougher by the minute as we pulled away from Southern Ireland and the afternoon was rapidly turning to dusk . . .

* * *

The fishing boats and the U-Boats: It was a dark night in the Irish Sea as the Sweetbriar continued to escort the Plover, I was glued to the 271PQ screen in front of me trying to pick out U-Boat periscopes from the flotsam and jetsam that floated listlessly in the waters around us, and of course, any surfaced mine that might have the name Sweetbriar stenciled on it. No self respecting Kriegsmarine U-Boat captain would have dared to surface in these waters. I had relieved 'Whitey' about twenty minutes ago after standing on the bridge keeping watch with Alf Cole. From our vantage point high up on the bridge we could see the Sweetbriar's bow wave and stern wake in the all enveloping darkness around us. Both were a brilliant foamy white riding on bright green phosphorous waves. Above us spread a million stars reflected off the sea below us. It was a surreal scene and one would never have suspected we were at war. As the green line rotated around the screen in front of me I thought of Ireland and County Cork not too far distant. My mind idly wondered what it would be like to swim there. I had always had a hankering to visit Cork especially after listening to the many fireplace stories both my grandfather and grandmother had delighted in regaling to the Chapman boys sitting on comfortable cushions by roaring logs casting their heat and orange glow upon us in the dead of winter. Those days were gone, dead and buried with the war along with Grandpa and Grandma O'Sullivan. I missed both of them and their Irish laughter and humor filling our house with happiness and mirth. I now inhabited a half life, a purgatory somewhere between life and death with little or no contact with both siblings and parents. My family now consisted of my shipmates aboard the Sweetbriar. At least that is how it felt since I was becoming estranged from my real one. It all seemed so long ago, an eternity in fact. Knowing Cork was not too far distant made me feel homesick, homesick for a place I had but heard about from my grandparents. I continued to focus on the screen in front as Alf popped his head through the hatch, "Would you like some hot chocolate?" he asked. "Of course . . . need you ask . . ." I smiled back at him. Alf duly went and got both him and me a steaming mug then settled back on his watch staring quietly at the briny sea surrounding us and the Plover not too far away on our portside. I took a sip of the hot brew in my hand. At the same moment my mug touched my lips I picked up three contacts that from their radar signature looked like fishing vessels. I spoke into my microphone, "Radar–Bridge, have contact, Sir, small echoes, suspect they have no indication friend or foe. Bearing 080. Distance 2 miles. I think they are fishing boats. Suggest you give warning of mine fields in the area. A submarine could be sitting with them as camouflage . . ." It was an old trick and one of the U-Boat tactics was to use other vessels in the area they were operating in to disguise themselves . . .

On the bridge in front of the radar hut Alf said, "Sound bell . . . Action Stations!" The bell rang and every man aboard jumped into action closing bulkhead watertight doors and leaping to their stations. Alf ordered, "Alter course to 080 degrees. Increase speed to 16 knots."

We barreled down on the contacts quickly and came across the first boat, an Irish fishing vessel as I had suspected. The skipper and Tom had now joined Alf up top. Tom hailed them, "Bridge to captain of fishing boat–You are too close to mined area. Warn your other vessels to move south! Repeat, you must move south . . ."

The captain of the fishing boat waved in acknowledgement and shouted back that he would comply with our orders. I went back to my radar set and continued my scan. Nothing seemed amiss and I couldn't find head or tail of a submarine. The Sweetbriar keeled about and returned to its escort position adjacent to the Plover. Not long after we escorted her back to Milford Haven. We had been with her in the Irish Sea for 42 hours now. I looked forward to at last getting some uninterrupted sleep . . . my eyes had become weary after a constant four hours on and four hours off radar duty and watch on the bridge due to insomnia and the stuffy decks below . . .

Sleep was not mine to have and in a few hours I would be back on duty again. Rays from the early morning sun struck my face as I reached the ladder to the bridge. The officer of the watch was just coming down and said to me, "Prepare for departure from the mine fields . . ." I breathed a sigh of relief, to me it couldn't be too soon. I climbed up the ladder to get info for my operational duties for the day. Dawn had broken fully over the Irish Sea while I was on the bridge discussing the day to come with Tom and Alf. Below me I could see the waves were becoming rougher due to the wind from the North West over Southern Ireland. The order to leave had come none too soon. If we couldn't see the mines we had a good chance of running into one. The waves and sea spray were now hitting the bridge. I went back down to the mess for breakfast. When I got there the cook noted, "Stan, we've run out of potatoes, could you get some for me, please?"

I popped up top to the locker just behind the pompom gun, opened it, *'No potatoes,'* oh well, *'we'll just have to do without,'* I thought. Down in the mess I told the cook we'll be in Milford in about two hours so why don't we just have some fried tinned sausages. Bangers and mash was a favorite on board so sour faces were the order of the day when everyone found out there'd be no mash. We sat down to have a meal with the second favorite added on our plates, tinned bacon rashers. I'd just had my first mouthful when 'Whitey', our radar mechanic, came down from the bridge, "Officer of watch wants you back on watch for an hour while the charts are surveyed and we leave the Plover here and then report back to Milford Base, Stan . . ."

I reported back to the bridge and was briefed, and they relied on my experience to pick out the correct return channel we would use. The responsibility lay heavily on my shoulders, one mistake and we would find ourselves blown to smithereens. After we finished with the navigation charts I thought, *'Now I can finish my breakfast,'* no chance, the officer of watch stated, "Now I need you to check the armaments list and the ammunition that was used . . ."

"Aye, aye, Sir," I said as I began my inspection and checking. Every time we made landfall and reported back to a shore base in Britain we would make a thorough inspection and account for every round, depth charge and shell that had been spent or used in action. Failure to do this and running aground could have serious repercussions. Harsh words from the Admiralty would be a lesser punishment, being sent to one of the Admiralty bases called Barrack Stanchions was more severe. This punishment was reserved for those who disobeyed orders or bad judgment calls and mistakes. Any costs incurred to the navy were always added up. There was never a, "Oh, hello, good on you old fellow, you returned safely . . ."

No, it was more like, "This is what you did wrong old man and you will pay for it . . ."

Whenever we arrived back in Liverpool we always waited tensely for the skipper to return with the leather bag with our instructions, whatever they may be. The skipper was accountable for all things and he had to tread lightly and leave no tracks . . .

Returning to Milford the sea was very choppy and the waves had become much bigger, they were now breaking over the bow. If we had stayed escorting the Plover we would have struck a mine for sure . . . I prayed I had made the right decision and chosen the right mine free channel for the Sweetbriar's return . . .

We made landfall at Milford without any problems and I breathed a sigh of relief and said a special thank you to God. We had another few hours leave and I intended to watch another movie I had seen advertized on a poster at the cinema . . .

After our quick leave and my movie I walked up the gangplank and was back on the ship again. It wasn't very long before the skipper returned with the ubiquitous leather bag, in short order we would be returning to Liverpool and readied for our next mission . . . The trip back would see us patrolling Southern Ireland and up the Atlantic coastline . . . When we shipped out of Milford Haven it was on a beautiful summer's day, the captain sounded the Sweetbriar's siren to say thank you to Milford and the awesome reception we had had from one and all . . .

\* \* \*

Patrolling the Atlantic seaboard of Ireland: The Sweetbriar slipped out of the Severn and made its way quietly and with as little fuss as possible to the coast of Southern Ireland. The size of the waves had changed considerably and instead of the big waves we had ploughed through on our way back to the Severn we now had good clear weather and calm seas. As I said, the weather in the Irish Channel is a fickle mistress, one day blowing cold and the next hot . . . We kept close to the coast and I kept a keen lookout for U-Boats and any suspicious activity around us. We had been warned to look out for German subs offloading operatives and fifth columnists onto Irish beaches. Once past Cork we headed north up the coastline. Most of the crew couldn't wait to get back to Liverpool and then back home on leave. I focused on the job at hand not wanting to jinx our good luck so far, for any lapse of concentration on my part could well send us to the bottom of the ocean with a tin-fish up our kazoo. With a stiff Atlantic swell on our port beam we rolled heavily. The waves kept on increasing in size and I was thankful after one and a half days of rolling swell when we at last turned eastwards to Londonderry. It was the border between

Northern Ireland and the farthest northern part of the Irish
Republic. We now had a stern sea which made walking on the
brine soaked decks a lot easier. It wasn't long before we entered
the Irish Sea from its most northern end with Scotland and the
Clyde coming up on our port side. The skipper always took great
interest in our radar and would always be delighted when he saw
the mouth of the River Clyde on my screen. He knew we were
now nearly home all in one piece, and he could breathe a sigh
of relief . . . *Another mission was over and we were still all alive* . . .

* * *

New orders: After we got back to the Liverpool and Albert
docks we were given shore leave with the prospect of a mission
to the Mediterranean on the cards in the future. When I heard
this I was thrilled at the prospect of revisiting Gibraltar then on
to Malta and the rest of the Mediterranean, hopefully. Granted,
we had a lot of work to do in the meantime, but that night
after I had received the *buzz* I dreamt of porpoises swimming
gracefully next to the Sweetbriar, warm sand between my toes,
the warm rays of the sun on my face, Spanish guitar music and
sweet Spanish maids. I couldn't wait to get to the Med; I thrilled
at the prospect . . .

* * *

Back to the Mediterranean: The time was nearly 2300 hours
or 11:00 pm at night for land lubbers, and a cold 1945 chill ran
up the Mersey out to the harbor and the Irish Sea beyond. We
had just loaded all our supplies and replenished our armaments
and were bound for Gibraltar and the Mediterranean. The sea
was relatively calm as we slipped out of Birkenhead opposite
Liver Building in Liverpool. Going out the Mersey runs very
fast as it does when the tide comes in. I had never heard of
anyone swimming across from Liverpool to Birkenhead, they
would be quickly whipped out to sea and never seen again even

though the distance across was only about one and a quarter miles. Other than, that is, our shipmate jumping overboard because of wife troubles. Going out with the tide didn't even necessitate switching on the engines as long as visibility was good. We hardly ever turned on ours when leaving with the tide. In the dark looming before us was a big Chinese freighter with its red bow light and stern green light gleaming bright under a moonless night sky. Naturally we headed to what we thought was the stern of the ship proudly displaying the green light, not wanting to run the risk of fouling her anchor chain. I had gone down to the mess to make myself a jam sandwich when the ship started to keel over. There was a loud grating and tearing sound under my feet coming from the hull of our ship. I bolted up the ladder topside still holding my jam sandwich. Reaching the deck and clawing for a railing I tried to hold fast. The ship was now at a 50 degree angle and in danger of turning turtle. I heard a loud tearing sound and knew our ASDIC dome had just been ripped off. Looking at the big Chinese ship while clutching the railing and trying to keep my feet on the deck I could see we were running up her anchor chain, some bright spark had put her green stern light on the bow and the red bow light on the stern. Our corvette was in real danger of rolling over and I prepared myself to leap into the dark waters below when of a sudden our ship lurched back and steadied herself, we were clear of the anchor chain . . .

Everyone on board was looking forward to our Mediterranean combat cruise, and now, due to someone's idiocy, we would be laid up for repairs . . . I remembered the jam sandwich in my hand and finished it off quickly, staring out into the dark sea beyond . . . *swell, just swell* . . .

\* \* \*

We all wondered whether we would get out to sea and back in action. There wasn't one soul aboard who didn't relish the chance, we loved our ship and the whole complement of men worked like a well oiled machine on her. HMS Sweetbriar was our home, our adopted mother and we would all defend her with every last drop of blood we had in our bodies . . . Besides, we all loved the Mediterranean, especially me in particular. I loved the Spanish guitar music they played in bars and restaurants, the food, the weather–everything about it was home to me and I relished the chance to get back to Gibraltar and Spain. Every night I prayed that the next day was to be the Sweetbriar's last in dock and that soon we would be underway yet again to the warm sunny seas and skies of the Mediterranean with its dancing porpoises flitting next to her hull.

* * *

The war was coming to an end: It was like an ocean swell that just kept on coming, war's end, and an unstoppable conclusion to all the fighting and strife we had experienced and been witness to. Events we had no control over were gradually overtaking us. The Mediterranean combat cruise with everything Hitler could throw at us, and we had all been looking forward to, might not happen at all. The Allied forces were gradually pushing Hitler's forces back throughout Europe with the goal of finally crushing him once and for all in sight. I understood Jimmy was still in Italy with his unit, where the end of hostilities had drawn to a close. The Italian fascists with their Germanic overlords had capitulated after stiff fighting and the loss of many Allied soldiers. Whatever gains had been made by the Allies was accompanied by the tremendous sacrifice of its foot soldiers. They laid down their lives for King and Country. On board the Sweetbriar things were morose, nobody knew what was going to happen after the war ended, not one soul wanted to leave the ship. We didn't have a small transistor radio on board the ship, they were too expensive, so any news we had was second hand, either from the dockies or a snippet shared here and there when we went ashore. The ship had grown very quiet and dull, the normal joyous banter between shipmates had ceased. Mail had all but stopped being delivered and I had not heard from dad or mum, or my brothers in a long time. It was hard to say whether the censors had scrubbed them or they had been disposed of, I couldn't tell. Maybe they expected us to be de-mobbed and it wasn't worth passing them on, but at any rate we were starting to feel cut off from the outside world and the Admiralty itself . . . Our reason for being was starting to evaporate . . . I cursed at the stupid sailors aboard that damned Chinese ship, they had ruined the Mediterranean cruise and our chance of laying over in Gibraltar, at least we could have consoled ourselves under the warm sun with exotic Spanish drinks listening to the gentle strumming of a guitar or joining in the camaraderie around a piano with other sailors, maybe even a smattering of *pongoes* as well if it came to the push . . . By the sad-sack look upon the skipper's face and those of Tom's and Alf's, they felt the same way . . .

* * *

Victory Europe: The war in Europe, Asia and North Africa had taken a tremendous toll on both humanity, resources and infrastructure, by June of 1941 Hitler had attacked Russia with Operation Barbarossa and the fates of both Allied and Axis powers had vacillated in North Africa. In November of 1941 German military might had reached the gates of Moscow. Around the same time Rommel had attacked Tobruk. In December the Russian winter had bit into the German advance and stopped it in its tracks; Rommel, too, was bogged down . . .

The following year on June the 28th Hitler began a renewed offensive against Russia eventually attacking Stalingrad in August of 1942. In North Africa Rommel pushed into Tobruk which surrendered in June. All the while the Arctic, Atlantic and Mediterranean convoys had come under concerted attack by the

Germans to cut off Britain, Russia and Malta from any supplies, thereby stopping them from waging war against their foe. The German U-Boat fleet did their utmost to smash convoys coming into, and leaving from, Britain. The Battle of the Atlantic was waged relentlessly and unceasingly by Hitler, and things seemed to be going well for him and his Germanic hordes . . .

Malta was a major thorn in Rommel's side and was under constant attack by everything the German's had at their disposal. Most of the ships leaving Britain to resupply the island were sunk, few managed to get through. The Pedestal Convoy barely scrapped through with a few ships but this managed to keep Malta going during the height of the German aggression . . .

Eventually the war in North Africa started to turn as Montgomery defeated Rommel at El Alamein on the night of October the 23rd and the early hours of the morning of the 24th in 1942. On November the 8th US forces landed in North Africa to kick the Germans out. A little later on the 19th the Russians launched a counter attack at Stalingrad and forced the German VI Army, under the leadership of Paulus, to surrender what was left by the end of January 1943. In an effort to halt the Russian advance Manstein launched a counter offensive but couldn't hold the Ruskies back for long. In June the German's lost the Battle of Kursk, a major mechanized tank assault launched by both sides in the Russian theatre. They continued to push the German forces back and by the end of the year the Russians had gained the ground they had lost and established bridgeheads across the River Dniepr. The tide had turned against Hitler and his jackbooted forces and on May the 13th 1943 the remaining Axis forces in North Africa surrendered . . .

The Allies invaded Sicily in July 1943, and in September they landed in Southern Italy. The Allies drive to Rome was stopped by Kesselring and by December a stalemate at Monte Cassino halted the Allied advance. In January 1944 Leningrad was relieved after a long and terrible siege, its people, on the verge of starvation, resorted to cannibalism to survive. Sebastopol was retaken by the Russian army in May while the Ukraine was taken by the Germans . . .

After a bombardment that saw over twenty thousand tons of bombs falling on the 15th Century historic buildings of Monte Cassino, destroying most of it and leaving little standing, it fell on June the 4th of 1944. After this the Allied forces had a cakewalk into Rome. Two days after it fell on June the 6th the Allies landed on the beaches of Normandy in France which signaled the beginning of the end for the German occupation. While the Allies fought from hedgerow to hedgerow on French soil the Russians pushed forward their counteroffensive seeking the blood of Hitler and the capitulation of Germany. In mid July they entered Poland and by the end of July they had reached the Vistula. While their fortunes waned against the Russians in August of 1944 the Germans took Czechoslovakia. However, Paris was liberated by the end of August and the Russians were on the outskirts of Warsaw in Poland. The Germans had no intention of letting go of Poland without a fight and crushed a gallant Polish uprising between August and September of 1944. Eventually the Germans withdrew and the Russians took Warsaw on October the 2nd of the same year. While the Russians advanced through Poland the Allies advanced toward the Rhine . . . Hitler's back was broken and his forces were on the verge of defeat, his Thousand Year Reich was coming to an end, his factories and cities were being bombed day and night by British and American bombers and the crème and might of his army with its stalwart young men had been emaciated on the field of battle on all fronts, leaving only old men and young boys to take their place. Hitler lost the Ardennes in the Battle of the Bulge to Allied forces in December of 1944 and the Russians continued to the Oder River which they reached on January 31st of 1945 . . . In a last ditch effort Hitler tried to retain the Balaton oil fields on the 6th of March. The following day the Allies crossed the Rhine over the bridge at Remagen. On April the 12th the Allies reached the Elbe. Vienna fell to the Russians on April the 14th and by the 16th the Russians approached Berlin from two fronts. On April the 30th 1945 the Reichstag fell . . .

It was said that Hitler died in his bunker after taking a cyanide pill with Eva Braun by his side in Berlin as both the American and British forces approached from the west and the Russians from the east. A fortune in gold, diamonds, precious works of art and counterfeit currency disappeared as Germany and the Third Reich fragmented and broke apart. Much of this was transported to far flung countries and away from war torn Europe. It was said the Germans even had a secret base in the Antarctic where they continued projects without the threat of Allied bombs and interference. Favorite places of refuge were South West Africa and Argentina. Land was purchased and a portion of Europe's spoils ended up there. Long range submarines left from Norway on route to them . . . The only way to escape the bunker in Berlin was in a hospital tank bound for Tempelhof airport. It was reported that Flug Kapitan Peter Baumgart took Adolf Hitler, his wife Eva Braun and certain die-hard loyalists by plane from Tempelhof airport in Berlin to Tondern in Denmark. At the time Tondern was firmly controlled by German forces. From there they flew to Kristiansund in Norway which was still under German control. A German submarine convoy had sat waiting for unusual cargo. The Junkers that had supposedly taken Hitler and his party to Norway returned to Tondern and dropped a message saying that the Führer had been safely delivered . . . A German submarine commander revealed under interrogation by the American CIC that he and at least ten other submarine commanders had received orders to be at constant readiness, 'Besonderen Verfugung', and directly under the Führer's command. Further CIC interrogations found that twelve flight captains had been issued with secret orders to be in a constant state of readiness for the transportation of Hitler to a destination unknown . . . On May 2nd 1945 a convoy of large U-Boats left Kristiansund and headed to the South Atlantic running silent and running deep . . . In the long voyage south one of them got lost, a U-Boat carrying enough cigarettes to last 30 years. Each submarine in the convoy carried a specific cargo, one gold, one filled with art pieces, one with ammunition, one with food, and so on . . . and one, the most precious cargo of all, the Führer . . . After the voyage a large party of Nazi die-hards and their supplies were dropped off on a deserted piece of coastline in Argentina and left in a convoy of awaiting trucks and automobiles . . . Since 1933 the Nazi Party had cultivated South America with its doctrine which was readily accepted. Especially since hundreds of thousands of Germans had settled in Brazil and Argentina. Donitz once claimed that his U-Boat fleet had been instrumental in setting up a veritable oasis in South America. Reports surfaced that Hitler had escaped to an oasis in South America. Admiral Donitz was made Commander in Chief of Germany by Hitler before he disappeared off the scene . . . Over the skies of Tempelhof airport German jets circled unceasingly to defend the airspace while Russian troops advanced from the east. The order of the day was escape from Tempelhof or be captured. At 4:15 pm on April the 30th 1945 a Ju-52 landed filled with SS troops all under the age of 18; they had come directly from Rechlin for the defense of Berlin. The gunner and engineer on the aircraft got out to refuel it. The radio operator jabbed him in the ribs and pointed to what looked like an Arado 234 or Messerschmitt 332 jet aircraft. The Arado's turbojets gave it a range of 4000 kms and it would be fast enough to escape from enemy fighters but would need a longer tar or concrete airstrip to land on. Standing in front of it was none other than Adolf Hitler wearing a field grey uniform gesticulating animatedly at some Nazi Party functionaries seeing him off while his plane was being fueled and readied for flight. The plane took off at around 4:30 pm. The engineer and radio operator were stunned at hearing of Hitler's death on the radio, they thought the aircraft had crashed. They were even more dumbfounded when they heard he had died in Berlin after committing suicide seven and a half hours after they had seen him. There was not enough time for him to get back, and, at that time, it would have been near impossible to reach the bunker. And, it seems illogical that it was his double, the baker, at Tempelhof airport . . . Months before Hitler had ordered a special aircraft to leave Berlin with medical and dental records of top Nazis for an unknown destination . . . The Germans, with their normal efficiency, had paperwork and information on every German citizen, so even with the turmoil which had reduced much of the country to broken brick and masonry it was still possible to account for every individual German citizen. The Germans were incredibly fastidious when it came to paperwork . . .

Lieutenant Heimlich of the American CIC had the responsibility to check on all rumors and reports relating to the whereabouts and death of Hitler. In the end he came to the conclusion that Adolf Hitler, his wife Eva Braun and Martin Bormann were still alive as there was not a shred of verifiable evidence that they had actually died . . . An INS report indicated it would have been impossible to reduce a corpse to ashes with one can of gasoline in an open space. Stalin stated that Hitler had escaped to Argentina. Still, the war against Hitler and the Nazis finally ended on May the 8th 1945 when Germany officially surrendered . . .

* * *

Victory Japan: On December the 7th 1941 the Japanese attacked Pearl Harbor and the United States officially entered the war. The Japanese had already taken China, Korea and Manchuria and within a short while followed their conquests with a vast swathe of the Pacific islands, Malaya and Burma. The government of the Dutch East Indies surrendered to them on March the 8th 1942 with the remaining British and American forces in Bataan, Corregidor and the Philippines surrendering in short succession. Little thought did the Allied soldiers give to incarceration by the Japanese at that time. They were soon to learn what capture meant to the Japanese, by the beheadings and the utter disregard of life and the complete disdain of prisoners by the Japanese; blood flowed by the gallon in Singapore harbor as thousands of residents were beheaded or butchered and cut into pieces then thrown into the water. The conquered indigenous populations were used for live bayonet practice and others used as targets for their riflemen. Japanese savagery was unbridled as surviving sailors from Allied shipping were forced to run a gauntlet of knives, clubs and swords off submarines and ships, in the end plunging into shark infested waters of the Pacific Ocean and China Sea. Prisoners, by the thousands, died on forced marches. Imprisoned, captives were fed little or nothing and ended their lives as emaciated skeletons . . .

By May the 15th 1942 British forces withdrew behind the River Chindwin. Between May the 3rd and 8th the Japanese tried to seize Port Moresby but were stopped in the Coral Sea. On June 4th 1942 they suffered another defeat when the tide turned and they lost the Battle of Midway. Far to the east the US Marines were struggling to get a foothold on Guadalcanal. The war in the Pacific was waged one island at a time, one atoll at a time as the US forces forged across the now bloody Pacific. In June 1943 they were fighting for control of the central Solomon Islands. In November they took the Gilbert Islands and in February of 1944 the Marshall Islands . . .

On the East Asian mainland the British launched a second Arakan campaign in December of 1943, however, by March 1944 the Japanese countered with attacks on Imphal and Kohima. The Japanese were now under pressure and in June Kohima and Imphal were retaken . . . In the Pacific the Battle of the Philippine Sea raged and enabled US forces to land on the Marianas. On October the 20th American forces returned to the Philippines and Leyte after the Battle of Leyte Gulf. In February and March of 1945 American Marines fought bloody battles on Iwo Jima, eventually crushing the Japanese . . .

With sheer brilliance, Slim's 14th Army recaptured Meitila and Mandalay in Burma. The Japanese were now being defeated on many fronts. The next island to fall under the control of the Allies was Okinawa on April the 1st. It was a crushing defeat on the homeland doorstep for the Emperor of Japan and his cronies. Not long afterward on May the 3rd Rangoon was retaken, and after stiff fighting on the Island of Okinawa all hostilities ceased in the third week of June. Mopping up operations continued in the Philippines as Operation Olympic, an assault on Kyushu, was scheduled for November 1945, and Operation Coronet was scheduled for March 1946; this was to be an all out attack of Honshu, the biggest island in Japan. To save American lives the first atom bomb was dropped on Hiroshima on August the 6th – the second on August the 9th. The Russians, ever eager to gain territory, declared war on Japan on August the 9th when they were sure Japan was finished and unable to defend itself. Russia invaded Manchuria on the same day to seize it before Japan surrendered. The atomic bombs were the last straw for a defeated and crumbling Japan . . . On September the 2nd of 1945 Japan formally surrendered on board the USS Missouri in Tokyo Bay . . .

In the end Britain's Empire days were drawing to a close, Germany and much of Europe had been reduced to a pile of rubble. Many of Germany's historical buildings had been destroyed, its population now bitterly regretting the part they had played in Hitler's rise to power and the war itself. The lives of European Jews stood in tatters with over 6 million having died of starvation in concentration camps and so many gassed to death. The bombs dropped on Hiroshima and Nagasaki had ushered in the nuclear era, a new way in which to forge weapons of war and de-ploy them. 55 million people had lost their lives in the Second World War as a direct result of warfare and 25 million died as a result of disease and starvation. Society had fractured and family closeness with it, *the old world was dead and in its stead stood a brave new world* . . .

# Chapter 13

## De-mob

**F**our years I spent on the Sweet 'B' with so many near death experiences I had lost count. I had done my duty and fought high seas and wind and German submarines to escort the nation's vital supplies to her in a time of need. We had been attacked by Jerry aircraft, U-Boats and their tin-fish, and battleship formations all intent on sending us to the bottom of the sea, and done our duty at D-Day. On our corvette with a complement of seventy three men you would be hard placed to find somewhere to sling your hammock. My radar hut was one and a half yards square, a refrigerator in winter and an oven in summer. Day in and day out it had to be manned . . . I now felt lost–empty–my reason to exist had departed in my mind–I was now worthless . . . flotsam thrown to the wind . . . none of us received a hero's welcome, the war had ended and that was that . . . no ticker tape parades, no jolly well done my man, no sexy broads taking you in their arms and planting a wet kiss on your face, no, to me the war had ended not with an epiphany or an exalted joyous shout, no, it had just fizzled out to nothingness . . . All those men who had sacrificed their lives and their futures now lay in white crossed graves across Europe, or, they lay rotting quietly at the bottom of briny oceans, and in the end nothing would be left of them except maybe a solid pair of naval leather boots. There would be no grave markers for those men, but for as long as their close relatives kept them in their prayers they would be remembered. And for how long, even they eventually would succumb to Death's gates . . . and in time their sacrifices would mean nothing, no more than just a grain of silicate on a beach somewhere being trod underfoot by a beachcomber . . .

\* \* \*

Leaving HMS Sweetbriar to HMS Blackcat: While repairs were being done on the Sweet 'B' new orders came through on the seventh day, the war for the Sweetbriar was over and we were to be de-mobbed. Every single man on the ship was shocked speechless. I couldn't believe it. I didn't know what I would do or what the future had in store for me. I was totally unprepared for what would happen after the war. This was our way of life the war, pure and simple, but now we were warriors without a battle to fight. Actually, I never thought the war would end, that it would continue on forever and ever. It never occurred to me that at some point it would end. The Sweet 'B' was my life, my love, my family. There was no-one now I could count on, mum had grown older and so had my brothers. In my mind I had grown distant and apart from the nurture I had been given growing up, I, like Romulus and Remus now suckled at the teats of a new mother, the Sweetbriar. I had grown fond of her and viewed her as a substitute parent. While we were berthed at Albert dock waiting for our de-mob a stoker onboard the Sweet 'B' fell overboard between the ship and the jetty. Lucky for him we managed to get a rope around him in cowboy fashion with a noose and pulled him aboard. What an ignominious end it would have been for the stoker, going through the whole war on the Sweetbriar then drowning a day or two before being de-mobbed . . .

There was nary a word said to the crew as we boarded two trucks headed for HMS Blackcat, a shore station in Manchester.

No final line-up, no de-brief or thank you from the captain, no nothing . . . A simple heartfelt adieu would have been nice . . . it would have made the world of difference . . . as navy men we had shed our blood and tears in wild abandon on the open seas fighting our enemy, and now, at war's end, nothing . . . not even a perfunctory nod of acknowledgement . . . *Inwardly I felt disgusted* . . . If I had been the captain I would have shaken the hand of every man aboard and piped them off with their chins held high like a hero, for, to me, every man who had served aboard the Sweet 'B' was . . .

\* \* \*

25 pounds and a new suit: Arriving at HMS Blackcat we jumped out of the trucks and headed for the living quarters. I must say I was impressed, they were very neat and clean and for wont of a better word, charming . . . We were allotted beds where we deposited our kitbags then escorted toward a row of huts and the central building that housed an excellent canteen for a decent meal. After a day and a half we were taken to a clothing factory where we received one new suit, one pair of socks, one pair of shoes and a shirt. We were then instructed to stay in the main building and await further orders. We had forms to fill in and medals to be issued. The next thing on their list was the issuance of the £25. The men with me were handed train tickets to anywhere in the British Isles. Since I was the only radar officer there I had to go the following day . . . After a decent night's sleep I wandered down to the canteen for breakfast. I was the only one there apart from two cooks behind the long counter. One of the cooks said, "I've just been told you're the only one here. Do you like eggs?" I looked at him and the big tray of eggs before him, and replied, "Sure, just give them to me . . ." I hadn't seen eggs like that since before the war, my eyes got bigger and bigger. He gave me five which I scoffed down, then said, "Here, you may as well have all of these . . ."

He then deposited thirty eggs on my plate. I polished them all off in short order. The best thirty eggs I'd ever had . . . After breakfast I was called into the office and given my medals and a railway ticket. I didn't use the ticket just in case I needed it for the journey to Buntingford or wherever. I thought I may as well head back to Liverpool to start my new life as a civilian . . . After a short stay in a bed and breakfast establishment I found an apartment in Sefton Park and settled into it with my navy kitbag and my hammock . . .

\* \* \*

The ferry across the Mersey: My options were limited so I decided I may as well stay in Liverpool and find work. I approached a small vehicle repair and alterations factory, I figured with my coach building experience and the work I had done assembling the Mosquito main-planes it would put me in good stead. I got a job immediately and started the very next day. I would go everyday across the Mersey by the ferry to Birkenhead where the factory was. I missed the Sweet 'B' a lot and would always look out for her, but I knew her days were numbered and shortly she'd be at the mercy of the wrecker's ball or whatever they did to rip apart her steel innards. It wasn't a nice end for such a stout ship that had served Britain in her time of need with distinction. Military hardware was just viewed for the money it could bring in. She had weathered the North Atlantic storms stoically, never complaining, never giving in to the ravages of the war. I wondered what shape she was in. Standing by the railing of the ferry I would look for her like a lost lover in a crowd, knowing she was out there somewhere . . . somewhere . . .

At the factory workshop we would sit outside where the vehicles were parked for repairs or ready for collection during our lunch or tea breaks. A Flying Standard with a Union Jack emblem on the bonnet just behind the grill had been standing

there since the beginning of the war due to fuel rationing.
A client had recently bought the car and had been scouring
the country for bright new bumpers and other parts. Since no
luxury cars had been built since the beginning of the war the
Standard was a little beauty. The car had been meticulously
restored to pristine condition and after it had been re-sprayed
to perfection this mint stunner now stood outside waiting for
collection by its proud owner. We had a moronic apprentice
who never let the opportunity pass to jump into the finished
vehicles and set off on journeys within his mind's eye. One day
I sat watching him and advised, "Be careful what you touch in
the Flying Standard, the owner's going to collect it shortly . . ."

Peanut brain, as we called him, just looked at me and grinned
stupidly, then in a cocky arrogant manner he climbed into the
Standard. He started the car up and put it in gear. The car
started rolling forward so he put his foot hard down on the gas
pedal. The Flying Standard went flying forward through the
doors of the repair shop toward a parked truck in the midst of
servicing. There was a loud bang and the Standard hit the back
of it and ended up under it. The idiot apprentice was fired on the
spot and the once proud owner nearly collapsed in tears when he
saw what was left of the car. It was while working there I met an
interesting scientist who drove a big Utilicon with sand tires . . .

* * *

William Caird Peak and the two cottages: I met a Scotsman
called William Peak in Liverpool one day while I worked in
Birkenhead, he had been one of the scientists working with
Barnes Wallace on the bouncing bomb that had destroyed a
dam in Germany and taking a fair portion of the Nazi industrial
war machinery with it. The project was immortalized in film
by 'The Dambusters'. William and I got on well and he asked
whether I could improve two cottages he had bought in Wales.
The cottages were built around the year 1700 with horse hair

plaster, roughly sawn roof timbers and thatched roofs, wattle and stone. All the doors were hand made in the 1700s. The fireplaces were constructed of stone slabs from local material. They really were a piece of history. He wanted me to cut through the rock in one wall and put in a window. The wall was about four yards long and one yard in thickness. I didn't want to do it but he insisted. As I progressed cutting through and removing the rock I could clearly see it wasn't going to work and my fears about a collapse of the whole wall were rapidly turning into reality. I stopped and showed him what was about to happen if we continued on this course. He agreed with me at last and I set about repairing the damage done. After that he listened to my advice . . . The two cottages were about a mile apart so I used one of their horses, a beautiful black mare called *Beauty*, to get from one cottage to the other. The one cottage was up a hill called Ty Du and the walk was difficult and tiresome, that was where I stayed while working. The cottage by the main road was called Llyn Du and was the main house where the Peak's lived. *Beauty* loved nothing more than to wait outside the cottage I was working on then canter up or down the hill with me on her back. She really loved me and the attention I gave her. When I woke up and came out of the cottage in the morning she was always there waiting expectantly for me. She was quite tall so I would climb onto a fence then mount her. One day I had made an early start and was climbing the fence to see where *Beauty* was when she caught sight of me. She galloped at full speed from across the paddock then reared up on her hind legs right in front of me to stop herself. I got such a shock I fell back off the fence and landed in some manure. I didn't know whether I should laugh or cry looking up at *Beauty* from the pile of steaming muck. She stuck her nose through the fence and nuzzled me. Later on when I told Bill Peak and his wife what had happened we laughed our heads off and I never got over the ribbing they gave me . . . *Wherever I went on the farm Beauty was always two steps behind me . . .*

During the repairs of the cottages I would spend weekends back in my flat at Sefton Park in Liverpool. One weekend the weather deteriorated so badly that I had to use Bill's 4x4 Utilicon army truck. The road back was misty with sleet and snow obscuring my vision even more so. Soon the fog lifted because a stiff wind had started to blow driving both the sleet and snow and me across the road. The road was rapidly turning into an ice rink as I took a sweeping bend in the Utilicon. Even the 4x4 had no chance against the Welsh weather and she spun out of control. The next second the rear bumper impacted with a stone wall running by the road and the windscreen wipers jumped forward off the windscreen. I sat there for a second before I got out checking the damage. The rear bumper of the Utilicon is a thick piece of steel, the stone wall didn't even dent or scratch it, but I had inadvertently knocked down a section of the wall. The damage wasn't bad and only a few levels of the stone had fallen off the top. There were some cottages a little further on and an elderly lady came out and asked if I was alright. I said yes and she ambled off to the warmth of her Welsh stone house. There was a big tree and a water trough near the hole I had made, *'For the cattle in summer,'* I thought. I got back in the Utilicon and carried on to Llyn Du. Two months later while I was renovating Ty Du the phone rang and Bill Peak on the other end said, "Stan, there's a policeman here looking for you . . ."

I dropped my tools quickly and got on *Beauty* heading for the main cottage. I thought, *'What on Earth could he want,'* I was dumbfounded. Sure enough when I reached Llyn Du there was a policeman standing next to a bicycle waiting for me. The policeman said, "Are you Mr. Stanley Chapman?"

"Yes, why?" I enquired.

"We have a complaint from a farmer that you knocked down a wall . . ." The policeman then proceeded to rattle off the time and date and the vehicle I was driving. I told him what had happened then he said, "Well, the farmer either wants £30 to repair the wall or you can do the repairs yourself . . ."

I said, "Don't worry. I'll go down and do the repairs myself . . ."

Satisfied, the copper left and the following weekend I borrowed the Utilicon loaded it with cement, sand and tools and headed off to repair the hole. When I arrived I couldn't believe my eyes, the cows at pasture had rubbed against the wall and made it far worse than the hole I had made. I set to work and made the repairs regardless. In short order I was finished, not perfect but it would do . . . I never heard anything about the wall again and continued driving past it . . . *It remains solid to this day . . .*

The trips to the Peak's cottages were always eventful, one day after having left Liverpool at five in the morning I battled through heavy driving rain all the way to Wales. The Peak cottages were about eighty miles due south of Colwyn Bay on the north coast of Wales. At one point I would turn left not far from where I knocked over the wall and cross a small bridge going over an even smaller river. As I approached the turning a bread van passed me flashing his lights. I just thought he was being friendly and flashed him back. As I turned the corner a wall of water confronted me. I slammed on the brakes of my Flying Standard. It didn't do much good as the vehicle continued across the bridge into the water which flooded over it. The car stopped right in the center. The engine stalled and wouldn't restart. The water was flowing two feet up the door, I thought, 'Oh, Shucks! What am I going to do now?' Luckily for me the sides were high enough to stop the car sliding off into the river. While I sat there water started seeping into the car through the doors at the bottom. *'What a fix,'* I thought, the engine was flooded and there was no help in sight . . . Within a couple of minutes though a tractor rounded the corner led by an angel, I was in luck! In short order the friendly driver hooked up my front bumper and pulled me out . . . It took two hours of waiting before the engine was sufficiently dry and I could continue on towards the cottages . . . *What a day . . . Phew!*

\* \* \*

The ghost in the attic: I really hadn't thought of what I would do after the war ended, in fact, I thought it would go on forever, the ship was my home and the enemy lurked beneath the waves, this was now my lot in life and I had learnt to love it, reveling in the comradeship of my crewmates, the heaving deck beneath my feet, the salt spray in my face, the reassuring sounds of our guns and sea swelling explosions of our depth charges, the scent of engine oil and cordite. Life in the navy had been hard but it had also given me a great sense of belonging. I was still in Liverpool, where else could I go? I felt restless and ill-at-ease. I had made friends with an Italian family making statues for the Catholic Church. There were two sons, Vince and Mario. One time I hid in the basement where the statues were stored and I stood motionless in the midst of them. A little while later Vincent came down the stairs totally unaware. As he passed me by I leaned over and groaned, "Oooaahh!" Vincent nearly had a heart attack and ran back up the stairs.

Once Vince, Mario and I put a statue outside an elderly lady's house on her doorstep, we put a lit cigarette in its mouth, rang the bell and then hid behind some bushes. The lady opened the door and said, "Yes, what do you want?" The statue remained mute. "Well, what do you want, man, speak up, I can't hear a word you're saying!" She looked the statue in the eyes, then expressed, "Hmmphh! Idiot!" slammed the door and went back to her knitting . . . Another time we put the same statue behind a hedge with a cigarette in its mouth. A young couple walked by and got such a fright they nearly died on the spot.

Vincent had recently become engaged and he and his fiancée had bought a large house on a corner near to his parents' house. I had now started a business repairing and renovating houses and had employed a young man by the name of John Grey. We were always joking with Vince and his brother and they were always playing pranks on me, one time Vince hid the legs of a piano I was repairing for someone and I thought one of these days I'd get him back. The house was undergoing some major repair work since it was quite old, John was inside the kitchen helping the builder and a friend of ours, a commercial artist, Martin, was busy chatting to Vincent. They left the front door open and were busy discussing the project as John came upstairs to help me. I figured it was payback time for all the pranks perpetrated by the two brothers. John and I went to the bathroom and saw a hatch into the attic. The bathroom door was off its hinges and lying against the wall. I climbed up with the help of John then reached down for him and pulled him up. We had found an old chain and started rattling it to and fro, then, spitting into the bathtub crying, "The blood! The blood! The blood! Ah-ah-ah-ah–"

The voices stopped downstairs and the house became quiet, no voices, chatter or the banging of hammers. Two voices broke the silence, that of the painter and plasterer, "Well, it's getting late now so we'd best be off . . ." I could hear them packing away their tools as we lay in the attic stifling our laughter. Martin disappeared in short order; we didn't even hear him leave. Vincent's fiancée arrived and the pair of them left the house quickly and stood outside by the corner, we could hear their discussion, "The house must be haunted, I'm not living there," said Vincent's fiancée. "But we can't leave it, I've already paid a lot of money for it," noted Vincent.

"Why don't we call the police then?" suggested Vincent's fiancée.

It was at that point I remarked to John, "I think we'd better get down and pack this in . . ."

"I think you're right," answered John. Clambering down we headed for the stairs. It wasn't windy or anything just dark outside with a bit of drizzle, the house was dead quiet. Suddenly one of the doors behind me slammed shut by itself sending both John and I madly rushing down the staircase. When we got to the front door Vincent almost fainted, *"Y-Y-YOU!"* he stammered, "Oh my God! Oh my God!" he almost cried with relief. I still had my navy coat on and a dark ocean bronzed

face to go with it. Vincent nearly fell to his knees in relief. Me,
I looked back up at the house and could have sworn I saw the
shadow of someone in one of the windows . . .

* * *

I was reticent about leaving Liverpool since our ship had
been berthed there and I had made many friends in the area. I
just couldn't get over the fact that the war had ended; I still felt
I was on active duty and I seemed to be stuck in time, in limbo.
I went down to the docks and walked around half expecting our
ship to be in port, half expecting my crew-mates to be there. All I
saw were empty untied stanchions and an empty berth. I turned
and walked away as it started to drizzle . . . My mind drifted to
roiling and rolling seas, to the sometimes smiling faces of our
crew, of the fights we had won and of the subs we had sunk. It
drifted to the beaches of D-Day, to the valiant men who had
stormed the beaches, to our brothers-in-arms on their ships
at the bottom of the ocean. To the wickedness of our enemy,
which, at the time we gave little thought. To the warm days in
the sun in the Mediterranean, to the cold inhospitable seas the
Sweet 'B' had forged through, yes, I had many memories and in
my mind I was still there . . .

I had met an attractive girl, a Liverpudlian, when I started
playing soccer for Prescott Cables in the Third Division. I soon
realized she was only looking for a meal ticket and I dropped
her like a hot potato. I was a very good soccer player and was
just about to join the Second Division when one of the other
players kicked my leg on purpose in an ugly tackle. He knew
the coach from First Division Liverpool had his eye on me
and had told our coach. There was an ugly snap just above my
ankle and I went down onto the pitch. I had no insurance and
no benefits I could claim. It was impossible to continue house
renovations and vehicle modifications to earn my living while
hobbling around on a painfully swollen leg in a cast. I was at

that time converting light army vans into usable automobiles called shooting breaks. My life in Liverpool was unraveling fast, my money was running out and I had no option other than to head home to Buntingford . . .

I stood just outside Liverpool on Highway Number–1 with my leg in Plaster of Paris and a walking stick in my right hand with my navy kitbag sitting next to me, it was cold so I had my navy overcoat on. After several attempts of holding my hand out with my left thumb extended upwards a Rolls Royce pulled up next to me. A respectable gent popped his head out the driver's window and said, "Where are you going?"

"To London–" I answered.

"Well then, jump in, I'm headed in that direction, son . . ."

I couldn't believe my luck. At first we said nothing until the ice broke and we started chatting up a storm. I told him about my years in the navy and he reciprocated by telling me about his life. In the end he asked me what my destination was and I told him Buntingford, but I could get off at Dunstable and hike the rest of the way, he said, "Nonsense, son, I'll take you all the way home–"

He dropped me off and gave me a friendly wave as he left, turning, I strolled up the pathway to mum's cottage. Getting to the door I dropped my kitbag and was about to knock, I changed my mind and tried the door handle. Turning the handle I pushed it and the door swung open, I could hear mum in the kitchen busy with chores. "Mum!" I called out, "Mum!"

Mother came out of the kitchen holding a tea cloth between her hands drying them, a look of shock on her face, she couldn't believe it, she started to cry, I had come home at last . . . *The war for me was now truly over . . .*

That night the family sat down together for the first time since the beginning of the war at number 41 Greenways in Buntingford, we were whole again, the sounds of German aircraft flying above and dropping bombs on us had stopped and all was quiet, no sounds of screaming Merlin engines from

Spitfires or Hurricanes nor the distinct throbbing sounds of Heinkels and the like, no, for once in such a long time we sat down to a peaceful meal. My childhood and the innocence of Britain had ceased abruptly and we were now living in the new world. Ted and Alf were brimming with excitement, having their missing brother back again after such a long time. Ernie, the eldest of the Chapman boys and chief engine room artificer on the HMS Arethusa, told me how he had entered the canteen then turned around to fetch something closing the hatch behind him. It was at that exact moment a torpedo hit the side of the ship and killed everyone in the mess. Out of the two hundred that died many were his friends. A part of him died then. I had heard very little from both Jim and Ernie throughout the war, letters were scarce and any news came from my mother. Not that much could be said anyway, censorship and the thought of a careless word here or there could mean the death of a loved one; any letters had to be carefully worded. Jim had served in the Eighth Army for the duration of the war after his anti-aircraft days during the Blitz; he had served in Egypt and Italy and been one of the *pongoes* who had kicked Rommel out of Africa. At mid-night after Teddy and Alf had gone to bed and mum kissed me goodnight and went off to bed with dad, I sat in the darkened living room with so many thoughts flooding my mind. Of oil blackened sailors swimming towards our ship being swallowed up by fast spreading flames, while we screamed at them to 'SWIM FASTER!' Of our captain ordering the helmsman to get closer to the searing heat and raging inferno . . . Of the injured man I carried on my back in London while I ran as fast as I could as bombs fell all around us. Of the bomb that exploded behind us and his hand gripping tightly around mine before he slipped into everlasting darkness . . . Of screams, of pain, and of death . . . So much of it . . . Eventually I hobbled up the stairs with tears in my eyes . . .

# CHAPTER 14

## Post War Britain

The Berlin Airlift had just started, the year was 1947, and I was soon to become–Lt. Sg. Stanley W. Chapman USN . . . After a brief respite I was now at war once more, Berlin was in trouble, Communism was on the rise and the *Cold War* had now begun. It was a war waged with words, rhetoric and bad intentions, a war where the spies of many nations, especially those of Britain, the United States and the USSR, had now come to the fore. It wasn't possible for rail and road traffic carrying goods and foodstuffs to get into West Berlin. The communists had built a blockade wall around it, sealing it off from the West and the rest of free Germany . . .

Dad had told me about the United States needing assistance at Stansted Airport about twenty miles from Buntingford. They were in dire straits in having to supply everything that West Berlin needed to stay independent and free; the US Forces there were also sending back injured personnel. I borrowed dad's Austin 7 and headed over to see Commander Chadwick of the United States Navy, he was in charge of all air and ground operations at Stansted Airport for the US forces. Commander Chadwick had been in the Royal Navy during the war and he was delighted that I had come; they were in a bind and needed an experienced navy man like myself. I started immediately and became the 2IC to Commander Chadwick. My rank under the commander would be that of senior grade lieutenant (USN), with my salary paid for by the United States military . . . Our mission was simple, to organize all supply flights and flight crews from Stansted Airport, to obtain and supply the transportation for supplies, equipment, food, medicine, the sick, the injured and personnel going in and out of Russian blockaded Berlin. *Well, maybe not that simple, more like a logistical nightmare . . .* The aircraft going in and out of Stansted Airport in Essex would be flying under the *Skyways* banner. I was now a participant in the *Cold War.* The aircraft at our disposal were converted Lancaster and Halifax bombers from the RAF, and durable dependable beasts like the B-17G from the USAAF. They had been stripped of all their guns and armaments and reconfigured for a life less hazardous than the one they had endured during the Second World War . . . *Then again, maybe not . . .* The C-47 Dakota and C-54 with the R5D variant were also available to us, in fact anything we could get hold of and commandeer we could use. Our biggest nightmares were the drivers of the fleet of trucks, buses and vans under our command. These vehicles were on 24 hour standby and our staff was pooled from a core of civilians living near to the airport. I thought I had seen it all on the Sweetbriar, not a chance! I would grab a few hours sleep on the couch in my office before the next flight came in or some idiot didn't turn up for his shift and I would fill in for him. We had thirty five drivers and four motor mechanics, not to mention the mass of personnel working all the time in stores assembling the supplies to be shipped out on the next flight. We were shuttling aircraft in and out like nobody's business. On the odd days I actually managed to get home my mother would say, "What on Earth are you doing there, you hardly ever come home now!" All I can say is the Berlin Airlift was one of the most intense, nerve wracking and stressful periods in my life, there was just no letup. However, I knew what I was getting myself into and for me, it was important. How could we leave them to the mercy of starvation and sickness, to the mercy of a Russian government intent on crushing them into submission? At least that's how I consoled myself as I drove hell for leather in a double-decker bus through narrow country lanes in the early hours of the morning with overhanging branches scratching its sides and top picking up personnel all because some bright spark had decided not to pitch up for work thinking that the aircrews scheduled to fly the Lancasters and B-17Gs that day could find their own way to the airport; and in no way did it matter that we had to get valuable supplies out and receive a medical evacuation aircraft full of hospital cases. Food rationing was still in progress at that time, with many items still not available in Post War Britain, so it must have been hard obtaining the valuable supplies needed for Berlin; sacrifices no doubt had been made. The one bonus was because I was now working for the US Navy and the US Military Command in Europe our food was excellent, all our food came from the US so I couldn't complain, rations to me, had never been better . . .

During the airlift even we had casualties, a common cause of crashes was the under-carriage of the old bombers collapsing due to overloading. Our aircraft were all jam-packed with supplies and calculations were left to the pilots. Probably metal fatigue played a great part in oleos breaking and wheels flying off as the bombers struggled to get airborne or came in for a landing. The aircraft we used had already seen a lot of action over Europe and Germany in particular, and no doubt the under-carriage on these bombers needed to be beefed up. Accidents caused by overloading increased as time went by, especially with the Avro Lancaster. One time as I stood on the edge of the runway looking at a Lancaster taking off and approaching V1, the portside oleo just collapsed which sent the bird careening down the runway on its left wing bending the props and tearing the under-carriage off. The portside under-carriage ended up penetrating the fuselage as the aircraft slid down the runway. Luckily it didn't burst into flames with its full fuel load. There had been twelve passengers aboard, fortunately no one was killed but some of them were seriously injured. After that we had to seriously regulate the amount of cargo permitted on our aircraft, as things were getting seriously dangerous. Many times Commander Chadwick would catch a flight with our planes to Berlin to take care of problems that side while I remained and handled everything this side. It wouldn't be on to have a US Navy commander in full uniform buying a farm in Europe or Britain, especially when he was in charge of operations at Stansted, and the servicing of the aircraft. I also had no desire to go down in one of our aircraft, or to let anyone else take their lives in a throw of a dice . . . The airfield at Stansted was long enough to cope with crash landings, which at the time, were numerous. Most of the pilots and aircrew involved in prangs managed to jump out and walk away. Our emergency crews at the airport were kept quite busy. The other problem we had was accidental damage to our ground vehicles. Any problems would illicit the words from Cdr. Chadwick, "Sort it out, Chapman . . ." To which I would reply, "Yes, Sir!" There was no lee-way for tardiness in my position.

Sometimes the aircraft would be ready but the supplies had not arrived, or the volume of supplies to be loaded on board was just too large to be contained in one aircraft. This would throw our scheduling out and we'd have to scramble for another aircraft. Because of the great need for supplies in Berlin our phones never stopped ringing. Our typist, office clerk and staff were under tremendous pressure. The officers in charge of Airlift Command really had their work cut out for them; they incorporated other airfields around Hertfordshire that had been used by Bomber Command during WW2. Pilots and aircrew were in high demand. The supplies we sent were never enough but it kept Berliners from starving and kept West Berlin out of communist hands. If it had not been for the supreme efforts of the US forces and the relief they delivered Berlin would have crumbled to dust . . . Because of the Cold War and the serious nature of the communist threat in Europe a portion of our work was highly confidential, and I was asked by Commander Chadwick to deliver a briefcase to a certain high ranking officer at Tempelhof airport in Berlin . . . It had been raining for days and there was no letup, rain pelted the windows of the operations building as I glanced outside, barely catching sight of the B-17G standing outside being loaded. The briefcase wasn't all that heavy, I assumed it carried papers, but the handcuff around my wrist attached to the handle of the case chafed a little. Commander Chadwick had entrusted me with an important mission and I would not let him down, but . . . the weather outside looked truly atrocious and I wondered how the ex-bomber boys would fare taking us all the way across Europe to our destination – Berlin! I picked up my dark blue raincoat and headed out the door grabbing an umbrella as I did so. I had just polished my shoes and didn't relish the thought of dirtying them as I joined the other passengers bound for Berlin, soldiers, medical personnel and a few non-descript men belonging to intelligence I guessed. I pulled the brim of my naval cap down just before I made a dash for the plane and the ladder I had to climb up. As I settled into a small canvas seat I wondered what would happen if we didn't quite take-off, I'd seen too many over-laden planes not quite make take-off speed on stormy days and nights. I put the thought out of my head and glanced around at the other passengers; they seemed more worried than I was which put my mind at ease. The four radial engines burst into life and soon we were clear of the airfield. I had nothing to worry about. This time there would be no heavy German guns aimed at me, there would be no coastal shore batteries belting out shell after shell at the Sweetbriar, no, it would be just the Fortress battling the driving rain and gusting wind that threatened to blow us off course . . . Of that I could be thankful . . .

It rained all the way across Britain and all the way across the English Channel, in fact, it rained all the way to Berlin.

The cabin was freezing and I thanked the Lord for my thick naval pants and jacket, though a sheepskin jacket and pants would have suited me better . . . The wind was gusty and tried its best to blow the Fortress off course but the pilot greased the strip just like the pro he was. He had taken part in the bombing of this self-same city during the war and now he was here delivering food stuffs and medicine on a humanitarian mission . . . how fortunes and war change. The rain pelted Berlin with the same violence it had Stansted Airport and I looked through a rain streaked window hoping I could get a hot cup of coffee after the briefcase was delivered. Through the rain a covered Willy's Jeep splashed through puddles and pulled to a stop next to the fuselage. I figured this was my ride and climbed down the ladder. A sergeant wearing US Army fatigues under a heavy raincoat greeted me, "Are you Lieutenant Chapman?" he said after saluting. "Yes . . ." I replied saluting him back. "Could you come with me please?" he added. I had no wish to stand in the rain sheltering under the wing of the Fortress so I quickly climbed in the Jeep. The sergeant shoved the vehicle into reverse, spun it around and headed for the operations and terminal building. The rain, if anything, seemed to be getting heavier. . . .

At the terminal building the sergeant and I were met by a high ranking army officer, the one I was to hand the briefcase to. I undid the handcuff around my wrist and handed the case to him. He checked the lock hadn't been tampered with and left with a great sense of urgency . . . my mission, it seemed, was over . . . now all I had to do was get home . . . The rain continued to pour and pour and pour as the B-17G crossed Europe and headed home, this time full of med-evac cases and some refugees that would be vetted in due course. Looking at them I wondered which of them we had fought . . . The rain pelted the aluminum fuselage sounding all the while like shrapnel as we winged our way across the channel, and soon, we would be landing and I could get a good cup of strong coffee before curling up to sleep in my cot and get ready for tomorrow.

When we touched down at Stansted I breathed a great sigh . . . home, hearth and a hot dinner would be mine shortly . . .

As time went by we received information that the Russians would relax the embargo on Berlin. Only because the blockade had failed to produce the desired results communist leaders had been salivating over. Eventually a ground corridor was created allowing access to Berlin. The airlift was no longer needed and Commander Chadwick received a posting to Washington D.C., I would be transferred to the naval base in San Diego for more formal duties where I would also receive further advanced training . . . After having spent nearly six years of my life at war with the Germans and seeing so many people die around me I really wanted to stay in Buntingford for a while, my mother implored me not to leave as well. The memories and the horrors of war were all but too fresh, I had had my fill of rough mountainous seas, torpedoes, bullets and high explosive shells exploding around me, of men being fried alive and blown to bits, so in 1949 with the airlift over I resigned my commission and left . . . *Was it the right decision, probably not . . . for it turned out to be a decision I lived to regret . . .*

* * *

I was no Mario Lanza: After the hectic time I had during the Berlin Airlift I carried on with my carpentry but my interest in it had waned. I met Richard Tauber a singer and musician, and Jack Hulbert an actor, they implored me to get on the stage and explore my talents. They had heard me sing as I played the guitar and were very impressed. But I was of two minds to take it up seriously, besides, even though I could sing and play the guitar I couldn't read a note of music. They said I had a stage personality even though I was a tad nervous in front of a crowd. The confidence, they said, would come in time. "Rome wasn't built in a day . . ." they implored trying to encourage me. I took to heart what they said and approached a record company, did an audition and impressed the recording manager at their studio. They asked me to record some songs which would then be pressed onto records. The 'A' side of my first record was, *I've Never Been In Love Before'*. During this period I sang Country and Western songs to entertain both myself and others at a variety of venues. I was popular and started to seriously consider other ways to carve out a stage career for myself. I was told the Windmill Theatre was looking for acts and anyone with talent and ambition, so I signed up for an audition and went up to the West End one morning. When I arrived the stage manager came up to me and said, "Do comedy, we need comedians, just do a joke or two . . ." He gave me the thumbs up sign and pushed me through the stage entrance . . . As I stood on that big expansive stage my nerves seemed to shrink back and I lost all feeling, my mind went totally numb . . . my mind went blank . . . In front of me in the seats below the stage sat twelve people who would decide on my fate. I stuttered a little not knowing what to do, my nerve was truly gone and with it my composure. I tried to sing and all that came out was a croak, I tried to do a joke and the words got stuck in my throat, there was now only one thing I could do . . . a harmonica impression . . .

The harmonica impression went down like the Titanic with no survivors and I was pulled off stage in short order by one of the stage hands at the behest of the twelve prophets of doom sitting below in sumptuous red velvet chairs. I stood for a second or two with perspiration pouring down my face and staining my armpits . . . As I left the building I wondered why I hadn't brought my guitar or the puppets I had begun practicing with . . . Why did I do the stupid harmonica impression . . . God only knows . . . My stage career now lay at the bottom of the Atlantic with the Titanic . . . *and with it my nerves* . . . The posters I had pasted up on the walls of my mind now had 'Cancelled, Until Further Notice!' scrawled over them in red, especially after I heard Tom Jones sing at a concert, *'How could I possibly compete against him,'* I thought . . .

* * *

Dunstable Commer Carriers 1949-51: I had decided I might as well get back into carpentry and start a business down in Buntingford as even though I liked the stage, the stage didn't like me. I had all my tools picked up in Liverpool that had been stored for me and began marketing my skills. It wasn't long before I picked up quite a few alterations to buildings including a very old farmhouse that needed its rafters repaired. I also raised the roof of a military van to turn it into a commercial vehicle. One of the strangest jobs I picked up was turning a large room in a mansion into a chicken coop. The lady who owned the mansion was a very large woman who worked at the BBC as a senior director. Why she decided to screen the doorways with chicken-wire and house several hundred chickens inside the house I'll never know. She had adequate out-buildings that would have served the purpose perfectly. I did it anyway without protestation and built the roosts and everything and even helped her relocate the chickens. Personally, I could have thought of about a million other ways to use the building, a chicken coop would have been my last choice. The other job I did for her was to fashion a shaft for a horse rig which had broken; I shaped it then used a spoke shave, filed and sanded it, smoothing it down for varnishing. When I had finished with it the shaft looked exactly like its right hand mate that would slip over the right hand side of the horse. The shaft worked like a charm when the whole assembly was hitched to a two wheel cart and a horse pulled it down the driveway under majestic old trees through the old established garden that once was the pride and joy of occupants long gone. If the place had been mine what a pleasure it would have been to restore it to its former glory . . . but it wasn't, so when I packed away my tools and stowed them in the Austin, and started the old girl up, it was the last I saw of it . . . It left me feeling unfulfilled and wondering, *'With all my ability and skills is this what I had been reduced to?'* I wanted so much more out of life . . . and I could have kicked myself for not going to the naval base in San Diego . . .

A little while later I heard from Thurgoods that the new-town of Milton Keynes was to be the center of commercial and manufacturing industries encouraged by the government to decentralize business and encourage work outside of the large cites. One of the companies, the Rootes Group Vehicle Manufacturers, had started a new operation called Commer Carriers. They were starting up in Dunstable and were looking for skilled coachbuilders and they needed vehicle and truck inspectors on the finishing line in their vehicle assembly plant. I applied for a position there and was hired on the spot as a finished vehicle and truck inspector. I started the following day as they badly needed inspectors. Problem was, I wasn't eligible for a house as I was single and unattached. So I moved from place to place and really wasn't settled at all. Accommodation proved to be a real drawback and I wanted a real career, something that I could sink my teeth into that would give me satisfaction . . . In the end Commer Carriers just wasn't for me . . .

* * *

The vending machines and the baker's tins full of money 1952-57: After leaving Commer Carriers I began searching for a good business, then I came across the Viegandt & Deutsch Wagon Master vending machines selling hot and cold drinks, cigarettes and other things. I had met a retired baker near Royston who had recently sold his business; he was very wealthy due to his black market activities during the war. His confectionary sales included sugar and flour which was severely rationed. At that time he was busy buying up old church organs for their pipes from all over Britain. The baker said he'd like to invest in a drink machine I had on site at Woburn Abbey, the Duke of Bedford's zoo. I agreed to sell him shares in it since the machine was large and cost around £2,500. He offered me £950 as his investment portion which I gratefully accepted. We made arrangements for me to come to his house to pick up the money in a village near Royston on the road to Bedford . . . When I got to the house in my Morris Oxford he led me upstairs to one of the bedrooms to fetch the money. I couldn't believe my eyes when he opened the door, the room was filled wall to wall and from top to bottom with small bread oven tins filled with 2 shilling and half a crown coins which he'd collected during the war from his black market trading. I carried a big basket up and down the stairs several times to get the money and deposited it in the trunk of the Morris Oxford. The weight of all the coins was so much it nearly lifted the front wheels off the ground. I had difficulty steering the vehicle home but was pleased with his investment. The baker was obviously worried the tax office would take issue over the undeclared income he had earned during the war and was afraid to declare it even though hostilities were now over . . . That had nothing to do with me though; I was more concerned with getting the vending machine business on a roll . . .

* * *

The day that changed my life: It was a warm sunny day and I decided to stop at the Royston swimming pool and go for a swim. I parked the car and headed to the changing room after paying the entrance fee. I strolled out to the bright blue pool with my towel in hand. Going to the pool side I dipped my foot into the water, *'Not too warm and not too cold, just right,'* I thought. I picked out a chair and spread my towel across it. Going to the poolside I dived in and swam up and down the length of the pool a few times to limber up. Feeling refreshed I stopped and looked around at the other patrons. While I was treading water and casting about I saw a beautiful fair haired girl swimming not too far from me. I smiled at her. She smiled back. I swam toward her and for some reason she did the same, swimming towards me. We were near the pool's edge and she placed her hand on it to steady herself. I put my hand over hers and we started talking up a storm laughing at each other's comments about life and the universe. I tried to contain myself and not be a blabber or jabber mouth but it was awfully hard. She was truly beautiful and wonderful to behold. We carried on talking and I made a date with her . . . Our date went well and I fell head over heels in love with her. Her name was Elizabeth Katherine Langridge, she had been educated at a Catholic convent school, swam and played tennis for Royston clubs and loved playing the piano and singing. After the first date we saw each other as much as we could, reveling in each other's company. I couldn't get Elizabeth out of my mind and nor did I want to. We started seeing each other every day and still couldn't see enough of each other. At the time I had a small flat in Cambridge and it wasn't long before I was invited to her home to meet her mother Iris, then her brother David and finally her father, George. The family name Langridge was Nordic and actually means *Place of the Long Ridge*. Elizabeth's father liked me a lot and the feeling was reciprocated. Their house was in Orchard Road in front of the Farmers Fertilizer Company that George was the manager of. It had three bedrooms on the top floor, a kitchen in front with a dining room overlooking the garden at the back with a lounge and sitting room between it and the stairs. Ivy ran up the side and back of the house giving it an old world feel. George was not only an excellent manager and chairman of the Royston Golf club, but he also made sure the working environment around the factory was stunningly beautiful. He even had the railway sidings nearby planted with flowers by his wife, Iris. The factory was so neat and tidy with not a blade of grass out of place. George was too young to enlist for the First World War and too old to be on active duty in the Second World

War, instead he joined the Home Guard and was on the housing committee for evacuees from London. His job as the manager of Farmers Fertilizer Company was important, for without it the farmers wouldn't be able to produce their much needed crops. Iris, Elizabeth's mother, was a wonderful cook and kept the house to a high standard, her garden, which she loved, was straight out of *Alice in Wonderland* with arches festooned with flowers and expertly arranged, it seemed so natural and flowing with little pathways running up and down. Iris also had a vegetable plot, which had been her Victory Garden, behind the house and in front of the fertilizer factory. The house had a high hedge running around on the left adjacent to an access road to the factory and the garage where George kept his pride and joy, his Morris Oxford. I have never seen anyone, other than myself, take such pride and care with an automobile, George had such a tremendous respect for his car, I think he loved it as much as he loved his wife. In winter he would put a blanket over the engine which was always spotlessly clean and he would never take it out on the salt strewn winter roads when the bodywork would be exposed to rust, and if he did, he would always wash the car down to remove the salt. The other things he prized were his Billy Record II camera, a brown Bias tie with green dots and a silver tie clip with cowry shell inset, his silver cigarette case and a pair of gold cufflinks made in 1914 in Cambridge by Munsey & Co in a small tortoise shell rectangular box. His shoes of choice were Grenson, black or brown of the finest leather available. The color made no difference to him. Grensons were all handmade in London to traditional standards with a history going back long before the Great War. George appreciated good workmanship . . .

Behind the house was an expanse of lawn on which Elizabeth and I spent summer days lounging in the warm rays of the sun with me playing my guitar and wooing her. Elizabeth and I would go on double dates with David and his girlfriend, Judy, a very bubbly vivacious young lady. We would all pile into my car and spend the day at her parents' house. Elizabeth and I were very much in love with each other, going to Sitges in Spain, and to Rimini in Italy. We met another couple, George and Audrey Lee, whom we got on famously with and went on holiday. George worked at Hollerith Computers in Letchworth, the same company my Uncle Edward worked at. On these trips I never left my guitar at home. I would take it with me wherever we went playing and singing to my fair lady love like a medieval bard of old on our day trips to Walton on Naze, Clacton and everywhere else we went. That chance meeting on a warm summer's day changed my life forever and made me a better man . . . was it fate, was it destiny . . . Yes –

\* \* \*

It was 1957 and my business was expanding to such an extent I felt a partner with prestige and character would really provide added value to the product lines I was developing. I had installed a Viegandt cold drink machine at a rocket site in Norfolk. At the time I really hadn't considered what they were doing as top secret. Russia was now the new enemy according to the newspapers. In the course of my regular trips to the site to service the machine I had befriended Squadron Leader Brian Hearn. He was looking for something to do when he retired from the Royal Air Force and felt we could really exploit an untapped market with my machines. He joined me in my new project that of a biscuit and cake dispenser machine that I had converted from a cigarette dispenser. It would now give out packets of biscuits and slices of cake. A very large manufacturing company called Huntley and Palmers, a leader in the biscuit business, were incredibly enthusiastic about my designs and the prototype I had built. Within two months I received a call from their sales director requesting me to demonstrate the machine at the British Railways Company head office in Euston Station, London. The appointment was duly made and I told Brian the good news. He was really excited at the prospect of getting the machines onto the platforms of the BRC. I arrived at Euston Station and met the General Manager of British Rail. She was taller than me, both in girth and height, a really big woman. Full of herself she made me strip the whole machine apart down to its nuts and bolts, examining it in detail. After that she said, "Ok, you can go now–"

I thought, *'How rude!'* I packed up the machine and left without even a handshake from the obnoxious broad. I couldn't believe how full of it they were. About two weeks later I received a phone call from the sales director of Huntley and Palmers to go and install the machine at Euston Station. He said, "If all goes well you'll be installing them in all British Rail stations throughout the British Isles. Providing, that is, they operate well . . ."

Calling Brian I let him know of our success, he said, "Great, I'm all the way with you on this project and I'll put some money into it as well–"

Brian had been a fighter pilot during the war and had crash landed three times with a Spitfire in combat without a scratch. On the day of the delivery I picked him up at the base in my brand new Rover. I wore my cavalry twill overcoat since it was cold and we headed down the A10. It was 7:45 am just as we passed Braughing. There was a café about five miles away on the right with about a mile on either side of it of dead straight clear road. Just as we approached the café a huge sand and gravel truck pulled straight out in front of us blocking the entire road. The road had been clear on both sides of the café except us. I had seen him waiting at the café and not expecting anyone to be so foolhardy and pull a stunt like that. It seemed as though he had done it on purpose. Swerving I tried to get the Rover 90 up onto the kerb but it was no use, they'd just laid new ones that were quite high. I pushed as hard as I could on the brakes without locking the wheels but the ton and a bit Rover slammed into the left front wheel and cab of the truck and came to an abrupt stop –

I woke up groggily, my face was wet, I ran my hand over it to wipe it off, looking at it through the mist of my concussion I noted it was red–blood . . . my nose was painful and every time I breathed pangs of pain shot through my rib cage. I had broken my nose and also a rib. The bulkiness of my cavalry twill overcoat had saved me from further injury. I had been driving for twenty years and never had an accident–and now–I looked over at Brian . . . he had hit the windscreen face first and was now covered in lacerations from the glass. At that time seat belts in cars were nonexistent. I blacked out –

I lapsed in and out of consciousness for some time. I had been taken to Ware General Hospital. I didn't know what was happening and continued unconscious for most of the time. The only thing I remember was being slapped in the face by a nurse repeatedly as she cried, *"Wake up! Wake up! Doctor! Come quickly he's going into a coma!"*

When I was released from hospital I stayed with Elizabeth and her family but the concussed feeling stayed with me for about four to six months. I couldn't contact Brian at all; I didn't even know where I was half of the time. After six months I got my Rover 90 back from the repair shop. I didn't claim for my injuries but I should have, it was nearly a year before I could start work again. The Rover was never the same; it seemed to move crab-like down the road and wore out tires rapidly. While I was semiconscious in hospital a representative of the truck company and their lawyer came and had me sign a statement absolving them from all responsibility, my insurance company Eagle Star of London, a subsidiary of Lloyds, weren't interested in helping either. I never heard from Brian and I felt too embarrassed to contact him when my mind had cleared and I was well enough to work again. The funny thing was that at the time I started working on the project with Brian I felt unseen eyes on me as though someone was following me, watching me. His work was very sensitive and highly secret. I often pondered over whether someone had arranged the accident on purpose . . . and was it an attempt to end our association?

* * *

Courting and getting married: Fate had been kind to me on that summer's day I had met Elizabeth. I wasn't a particularly sociable man and had just a few good friends, with Kenneth Carr and Victor Haynes being my closest compatriots. I wanted good companions around me, and since I didn't smoke and wasn't really a drinker I wanted men of good sorts who felt the same way. Elizabeth's family had helped me get over my concussion and injuries with Elizabeth's mother doing her utmost to make me comfortable. The accident was fast disappearing from my mind and I proposed to Elizabeth eighteen months after our chance meeting at Royston swimming baths. The word chance is loaded and I felt, and still do, that we were destined to meet. We both fell in love on that day . . . and no other woman in the world could have made me happier . . . and if you're wondering, "Yes," was Elizabeth's answer . . .

I was still staying with the Langridge family in Orchard Road, Royston and that is where we made our engagement and marriage plans. Accommodation was hard to come by and we eventually found a small filling station with living quarters at Arrington, just outside Royston.

We had a beautiful wedding reception at The Banyers Hotel. I was an old patron there and the manager knew me well. George, Iris, David and Judy were there of course and so was Victor Haynes, plus a whole lot of Elizabeth's old friends and extended family. The hotel staff and the manager didn't want to be left out so they were in attendance as well. George Langridge escorted Elizabeth to the podium where the vicar and I waited. The ceremony was very sweet and after our, "I do's . . ." the reception party began . . . During the festivities David slipped out and put a fish on top of the engine and attached a string of balloons to the rear bumper of the Rover . . . After the reception meal and a lot of clapping and confetti throwing we headed to Devon and Cornwall on our honeymoon. Our first port of call was Swindon and the Station Hotel. On the way I smelt something odd, frying fish, I stopped the car lifted up the hood and removed the burnt offering from David and cast it into the bushes at the side of the road. When we eventually got to Swindon and our hotel room we had a surprise in the form of tons of confetti erupting from our suitcases when we opened them . . . *On that day my feet never felt the ground and it was the second happiest day of my life . . .*

* * *

The garage and the motorcycle club: When we returned from our honeymoon we set about renovating the little service station half a mile from Arrington and about three miles from Royston. The property was owned by a Mr. Pigg, it had a piece of ground at the back which set me thinking. The station was quiet but I thought if we could stimulate some interest in the area like a motorcycle club we could make a go of it. Elizabeth was working as a secretary in the offices of the US Base nearby so for her the station was ideally situated. Elizabeth had very high standards passed on to her by her father; she was very well respected at the base. The filling station had two pumps for Cleveland Oil and we soon realized that the profit margin in selling gasoline was small. The only real profit came from selling fifty gallon drums of oil to the farmers in the area for their machinery. I tried to restart the vending machine business but after having been out of it due to the injuries I had sustained in the car crash I found that the opposition had moved in, taken over my contacts, and started to monopolize the whole business . . . It could have possibly worked but organized criminals had stuck their noses into the business, they sent one of their men packing a firearm to come and see me. The risks to my new family were too great so I decided the better part of valor would be to leave the business altogether. I set to work in earnest at remodeling the station. The building looked like a country cottage with a bedroom, bathroom and toilet, kitchen and lounge with an office near the pumps. I spent my money to upgrade the building and make it more habitable without one iota of assistance from the 'genial' Mr. Pigg who was only interested in his £150 per month . . . We had a beautiful cat, a short haired tabby, and Elizabeth was three months pregnant, at the time there was no way to tell if it was a boy or girl, to me a healthy bouncing baby of either sex would be a boon. We had an electrician in to put in new plug sockets on the Friday; he didn't finish the work and left in the afternoon leaving bare wires sticking out of the socket. Our tabby started playing with the wires. Naked electricity coursed through the poor feline's body and he started to writhe and shake uncontrollably. Elizabeth reached out and tried to snatch him from harm's way, I stopped her just before her fingers touched his fur. Quickly I went to the kitchen and turned off the main electricity supply. It was too late to save our young cat that was dead when I picked him up. Both Elizabeth and I loved cats and we both mourned our loss. But, it could have turned into a tragedy if I hadn't stopped Elizabeth from trying to save him . . . The motorcycle club we started turned the little business around and our gas station started to turn a profit. I made an off-road course on swampy ground behind us on two acres of land. Everything was going fine. We now had twenty members in our group . . . Then disaster struck in short succession . . . one of our riders was killed hitting a telegraph pole as he took a bend too fast on a country road not far from us, then, a month later, one of our club members and his girlfriend had an accident when a big truck pulled across the road in front of them one evening just past the Royston golf club. Their motorcycle slid under the truck and they both died on the spot . . . This put a damper on things and took the enjoyment out of our riding and the motorcycle club.

Elizabeth was six months pregnant with our first child when a Reverend from the local vicarage came calling. Elizabeth was twenty one at the time and the Reverend was not on a social visit, he had other things on his mind . . . When I got home that evening Elizabeth told me what had happened. I wanted to sort the fellow out but she implored me not to, that it wasn't worth it . . . We left it at that but the sour taste in my mouth remained . . .

* * *

Tina being born in Cambridge: She was our little bundle of joy our Tina Louise Chapman, a bright spark in our lives. Elizabeth had decided upon our little girl's name as I kissed her on the forehead and she cradled her in a warm loving embrace. On that day in the middle of February when she was born in Cambridge everything changed for me. It was now the three of us, and our future as a family was foremost in my mind. I wanted to give my little girl the Earth and for her to attain great heights; for she was a bright shining star in a dim grey world . . .

Everyone fell in love with Tina, she was the most gorgeous baby ever, and I was her proud doting dad. It really amazed me how people fussed over her; George and Iris were so thrilled to have such a beautiful granddaughter. I wondered about our future and a better income for our burgeoning family as Elizabeth was pregnant again with our second child . . .

Teddy, my brother had moved permanently to Wales marrying his sweetheart Valerie, they had two children and lived in Borthygest near Portmadoc. Ted suggested we visit and I apply for work at the atomic power station project at Blanau Frestiniog because there were plenty of positions available there. The power station project was about 15 miles from Portmadoc so we packed the filling station business in and off we went in the Rover to north Wales with our precious little baby girl. Tina was growing up so fast and even at twelve months she was already walking, she was turning into a little dictator, one that people just fell in love with at first sight . . . To document her growth I began to take more than the usual amount of photographs with our little *Brownie* camera. The quality of photos it took was amazing and I wished I had taken more onboard the Sweetbriar . . .

* * *

Teddy: Teddy had served with the marines after the Second World War and gone to Malaya with them; before he left he had given me his motorcycle to sell while I was doing carpentry and coach building work in Buntingford and other parts of England. One day while I was up a ladder in my workshop converting a military van to civilian specification a friend brought in a funny looking fellow with an oddly shaped head and malformed dark face. He said, "This man wants to buy the motorcycle . . ." The man groaned and grunted out something unintelligible. I gave a slight shiver; he was the weirdest character I had ever come across. He uttered something again out the corner of his misshapen face. "Urrggghhaa!" He started to walk toward the ladder I was on. I moved one step up. He made another noise and grabbed hold of the ladder, uttering, "Uuuuurrrgggaaahh!"

He shook the ladder below me and made another noise. I nearly had a heart attack, until that is my friend started to laugh his head off and the weird character below me started laughing as well, so much so he had to take the misshapen mask off his face . . . After that episode I sold the bike for Ted and wired the money to Malaya. *'Someday,'* I thought, *'I'll get my friend back for that prank . . .'*

Both Ted and Alfie loved Wales after being evacuated from London and I suppose they would eventually end up back there, which they did. Wales is a beautiful mountainous kingdom and its people are warm and friendly. Ted had started making pottery and was a gifted artist. He eventually purchased a windmill, a yacht and had his own BBC TV series called *Ted* which was widely acclaimed in Britain . . .

Our little family was warmly welcomed by Ted and Valerie, so we settled into the farmhouse with them while I looked for work and more permanent accommodation . . .

* * *

The Adventures of Stanley and Ted: It was around 7:00 am when my brother Ted and I decided to walk up Mount Snowdon in North Wales. It wasn't far from Bedgelert where Ted and Valerie, his wife, had a small farm owned by Valerie's mother. Valerie's father was the managing director of The Danish Bacon Company and the brand had stores all over Great Britain. Ted had a small art and pottery gift shop in Bedgelert . . . On that day our feet were shod with plimsoles as we made our way up a gradual slope on the southern side of the mountain. After about two hours we decided to take a break. The mist had started to get thicker and thicker. It was really cloud but when walking through it seemed to be harmless mist. We carried on climbing up the slope as what had once been a gentle incline was now a scramble up. The mist became very thick and we couldn't see more than a few feet in front of us. We found an outcrop of rock with grass around it to take a break from our exertions. Sitting down we decided to wait until the cloud thinned and we could once again see where we were going. When the whiteness around us cleared we got a shock, just in front of us along the path we were taking was a chasm about three hundred feet in depth. One more step and we would have plunged to our deaths – After that, it was homeward bound – no sense in being stupid and losing our lives just because we wanted to climb up a mountain . . . We had climbed about 1500 feet up the mountain. On the way down we met other climbers who told us that every year one or two people succumbed to Snowdon's charms and never returned home. When we got back to Bedgelert Elizabeth was waiting for me, she was just a tad angry and said, "Where in tar nation's sake have you been, the dinner's been in the oven for over three hours . . . Ted and I had learnt our lesson but the message hadn't sunk in, *well, not just yet . . .*

The sailboat: Jim, Teddy's brother in law, offered the use of his small boat with a sail. He was off with his wife to live in a croft in Scotland; it was offered free and had enough land with it for sheep, cows, pigs and some crops. He wanted to try and make a success from living off the land and be self sufficient. There was also an incentive in the way of social benefits. It was a way to make the inhospitable countryside of Scotland habitable and populous. Ted and I picked up the boat and put it on a trailer; we headed down to Portmadoc which had a wide river running into the sea and an estuary of sorts. We unloaded the boat and launched her into the river. I pulled up the sail and we were off. The river was fast flowing and it wasn't long before we reached a buoy at the mouth of the estuary, it was bigger than the sailboat. I hadn't checked the ropes on the sail; at a glance they looked strong enough. There was a stiff wind and we flew on until the rope stays broke and we headed out to sea with only a small paddle as we had no oars. We had pulled down the sail as it was flapping in the wind and the rope kept breaking every time I tried to repair it. There was no way the little paddle could get us home so we decided to head for the nearest piece of solid land or stretch of sand. Sure enough, not too far away we spotted some sand banks and headed for them. By the time we got to the nearest one we thanked our lucky stars. The tide had been going out and we had left home at eight in the morning. We had both promised to be home for the lunch Elizabeth and Valerie were cooking for us.

We had landed on the wrong side of the estuary and tried pushing the boat back closer to where we had launched it. Our feet kept sinking into the soft sand and the current was deceptively strong, one slip into the water and you would be dragged off into the sea beyond. The current was also undercutting the sandbank so one false step would collapse it and leave you waist deep in muddy water. We had dragged, pushed and fumbled our way up the side of the sand bar, but the closer we got to the river running into the estuary the faster the current became. Portmadoc was further up the estuary and a river joined it opposite a small resort with a beach. We decided to cross the eighty so yards of the river mouth using our small paddle; we had no option for we were now up to our knees in water and in danger of being swept away without the boat. Taking turns we made our way across and were nearly to the other side when the current took hold of us and pulled us into the estuary. We were now heading back out to sea. As luck would have it the current also took us toward the little beach on the opposite side. We waved and called to the people lazing around and playing ball on it. All this elicited were friendly waves back. Eventually someone on the beach realized we were in trouble.

We had one good rope left that hadn't broken which we threw to a man who had waded out into the current. He caught it and dragged us to shore with the help of another kind Samaritan. By the time we returned at 5:30 pm Elizabeth was furious, the roast and our beautiful Sunday lunch were ruined. Valerie was thankful we had got back in one piece. Ted slapped me on the shoulder and said, "Well, that's another fine mess you've got me into, Stanley . . ."

\* \* \*

Shaun being born in Wales: On a beautiful summer's day in May while we were still staying with Teddy, Elizabeth went into labor and had to be rushed to hospital in Pwllheli on the coast near Portmadoc. The small hospital was once the residence of Lloyd George, a great statesman and the Prime Minister of Britain during the First World War. Shaun was overdue and had no intention of leaving his mother, but, nature being nature, he had no option. He was ten pounds and two ounces when he entered the world and a long time coming. Ted and I had stayed behind on the farm to look after my little daughter, Tina. I waited patiently at home by the phone with Tina alternately walking and running around me. When the phone eventually rang I picked up the receiver swiftly and heard the words, "You have a son Mr. Chapman . . ." What glorious words they were. Elizabeth had named him Shaun. He was big, but not fat, very quiet and very healthy . . . Shaun would sit and watch the world around him with great interest, reflecting and pondering on the world without. Tina was thrilled and enthralled at having a little brother, and at that young age she was very protective of him, and even though she still wore diapers and was only about seventeen months old and could hardly reach the handle she would delight at pushing his pram around as though she was an adult. Shaun would look on from out of the pram in feigned amusement at her. I was now the proud father of two beautiful and delightful children and the husband to an equally beautiful and lovesome woman, Elizabeth . . .

\* \* \*

The Nuclear Power Station: I had an interview in the project manager's office at the construction site at the new soon-to-be-built nuclear power station at Blanau Frestiniog. They took me on immediately as a carpenter not realizing my abilities as a draughtsman. It wasn't long before my job description changed and I was redeployed to the planning office on the construction site where they needed my skills. I then started on detail drawings of the project and copying work sent in from London. The work was very interesting, and we had to construct two cooling towers with each taking between three to four months to build. The erection of the towers required the use of massive Goliath cranes. I was really in my element and loved the challenge. I spent my time in the planning office on my board with a drafting pen in hand and on site liaising with the engineers. However, the problem Elizabeth and I faced was where to live; we couldn't share a home with Teddy and Valerie forever. I approached a tall Irishman who was working on the project and he suggested we run a big old house he'd bought as a guest house. The place would have to be fixed up first and needed painting but I thought it would be right up my alley after the renovation work I'd done for Mr. Peak on his two cottages. When we got there Elizabeth and I couldn't believe it, the place was filthy with dust and full of rats, it hadn't been used in ages, I thought, *'Oh God, what have we let ourselves in for!'* We did our best though and started to make the place habitable. Work was going fine at the nuclear power station and my salary was excellent, that was until four men were contaminated by a loose cooling rod. The engineer and three workers went red in the face very quickly; they had been irradiated and burnt. I knew all four well and they died within six months of the accident. I thought long and hard, seriously considering what would happen to me and my little family if something went wrong while I was in the plant. Later that day when I got home, I said to Elizabeth, "Maybe it's not such a good idea to work at the nuclear power station . . ." *Yes, I needed work, but at the risk of my life? I remember their faces clearly all glowing and shiny red; it was a pitiful sight indeed . . .*

# CHAPTER 15

## The Sea Calls

**W**inter had set in and it was decidedly cold in Wales, snow fell on mist covered hills and mountains and ice covered the roads. It was a winter wonderland but I didn't feel like Santa Claus and my secondhand 1940s Austin pick-up was no sled, though by the way she slid around corners and over the ice crystals that had formed over the tar macadam I was driving on I was beginning to wonder whether in fact she was. Snow whipped past the Austin and settled on the hood as the windscreen wipers struggled desperately to keep the glass clear. I tried to see through the white windblown crystals accumulating on the windscreen, in front of me was a white road, to the side white stone walls, and past them, white snow covered mountainsides with fields running down the slopes . . . Every Sunday for the past few weeks I had scanned the newspapers for a better place to live and a better life for Elizabeth and our two young babies. And every Sunday I would see balmy sunny weather and a warm comely climate in Brisbane, Australia. Winter in Blaneau up in the Welsh mountains was on the opposite side of the spectrum; it was bitterly cold and had a chill wind that would bite the very core of your soul, not unlike Nimir, or a mythical Norse frost giant casting its frozen hand out at you. Elizabeth had never once complained about anything, she was a wonderful caring mother to Tina and Shaun, and had spent her time cleaning up the guest house making it warm and homely. Now, with all her work, the rambling old building sparkled and looked like a new pin . . . The stone walls had now disappeared and I started down a steep mountainside, but, for some reason, the Austin refused to slow down as I pushed down on the brakes, I pushed harder, almost to the floorboards. I was going down a very steep hill with sharp bends every hundred yards or so as the road threaded down the side of the mountain. I pushed even harder this time, all the way to the floor boards. I grimaced as the brakes refused to work and the pick-up slid from side to side all over the road as it picked up speed and I tried to keep it under control. As I changed down through the grating gears I could smell the asbestos lining of the clutch plate. Another bend loomed in front of me as I looked down the steep declivity on my right, I envisioned myself flying into space and crashing in flames at the rocky bottom. I gritted my teeth and tried to keep the Austin under control. The Austin scrapped the rock on my left and bounced over some rocks as it skewed round on the ice on two wheels. It was now on the verge of going out of control with me at the wheel guiding it to an untimely end. As the road wound down the bank on my left going up the mountain got broader so I let the Austin run up hoping the muddy slope would impede its progress to Valhalla, *it worked!* I now had a modicum of control and was able to slow her a little. I approached a large bend, the automobile was now in first gear and the smell of burnt asbestos filled the Austin. My clutch was pretty much finished now; the muddy slope would be my last chance. As the Austin came into the bend I let her ride up the earthen snow covered side of the mountain, the Austin slowed then came to a halt at a rakish angle on the steep mountainside. *I was safe at last!* I sat staring through the cold frosty windscreen; snow was gradually adhering to it. The wipers had given up the ghost when I shut off the engine. I got out and lifted the hood,

I thought, *'If I don't fix it I'll be sitting in the frozen hunk of metal till summer sets in . . .'* I set to work fixing it . . .

Eventually, after making some repairs and on my way home, I kept thinking of Brisbane and a warm sky spreading its expanse over me and mine, I made up my mind to do something about it, this was no life for Elizabeth and the little ones, definitely not . . . Not long afterward I picked up a copy of *The People*, a popular national rag in Britain, and saw an advertorial stating *Australia Needs People of all Trades and Businesses*, free travel for approved applicants, *We Need Young Families*. There was a £10 application fee which Elizabeth agreed we should send off immediately. She was as tired as I was of the cold British weather. I had had enough of storm tossed seas and cold biting ice-filled winds striking my face in the navy, I felt I deserved a break, that my family shouldn't suffer what I had during the war. The guest house was cold in winter; it had large stone fireplaces that even when full of burning wood and stoked to keep the embers alight never seemed to keep the stone building warm enough. It took two weeks for a large manila envelope to return full of forms, tickets for the voyage, tickets for the rail journey and £50 for expenses. Both Elizabeth and I were thrilled, me even more so, I would once again be at sea and would be cruising to my beloved Mediterranean. I had never sailed in the Indian Ocean and was looking forward to the experience. A note in the envelope said, "The passenger ship, the RMS Orion was now at Barking docks and ready to sail to Australia. Your berth will be on 'E' deck and you should be ready to board within five days at the quayside. A purser from the RMS Orion will meet you there and take you onboard to your cabin . . ." Elizabeth was ecstatic and I couldn't wait to leave . . .

I had met a tourist by the name of Lou Armitage while we were in Wales, he was from New Zealand and had recently lost his wife there. He was touring around Britain in an old Riley he intended to take back with him when he left. We got on like a house on fire and I had his address and telephone number in my wallet, if we ever went to New Zealand I would be sure to look him up since he had been most adamant I should. The owner of the guest house wasn't happy we were going; it would be a hard slog for him to keep it open, what with the constant upkeep and all. He was pondering about returning to Ireland and selling the place if we left. But the die was cast. I sold the Austin pick-up and we bought a beautiful new pram for Tina and Shaun. The pram was like a new toy for Tina and we just couldn't stop her from pushing Shaun around in it. I would scream, "No! No! Tina, you're going to fall over . . ." she never listened. I may have been their father, but Tina, she was his big sister. Shaun was her new baby brother and she called the shots, whatever I said fell on deaf ears . . .

\* \* \*

It was ten in the morning when we left the old stone guest house in Blaneau. A cold icy frost covered the road an inch thick, our feet crunched on it as we trod carefully down the straight road to the station. I carried two suitcases and Tina while Elizabeth pushed our new pram with Shaun tucked snugly inside and another two cases perched on it. We had sent the rest of our trunks to the ship already. The station was only about five hundred yards away, a slippery treacherous five hundred yards. A Welsh chill spread through the frozen air, our vaporous breath hung in the cold morning mist until it disappeared, whipped away by a slight breeze. I breathed a sigh of relief when we reached the station without slipping and falling. After waiting a short while on the chilly platform a two carriage electric train arrived and we boarded it, we had now started our long journey to Australia, the first port of call would be the main station at Colwyn Bay . . . The electric train arrived at Colwyn without any fuss or ado and a wait of one hour saw us boarding a high speed express train to Euston station with only one stop on the way . . . The express had come from Holyhead where the ferries cross to Ireland. We had a compartment all to ourselves which was a blessing because of the nappy changes, clothing changes and feeding Tina and Shaun. In summer-time you would be hard pressed to find a vacant seat let alone a vacant compartment. The spacious compartment made the trip so much easier for Elizabeth, especially at changing times. The train only stopped at Rugby then finally at Euston. In the morning we would have to be at King's Cross to catch the train for Tilbury docks . . . When we disembarked at Euston we were in a quandary about our lodgings for the night but the railway attendants were so helpful and found us accommodation at a guest house not far from King's Cross station. The packing and journey with two babies in tow was tiring and we only managed to sustain ourselves on snacks. Our attention was focused on the comfort of our two young children. That night the Welsh winter chill had followed us and London was bitterly cold, I spent most of the night putting shilling pieces in the gas meter to keep us warm. Elizabeth and I were pleased when a cold winter sun in a mist filled sky peeked over the horizon from the east. We went down to the dining room and had a breakfast of toast, egg and tea. Elizabeth was so excited about the prospect of new horizons and opportunities open to us in Australia. We packed quickly and were off again to catch the train for the docks. When we got to King's Cross the train was waiting for us. The carriages were already full of eager emigrants, all just as excited as Elizabeth and I; they all wondered what the voyage would be like and what life in Australia would be like. Tina was made a fuss of as usual and Shaun just sat in his pram, his normal stoic uncomplaining self. It wasn't long before the train pulled up to a platform on the docks which was right next to the Orion's berth. I had a shock when I saw the liner; I had no idea a ship that size, an ocean going liner, could even get so far up the Thames River. The day before D-Day, when we had picked up the liners under our protection, they were much further down the Thames. The purser meeting us on the dockside was very nice and led us aboard to our cabin on 'E' deck, it was snug, Elizabeth didn't complain, she took everything in her stride and got to work organizing our living quarters.

At any rate, Elizabeth and I were pleased to be aboard, and after we settled in we went to the dining room which could seat between three to four hundred people at a time. Sitting down at our table who should waltz over to serve us but the head waiter from The Banyers, Bob Nelson, both Elizabeth and I smiled broadly. He was also surprised to see us and said, "If I'd known you were coming aboard I could have arranged a lovely cabin for you on the upper decks and all the perks you could possibly require . . ." but, he didn't know, how could he, unless he'd seen the purser's passenger list, and we hadn't been to The Banyers in a while. He had even been our head waiter at our wedding reception. After a little chat he brought us lunch, a sumptuous feast which we really enjoyed after all the fuss and bother of catching the trains and the cold night at the guest house. Soon, it was all forgotten and we thrilled at the thought of seeing the back of cold inhospitable England and Wales once and for all . . . The Orion had been at Tilbury docks for a week fueling and preparing herself for the voyage to Australia and once all the migrants were aboard she set sail in the afternoon. I stood near the stern on an upper deck in my cavalry twill overcoat, it was bitterly cold outside and Elizabeth was with the children inside our warm cabin. She had worn the mink coat I had bought for her as a present on board, but it was just too cold to take Tina and Shaun outside to watch the ship slip gently down the Thames to the English Channel. It was now late afternoon as I stood there on the deck resting my elbows on the thick wooden top railing. I said my goodbyes to London, England and Wales and all the trouble and strife during my years at war. I said goodbye to mother and father and my brothers whom I figured I would never see again. I said goodbye to the cold and the frost, and the mist and fog. Thoughts of my family during the Blitz came into my mind, I thought of Grandfather and Grandmother Chapman and Grandmother O'Sullivan, of Uncle Percy and Aunt Mary . . . A film of mist covered my eyes and I tried to contain the tears, I turned and headed back to our cabin on 'E' deck pulling the lapels up even closer to my neck to stop the chill that had started to envelop my heart . . . In the encroaching darkness, the docks, the city of London and the River Thames slowly disappeared . . .

\* \* \*

As we sailed through the English Channel thoughts of the D-Day landings flooded my mind, there was just no escape from it, the smell of the ship and the gentle vibration from the screws on the hull, waves hitting the Orion's sides eliciting a gentle swaying motion from her. Vivid memories I had tried hard to forget came back. I had visions of troops disgorged by landing craft, of transport ships in the hundreds, of blood spilt on the beaches of Normandy, of gliders and aircraft by the thousand filling the sky above me, waves upon waves of them . . . And then I saw my two beautiful children sleeping peacefully and gazed into Elizabeth's eyes while we sat down to dinner . . . *'Did I deserve this when so many had sacrificed their lives,'* I asked myself. I reminded myself to cherish each moment with them. I was restless, an old sea-dog wanting to greet his old mistress. I left Elizabeth and the babies sleeping in our cabin for the night and continued my stroll on the top deck. The temperature was now dropping drastically so why disturb them just for the wont of company and the cold night air. The memories of the D-Day landings refused to stop so I let the thoughts overpower and immerse me within their folds. *'A little self indulgence and remembrance wouldn't hurt,'* I thought, at the very least I would be paying homage to the men that had died . . . I continued to gaze out at the dark seas around us as the ship carried on its southward course, I knew that the air would be warmer the further south we steamed. I thought of Tina and Shaun safely tucked in their bunk, warm and contented, it was a far cry on that day seemingly so long ago, that sixth day in June of 1944, when German shells bombarded our ships and submarines attacked us from these self-same waters. *'How the world had changed,'* I thought. After a while I decided to go back to the cabin; I didn't want to be away from my family too long. It was going to be a long voyage and I reveled in it, no more four hours on and four hours off with my downtime spent on the bridge with a pair of binoculars around my neck, with mountainous waves threatening to swamp us, German dive bombers swooping down out of the sky like hungry vultures lusting for our blood and U-Boats rising from the depths to tin-fish us, no, this would be a pleasure cruise I would enjoy . . .

* * *

The lights of Lisbon twinkled in the distance; it was early morning when the Orion sailed into the harbor and I left Elizabeth in the cabin with the babies to stretch my legs. We tied up at a buoy just off the promenade. It was a lot warmer now; there was no snow or ice and driving cold rain, just a light windblown early morning chill from the west. I smiled to myself; I was back in Lisbon harbor. Breakfast would be served at seven and the sea air had invigorated me, the hunger I had felt in my soul for a new life had been replaced by that of a hearty meal. I went back to the cabin with a new spring in my step . . .

During the day the ship's boat shuttled back and forth bringing fresh supplies of fruit and vegetables. Britain in winter is not the best place to procure fresh vitals, it was by far better to purchase such things for a long voyage in a country graced by sunshine and warm nurturing weather. After the ship was refueled we left Lisbon and the promenade lined with statues and its stucco faced buildings for an Atlantic beam sea and the prospect of warm Mediterranean seas and skies. That night we sailed through the Straits of Gibraltar. There would be no stopover there and all I saw of my wartime Gibraltar was its warm inviting lights under a clear starlit sky as our bow cut through phosphor tinted waves. We left Gibraltar in our stern wake heading for Sicily and Malta.

Life on board was relaxing and calm with our happy little family, our waiter from The Banyers in Royston really did his best to make sure we had everything we needed, especially at meal times. He was the first friend we had made on the voyage, but it wasn't long before we found other new parents to while away our time with. We laid blankets out on the deck for the children and babies to play. I spent a lot of time running after Tina who delighted in making me chase her. She would giggle at first then try to worm her way out of my firm hold. I had no intention of losing sight of her. Shaun, still only six months old, was happy on the blanket with his doting mother keeping an eye on him. He was happiest with a crayon in his hand and a piece of paper on which to draw. Life was idyllic on the Orion as we sailed toward Greece. The Mediterranean had given us her best, gentle waves and warm sunny skies. I felt at home, and even though it had been a long time she embraced me with all the love and joy she could muster. In the intervening years I had missed her greatly and now, our ill-fated voyage at war's end was but a dream, I was back in her warm loving arms, and that was all that mattered. I only hoped she wouldn't be jealous of my beautiful wife and children . . .

* * *

Pirea loomed before us in the Mediterranean sunlight; it was the biggest and busiest shipping port in Greece. The first thing they did once we'd berthed was to put chains and locks on the doors leading to the lower decks with 'No Admittance' signs on them. I asked our waiter friend why they did it, he replied, "Stan, you won't believe what you'll see in two day's time. I'll take you down then . . ."

We were in Pirea for a day to replenish supplies and pick up the passengers from Greece, by nightfall we were on our way again heading for the Suez Canal. Elizabeth and I put the small ones to bed and went down for dinner. Our waiter, Bob, kept smiling as I told Elizabeth of the locks on the doors, he reiterated his previous comment to Lizzie, "Just wait another couple of days Elizabeth, I'm taking Stan down to show him, you'll understand then why we have to take such drastic precautions . . ." I shook my head in wonderment and Liz noted, "Isn't that a bit harsh, Stan?" I just shrugged my shoulders, what could I say . . .

After two days at sea a horrible smell seemed to permeate every nook and cranny of the ship. Elizabeth wrinkled up her nose, "What is that nasty stench?" Not long after Bob Nelson, knocked on our cabin door and said, "Stan, come with me, I want to show you something . . ." I followed him and we went down to the lower decks through the chained and locked doors. One deck below us he opened the door to the toilets and I couldn't believe my eyes, the walls were covered in dripping excrement with streaky finger marks everywhere. I clutched my nose and mouth in my right hand, turned and fled from the stench. I didn't bother waiting for him and headed for the stairs to go up top. Catching up to me, he said, "Before we go back up I want you to see the lower decks. I didn't really have the stomach for it but he insisted so off we went. It didn't get any better and I was glad to get back to an upper outside deck and smell the aromatic salty scent of the sea. By the time we reached the Suez Canal nearly everyone on board had dysentery . . .

It was another sunny Mediterranean morning and at the entrance to the canal the ship was surrounded by a flotilla of little boats, their occupants proffering all sorts of goods from tea, coffee to locally made craft items. Nothing tempted Elizabeth or I so we headed back to our deck chairs where our two babies were being watched by some of the young parents we had met on board where Elizabeth and the other mothers had set up a crèche of sorts with blankets and toys to keep the small ones entertained until feeding or changing times . . . Another two days saw us reaching the port of Aden where we and another couple with small children decided to go ashore and sightsee. We were all excited as we toured the shops and surroundings adjacent to the Orion's berth. It didn't last long though. The locals were very hostile and scowled venomously at us, even going so far as to spit on the ground in front of us. Elizabeth and I had had enough, so to the couple we were with; we hurried back to the ship through a gamut of angry faced white robed hostiles. As far as I was concerned they could swallow all the sands of Arabia. I hoped it would get stuck in their throats along with their spit. With its refueling finished the Orion set sail into the Indian Ocean; I for one was pleased to see the back of Aden. We were now very near the equator and the temperature rose dramatically. It was a little too much for Liz and the babies who stayed in the shade and sought out any comforting breeze the ocean had to offer. The conditions in Aden left a lot to be desired and those who hadn't had dysentery along with Elizabeth and our two babies now contracted it. They had a severe case and ended up in the infirmary with air-conditioning. Because of the severe equatorial heat it was the one place on board that offered some respite from it. In a way Elizabeth was happier there . . .

* * *

Shaun had been sick for the past week but sunny skies and the nurse in the infirmary had done wonders to his health and he was his old perky happy self. "Let me take him out for some air," I said to Elizabeth, who was still a bit under the weather herself, after picking up the same tummy bug. Leaving our cabin I strolled down the wooden decking with Shaun wrapped in a blanket. The lower decks with the steerage passengers from Greece were still gated and locked so there weren't many people on deck that afternoon, this gave me a chance to think and reflect, on the recent past and the future, and, what it had in store for us . . . I strolled unconcernedly up and down the deck eventually ending up in the aft section . . .

As I stood there on the aft deck looking at the sun setting on the horizon and the frothy wake of the ship disappearing into the distance amidst the endless waters of the Indian Ocean my mind travelled unconsciously back to the war, the pain, the suffering, the men lost at sea, drowning in oily muck or shivering uncontrollably until they lost consciousness and slipped beneath the waves never to be seen again, their families grieving and heartbroken. This had left an indelible mark upon my soul . . . I thought how future generations may not realize the peril civilization faced by the evil that pervaded Europe and the Far East in that last great war. But we did. We rolled up our sleeves and stepped into the fray, whether on the home front, tilling the fields or working in factories building tanks and aircraft, producing the ammunition and bombs used against those Axis forces, and the men who fought on the front line staring death in the face each day . . . It was because of us that the Nazi flag was set aflame then drowned in a sea of blood, both ours and our enemies, never to rise again . . .

Standing there holding my six month old son, with a cool breeze whipping around us and the ship's flag fluttering, the heaving deck beneath my feet, I thought, *'Yes, we had done alright, we had saved the world from an evil that would have dominated the Earth for one thousand years, the Third Reich and Hitler had been beaten, so future generations like my son could be free from the heel of oppression, crushing and beating them into submission,'* I couldn't help but wonder though, what future challenges would face him and the rest of humanity in the years to come . . . Even though the war in Europe and the Pacific had ended the world was still not at peace with itself. Bob had commented that we would dock in Ceylon for supplies and fuel; both Liz and I looked forward to it, even though fighting had broken out in some parts of the country.

\* \* \*

As the Orion sailed smoothly across the Indian Ocean the war in Ceylon began to hot up and a festering mass of discontent boiled over creating an environment of hostility throughout the country. Their ports were now off limits to passenger liners so we headed for Bombay in India for refueling and supplies instead . . . Sailing to India under bright sun filled days and star filled nights was a far cry from the hectic waters of the Atlantic in mid-winter. I relaxed in a deck chair with a magazine in shorts and a short sleeve shirt, yes, this was a far cry from my navy days, and I was beginning to enjoy it immensely. As with any good thing though, it wasn't going to last forever and one evening the Orion sailed into Bombay and tied up at a wharf. That following day Elizabeth and I decided to visit the city of Bombay proper and immerse ourselves in the markets, the oriental spices, its delights, smells and sounds. When we told Bob, our waiter, of our plans he screwed up his nose and said, "It's not a good idea, the place smells awful and the conditions in the city are not very sanitary, honestly I think it would be better to stay aboard the ship . . ."

After discussing this with Elizabeth and the couple we were to accompany onto the streets of Bombay it was decided that the gents would foray out to reconnoiter the place and the ladies would stay behind with the young children. It took us one hour of walking through filthy streets and jumping over open sewers, with prostitutes hanging in baskets in front of shops beseeching passersby for business, to decide it wasn't worth the effort. We headed back to the ship with a rotten taste in our mouths and the stench of open sewers assailing our nostrils and clinging to our clothes . . . Only a few hours after we returned to the ship she was heading out into the ocean once more . . . After giving Ceylon a wide berth it took us five days of large ocean swells to reach Perth and Freemantle where the ship docked. It was a beautiful day when the Orion arrived. The weather was perfect, not too hot and not too cold. Elizabeth got the babies ready and we walked down the gangway with them and took

our first steps onto Australian soil. The town was very quaint
and homely and looked very much like Ilford in Essex in the
olden days. We both fell in love with it and decided this was
where we should start our new lives, especially since there were
'Situation Vacant' signs everywhere. I knew I could get a job of
some description immediately. When we returned to the ship
I found Bob Nelson and told him we want to get off the ship
here. Bob said, "You'll have to see the purser about it, he's the
only man who can give you permission . . ." Elizabeth and I set
off to see him immediately. When we located him he said very
politely, "By all means, if that is what you want to do but there's a
little problem, you see, your luggage is at the bottom of the hold,
impossible to get at until we reach our last port of call, from
here we go to Adelaide–Melbourne–Sydney and then Brisbane
– your destination. We'll only return to Perth in six months
time." Both Elizabeth and I were shocked, the pram, the babies
clothes, toys and cots, our radio and clothes, personal effects,
bedding and household items were now unreachable with tons
of other stuff stacked on top of it. We realized we had no choice
but to stay on board, it would have been a miserable situation
indeed to leave the ship without them, life would have been nigh
impossible. So we stayed with the ship hoping that Brisbane
would be the same . . . The journey around the south coast of
Australia proved uneventful and we soon arrived in Adelaide.
It was Eastern European in flavor with many Yugoslavians
and Ukrainians settling there. It was a vast vine growing area
with many wines being produced and it seemed the languages
spoken were of Eastern European origin. The temperature got
colder the further south we went and by the time we reached
Melbourne the seas had turned very rough in the Australian
Bight and the skies were grey and overcast. Going into the port
of Melbourne the wild sea tried hard to upset the stomach of
everyone on board. Our two small babies were not happy at
all so when we docked Elizabeth stayed to comfort them and I
went ashore under grey cold skies . . . The place reminded me

a lot of Britain as the people were very reserved and not very sociable. The buildings in Melbourne matched the skies, grey and miserable. The atmosphere of the place was much the same so I headed back to the ship with nothing to report, I didn't like leaving my little family for long . . . After two days in port to refuel, resupply and drop off passengers we were off again, to Sydney this time . . . By now Elizabeth was getting tired of being on the ship, even our babies had had enough of it and couldn't wait to feel grass and sand between their toes again. Tina had now begun to talk and her intelligence shined through, Shaun, of course, remained taciturn. All the passengers on the ship admired Elizabeth and our babies. Bob Nelson would always bring little presents of food and things he thought we needed for the babies and Elizabeth. I was use to ship life so the time spent aboard didn't bother me . . . then the seas got rough, very rough. Huge waves lashed the ship and cold Antarctic air from the south made me pleased we had brought along sweaters and coats. I was told it was normal for this time of year; I yearned for the pleasant climate of Perth, for a walk on the decks outside was now hazardous and out of the question . . . Two days of this saw us reaching Sydney and calmer waters . . .

* * *

The Orion entered Sydney Harbor after breakfast one morning with Elizabeth, the babies and I standing on deck next to the railing gazing at the vista it presented. It was a beautiful harbor indeed with a wide entrance and verdant growth on both sides, and a bridge Stevenson would have been proud of crossing the harbor. We were all so excited at the prospect of getting off the ship to sample dry land in a civilized city at long last . . . Once the ship docked we were off the Orion and walked through the dockyard area where the shops were old and scruffy, but eventually we entered the High Street and all this disappeared being replaced by rows of attractive well appointed and stocked shops. It seemed we had walked into a totally different city. Sydney was at least warm compared to Melbourne and Adelaide; the buildings of the city proper were old, but well cared for and not overly tall. Elizabeth and I headed for a bus terminus for a day trip over Sydney Harbor Bridge with the children to the zoo, this brought a little bit of normality into our storm tossed lives. My little family appreciated both the outing and terra firma under their feet, and the opportunity for Tina and Shaun to hold and cuddle a koala bear . . . The ship had arrived in the morning and by the following evening she had departed for Brisbane, our final port of call and destination . . .

I had no idea what Brisbane would be like when we arrived, my knowledge of it was derived from the temperatures it presented to the world in the British Sunday newspapers, I thought the work situation would be the same as that of Perth with vacancies abounding. The temperature increased by the day the further north up the east coast we steamed. In two days we made landfall . . . We had made many good friends aboard the Orion and were invited by a young couple to stay with them until we found a decent place to live . . . Australia, with its vast open spaces, kangaroos and aborigines, was now our home . . .

# CHAPTER 16

## Australia

I was looking forward to a new beginning in Australia and getting away from the memories of the war, the death and destruction I had witnessed, but most of all relishing the thought of my own family and the joy they would bring in the future, seeing them grow and prosper. I still suffered from nightmares of the German bombs, the whistling noise they made before they exploded, of black painted aircraft adorned with swastikas bearing down on me and ending my life and those around me. I had witnessed firsthand the effect war had had on families, even our own, taking away our home, our lives, family members, and our way of life, reducing it all to ashes. My family had never been the same after the war, we had grown apart, become restless, always yearning for and seeking for something that had vanished and would never again exist on this mortal plane of ours. The closeness we had as a family was gone; it had evaporated along with the innocence of my younger years. Everything had been ripped apart by falling German bombs and endless ocean rollers . . .

\* \* \*

It wasn't long before Elizabeth and I found a cottage on the beach at Clontarf. Setting up house again wasn't easy but we did it anyway and before long we had a comfortable place to call home. We attended a meeting of immigrants from the RMS Orion and found out that each state was very different when it came to work, Australia is a very large country and Queensland had recently experienced a typhoon which had impacted very negatively on it. Farms and villages had been swept away leaving the survivors penniless. Pulling up at a gas station in Redcliffe one day an attendant came up to me. I thought he must be the owner or manager of the station. He was in his late forties and looked to me to be a man of superior intellect and high standing. We began to chat and he asked many questions about Britain. He said, "I haven't been there in a while; the last time was over twenty years ago . . ." As he pushed the gas pump nozzle into the tank he continued, "So what are you doing here?"

I told him of my years in the navy, the Berlin Airlift and the work I had done since, and the fact that I wanted to establish myself here in one business or another.

"Maybe you have some ideas or would like to assist in some manner?" I said.

He looked up and smiled at me, "If you had asked me eight months ago I could have helped you, but now," he laughed, "I'm just a petrol attendant here . . ."

"You're joking . . ." I replied.

He shook his head and a serious look came over his face, "I wish I were . . . I use to have over a thousand head of prize cattle on my farm and exported all over the world . . . But now, after a bad storm I lost my farm. My land was covered in mud one yard in depth. My house and all my farm buildings were destroyed and washed away with all my cattle and farm equipment. Now it's taking all my time just to try and rebuild our home, the banks won't help me. At the moment my family and I are sleeping under what remains of our house. The strong sun burns our dog and cat, who were the only survivors of the storm . . . When I see a storm brewing and hear lightning now

I panic . . . I can't afford to buy anything now; it's all I can do working here to buy food for the family . . ."

The little chat we had gave me a healthy respect of storms and the power of nature in Australia. When I left I gave him some notes to assist his rebuilding work. It just goes to show you how fragile life can be and no matter how hard pressed you may feel there are always people worse off than you . . .

My first meeting in Britain with immigration officers had led me to believe that with my experience in civil engineering and drafting I would get a job immediately. This didn't happen so I went straight down to Home Affairs for assistance because there didn't seem to be any openings at all. When I arrived at the immigration offices it was full of men seeking work, most of them were Italian and Greek, and they all looked a tad shabby. Standing there in my blue blazer and pressed trousers and shirt with tie I couldn't see a board with work vacancies on so I decided to go straight to the manager, since the queue was far too long. I looked like a professional cricketer with my attire and the office staffers were all a little taken aback when I knocked on the door and strode in. I was on a mission so niceties could wait, right now I needed work and nobody was going to stop me from getting it. They called the manager and he came immediately. I quietly explained to him that the Sunday newspaper *The People* had fabricated the opportunities available in Australia, and in particular Brisbane, or was it the Australian government? I had looked for work but had come up with nothing, I said, "Look, my brother is a journalist with a paper in London and I will be contacting him as soon as I leave the office . . . So either you can find me something, or . . ."

Within twenty four hours of me leaving the office they found me a position with an engineering company. The offices had no air conditioning so it was rather hot and stuffy inside when I arrived on my first day of work to start as a draftsman. Liz and I now had a home and work. The cottage was separated from the beach by a tar road and was one and a half miles from Redcliffe,

a small seaside town to the north that catered for holiday makers
in the high season. It had the normal amenities for a town that
size, hotels, shops, arcades and entertainment areas with many
wood framed holiday homes lining the shore on both sides. To
the south a ten minute bus ride took us into Brisbane. Redcliffe
was developing slowly and the area reminded me of something
out of Africa. Offshore were islands and the Great Barrier Reef
that separated us from the Pacific Ocean. There were plenty
of sharks and crocodiles in the area so you would always have
to be mindful of them when taking the children to the beach.
Even though our bungalow was made of brick and very quaint
we decided to move to another house in a more private grassed
area a couple of streets away from the beachfront when one
became available, mainly because the road outside was always
busy and we were worried that one of our toddlers would run
out onto the road. If we could find one with trees in the yard
that could provide a modicum of shade for Elizabeth and the
toddlers it would be a bonus. Within three months one became
available, a two bedroom cottage three streets away from the
beach with ample living and dining room space, it even had two
little trees in the garden with plenty of lawn area for Tina and
Shaun to play in. Shaun was beginning to walk and Tina was
irrepressible, a little firecracker who demanded more space to
play in. So we moved and set up home again. But a day before we
left I saw a big green and gray snake go under the water heater
in the bathroom, I hurried outside to find someone since I
didn't want the snake to bite one of the toddlers or Elizabeth, a
young man was walking by looking for a place to rent, he came
in with me and went to the immersion tank where he pulled out
a big green and gray lizard with a blue tongue. "Don't worry, it's
harmless unless it's attacked, and even then they'll only bite."
Then he added, "These lizards grow to about four or five feet
in length . . ." He took it over the road and released it onto the
beach; so much for what I thought was a snake . . .

When we left the cottage I had mistakenly left two of my expensive blue and white check Tern shirts there, by the time I returned to fetch them a pastor and his wife had moved into the cottage, I knocked on the door and the pastor answered, I enquired, "Excuse me, but I lived here not long ago and I mistakenly left two of my shirts, they are blue and white check Terns . . ." He answered, "No, never seen them." His wife was just behind him and when I repeated the question to her, she replied very sweetly, "No . . . I've never seen them either." The pastor then closed the door. I shook my head as I headed to my automobile at the roadside, *'Damn,'* I thought, *'they were expensive . . .'* Not two weeks later I was late for work and driving down the same road and what did I see hanging on the rotary line in the back garden of our old cottage, *my shirts!* I stopped the car and jumped over the low wall to the back and grabbed them off the line. The pastor's wife came out of the house and saw me; she flushed red and went back inside quickly, closing the door behind her . . .

* * *

Salesman Stan: I had been in the drafting office for over three months and was getting tired of the drudgery. There was just no challenge to the work and my abilities, especially after having worked at the nuclear power station. I wasn't happy there and decided I should look around for something else with more prospects and money . . . Walking along the seafront one day and thinking about my friend Lou in Auckland and how he was doing, I saw a tall well dressed English looking fellow standing at the entrance to a big store with a large sign above stating, 'H.G. Palmers, Radios, TV & all types of Electrical Goods,' I said, "Good morning . . ." He replied, "Morning . . ." Then we got chatting, I asked, "Are you buying something here?" He laughed and said, "No, I work here, I'm the manager . . ." We carried on talking and I told him of my experience in the navy on radar and construction projects. I said, "You've got a nice cushy job, I wish I could do the same." He replied, "Well, why don't you apply for a job then with H.G. Palmers? They're all over the country . . ." I nodded and it got me thinking, why not? It wasn't legal for any immigrant to leave a job for two years but I just couldn't stand being in the hot, dusty and stuffy office anymore. As he led me into the air conditioned store, he asked, "Have you had any sales experience?"

"No . . ." I replied. "Well, if you go for an interview, don't say that . . ."

During my lunch break one day I went to Fort St. Valley in Brisbane to the head office of H.G. Palmers and asked to see the manager, everyone was very cordial and I soon stepped into his office. I sat down and asked whether he had any vacancies. "Yes, why?" he answered. I said, "I've just arrived from Britain and am looking for a position . . ."

"Do you have any selling and electrical experience?" he queried. I replied, "Yes, indeed I do."

"Well then, you can apply for a position," the manager stated, "I'll set up an appointment with our sales manager from Sydney, he's coming up next week . . ."

Two days after my interview I received an appointment letter and was employed by H.G. Palmers. With the job, which was selling and repossessing items in arrears, came a smart split screen VW Kombi with big chrome bumpers. It was mine to use for work and home. H.G. Palmers sold their goods on a deposit or no-deposit basis, which, for sales, was a good tactic and helped me no-end . . .

The drafting company weren't happy at all that I had left them and kept on calling. Eventually two gentlemen from the immigration department came to our house. Elizabeth answered the door and invited them in for tea and cake, after she had explained in an eloquent manner the reason why I had found it necessary to obtain another position with a better salary and perks to look after our family they went away smiling. Her rational and intelligent reasoning satisfied them and they were happy I had found a better position with H.G. Palmers . . . we never heard from them again . . .

* * *

We had moved from a brick house to a framework wooden house on stilts, the reason for this was the amount of water from typhoons deposited around Queensland and New South Wales. Elizabeth and I always had a sinking feeling as we walked from one room to another and after several weeks of this we found another sturdier and bigger house closer to Redcliffe. It was much better and easier for Elizabeth to take the babies out shopping. The house had a huge tree growing on one side of the garden and provided the shade Elizabeth so desperately wanted and needed. Elizabeth and the babies were not the only ones that gravitated to the tree, we had resident Kookaburra birds who loved to make a noise in the morning, and their laughing jackass 'Hoo–hoo–haa–haa' sound could be irritating. At one stage we were invaded by flying foxes which made an even more hideous grating noise. Those flying creatures we could live with, the mosquitoes however, proved unbearable, they seemed to love biting Elizabeth and attacked her with relish, so much so that her ankles would swell up to the size of her thighs nearly. Even so, we had some wonderful days and parties in the garden under that big tree, in the heat of summer and winter it provided welcome relief from the sizzling rays of the sun. Tina had her second birthday in this house and Shaun had his first birthday with all the kids of the neighborhood in attendance . . .

I had made friends with quite a few of the residents in the area, one even lent me his rowing boat so I could go fishing on the weekends. One quiet beautiful Sunday morning I pushed the boat into the blue Pacific waters and headed out towards the islands in the far distance. I had rowed out about a mile and was sitting peacefully in the calm azure briny expanse with my fishing line hanging over the side when my world seemed to suddenly end. Right next to the boat the sea came up into a large rolling mound nearly turning the dinghy over, shocked, I grabbed the sides to stop myself from being tipped into the water. When I got over the surprise I looked intently at the thing that had risen next to me, not the bottom of the ocean but a giant sea turtle whose shell was well over two yards across. The turtle didn't stay up very long and shortly disappeared into the briny depths. I only realized then the risk I was taking, if the boat had tipped over sending me into the water how long could I have survived with the multitude of Great Whites and other sharks in the area, let alone the massive salt water crocodiles, I was taking a huge risk. Next time, I reasoned, I wouldn't row so far out. I wasn't afraid of the sea but Australia had some mean toothed sea creatures that could swallow you completely in one gulp and others who had such a venomous bite the poison would kill you in half a minute or less, let alone the stone-fish that loved to lie on the bottom in shallow water, these fish had poisonous barbs that would ruin your day if you trod on one without some sort of foot protection. Sea snakes were also in abundance and could kill you if you were bitten . . . I'd had enough of fishing for the day so I pulled in the line and started rowing back toward the beach and Redcliffe in the distance . . .

* * *

When I'd had the interview with the sales manager he had asked many questions about life in the navy and my experience on radar. My past experience held me in great stead as H.G. Palmers was starting to push TVs and other electrical appliances heavily in their advertizing. They even supplied the Australian Navy with electrical goods. The sales manager felt with my unique working knowledge of the electrical systems on ships I would be of great benefit to them in the future. There had been three other applicants for the position I was after. The sales manager was impressed with me and had given me the opportunity in the end as well as a three day sales course that proved invaluable . . . We had begun to make friends in Clontarf which included the manager of the Redcliffe branch of H.G. Palmers who had given me the impetus to approach their head office in Brisbane. He and his wife had arrived from London just a few months earlier and relished the company we provided . . . In my sales course I learnt the basics of selling, the first lesson was always stand at the front door of the shop, no matter how big or small it is. When you see a possible client enquire what they are looking for, when you ascertain this take them around the store and show them a potential make or model of the item. This is stage one, the next step is, do they like the color? Yes, good, now where would you put it in the house? This is stage two. Now go to stage three, the payment of the item. 'But I haven't got the money for it!' Okay, how about a small deposit? Next month maybe, we can arrange it on terms, no deposit and pay as you go? Sold . . . If they leave the shop without buying something or taking an item on terms you have lost both a sale and a potential client . . . After four months at H.G. Palmers I became the second top salesman in Queensland which had forty five stores in total. They had a corporate magazine that was printed monthly and both Elizabeth and I were proud to see in second place my photograph next to H.G. Palmer's best salesman in such a short time!

\* \* \*

Every now and again I would phone Lou Armitage to see how he was getting on, he was pleased that we were now close by in Australia and asked whether we had considered New Zealand as a land of opportunity. He made convincing arguments that life would be better in the land of the long white cloud, or, *Ao-tea-roa,* as the Maoris had named it. When the Dutch arrived they called it *Nieuw Zeeland,* this was later anglicized to New

Zealand by English explorers. I told him Elizabeth and I would give it some thought. The seed had now been planted . . . The Kombi was a great vehicle with excellent suspension, perfect for sightseeing and just the thing for taking the little ones on outings. We took advantage of it and travelled all over the place as much as possible with our two bouncing irrepressible tiny family members in the back. It was a moving playpen for Tina and Shaun . . . One morning I was running late so I took the car which was parked behind the Kombi, blocking it in, normally I had a particular parking spot which I used, but because of my lateness I had lost it, so I parked it in another spot. When I left work at six in the afternoon I couldn't find it, I thought, *'Oh God, it's been stolen!'* I ran as fast as I could to the police station. The police station was one and a half miles away in Brisbane City; the store I worked at was on the periphery of Brisbane, a large double fronted store with doors to match. I eventually bounded up the stairs of the station building when all of a sudden I realized what had happened in the morning and where I had parked the vehicle. I had to find another parking lot altogether because my normal one was full, *'What a fool I was,'* I thought, *'all that running for nothing . . .'* I ran all the way back thinking I'd better not be late or Liz would worry . . . Besides, after the incident with Ted and nearly being washed out into the Irish Sea without paddles, I knew she'd be unhappy if I was late for dinner. My little boy and girl would also be waiting expectantly at the front gate for me to come home . . .

To earn a little extra money I picked up a small job at the Redcliffe Hotel singing and doing impersonations every Sunday between 12:00 and 2:30 pm. I enjoyed performing on stage now for I had gotten over my aversion of being in front of an audience. I had picked up many a compliment from the patrons; at any rate I was never booed off the stage . . . At the hotel I met a Russian waiter who invited Elizabeth and me up to his apartment for a meal. We had never tasted true Russian cooking so were eager to try it. We left the babies with our babysitter and drove over to the building he lived in. He had made a delicious rabbit stew mix for us, it was very hot but very tasty . . . unfortunately Liz never managed to get the recipe . . .

To brighten up our home Liz and I went over to a garden centre in Redcliffe, walking in we were surprised to see a twelve foot long carpet snake wound around a roof beam. Initially I had thought it was a boa constrictor. The owner of the centre explained to us that he kept it in the store to take care of the rats, cockroaches and other vermin . . . I wished we could have had something like that to feast on our mosquitoes . . . but not that big.

* * *

While we were in Clontarf a little settlement called Townsville, just north of Brisbane, was having its roads upgraded with new tar macadam. Old runoff trenches were being cleaned and concrete pipes were being laid. One of the laborers, a digger, accidentally slipped and fell into one of the old trenches, almost immediately he was attacked by giant ants that had a nest in it. He couldn't climb out because the soil broke apart in his hands and his boots slipped on the sandy dry soil. The ants swarmed all over him and killed him, it was like something out of a horror movie . . . At around the same time over a period of several months dogs started disappearing from Clontarf and Redcliffe, it was a mystery. Then, one morning at 5:00 am when our milkman was doing his rounds, he came across a mammoth 20ft crocodile doing his rounds on the streets of our town and in residents' gardens looking for dogs to munch on. The mystery was solved, and the only thing that remained was to dispatch the beast to crocodile heaven because it would only be a matter of time before this giant reptile would be feasting on tastier two legged prey . . . The bush and wild coastal areas of Queensland were known for its dangerous fauna, and I wondered how long it would be before our babies would interact with them. I began to have my doubts about staying and raising a family there. Shaun was very inquisitive and even though young displayed a fearless attitude to all things creeping and crawling. I shuddered at the thought of what might happen should he inadvertently stumble across a big crocodile, let alone a poisonous snake or spider . . . And then, one day it happened, something that Liz never dared tell me at the time. While I took off to work Elizabeth, Tina and Shaun stood at the door to wave goodbye. The kettle was on the boil and Liz hustled Tina into the kitchen with her, Shaun however, pushed the screen door open and clambered down the steps looking for his daddy. In the garden he sat down on the grass playing with one of his toys as a huge crocodile ambled slowly down the road towards him. Shaun got up and went to greet the massive reptile. Elizabeth gave a scream of horror as she looked out the kitchen window and leaped for the front door. Rushing down the steps she grabbed Shaun and pulled him away from the crocodile and ran inside slamming the door shut behind her . . . *From the jaws of the very beast doth she snatch away our youngest . . .*

\* \* \*

At work I would wear tailored shorts with an ironed shirt and tie with long socks and smart shoes or a safari suit with shorts or long pants. Whatever the dress it had to be smart and professional, even your sandals had to be dress sandals if you wore them to work. I preferred wearing safari suits; they were more comfortable to wear, especially in summer. If we drove anywhere after work it would always be as a family with our two babies in the back. I was a very proud father with a beautiful wife. Wherever we went people admired our babies who were scrupulously clean and decently attired by their caring and attentive mother. Driving down toward Koolangata along the Gold Coast in the red split screen Kombi was always a journey of discovery. The kids loved to play on the sandy beaches where we would lay out our big dark blue checked blanket, set up the umbrella and turn on our portable radio to enjoy a picnic by the sea. Swimming wasn't always a good idea, especially on deserted beaches, for there was an abundance of sharks along the coast and the sand dropped sharply from the shoreline because of a strong undertow. If you stood up in the sea there was a pretty good chance of being knocked over by the big waves and washed out with the current. The sea, however, was stunningly blue and enticing . . . very deceptive, considering what swam around just under the surface . . . but, we found pleasure on those sweet deserted white sands and under those azure blue skies with white puffy clouds. I wanted those days to last forever, though I wondered what life would be like for us across the Pacific Ocean just south-east of us on the same latitude as Tasmania . . . and would I ever see Tom Brocus and Alf Cole again. I often wondered what had become of them after we left the Sweetbriar . . .

* * *

While working at H.G. Palmers I had several customers who raved about the Gold Coast, an area along the coastline south of Brisbane. Koolangata was also a place to go for entertainment, and it boasted a big fairground and zoo for our babies. The Gold Coast itself was a wild playground with lots of attractions, and along with Bondai beach outside Sydney, was a premier destination for rest and relaxation in Australia . . . Koolangata was only about fifty miles away from Brisbane; Elizabeth wanted to go so we packed the Kombi for a day trip one weekend and set out with the children. It was extremely hot and the tar road down to Koolangata shimmered, radiating rippling heat waves skyward. The Kombi was a perfect family vehicle and very spacious, nice to carry surfboards too. When we arrived we headed to the zoo for the kids and spent a few hours wandering around looking at the animals with Tina and Shaun. My little boy was enamored with all creatures great and small and wasn't happy when we left. After that we headed for the fairground and its entertainments. Candy floss and ice-cream were of more interest to the kids than anything else so after pushing Shaun around in the pram and half carrying Tina we left for the beach . . . The waves came nearly up to the road and gouged out big holes in the sand due to the undertow. Good for surfing and strong swimmers but not child friendly. We watched the few surfers as we stood by the road munching and licking on Australia's finest ice-cream cones. Shaun made a mess of himself and his bib but was incredibly happy to be out with his father and mother, but even more so with the ice-cream. Tina wanted to run everywhere and we had difficulty trying to restrain her; she was very attentive to everything happening around her. Our young girl's vocabulary was also increasing from day to day. Shaun was rather silent and not vocal at all but he never missed a trick, he had the eyes of an eagle and they flashed around–nothing escaped him . . . The beaches were literally empty; most people were at the *Mickey Mouse* style fairgrounds. The various rides and entertainments were rather expensive so after a pleasant meal of fish and chips Australian style we headed home to Redcliffe . . . with lots of ice-cream of course . . . Antipodean chips, by the way, served in a paper cone are the best in the world . . . That said, Elizabeth and I had made up our minds and were determined to make a home for ourselves in New Zealand . . .

\* \* \*

Leaving Australia wasn't something I really wanted to do, we had made some good friends and were enjoying life along the Gold Coast up to a point, it was wild and untamed but it did have a charm all of its own. The extra money I earned at the Redcliffe Hotel was put aside for the day we left for New Zealand. The mosquitoes had really had a field day with Elizabeth's legs and they had swollen up pretty badly. We thought long and hard about leaving the life we had begun to enjoy, had it not been for the mosquitoes and a call to Lou Armitage we would have stayed. I had no intention of letting Elizabeth suffer any longer and Lou convinced me that New Zealand would be a better option than Australia and I was sure to find even better and more fruitful employment, work that would not only satisfy my thirst for fulfillment but also reward me financially. I had dreams of financial independence and security for my family, and social upward mobility and stature for us. Elizabeth shared these dreams. I wanted to make something of myself for my family, and maybe Australia was not the place for these dreams to come true. I also had a restless spirit always wanting to see what was over the next hill, I suppose I've always been like that, more especially so since my days in the navy, my soul yearned for greener pastures to satisfy it . . . H.G. Palmers were very understanding when I told them of our intention to leave and head south; they even gave me a bonus for their appreciation of my hard work and service to the company, no matter how briefly I had been there. Elizabeth never once complained but I could see the insects were taking a toll on her. I had seen an advert for a lovely guest house in Auckland just a stone's throw away from Auckland University. The place seemed so quaint and inviting Elizabeth and I couldn't wait to get there . . . We decided to leave in October and I didn't give one thought about being able to find employment immediately with the December holidays looming . . . on the surface New Zealand seemed to be the land of milk and honey . . .

To lighten up our load we sold what we could and packed the necessities and caught a taxi to Brisbane airport for a British Airways flight to Whenuapai, an international airport just outside Auckland. When we packed our belongings Elizabeth said, "This is the last move!" I could understand why, travelling with two small children and shifting a household was very stressful, it was a huge task, but I was looking for our

Shangri-La, a place we could really call home, I didn't feel that Brisbane was it, had we got off at Freetown and Perth things would have been different, it was what we had been searching for, but unfortunately, things had not worked out that way . . .

We boarded the four engine turboprop airliner and relaxed in the comfortable seats. The air hostesses fussed over our two small infants and made sure they were extra comfy. The aircraft plied through sunny calm summer skies southward, its engines humming smoothly. After about two hours I noticed a strange smell had begun to permeate the cabin, several passengers began looking around and sniffing, trying to ascertain where the smell had its origins. All eyes were on us and our two children. Unfortunately the smell had originated in Tina's pants. Tina looked at me very innocently and said, "Daddy, I'm pooing!" I picked her up out of her seat and passed her to Elizabeth who trotted her off to the toilet for a change and cleanup. It was the first time she had been on an aircraft so I supposed it had frightened her, normally she would ask for her potty. Once Elizabeth got back several of the passengers close to us made a fuss of Tina and Shaun, keeping them busy with little games until they fell asleep . . .

# CHAPTER 17

## New Zealand

Our plane was late when it arrived at Whenuapai, Elizabeth and our little children were dog-tired. It was a new country to us and we didn't really know what to expect, but Liz was marvelous about mustering the babies and luggage. We found a taxi at the airport and drove to Auckland. The driver was extremely helpful and within short order we were at the steps of the guest house. When we first saw the advertisement we pictured the quaint houses in Cambridge near the universities with cobbled streets and old world charm. The guest house was old world alright, but not any world that I'd lived in . . . What we expected was not what we got, in fact it was totally the opposite. We climbed the steps to the front door with suitcases and pram. It was a grim looking house and I wondered inwardly what spirits of the undead populated it. Tina twitched and turned her nose up at it. It was 9:00 o'clock in the evening now and dark. I envisioned a tall pale man in dusty creased butler's attire answering our call when I knocked on the door. What creaked down the passage inside and opened the door was even scarier! A middle aged wrinkled face peered out into the darkness, her face was covered in a whitish cream and curlers festooned her hair. The nightgown she wore reminded me of a shroud . . .

"Evening," I said, "we answered your advertisement and made a booking for today . . ."

The lady scrunched her face up and said curtly, "You're late!"

"I'm sorry, but our plane was late arriving . . ." I apologized.

She then turned her back to us and headed up the passage without a word. We followed her into the dimly lit house. Without saying anything she climbed the stairs with us behind her. Getting to a room at the end of the first floor she opened the door, and said, "This is your room . . ." With that she turned around and left us. Tina was the first to rush in and glanced around the room; she looked at the old iron bedstead disgustedly, and then turned to me pointing at the bed horrified, "Ooh, Daddy, look at the sheet, it got holes in it . . ."

Someone had been smoking in bed and had left so many holes in the sheets it looked like a sieve. But what could I say to the woman, we were all so tired by now holes or not we all fell asleep in quick succession . . . In the morning we went down to the dining room for breakfast and had the food literally thrown at us. Both Elizabeth and I felt disgusted at the treatment and we vowed to get out of there as soon as possible. By 10:00 am I had phoned Lou Armitage. He picked up the phone and said, "Ah, you finally made it . . ."

"Yes," I answered.

"How are Elizabeth and the children?" he continued.

I replied, "Fine . . . well, so, so . . ." I then explained the problem with our accommodation.

There was silence on the other end for a few seconds, then, he queried, "Are you running against the wind?"

I said, "More like a hurricane . . ."

Lou was quiet for a moment then noted, "Stan, I'll be there in half an hour to pick you and the family up and you can stay with me until you find a house . . ."

We left the grim looking guest house and the woman who reminded me of a dark Dickensian character and headed with luggage and children to Lou's house on Forrest Hill Road in a suburb on the outskirts of Auckland called Milford; which was near a peninsular with a port called Devonport where the Royal New Zealand Navy had a base. On the other side was Rangitoto, an extinct volcano. The drive to Lou's house in the old Riley he'd brought from England was like manna from heaven, it was as if a breath of fresh air had rushed in and swept the badness away. When we arrived at the house it had a big expansive lawn, so there was plenty of space for the children to play, Lou's sheets on the spare beds were as clean and fresh as a whistle, and Elizabeth smiled. I was happy she was happy. Lou was pleased too, since his wife died he had been alone and he was more than happy to have company in his big lonely house. Once we were settled in with Lou I went out immediately to look for work and found a job in a carpet business the following day by 10:00 am. The bus service in New Zealand is excellent and will get you anywhere on time, so it didn't take me long to catch one into Auckland city going across the Auckland Harbor Bridge to work. At present I didn't need a car. The ride took me past a factory manufacturing bitumen, where a strong sulphur smell permeated the air . . . I was lucky finding a position in early November since most of the businesses and shops close on December 15th and only open on the 15th of January. In the carpet business however, the month of December is a busy time, measurements can be made in peace and old carpets can be removed in offices and replaced with new ones without the necessity of interrupting workers and their day to day activities. So while I went to work that week Elizabeth went out house hunting. She found a house quickly on the same high road as Lou's about a mile down the road on the opposite side facing south east. Since it was on top of the hill it had a commanding view of the sea some two miles away. All the roads led down to the beach and the weather was placid, warm and calm, just perfect for Elizabeth and the babies . . . and there were no snakes or crocodiles wandering around, nor, masses of mosquitoes . . .

*We had found our Shangri-La at last* . . . I just wished I had a better job . . . *He manako te kōura, i kora ai* . . . which, in the indigenous Maori tongue means, *Wishing never caught a crayfish* . . .

\* \* \*

Looking for a new job would have to wait until sometime after January the 15th, leaving before would create problems, well, even after. The manager of the business was afraid that the owner would be so incensed and angry he would report me to Home Affairs for leaving. The same rule applied in New Zealand as it did in Australia, new arrivals would have to work in the same position for a period of two years before applying for other work. I was doing very well for them, both in sales and fitting, I had turned into a big asset even though I'd only been there for a month and a half. I continued to scout around for something more challenging and suitable though. In the end I came across a civil engineering company by the name of *Vinele* who had entered into a joint venture with a construction company. The newly formed business was called *Vinele Mcleod Construction* and had their newest construction project at 246 Queen Str. in Auckland, where they would develop nine floors of offices and three floors with shops. The building would be the tallest in Queen Str. with escalators and lifts connecting all the lower floors. I had an interview with the manager Jack Melvin, an American from California, within half an hour I had a new job as Site Engineer and Planning Officer for both companies starting immediately. I went back to the carpet business and told the manager. He had no intention of informing the owner, he said I should do it; he was dead scared of any repercussions if he should do so. The owner was a very angry man . . . at least that was how he was perceived to be . . . I handed in my resignation and left. The job with *Vinele* was what I had been looking for with plenty of room for advancement. Within weeks I was promoted to Assistant Manager under Jack Melvin. I would now organize and co-ordinate the project while Jack was away on business; *Vinele* had projects going on all over the United States and the Pacific which he had to manage. When 246 Queen Str. was finished *Vinele Corp.* had requested I start on a new project for them in Guadalcanal in the Pacific and then move to California for them where their head office was situated. While work was going well with *Vinele* the owner of the carpet company had called Home Affairs to report that I had left his company. They called on Elizabeth at home one day to make their enquiries. Elizabeth was able to appease them and turn them around, making them understand that a person of my experience would be wasted to the economy by fitting carpets and that I was much more of an asset to them in my new position . . .

Our first December month in New Zealand was very tight financially but that Christmas Santa Claus brought Shaun a tricycle, toy cars, a plastic aircraft plus a whole lot of other goodies, he brought Tina some dolls, different outfits for them, books and other things, for she had a love of clothing and fashion even at that young age. While at 270 East Coast Road I decided to make a sand pit for the children because they had a tendency to play on the front lawn, and I was very worried they might wander on to the main road. While I was assembling the wooden frame of it I bent down and thought I was getting dizzy because everything was wobbling to and fro. I stood up and began to stagger around as though I was drunk. I felt wobbly and thought I was going to collapse, then I realized that it wasn't me but the ground beneath my feet, it was an earthquake, I thought, *'Boy, this is a swell greeting from New Zealand. . .'* I'd never had the earth shake beneath my feet like that in all my life . . . Reports of it in the newspapers said it struck both Auckland and the Coramandel Peninsular in a straight line, a distance of eighty miles. I then remembered Lou telling me how frequently New Zealand experienced minor earth tremors. In Napier many years ago a battleship ended up high and dry on a sand bank in a river that disappeared after an earthquake. The river eventually returned but only as a trickle of its former self. Such was life in the *Land of the Long White Cloud* . . . The sandpit, once finished, turned into a major highlight for our children, they would spend most of their time playing in it and it was inordinately difficult to get them out of it except for when the neighborhood cats would use it as their bank to make deposits . . . Tina and Shaun were very disgusted when they did this, for it was their play area, not a toilet for all and sundry . . .

After building the sandpit I decided to build a catamaran, a twin hulled boat. I had become good friends with a few salty sailor type characters in the boat business. They insisted on helping me, especially Con Bree who provided a lot of the wood and other materials, and it wasn't long before a five yard twin-hull catamaran called 'Breezy' was built in our back yard on east Coast Road. Con wanted to launch it immediately so one fine day we took it to the beach and set sail. Con was the first out, he wanted the privilege so I helped him rig the sail and out he went. He went so far out I lost sight of him. I was glad we launched her in a calm sea because a light catamaran could easily be tipped over in bad weather and righting her would be difficult. In a short time I saw Con barreling toward the beach and breathed a sigh of relief. The catamaran was seaworthy and handled like a dream. Con and I had many days fun out with 'Breezy', but in the end I sold her, not least in my mind was the safety of Tina and Shaun should something happen, plus our new house was being built and the extra money would come in handy . . .

\* \* \*

While working on the construction of 246 Queen Str. we had steel reinforcing and iron girders projecting out of every nook and cranny. We had an excellent steel construction team working on the project on the fifth floor. Two floors below starter bars were still exposed while structures and escalators were in the process of being completed and installed. I was busy instructing the men on the work that day when one of the steelworkers, a huge gladiator of a man, a Maori named Dean, overbalanced and slipped off the fifth floor a short distance from where I and the team were. He fell down two floors and landed on his back with his head about ten inches from a protruding starter bar. He grunted then picked himself up, shook himself, then climbed back up the scaffolding to the fifth floor where we were. He was wearing a singlet which bore a few scuff marks and had a few grazes on his back. We had all been worried he had been seriously injured, but all he said was, "No worry, I fine . . ." He was a very tough lucky individual . . . My office was on the fifth floor and protruded over Queen Street. It was solid even though constructed with scaffolding, and the view over the street below was fantastic. My bird's eye view enabled me to see up and down the street and into the shop fronts. One day Jack Melvin told the foreman of the reinforcing structures team that there was a vacancy for a man of his ability in Guadalcanal working on the airport infrastructure there. It was the same project they wanted me on, building a control tower, an airport terminal and barracks for US Navy personnel. He was very keen to get the job and they kept discussing it. During tea break I would watch them go into a local pub below for sandwiches and a drink at around 10:00 am every morning. Playing a prank I phoned the pub and the manager who knew about the coveted position because that was all Melvin and Kelly talked about, I said with an over-the-top American accent with a Kentucky drawl, "Haalloo, I'm calling from Guadalcanal, is there a Mr. Kelly there?"

The manager said, "Hold the line, I'll call him . . ."

Within thirty seconds Kelly was on the line. I said, "Haalloo, are you Mr. Kelly?"

Kelly, excitedly answered, "Yes, yes, it's me!"

I replied in my Kentucky drawl, "Hold the line please . . ." With that I hung up.

When tea break ended Melvin and Kelly climbed back up to the fifth floor, the foreman wore a nasty scowl on his face, he was absolutely livid. In my capacity as senior engineer, I said, "Is everything okay?" He gave me a foul look then proceeded to tell me what had transpired. I slapped him on the shoulder and said with a sad-sack facial expression, "Don't worry, I'm sure it was just a harmless prank."

I continued, "Look if you want to call the island and see who phoned you can use my phone . . ."

Kelly shook his head, "No, don't worry . . ."

Seven days later he got the job and his countenance changed from somber to ecstatic. He would be getting twice what he was earning at 246 Queen Street . . . Whether he found out about me playing the prank I'll never know . . .

\* \* \*

The project at Queen Street was nearing completion and Jack Melvin called me into his office. Jack sat back on his chair and said, "The job in Guadalcanal is waiting for you, your position will be Senior Engineer and Site Manager. As soon as we wrap up here you'll ship out . . ." He continued, "After Guadalcanal is finished there are plenty of projects in the US you'll be transferred to . . . I see great things ahead for you, Stan . . ." It was a fantastic opportunity, but what of my family, how would they react, I would be uprooting them yet again . . . At home Elizabeth wasn't happy when I told her, and I could understand why. The move would be hard on her and the babies who loved their home in Auckland. In the end I had to reject the offer, for my career it would have been a tremendous boost, but for my family it would have meant continual wanderings in the Pacific and the United States. We needed a modicum of stability for our family . . . I started job hunting once again in Auckland and soon found a position as Sales Engineer for a company called Turnbull & Jones. I was given a large office where my drawing board was set up. The job entailed travelling all over New Zealand by plane, train and automobile. One afternoon when work was finished I hopped on the bus heading home to the North Shore and East Coast Road, when I spied someone very familiar sitting quietly at the back of the bus. I smiled and tried to keep my face turned away from him as much as possible. There was only one vacant seat on the bus and that was right next to him. As I sat down I gave him a shove. He glared at me crossly, until, that is, he recognized who I was and a broad smile crept over his face. Tom Brocus's hand shot out and grasped mine then he gave me a hearty slap on the shoulder, "Stan!" he exclaimed excitedly. "My God, it's been years . . ." he continued happily.

"Yes it has," I beamed.

We chatted on like the world was coming to an end and he invited me over to dinner the following week . . . He was ecstatic to see me when I arrived and a lot of our talk was on the war and the Sweetbriar in particular. He told me he was very unhappy about the way the men had been dismissed after years of good service to the navy; if it had been up to him things would have been very different. He was most upset when I told him of my demobilization. Our conversation vacillated back and forth about those last days on the Sweet 'B' and how the men hadn't received a word of thanks or been piped off by the captain. "At the time there was nothing I could do," Tom stated, then continued, "the captain called all the shots. I really wasn't happy by the way the men were treated, but I couldn't say anything, he was behaving more like Bligh on the *Bounty*," he laughed.

Over coffee Tom explained how Alf Cole was now Secretary of the New Zealand Navy. The most important position a naval man could obtain. "You're joking!" I exclaimed.

"Not at all . . ." said Tom, "He deserved it though . . . and you also deserve a decent shake, after all your time on the bridge and the hectic seas we sailed. Alf and I oft wondered what had happened to you after you left the ship. I know Alf would like to see you again . . . if it hadn't been for you the ship would have sunk more times than I'd like to remember . . . Crikey, we were living on the edge then, weren't we?" he grimaced, reaching from his comfy chair for a bowl of crisps and offering me some. I nodded, yes, we had faced certain death on many occasions, too many . . . I left Tom's house with Alf's contact details at Naval Headquarters in Wellington and gave him my assurances that I would indeed give him a call and go visit him when an opportunity presented itself . . .

*  *  *

I was always on the lookout for our special Shangri-La in Shangri-La, a place our family could call our own. One of my failings was that sometimes I never really appreciated what we had. I had a beautiful and creative young family with huge potential before them. Tina loved fashion and all she ever thought of was designing clothes and outfits for her plastic and paper dolls even at her young age. Shaun loved aircraft and tinkering with things, and even at two years of age managed to dismantle my watch completely. He loved finding out how things worked and were constructed. I now had an automobile that came with my job at Turnbull & Jones, a six cylinder Holden that looked very similar to the old yellow taxi cabs in New York City. And, I made sure, Shaun never got into the engine. The back shelf above the back seat was so broad Shaun would lie there to see out the windows. One day the kids and I were driving down the shore road when out of the car in front of us they threw a little kitten. Both Tina and Shaun screamed at me to stop so I jammed on the brakes. There weren't many cars around so I climbed out and picked the kitten up off the road and headed back to the car. Instantly, both children and I fell in love with her, and by the time we had reached home on East Coast Road the diminutive white ball of fur with black and grey markings had a name, *Muffy* . . . Our rented house was not ours so I approached the State Advances Corporation for a house loan. Because I was highly skilled they said, "No problem, there are several home builders we'll put you in touch with . . ." These builders were approved by the SAC and had stands close to where we stayed. Number one Arrow Road was to be our own Shangri-La. A sales executive from Keith Ray Homes showed me several designs, Liz and I chose a two bed-roomed house with lounge, kitchen, dining room and bathroom with toilet. It had glass sliding doors at the end of the lounge and the area had a great view of the sea in the distance. It took twelve months to construct from choosing the design. Once we moved in I built a nice big timber framed wooden sundeck in front of the lounge and Elizabeth and I spent time cultivating a nice big lawn with flowering plants in borders and trees dotted around. One of my next home improvement projects was to wall off our garden from the neighbors which proved a contentious issue for one in particular.

* * *

Life at Arrow Road couldn't be better, it was the nicest house by far that we had owned and I was continually putting my carpentry experience to good use. Elizabeth and I discussed having another baby in the future when we were more financially secure as Tina and Shaun were growing up fast. Shaun was a tear-away toddler who had a tendency to get into scrapes, one afternoon he pulled a pot of cooking food off the stove onto his head and face ending up with a nasty cut just above his right eyebrow. How he avoided getting scolded was beyond me . . . When the time came for Shaun to go to kindergarten he wasn't happy, he was three years of age and loved being around his mum. Elizabeth took him to the crèche about two miles away and left him in the care of the teachers and child-minders there. Shaun took the experience of being parted from his beloved mother in his stride and seemed to socialize with the other young children quite well. After Elizabeth left Shaun found a tricycle not so dissimilar from his own back at Arrow Road in the back garden near the sandpit. After mounting it and cycling a few feet one of the older children came over and told him to get off it and go away. So, that is exactly what Shaun did, he walked through the classroom, past the child minders, from the back garden and left through the front door then carried on down the short front path and up the road in the direction of home. When Shaun got to a busy road he saw an elderly lady trying to cross it, he walked over to her and said, "Don't worry, I'll take you across . . ." with that he took the elderly lady's hand and took her across the busy road safely, bade her farewell then carried on walking home . . . After walking down the driveway to the back door he heard Elizabeth in the kitchen washing dishes, he entered quietly and tugged at her dress. Elizabeth turned around and nearly dropped the dishes she was holding, she was so surprised. She knelt down and asked him, "How did you get here?"

Shaun replied, "I walked . . . I left because the other children are mean . . ."

Elizabeth was very cross, "That's the last time you're going there . . . They can't even keep an eye on you . . ." After her anger with the kindergarten had subsided she opened the fridge and pulled out a bottle of milk. "Would you like a glass of milk and a jam sandwich?" she asked Shaun.

"Yes," he answered.

"Good, now go and wash your hands and we'll sit at the table . . ." Elizabeth added, putting the kettle on the boil to make a cup of tea. Needless to say that was the last time she let Shaun out of her sight or entrusted our young son in the care of another person until he went to Forrest Hill primary school right next to us . . .

It was the end of November when I bought two puppets called Sooty & Sweep to entertain the children. I had seen similar ones in England on TV and thought they would be a good teaching aid and comedy act. I put on little shows for the kids at home using the puppets to tell stories with a squeaker in my mouth. I started a little act with the puppets and it became very popular with our youngsters . . . Milne & Choyce had a large store in Queen Street, Auckland, the top floor was an entertainment area for children where parents could leave them while they shopped or sat down at the café and watched over them while they played. They had bumper cars, bikes, roundabouts and jungle gyms, you name it and it was there. They had a puppet box on a stage stand and I would put on half hour shows for the kids. Sooty, though, would always come out on top at the end of the show. One of the stories I told was of Sooty trying to cook using flour. Sooty, being Sooty, always spilled everything. The flour invariably ended up on me. The first time Shaun saw the act was at a Christmas party for Turnbull & Jones. I was in a puppet box on a small platform with about forty five children and their parents sitting around. Sooty threw some flour on me and my three and a half year old son was horrified at what he'd done, he jumped up onto the stage and scalded Sooty, "Don't do that to my daddy Sooty, you are very, very naughty!"

He then looked at me and said seriously, "Daddy, Sooty is very naughty; I won't let him do that again . . ." All the adults in the audience burst out laughing because Shaun was so serious . . .

While I was putting on the puppet shows I met Graham Kerr, a chef, who had a very popular TV show called *The Galloping Gourmet* in New Zealand that was syndicated around the world, he and his wife were so enthralled by me and Sooty & Sweep, that he wanted me to do a puppet show for TV with them. Unfortunately, due to my full-time employment with Turnbull & Jones, there just wasn't time to do it. We became very good friends and I even helped him with the big catamaran he was building in a barn. Graham's choice in wines was impeccable and whenever he recommended one on his show they would fly out of the stores like there was no tomorrow . . . When Christmas came we decided to make it a real jolly affair for

the children, Tina was now four and three quarters and Shaun
was three and a half. I wanted to convince them that Santa, his
reindeers and sleigh were real, and that he travelled around the
world giving gifts to deserving children. On Christmas Eve Tina
and Shaun stood on the sundeck looking at the starry sky above
trying to spot Santa, sleigh and all, flying through the heavens
above, shouting, "Go Donna! Go Blixon!" A satellite moved
across the night sky and I pointed at it, "Maybe that's them!"
Then I said to Tina and Shaun, "All the reindeers have names
and maybe, just maybe, they'll come here and bring you some
presents . . ." They both looked at me amazed with their saucer
plate sized eyes wide open. "Maybe they'll even come down the
chimney . . ." You could have heard a pin drop it was so quiet, I
then whispered, "But we'll have to put out some milk in a glass
for Santa and cookies for the reindeers . . ." They couldn't wait
to go to bed when I told them Santa and the reindeers liked to
leave their gifts only when children were fast asleep. So off they
went to bed and fell into a deep slumber with *Muffy* sleeping, as
normal, between Shaun's legs . . . I put some soot on my fingers
and made reindeer footprints on both sides of the fireplace,
and, ate the cookies, washing it down with the glass of milk. I
put some milk on the plate for *Muffy* who had joined me in the
living room and was curious as to what I was up to . . . In the
early hours of the morning Tina and Shaun got up bright eyed
and bushy tailed heading straight for the fireplace where two
big red paper bag stockings hung full of gifts. They looked at
the hoof marks and ran straight into our bedroom shaking us
awake, "Come and look, Daddy! The reindeer and Santa have
been here!" they burst out in chorus. They dragged Elizabeth
and me out of bed and we followed them to the fireplace. Tina
and Shaun proudly pointed to all the goodies they had been
left. They were ecstatic and the excitement on their faces was
contagious as they showed me every hoof-print and how Santa
had drank the milk and the reindeers had eaten all the cookies.
I smiled and said, "I told you Santa leaves presents for all the

good children . . ." Our two little children were in absolute awe, and from then on did their best not to incur Santa's displeasure.

Shaun really loved his tricycle and would tear up and down the driveway on it; however, it nearly proved the death of him when one bright sunny summer's day he was going to the shops with Elizabeth, minus Tina who was at kindergarten. At the top of Arrow Road a neighbor's Alsatian went for him, he got a fright and put on a burst of speed which sent him barreling down the hill. Shaun managed to turn the corner at the bottom of Arrow Road but at the corner house his left wheel slipped off the sidewalk and stuck fast in the gap between grass verge and concrete. My little boy went flying over the handlebars and ended up smacking face first onto the concrete pathway. He sliced his chin open and scrapped the enamel off his front teeth. The person whose driveway he landed on saw what had happened and rushed out just as Elizabeth ran up to where Shaun lay. The homeowner took Shaun and Elizabeth to the hospital after putting the tricycle in the trunk and newspaper on the back seat of the old fashioned automobile, with running boards, to stop the dripping blood from staining the leather upholstery. A doctor at Takapuna hospital patched him up and sent him home with a new, soon-to-be scar, on his chin. It was around this time that Elizabeth and I took the children shopping for new shoes, nice shiny black ones for Shaun with a strap and a buckle on the top and a similar pair for Tina, if we bought for one we had to buy for the other. Shaun was so enamored with them at the shop he insisted on wearing them home. He wore them the whole afternoon and at dinner time. Elizabeth changed them for bed and tucked them in, when I came in to read them a bedtime story Shaun had fallen asleep and I noticed something odd under the sheets next to *Muffy* who would always lie on the bed between his legs on the blankets. I gingerly pulled the blanket and sheet back without disturbing *Muffy* and peered underneath. Shaun had put his shoes back on . . . I called Elizabeth in and we both had a little laugh then tucked the sheet and blanket back covering his shiny black shoes and the feet that were within . . . *Kids can be so darned lovable . . .* As the kids got older and our little toe tweaking ditty of, *"One little piggy went to market, one little piggy went home, one little piggy had roast beef and one little piggy had none . . . and one little piggy went . . . wee, wee, wee, wee . . . all the way home!"* got less, sibling rivalry played a part in the injuries accrued. One evening I was playing horsey with the kids with Tina on my back pretending to be a cowgirl when Shaun, jealous that I wasn't giving him some attention, pushed her off my back. Tina ended up with a broken left clavicle, a trip to the hospital and a sling on her arm. Not long after when she was better and the pair of them were sitting atop the wall I had built at the bottom of the garden, she pushed Shaun off the top, and said, "That's for pushing me off Daddy's back!" The wall was considerably higher than my back, and Shaun ended up with a broken right clavicle and his arm in a sling for six weeks. This said, Tina and Shaun were the best of friends and would play for hours together with building blocks, a train set and all their other toys, or making mud-pies outside when it rained. The pair of them dressed in yellow raincoats, hats and gumboots. Elizabeth and I would read fairy tales of *Rumplestiltskin, Rapunzel, Snow White and the Seven Dwarfs, The Princess and the Pea* and others for them every day, especially when we put them to bed. Tina would sit quietly for hours cutting and pressing out clothes from an activity book for her cardboard character dolls, but, her most priceless possessions were her plastic Barbie dolls. One night Shaun cut the hair off some of them and gave fringes to the others, this prompted Tina to take a pair of scissors to Shaun's hair while he was asleep. Shaun ended up with a big bald patch on the top of his head . . . *tit for tat . . .*

\* \* \*

Normally in New Zealand galvanized iron or IBR is a better option for roofing because of earth movement due to shifting tectonic plates in the region, but for our house in Arrow Road I chose Harvey Tiles, an interlocking tile that had just been invented and produced by clients of mine, Ian and Alex Harvey. Everything was going well at Turnbull & Jones, but even so, my ambitious nature wouldn't let up, I was always seeking that intangible Holy Grail to satisfy my hungering soul . . . Above me in the company was the General Manager, a Mr. Pascoe, and Don Young, the Sales Manager. My position at the company in Hobon Street was Chief Sales Engineer. Don was not only my manager but also a good friend. We had a client, *Skychef Catering Company*, and the owner asked me to design the bar and restaurant at Mangere International Airport. I did some designs which were loved by all but too expensive for the client, who repeatedly told me they were short of cash, could I not do something simple and cheap. Not wanting to compromise the designs I contacted Benson & Hedges and their senior manager. I included an advertizing punt for them in the design and they jumped at it. We now had the money for the project. *Skychef* were very happy. The overall theme woven into my designs was to illustrate the history of New Zealand and the discovery of it by the Maoris. To do this I commissioned a huge mirror with a Maori canoe etched in the foreground with twenty five oarsmen and another twenty five Maoris in various poses, all in all making up a complement of fifty in it. The mirror etching was completed by a silvery long white cloud in the distance to which they were rowing. The mirror was almost the width of the restaurant and had a big gold clock suspended above its center. Above this was a sign that said, *'Smoke Benson & Hedges'*. Even though I don't smoke I was really pleased that Benson & Hedges had helped pay for the project. The carpet inside both bar and restaurant was black with white polka dots with no expense spared. They used the high quality furnishings I had chosen and the mirror behind the bar even had the

Benson & Hedges logo engraved on it. The design proved to be a hit prompting Benson & Hedges to replicate it around the world. Out of that one project my reputation grew exponentially and my designs for the interiors of restaurants, bars, corporate interiors, catering establishments and the like were in great demand. Even breweries such as Dominion Brewery Works of Auckland demanded my designs for their new projects . . . My days were packed with work and home, in the morning I would drive to the office early, pop down to the YMCA in Auckland for a game of squash with Tom McFarlane before work started, then get busy on my design board after an energizing game in which some days he would win and on others I would. Tom, a computer wizard and genius, was a champion long distance runner just like my father, and ran for a club in Auckland. He was a very fit man. Our holidays with the kids were just as packed as my work days; we travelled to Mt. Ruapahu and spent a week on the slopes of the smoldering volcano at the chateau there. In the morning after our arrival, Elizabeth, the children and I were sitting at our table in the plush dining area waiting for our breakfast as the waiter came and went. He stood under the doorway leading to the kitchen as the hotel began to sway back and forth. All conversation in the dining hall stopped, and then after the hotel stopped swaying the conversation started up again as if nothing had happened, they were all quite accustomed to it . . . *including our waiter* . . .

Even though Ruapahu smoldered the trail leading up to its cone was open and the brave of heart could stand at the cone's edge. The trail up led past chalets and hot pools to bathe in. Nearby, at Lake Taupo, a motel served scrumptious Maori dishes and a *hangi*, a Maori earth oven, made by digging a hole and placing hot stones at the bottom which are covered by flax or palm leaves, fish or pork is then placed on these with another layer of leaves on top. More hot rocks are put on top with a layer of soil on which a fire is built. After two or three hours the fire, soil and rocks on top are slowly removed revealing the most delicate of dishes below, mouthwatering and delicate fish, chicken and boar. The meat would just melt in your mouth leaving a taste of heaven-on-earth on your palette . . .

The Maoris built their *whare houses* on stilts to avoid the humid dampness of New Zealand. The traditional garb of the Maoris, their culture, art and music reflects a high degree of sophistication and intelligence, everything about them speaks of an untainted deeply reflective people with heart and soul. The more I travelled around New Zealand with my work and the more I interacted with the Maoris I realized that they are not as war-like as many make them out to be, but are a wonderful race of highly sensitive spiritual human beings . . . with a mystical grasp and a feeling of oneness with nature . . .

I felt New Zealand is the place where I am meant to be, a place I would never leave . . . It was the home I had always been searching for . . .

* * *

The beautiful scenery of the North Island held me in rapture, the birds of paradise, the fern forests and trees straight out of the cretaceous era, the hot springs and warm hearts of the New Zealanders who populated the land, it was everything I had always dreamed of . . . When Maui had fished it out of the ocean he had brought a little piece of heaven with it . . .

One summer at Christmas time we went up to Whangaparoa Peninsular for a holiday where we rented a self contained unit at a guest house. The white silicate granules of beach sand entranced both Tina and Shaun; there was just so much of it. They were in the sandpit of the gods and in their element with plastic buckets and spades. I set up the umbrella for Elizabeth and we laid out our towels to enjoy the sea air and blue Pacific waves rolling in. Up above the blue sky was dotted by puffy white clouds with the sun beating down on the sand making it too hot to stand on in bare feet. We made sure our young children

didn't venture into the water without us, for sharks and stinging
jelly fish were all too common on the coasts of islands in the
Pacific, including New Zealand. We hadn't been there long
before I met the Harbor Master and we chatted about my navy
days in the Atlantic and the Med, he asked whether I'd like to
go out fishing with him, as he had a pilot boat used for assisting
bigger ships in the shallow water. I jumped at the chance and
after telling Elizabeth where I was going the Harbor Master and
I set sail, so to speak. We each had a line to hang over the side
and a large fish box one and a half yards in length, one yard in
width and twenty inches deep. After sailing out into the bright
blue briny ocean the Harbor Master cut the engines just off
a sandbar outside the harbor and let the pilot boat drift with
the currents. *Schnapper* is plentiful around the coast of New
Zealand, similar to herring but with a lot more meat and this is
what we were after. I stood on the portside near the stern while
the Harbor Master stood a little way from me amidships. Every
now and again he would catch a *schnapper* and throw it into his
fish bin while I caught nothing. This went on for nearly four
hours and I thought, *'What the heck is wrong with me, I can't even
catch a single little fish.'* Then I got a bite and pulled in my line,
it was a little *trumpeter* fish. Its mouth was shaped like the end
of a trumpet, hence its name. Catching the midget made me
feel all the worse and I felt like kicking it all in and calling it a
day. Then my line jerked as the hook caught on something, *'An
old boot perhaps,'* I thought, *'or maybe the damned thing's caught on
a rock.'* I pulled and pulled trying to get the line in and free my
hook all to no avail. I figured I'd have to cut the line and call it
quits. I carried on like this for five minutes struggling with my
heavy line when all of a sudden something came up out of the
water straight at me, it was a huge *schnapper* attached to my line.
I pulled the line up hard in surprise and the thing flew over my
head and landed straight into the fish bin behind me. When
we returned to the dock the Harbor Master insisted I take it
back to the guest house with me, so, after I got back, I cleaned

it and cut it up into *schnapper* steaks which we had for breakfast, lunch and in sandwiches with tomato and lettuce for the next three days . . . Our holiday didn't end with the fish though, the kids had a whale of a time with *Gin* the horse and on the white sands . . . Just before Christmas Eve Tina and Shaun were alone in our unit. Tina opened one of the cupboards in our room and had the surprise of her young life. The big red and white paper Christmas stocking bags Santa was due to bring in two day's time. Tina called Shaun who was playing with his toys on the carpet in the living area, she said, "Shaun, come here and look at this . . ."

Shaun got up, entered the bedroom, and went over to the tall cupboard where Tina was standing. He peered inside and got a shock. "You mean to say it was daddy and mummy all the time!" exclaimed Shaun. Tina nodded.

Shaun groaned, "Oh no, I wonder whether the Easter bunny was them as well." Shaun shook his head from side to side as Tina closed the cupboard . . . Even after the kids had found out I was helping Santa we couldn't have asked for a nicer holiday . . . *And Shaun, his dream of being a cowboy came true, his broad smile while being on Gin was worth a million words . . .*

\* \* \*

Travelling all over the North Island for work gave me tremendous opportunities to visit nearly every town and settlement from tip to toe. Sometimes I would fly in an Air New Zealand Fokker Friendship and at other times a Viscount turboprop. Many times I ended up in a Cessna 172 landing on a grass strip to reach my destination. On one business trip to Wellington the weather had turned very stormy and windy. Tom had spoken to Alf Cole and said I would be coming down to see him, so when I got to Wellington I would give him a call. However, by the looks of the weather I was wondering whether in fact we would get there. Wellington was infamous for its inclement weather, especially with the rough seas and storms in the Cook Strait between the North and South Islands of New Zealand. Most people and motor car traffic used the big ferry that plied between the two islands. It was as big as an ocean liner and could handle anything that the ocean threw at her, well, not quite . . . Even this big ship ran afoul of the vicious storms off Wellington. The ship ran aground on rocks just offshore. Passengers were forced to flee across the rocks to safety near Wellington Harbor. The big ferry stayed where she was stranded on the rocks and became quite a tourist sensation for about three years. She was on the rocks near the airport which was located close to town and ran out on reclaimed land into the sea. Every now and then they would lengthen the runway to allow bigger aircraft to land and take-off. My plane took off from Mangere International Airport in driving rain and blustering wind. It had to pick up passengers at New Plymouth. The wings of the Friendship flexed abnormally as the pilot announced over the loudspeaker system, "The landing is going to be a bit heavy because of the inclement weather and due to the wind we will be approaching the runway from the seaward side, nothing to be worried about . . ."

The person next to me looked a bit airsick as we bounced up and down and headed over the ocean. As we banked around I looked below at the raging seas. They were very, very rough and I commiserated with any sailor who was out in them. Because we were heading in from the seaward side we would be landing on a grass strip. I figured the landing was going to either break the undercarriage or send it through the wings. I braced myself as we approached on our glide slope. When the aircraft touched down I could not believe it, it was the smoothest landing I had ever experienced. Taxiing to the terminal we were informed that it would be impossible to takeoff and continue to Wellington in the Friendship because the weather was so bad. Those that wished to continue to Wellington would have to board a Dakota getting ready for the next hop to an RNZAF airbase to pick up more passengers. Taking off the wings of the Dakota flexed a little more than usual causing the passengers to shift uncomfortably in their not so comfortable seats. After landing at the RNZAF base the new passengers boarded and a medium sized woman took the window seat next to me. After taking off and getting airborne we continued south toward Wellington, the bad weather seemed to intensify, the further south we went the worse the weather became. The lady sitting next to me turned out to be a doctor and she clutched the arm rests of her seat as the plane was buffeted in all directions by strong gusts of wind. As we bounced all over the place she turned and looked out the window, her conversation abruptly stopped and I wondered why. Her face turned white. I looked out the window to see what she was looking at; the wings were flapping like a bird's. I had never seen wings move up and down so much before and was amazed they didn't rip off . . . We were now approaching Wellington and the pilot reduced the speed of the engines to lose height. Every time he did so the wind just picked the big bird up and hefted it up into the sky like it was a feather. This happened again and again until eventually the old Dakota lost some height and he lowered the gear. Approaching the runway the pilot had to turn the nose into the crosswind at a forty five degree angle just to keep on course. The cross winds were so high they blew the rain horizontally across the runway. The aircraft dropped like a stone as it came in to land, then, just before it touched down another gust hefted it upwards; the Dakota floated up and down the runway until it reached the middle, it was then that the pilot cut the engines forcing the big bird downwards to the tarred runway. She hit the tarmac hard, real hard, so hard in fact I thought the undercarriage would pop through the wings. With torrential rain cascading onto the runway and hurricane force-like wind buffeting the Dakota all over the place a fire engine had already started rolling toward us. By the time the aircraft rolled to a stop ground crew were swarming around her to tether the metal beast to the ground with thick metal cables. They waited awhile for the winds to lower before they opened the door to let the passengers and crew out onto the gusty rain swept runway. I was thankful the pilot had slammed her onto the deck because I envisioned us careening off the end of the runway into the rough merciless waves beyond. By the look of the high seas I doubt if any of us would have survived . . .

While we were waiting for our luggage at the terminal I stood next to the doctor, she turned around and smiled at me as if to say, "Thank God we're still alive . . ." I realized we had been close to disaster, too close for comfort. I put those thoughts out of my mind and looked for the nearest telephone. I made a call to Naval Headquarters and within seconds I was put through to the Secretary of the Navy, Alf Cole. "Cole speaking . . ." came a voice on the other side of the line. "Chapman, Sir," I said sprightly. The person on the other side laughed, "I'd recognize your voice anywhere," said Alf Cole, "Where are you?"

"At the airport, Alf," I stated.

"Good, I'll send someone round immediately to pick you up," he replied.

"Thanks, I'll be waiting inside the terminal, it's raining cats and dogs here . . ." I answered.

I waited for fifteen minutes next to my small case before a naval petty officer walked in; he introduced himself smartly and then picked up my bag and case. We made a dash to the very respectable naval vehicle outside and jumped in, out of the rain and wind . . . When the automobile arrived at Naval Headquarters, Alf, who was standing at the entrance to the imposing building, came out to greet me. When I caught sight of him it was as though the intervening years had just melted away and I was walking up the gangplank of the Sweetbriar for the first time, being greeted by Lieutenant Alf Cole, RNVR. I choked as I got out of the car and he walked up and shook my hand warmly, "Good to see you, Stan," he said.

"It's been a long time," I noted.

"Yes, it has, hasn't it, far too long," answered Alf, "I'm really pleased you came . . ."

I looked at the imposing building in front of me while Alf dismissed the petty officer. "Follow me," he said, walking into the building. As we entered the reception area every person we met saluted Alf smartly. We headed down a passageway from the large ante-room, Alf smiled and gestured to me, "We'll go to the wardroom."

I followed him and within a short while we entered the room sat down and ordered some drinks. I had a healthy double whiskey and soda water and he had the same.

"Seeing you again brought back a flood of memories, Stan," noted Alf, "I often wonder what happened to the rest of the crew and where they all are . . ."

"I know, sometimes I still can't believe that we made it out alive with everything we went through," I commented.

Alf chuckled, "Remember how many times all the dockies cheered and clapped as we pulled into the docks after everyone thought we'd been sunk . . ."

"Yes . . ." I answered, "The big seas and huge waves that nearly rolled us over and finished us off for good . . . Not to mention the damned Nazi tin-fish . . ."

"Sometimes I pinch myself just to remind myself that I'm still alive and that it isn't some sort of dream while I'm bobbing up and down in those cold Atlantic waters drifting into unconsciousness . . ." said Alf.

We continued on like this talking about the war and about those that didn't make it and for them we held our glasses aloft and saluted them. We remembered the tears of the living and the blood spilt of good naval men and good merchant marine sailors. Of the many ships that were sunk by German U-Boats. Of our battle at D-Day and the valiant efforts of our crew to ensure the survival of as many as possible in those hectic hours until Juno beach was well and truly taken. On our third whiskey he told me one of the reasons why he wanted to see me, "Stan,

I'd like you to come aboard and join the Royal New Zealand Navy, we could do with your sort here, men of your caliber. I have such a heavy load with the old and outdated system that's in place. It all needs to be updated and I know with your planning ability you're just the man for the job." Alf grinned broadly, "Of course it'll mean a decent commission, especially after all your years in combat and your training in radar, and you'll have to move to Wellington, but there are worse places to spend your days and I can't think of a better person suited for the job . . ."

I pondered over both the drink in my hand and Alf's words. Of course it was what I wanted; it was all I'd ever wanted. And I had a real chance to shine and fulfill my dream of becoming an Admiral. "Yes . . . Of course . . . I could think of nothing less," I answered. But as soon as the words were out of my mouth I wondered about my family, my vivacious wife and my two beautiful young children. How would they react to the move, I would have to think long and hard about it . . . I then added, "Just give me a little time . . ."

"That's understandable . . . think it over, there's no need to jump to it at the moment. Just keep this in mind, it's hard for me to get everything ship shape down here . . . and while I'm doing the best I can, bottom line is, I need someone with your expertise, and someone I can depend on . . ."

After that our conversation switched to life in general for half an hour, then, looking at my watch, I said, "Alf, I've got to be at the office shortly . . ." In short order we were back in the reception area where the same car drove up. As Alf shook my hand to bid me farewell he said, "Don't forget your work is here and I'll be waiting for your call . . ."

The automobile pulled away as Alf Cole, Secretary of the New Zealand Navy, stood on the steps looking at the departing vehicle. As we disappeared into the Wellington drizzle Alf turned and strode into the building hoping I would indeed join him and bring New Zealand's seaborne force up to speed and into the 21ˢᵗ Century . . . *It was an offer that would be hard to turn down . . .*

* * *

When I got to our office in Wellington I made my calls and confirmed my appointments to make measurements and do some quick preliminary designs for our clients. Turnbull & Jones was a big company, one of the biggest in New Zealand and had offices in every major town. Alf's offer kept me wondering what life would be like back in uniform, would I indeed be shore based as Alf had indicated or would I get a posting to a ship. How would Elizabeth feel about it, she was happy at Arrow Road, we all were, even *Muffy* our cat . . . we were settled now . . .

After seeing some of our clients I gave Graham Kerr a call but his wife answered and said he was still at the TV studio taping his *Galloping Gourmet* show. I called the studio and got hold of Graham. "Hi Stan, I'm still filming but if you go to the house make yourself comfortable and wait I shouldn't be too long," said Graham on the other side of the line. I duly went over and waited and waited. It was getting late when Graham called and said they were now filming an introduction piece for Australian television, he implored me to wait a little longer. I couldn't though; I was getting sleepy what with all the excitement of the day. I bade his wife farewell and said I'd call in the morning and then headed for the hotel that Turnbull & Jones had booked a room for me in . . . The following morning I made more calls and measured up a restaurant, kitchen and bar for an installation then called on Graham. When he first saw me do my puppet shows in Auckland with Sooty & Sweep he had been so impressed, now he had spoken to his producer at the studios. His producer had also been enthusiastic and offered me a spot on a TV show to try me out. My visit was short because he had to go back to the studio to tape yet another show. He was very busy and in great demand now. His popularity was skyrocketing throughout the western world. In a way I was a touch jealous of his success and wondered whether I could attain such heights in my line of work or would it be better to throw the towel in at Turnbull & Jones and hit the sound stage with Sooty & Sweep. I chuckled to myself, *'That would be a thing, wouldn't it . . .'* But I had my family to consider, how stable would the work at NZBC be?

My flight was already booked and I decided I might as well head to the airport and wait the hour and a half for my flight back home there, no sense in heading back to the office, it would be a waste of time . . . I had received two good offers which would both lead to more instability for my young family. Life was like that, when times are good that's when the offers to a potentially better life crop up, not when you're struggling to make a crust of bread. Turnbull & Jones had been good to me and I enjoyed working there. TV work was a two edged sword, it could be that I'd strike it lucky and become rich and famous like Graham, on the other hand it could be the ruin of both me and the family, besides, at heart I was a navy man . . . and the sea salt is hard to remove from your veins. I thought long and hard about this and other things as my plane took off and headed for Auckland . . . Yes, things could be better, but did I want to risk the happiness of my family . . . I certainly didn't want to traipse all over the world unsettling them . . . As the flight winged homeward my thoughts were fixated on my wife and two small children . . .

\* \* \*

That evening as I pulled into the driveway my precious youngsters, Tina and Shaun, stood expectantly with *Muffy* at the front door waiting for me to arrive. I turned off the car and opened the door, instantly I was surrounded with excited cries of, "Daddy! Daddy!"

I smiled broadly as I walked inside with them and kissed Elizabeth at the doorway. The aroma of roast beef, vegetables and potatoes filled my olfactory senses. I put my case next to a chair in the living room and sat down for a few seconds before Tina and Shaun engaged me in play . . . After dinner Elizabeth brought out some freshly baked cookies and we sat down to watch the news on television. It wasn't long before Tina jumped up from the blanket where the kids were laying and said, "Daddy, is it true that when we lose a tooth the fairies come and put money under your pillow?"

"Of course it's true . . ." I replied.

Tina turned to Elizabeth and fiddled with one of her front teeth, "Mummy, I think I'm going to lose this tooth." She wiggled it again and smiled.

I looked at Shaun and could see how fast they were now growing up. Not so long ago they were mere babies, and now . . . I turned to Elizabeth and laughed, "I think they're growing up real fast Liz . . ."

I picked up Sooty, the puppet, and asked him, "C'mon Sooty, show me your mouth, perhaps you've lost one of your teeth?"

Sooty ducked under a side table and nodded his head; he refused to open his mouth just in case I tried to pull out one of his teeth . . .

After a little television Elizabeth put the children to bed at nine o'clock and I read them a story, one from their Hans Christian Anderson fairy tale book . . . It wasn't long before the pair of them fell asleep and I kissed them good night. I felt like some fresh air so I went through the lounge, where Elizabeth was sitting, quietly knitting a blue sweater with white flecks in it for Shaun, with wool he'd chosen at the store nearby. I opened a door to the deck and stood alone looking at the stars above, alone that was except for *Muffy* who had followed me out and was now rubbing herself against my legs and purring . . . Before I made a decision I would have to think long and hard about it . . . The image of myself in naval whites with three gold stripes on black epaulettes on both of my shoulders came into my mind, I smiled to myself, yes, that would be nice . . . On the

other hand I now had my family to think of, it wasn't just me . . .
But, joining up again would give more security for them . . . I
was in a quandary, I was now in two minds as to what to do . . .
Elizabeth of course would have to be told and we would discuss
it . . . I continued standing there, *Muffy* had now left me and
gone inside to make herself comfortable on Shaun's bed as she
always did . . . I turned and closed the door then returned to
the balustrade and looked up, my mind travelled back to the
bridge of the Sweetbriar at night and the stars shinning above
our convoy as we headed toward Newfoundland, the ghostly
figures of Tom and Alf stood next to me on the bridge as in the
distance explosions broke through the eerie quiet of night in
the Atlantic Ocean. A cold chill invaded my bones underneath
my big duffel coat. Alf's ghostly form turned to me, he smiled
then the form evaporated into the mists of time. Other scenes
came into solidity from the darkness. Juno beach spread before
us and German shellfire rained down causing the water around
the ship to erupt in plumes. I heard the screams of dying men
and saw men rent asunder with canon fire . . . Once again I saw
the sea turning blood red around the Sweetbriar and felt the
ship keel to one side to avoid shellfire . . . I saw myself on my
radar set frantically searching for enemy subs . . . The air around
rang with our claxon bell as the words, "ACTION STATIONS!
ACTION STATIONS!" came over the loudspeakers . . . My
ghostly spirit self was now at the Oelikon gun on the bridge
firing frantically at German bombers attacking us from the skies
as the sailor next to me kept a steady flow of shells coming . . .
Below me our grassy lawn had now turned into heaving sea
where men were burning in oil as their ships sank beneath the
waves. I saw myself trying to help them but they kept slipping
under the freezing cold water, others still, tried to breathe in
life giving oxygen when they surfaced, only to take in a lung-full
of searing flame . . . Men screamed in pain all around me and
I was powerless to help them . . . As quickly as the visions had
come they disappeared and with them my close companions,

standing on the bridge of the Sweetbriar, Lieutenant Tom Brocus and Lieutenant Alf Cole . . . I turned to the patio deck doors and saw Elizabeth sitting in the lounge looking at a film on the television while still at work on Shaun's sweater, her knitting needles clacking away . . . I thought long and hard while standing on my very own bridge, *'Should I take the position in the RNZN that Alf Cole had offered?'* What would Elizabeth, my darling wife think? Would she like moving to Wellington? I would definitely become a high ranking commissioned officer with Alf Cole's recommendation. I would start as a commander then move up the ranks to at least a rear admiral with my experience, or, would I put my family first instead of my career? I was in a quandary, with my family on one side and the sea and a commission on the other, she was hard to escape from, my mistress the sea. A mistress that I had been drawn to then wished to escape from. And now, I was in a position to be the master and commander of my own ship in a navy that truly respected its sailors . . . And there was always the possibility of New Zealand being drawn into the war in Vietnam to protect its shores from the communists . . . Not that the thought of combat bothered me in the slightest, I had suffered the worst an enemy could throw at us and survived, how much worse could Vietnam be . . . *This would be a decision not to be taken lightly . . .*

\* \* \*

Summer cast its warming rays upon New Zealand and I had decided to take Shaun out to Milford beach one night for a fishing expedition. We drove down to the beach at nine in the evening, parked the car and headed onto the sand to build a fire and put the lines out in the calmly lapping waters at the shore's edge. The full moon above cloaked the warm sand in its bright reflective glow as we sat on our beach towels listening to the waves lapping the sand in front of us. Everything was perfect as I lay back relaxing weary bones and letting the petty frustrations of the day melt away. I then noticed something odd, the sand around us seemed to be crawling with little crabs, I blinked once then twice, no, I wasn't dreaming, the sand around us seemed to undulate with the tiny creatures. I flicked on my big orange torch and cast it about . . . The sand around was crawling with sand fleas, big nasty ones that bite like mad . . . I hastily packed up the fishing kit and everything else and we ran to where I had parked the car . . . So much for a lovely evening sitting on the beach fishing . . . Never again would I go fishing at night . . .

That week I had a trip to Taumarunui to see a client in the midlands of the North Island. The rail system was very slow so I left from Mangere Airport and flew with New Zealand Airways to New Plymouth. Once again heavy weather blighted the flight and we flew in from the sea to avoid crosswinds. And again, we were forced to land on the grass runway, and once again the high-winged Fokker Friendship performed wonderfully and touched down with nary a bump. On the ground and de-planed I headed for the terminal and asked about a flight to Taumarunui. I was told that because of the lack of passengers the airline had stopped flying in that direction, so there were no flights to Taumarunui whatsoever, except maybe, if I was really wanting to fly there I could go to the aero club and inquire there. I stood at the enquiries desk pondering my situation, the rail system had no direct link with Taumarunui and it would take another day or so even to get to a town nearby, if I was lucky. In the end I had no choice so I found a pilot who flew with the club and he offered to take me there, but first I would have to become a member for insurance purposes. We went to the club house and I signed all the necessary documents to become a member of their flying club. The pilot I had fallen in with then took me to the hanger where his aircraft was, entering it I saw an old Tiger Moth with a dirty yellow fuselage and light brown wings, I thought, *'Crikey, now what have I let myself in for . . .'*

I didn't know too much about Tiger Moths but what I did know frightened me. I had heard that a gust of wind could blow it hither and thither across the sky. I gulped, oh well, the die was cast and I had clients waiting so I'd better swallow my misgivings and go where the wind blew, literally . . .

As we were pushing the aircraft out of the hanger the pilot told me we would be flying between mountains and that I shouldn't worry. *'Another thing to go wrong,'* I thought as I put on the leather helmet and 'Battle of Britain' style fighter goggles I had been given. I looked inside at my seat behind the pilot and the piece of antiquated plywood I would be sitting on, I gulped again . . . The one redeeming factor was that it had a cushion and a padded backrest, otherwise it would prove to be uncomfortable in the least. The pilot and I climbed into the fabric and wood aircraft and strapped ourselves in, contact, the engine turned over and spluttered to life as a club member pulled away the chocks and we started to roll from the taxi apron onto the runway . . .

I started to feel relaxed once we were airborne but his jerky control movements unnerved me somewhat, my misgivings about the whole flight re-surfaced and I held on tightly to whatever I could find that made me relax . . . The Tiger Moth wove through the mountains and I could see myself reaching out and touching them without that much effort, my toes curled up in my shoes and anchored themselves to the underside of the pilots seat in front of me. I had started to acclimatize to the bumpy ride and the closeness to the igneous rock at our sides when the aircraft suddenly dropped five hundred feet in an air pocket. The pilot pulled the nose up, after we had nearly touched the bottom of the valley we were flying through, and the aircraft climbed upwards with its prop straining to bite into the air and get us out of trouble. The pilot turned back, and shouted over the din of the engine, "Are you still there?"

"Of course, I'm not going anywhere . . . I'm right behind you!" I shouted back as I gripped anything that was sturdy enough . . . The pilot pointed to the clouds above that were threatening to drop down and obscure the valley we were in, "If we get stuck in those you'll never know which way is up or down, it's an inner ear thing. Plenty of pilots crash because of it . . ."

I nodded and he turned back to the mountains in front of us. *'Swell, just swell . . .'* I thought, *'this fellow does his best to make you feel at ease . . .'*

It took one and a half hours to get to Taumarunui and I was ever so pleased when I saw the airfield below us. I thought we would land immediately when we made our first approach over a small river just before the grass field that served as the Taumarunui air hub, I was wrong, just as the plane touched down the pilot yanked back on the stick and headed skywards once more. We circled the runway then he did the same thing again and only on his fourth approach did he deign to put her down. I breathed a sigh of relief as I once more set foot on terra firma. "Why did you do the aerobatic show?" I asked the pilot.

"Oh, there where sheep on the runway, I had to chase them off first . . ." he replied.

I laughed heartily and my nervous stomach righted itself as we headed for the airport building. When I saw my clients I asked why they hadn't chased the sheep off the runway, but even they thought the pilot was showing off and giving them a demonstration of his skills. With the excitement over we headed for a restaurant in town to discuss the job I had come to sort out and do some sketches for. As we sat down and ordered something to eat I said to myself, *'Next time I'll take the car . . .'* When I eventually left I took a taxi to the closest train station.

\* \* \*

Bob Agnew was the General Manager at the Auckland Department of Health and a good friend of mine. One of his health inspectors had called on a restaurant called *'The Gourmet'* owned by a Dutch expatriate called Otto Groen. He had been instructed by the Health Department to remove the wooden bench they were using to prepare food with one made of stainless steel. Failure to comply with the instruction would mean closure of the restaurant with immediate effect. In New Zealand the Health Department didn't play games, if you ignored their recommendations your restaurant or eatery would be locked up and closed within twenty four hours . . . I called on the restaurant and measured up the food preparation area for fitting with a new stainless steel bench. I gave him the price, some fifty five dollars, and told him it would be fabricated in New Plymouth. I called Ed, who was our factory manager there and told him I needed it urgently, he said, "Don't worry, I'll get on it right away . . ." With my work done I was on my way out through the restaurant when Otto asked in a very friendly manner, "What would you like to eat?"

I sat down and ordered a fillet steak with mushrooms, roast potato and vegetables, with an orange drink to wash it down. I thought, *'Mighty friendly of him . . .'*

When I finished my meal I got up to leave and Otto came over with the bill. I was shocked. Elizabeth and I hardly ever went to restaurants as we had a family now and focused on making our income go as far as it could. I paid but I wasn't happy . . . When I got back to the office I decided I'd make him sweat a little for the bench. During the week that followed Otto kept phoning me with a greater sense of urgency in his voice each day, he was desperate because the Health Department were now threatening to close him down. In the end I said, "Look, the bench is in our factory at New Plymouth and the quickest way to get it to you is by air, but, you'll have to pay for the shipping . . ."

Otto readily agreed. The shipping and the bench cost him one hundred and sixty three dollars in the end . . . *If he'd been nice he could have saved himself one hundred and eight dollars . . .*

\* \* \*

Auckland is an idyllic and wonderful place to raise a family, the summers are warm and sunny and the winters aren't that bad, sometimes windy and cloudy with lots of rain, but not that cold. It is a very outdoorsy place to live in. In the garden Elizabeth and I planted trees running against the wall that had been built in Arrow Road to shield us from the neighbors. I was always mowing the lawn, as it is a national past time in New Zealand. The hum of lawn mowers could be heard far and wide *on any given Sunday.* This was because the soil is largely of volcanic origin and full of nutrients, especially nitrogen. Plants just spring up overnight giving rise to fern filled forests and carboniferous-like flora. This gave rise to large piles of compost which where a favorite spot for rats, a *Rat Vegas* if you like. In these piles they would play and frolic until it was time to burn or remove them. One Sunday while I was turning over our compost heap a large rat ran out of it, saw me and headed back. I threw the spade in my hand at it. Shaun had been playing nearby and the rat ran between his legs. The spade ended up stuck fast in the grass between Shaun's feet. He got a shock and the rat lost its tail. I chastised myself for being so stupid and throwing the spade in the first place . . . I was lucky, Shaun was lucky, and I was determined not to do something like that again . . . Many gardeners in New Zealand end up with three fingers because of the sticky wet and thick grass, the reason, not turning off the mower and removing a plug lead or two before trying to clear the grass from the blades. Even Lou had lost a finger because of this. In New Zealand it is a common injury . . . Underneath the house we had an earthen basement which I was still in the process of converting to a decent concreted one. We stored all our gardening equipment and other unnecessary things in it, including my fishing gear. *Muffy* loved the basement; it was cool on the hottest of days and probably boasted the odd mouse or two, though I never saw any. I had been fishing and had left a little of the bait on one of the hooks, *Muffy* had found it and taken a bite ending up with a vicious barbed hook through the side of her mouth. Shaun and I heard her crying and rushed down to see what was the matter. The hook and barb were stuck fast so we rushed her to the vet to remove it. It didn't take long and by the time we returned home she was as right as rain and happy when presented with a bowl of fresh milk . . . On the morning of every seventh day we would dress Tina and Shaun up in their Sunday best and take them to Sunday school at a church not too far distant from us. At ages five and four they would walk hand in hand to it. Tina would say they were quite capable of walking on their own and delighted in telling us they weren't babies anymore. New Zealand was a very safe country and Tina would always take charge, being the older one. Shaun would follow his big sister and listen to her. Our children were growing up. At church they were both very inquisitive and would always ask the priests at Sunday school questions, some of which they could not answer. One Sunday Shaun came back and said he didn't want to go there anymore because they didn't know much about God . . . We didn't force them and let them decide for themselves . . . He had asked the priest where did all the water come from in the story about Noah after being shown a picture of the ark floating on a mass of turbulent water, the priest couldn't answer him and told him not to ask such things . . . Another further two questions and Shaun lost all faith in what they were teaching. Even at five he had an enquiring mind . . .

I brought home a Bristol Beaufighter model for Shaun to build, his first model. He tried but didn't get it quite right, well, more wrong than right and it turned into a sticky mess of plastic and glue, but, at least he tried and the mess he made was all by himself. He loved aircraft, even more than cars at a very young age and absolutely loved the big Lancaster at the War Museum in Auckland. There were two Sunderland flying boats at the naval station outside Auckland near Whenuapai and I thought when he gets a little older, I would take him there . . .

The weekends at Arrow Road were not only taken up by gardening, but it was our time to relax, Tina and Shaun would do their best to make breakfast for us and deliver it while we were still in bed. They would get up before our Swiss Cuckoo clock in the lounge heralded in 7 o'clock and headed for the kitchen to make us toast and marmalade and tea and whatever else they could cook up. Being four and a half and six years of age it didn't always turn out the way they wanted it to, they couldn't boil the kettle, they weren't allowed to touch it so they used hot water from the tap to make our tea. The toast was either not done or as usual black, and the tea was lukewarm or cold. But their smiling faces could have melted the stoutest of hearts for they had tried their best for their mum and dad, Tina, the take charge gal, always beamed profusely as they brought the tray in to their mother wearing her embroidered red silk Chinese pyjamas . . .

Elizabeth was a loving mother but the one thing that she could not stand was a potty mouth child, any infraction of her *Potty Mouth Law* would bring out the soap and a trip to the bathroom for a mouth washing. Needless to say potty mouths were not very common at Arrow Road . . . A relaxing Saturday or Sunday would see Elizabeth in her red silk pyjamas next to our radiogram with her *Beatles* records, *The Sound of Music*, the soundtrack to *Oliver* and other favorites. At night when the airwaves were quiet Shaun would sit next to it twiddling the Short Wave knob in an effort to pick up interesting broadcasts from other countries and the regular pinging from satellites, that was, when he had finished playing with his tinplate toy police cars, colored bricks and things. Both Tina and Shaun would sit for hours in front of the TV on the lounge carpet building houses and humanity's future with all their toys, bears and dolls present to witness the *brave new world* under construction. The train set Santa brought Shaun one Christmas kept them thoroughly enraptured, but even so they never missed their favorite shows on television. Marionette animation programs like *Stingray* with Marina the mermaid, *Thunderbirds, Captain Scarlet and the Mysterons, Supercar* and *Joe 90* were firm favorites with them. Cartoons like *Speed Racer* with *Racer X* stimulated Shaun's imagination and kept him engrossed with his toy cars and his Fab One from the *Thunderbirds* TV series. *Voyage to the Bottom of the Sea, Lost in Space, I Dream of Jeannie, Daniel Boone, Skippy the Bush Kangaroo, Daktari, The High Chaparral, The Munsters, The Adventures of Jacque Cousteau & the Calypso* and a gamut of *Disney* cartoons and programs about animals kept them both enthralled and entranced. Shaun's favorite saying was, "Thunderbirds Are Go!" On Sunday afternoon there was always a *Disney* film on with *Lassie and the forest rangers.* This is not to say our children dominated the television, we also had our favorites like *The Dick Van Dyke Show* and a gamut of *Humphrey Bogart* films including *The Maltese Falcon,* and my friend Graham Kerr's program *The Galloping Gourmet . . .* naturally . . .

Elizabeth wanted professional portraits of Tina at five and a half and Shaun at four to send to her mother so she called a photographer in Takapuna. A bespectacled man of average height and build wearing black pants, white shirt with vest and bowtie came with a glass plate camera on a big wooden tripod. Shaun was fascinated with the glass plates and how the man had to duck under a large black cloth at the back of the camera to take a picture. He marveled at the large flash unit he had set up . . . When he returned with the photos both Liz and I were impressed, he really was a master of his craft, especially the way he made Shaun smile with the hand puppets he had, that was a nigh impossible task all by itself . . . Tina could smile when she wanted to, even at the drop of a hat, but Shaun, that was a totally different story all together . . .

Rainy days were the best days for Tina and Shaun for when they had finished playing outside in their rubber gumboots and raincoats in the garden making mud pies, they would come inside for a hot bath run by their mother and fresh clean clothes also put on by her. Then Elizabeth would sit with them and read fairy stories then give them something hot to eat. After dinner they would continue to play until TV time. And as the rain continued to drizzle Elizabeth and I would tuck them in bed by nine o'clock . . . whereupon Elizabeth would carry on knitting Shaun's blue sweater with the white flecks as we watched a late film . . . On sunny days the kids would be outside playing in the big orange tent I would set up on the lawn. Inside the tent they would have a school for *Teddy*, *Mr. Panda* and all Tina's dolls, teaching them how to read and tell the time with the aid of their books. The tent could be a hospital one day, a castle or frontier fort another. Shaun would run around it and the garden wearing his black double holster with six shooters, a silver star on his chest and a cowboy hat on his head and his feet shod with gumboots, his little friends would complain, "Why do we have to be the Indians all the time?" To that Shaun answered, "Because I'm the one with the cowboy hat, the cowboy holsters, guns and silver sheriff's star on my chest . . ." What more could a man ask for, for even if one were to possess the whole world it would be worth naught against the enjoyment I experienced through the eyes of my young children . . .

\* \* \*

One weekend while I was busy making Tina a cot for her dolls, Elizabeth was scanning through the newspapers to find a guest house in the country for us to stay at over the holidays when she came across an advertisement for one in Kumeu. The ad seemed rather inviting so we decided to pop down one Sunday and check the place out. After our first introduction to New Zealand guest houses we were a little wary now and tended to being more than a little careful. The Sunday drive into the country was just what we needed and as the kids played in the back and Shaun climbed up on the sill behind the back seat by the back window Elizabeth and I chatted about the scenery and what a relaxing drive it was. Shaun, laying on his back looked up at the telegraph poles and wires flashing by above, trying to count them all, while Tina wanted to play *I Spy With My Little Eye* which we all joined in. Arriving at the rambling farmhouse we entered the driveway and passed through an old iron gate and drove over the cattle grate and down the secluded and wooded driveway to a big grassed circle with a massive palm tree in the center. I stopped the car and we were immediately greeted by a beautiful female collie called *Mitzi* who made a big fuss of Tina and Shaun. As Doreen Mason came out of the house the kids were already in play mode with *Mitzi* who just fell in love with them immediately, taking them under her wing and showing them around the farm grounds. After talking to Doreen and sitting down at a green veneer topped table in the well stocked compact farm kitchen it took us exactly no seconds flat to become good friends with her. Our children now had an aunty, Aunty Dor, as we called her. She was a very loving compassionate woman who loved children. In the farmhouse adjacent lived her eldest son and his family. They even had children the same ages as ours, Simon and Sarah, whom our kids got on famously with and became best friends. Shaun with his holsters and cowboy hat on would go on little adventures in the area with Simon, Sarah, Tina, *Mitzi & Bruno,* and other children that lived nearby or were guests of Doreen's. The rambling farm covered quite a few hectors and had tracts of forested areas on it. Next door to Doreen's farm was a large manor type house on a hill with a long driveway bordered by trees leading up to it. At the back were apple and orange groves. It was a farming area so many of the more affluent members of the community would ride horses around to exercise them . . . When we left that evening after our first visit we didn't leave a guest house, we left two beloved members of our family, in the form of Aunty Dor and *Mitzi.* Driving back to Forrest Hill Shaun looked skywards at the gathering darkness and early evening stars, while telegraph poles with wire strung between them flashed by . . .

Our first holiday break with Doreen cemented our friendship with her and we invited her to stay with us one Christmas. The kids loved this and jumped all over her early in the morning after Santa had been. That Christmas Santa had left Shaun a big bright red fire engine with extending ladder. Our children had no relatives in New Zealand other than us, their parents. To them Aunty Dor was the only aunty they had in the whole wide world. Their blood relatives were far away in another country and it seemed unlikely that they would ever see them . . .

Being a widow Aunty Dor lived alone in the farmhouse. Her younger son had died in a tragic accident while wandering over the railway lines one night after having visited a local pub. When the points changed his foot got trapped between the rails. Struggling to release it he didn't see the train that was bearing down on him further down the line . . . Aunty Dor never truly came to the realization that her son would never return, she knew he was dead but didn't want to accept it; she couldn't for she loved him too much. His room was left exactly as he had left it on that fateful night. This tragedy was not the only one to befall Doreen; her husband had been in the thick of the fighting in Europe and had brought home a Luger which Doreen kept under her pillow at night. He was a poet and would wear a top hat and cape, carry a cane and fashioned himself on early twentieth century writers, artists and poets. His experience at war tainted his life forevermore, what he had seen and experienced had exacted a heavy toll on him mentally, eventually driving this sensitive soul to suicide with possibly that same loaded Luger Doreen kept under her pillow . . . The old farmhouse was well furnished and had a large living room for the kids to play in when it rained. Just outside the front door leading onto the veranda was a room where she and her husband stored their old newspapers, it had possibly every Auckland Herald paper from 1914, at least it seemed like it . . . Her husband's belongings, farm implements and old furniture were stored in an old barn with broken boards and tattered hessian hangings, in itself it looked like something from an old black and white horror movie starring Jack Belushi in *The Curse of the Mummy* . . . Doreen had the touch of the mystic about her too, being a little bit of a spiritual medium and would oft see people she knew had passed on. On one trip down to Hastings and Napier after a huge earthquake had demolished structures and killed many of the residents she greeted many of her friends as she walked down streets ravaged by the quake . . . The trouble was, they had all been killed in the earthquake . . . Doreen was a darling and always treated us like her own family . . . And Tina and Shaun, they loved her very much . . . and *Mitzi*, her collie . . .

\* \* \*

Shaun had two recurring nightmares from one to two years of age, one came from the television and centered on a fox puppet; this puppet would chase him through a forest and always tried to bite him when he was sleeping. His dreams were filled with its ugly visage. The other nightmare he had from when he was a toddler was that of black bombers filling grey skies dropping bomb after bomb on our house and Auckland. These black bombers always filled his dreams and wouldn't relinquish their grip upon his sleep-time. We never allowed our children to watch disturbing programs and kept them sheltered from the iniquities of the world around, for they would have enough of that when they got older we reasoned, no sense in spoiling their childhood now. I could only surmise those nightmares originated from my own experiences during the Blitz, experiences that had imprinted and embedded themselves in crystalline memory and then were passed on to him. I never spoke of what I had gone through to my family or anyone, what I had seen and felt was just too painful for words and I did my best to suppress the memories. And in truth it frightened the hell out of me as those black German bombers dropped their tons of explosives on everything I held dear and close to my heart . . . Then again maybe Shaun was just a sensitive young child that picked up on my own suppressed memories . . . We did, however, take the children to the biggest cinema in Auckland from a young age, movies like the *Sound of Music, The King and I* and *Oliver*. At the time going to see a movie on Friday evening was a big affair in Auckland, people dressed up for the occasion, just as they did when catching an airplane flight. Tina would wear one of her attractive tartan skirts with a pretty frilled little blouse with a little bow tied around her neckline, black shoes and tights with her hair tied in two little pony tails while Shaun would wear a satin shirt with his little black bowtie, trousers and black shoes. If it was chilly Elizabeth would wear her mink jacket and I would put on my cavalry tweed overcoat over my suit. After parking the car we would wait in line to enter the cinema, Auckland's finest, and it boasted glass domes in the ceiling that could be opened at night so you could see the stars. The seats and wall hangings were of plush red velvet which just about covered everything other than the carved wooden armrests which were also padded and covered in red velvet. The carpets inside were thick and plush. The expansive foyer was very art deco with a lot of wood paneling. Going to the cinema in Auckland was a real treat for any adult or child. Elizabeth and I picked the large screen movies very carefully for the young minds of our children, we had no wish to expose them to violence of any kind . . .

At times Elizabeth and I would have an argument, nothing serious, Tina and Shaun would be woken up by our voices, and, sitting up in bed, they would look at the wall separating our room from theirs, Tina would invariably turn to Shaun and ask, "Are they arguing again?"

One night we had a terrible argument about moving down to Wellington and me joining the navy, I threatened to leave and started to pack my suitcase. Elizabeth was so distraught she woke up Tina and Shaun and told them not to let their daddy leave . . .

Of course I stayed, what else could I do, as my two youngsters' grabbed hold of me and started to cry . . .

\* \* \*

Choosing a plot for our house right next to Forrest Hill Primary was probably the best thing we could have done, Tina was very happy to go to school there and took her first day there in her stride, she even said to Elizabeth, "I'm a big girl now; you don't have to come with me . . . I can go all by myself . . ." Of course Elizabeth took her on her first day and made sure she was alright and settled into her new classroom. Shaun on the other hand was a homebody; he would have rather stayed home and had no desire to go anywhere other than to stay beside his beloved mother . . . He had more than enough to do at home and plenty of books to look at. He suffered a lot from dyslexia and found it difficult to read as the words and letters all seemed jumbled up to him. His teachers would always say, "Why can't you be more like your sister . . ." When he started going to school he really didn't want his mother to leave him there. But, the big bonus for him was the sandpit, a real big one! The kids would all bring their toys and they would have a whale of a time at break. One child, Brett, would have his Green Thunderbird 4, another Thunderbird 1 and Shaun had Lady Penelope's Fab 1 with Parker in the driver's seat. That Dinky Toy was his most prized possession and could shoot matchsticks out of its Rolls Royce type grill when the front wheels were pressed up. Both Tina and Shaun had small brown cases for school and Elizabeth would make sure their lunch boxes always had a piece of fruit and a strawberry jam sandwich amongst other things. Children being children they would always compare lunches and even swop things they didn't like. In the morning at school all the children would line up in front of their classes as the New Zealand flag fluttered and they all sang 'God Save the Queen'. When they left in the morning Tina would always take her shy brother by the hand and take him to school just like any big sister would. Our house was right next to the rugby field of the primary school so Shaun knew his mother was nearby in case anything happened. He was very quiet in class unlike Tina who dominated her classroom; she was very bright and quick to learn while Shaun was slow and methodical. Tina was always the first to put up her hand and fire off any answer the teacher required. Her schoolwork was always neat and tidy unlike Shaun's, he focused on other more important things, like playing in the sandpit, for wasn't that what school was for? Besides, they had loads of good books to read at home . . . But, on the other hand they had a library at the school and he could always find something interesting there . . . The only real scary thing about school was the dentist, Shaun figured the lady dentist got a bonus every time she drilled and filled a cavity. And she got an extra big fist-full of dollars for the pain she inflicted upon the little children, and for the size of hole she drilled . . . At school Shaun met Brett who became his best friend, he lived about a mile and a half away from our house. His father built a big tree house in their garden for the kids to play in when Shaun visited them . . . *Shaun's days at Arrow Road were just packed,* and at the end of a hard day's play Elizabeth would make sure our children had a bath and then put fresh pyjamas on them, get them to say their prayers kneeling beside their beds, read a fairy tale to them, then tuck both Tina and Shaun in under the covers and switch off the light and leave the door ajar . . . *Muffy* would then push the door open if she was outside and climb onto Shaun's bed and make herself comfortable between his legs on the bedding . . . and there she would stay, keeping an eye on both of them as the dark of night closed in on our part of the world . . .

\* \* \*

There were lots of interesting places to take the family in and around Auckland, and for that matter, the whole of New Zealand. There were plenty of great museums, the remains of Maori defensive villages on the top of extinct volcanoes, a climb up One Tree Hill, the hot pools at Helensville, the bubbling mud, hot springs and geysers at Rotorua to name but a few. Holidays in New Zealand could be a voyage of discovery for the children, it was a cultural paradise steeped in history. Tina and Shaun were in awe of the giant Maori war canoe in the Auckland museum from a very young age, and it boasted a host of other exhibits detailing the traditional Maori way of life and their customs in days gone by. Near to it was Auckland University which I hoped they would go to when they were older. The zoo in Auckland with all its animals was also one of their favorite places where they could run around and interact with bunnies and other young animals in the nursery. But it was at Rotorua that we bought our prized Maori dolls and records with their traditional songs and ballads. They were not toys to be bandied about and played with, both Tina and Shaun were made well aware of this and they respected our request to leave them alone. Besides, Tina was too involved making and cutting out outfits for her cardboard cutout dolls and Shaun was way too engrossed with cowboy culture to be bothered about mere dolls, even if they were representative of the Maori culture New Zealand was steeped in . . . Above all this though was the fact that New Zealand boasted probably the best beaches in the world and to our young children it was pure unadulterated heaven. When on holiday plastic spades and buckets, sand castles and sand boats, which I would make for them, were the order of the day . . . It was everything a couple of young kids could dream of . . . New Zealand was a land of natural wonders, a pristine clean land free from trash and the useless cargo the western world promulgated . . . Going to the beach on a Saturday was a big occasion, what with our big beach umbrella, beach towels, balls, toys, a picnic basket full of food and drinks, and the kids favorite aunt, Doreen, all packed into the car. *Mitzy* stayed on the farm and *Muffy* stayed at Arrow Road. Sometimes there was just barely enough room for the kids, Elizabeth and myself to squeeze in. The sunny flat beaches were catnip to our family. At times I would leave Liz and Doreen to watch the kids while I went along the beach to explore. One day I came across a WW2 concrete bunker that would have been used as the first line of defense. It stood alone and neglected now. Sand piled high along its sides threatening to bury it. Standing with the bunker behind me I gazed out to the bright blue sea and sky above dotted with puffy white clouds. The sand filled the little gaps between my toes as I walked over the hot granules to take a peek inside the narrow slit that would have served as an observation and gun port. Inside was more sand, its occupants having deserted their posts many years before. I turned back to the sea half expecting the Sweetbriar to be out there somewhere riding the gently lapping waves. But the Sweetbriar, my mother, had gone, it was no-more, just a pale reminder of days past. Elizabeth called me breaking the spell cast upon me by the salt sea-air, sailing boats and the odd ship cruising in the far distance on the briny Pacific waters. Yes, the Sweet 'B' had gone leaving me to my own fate, master and commander of my own destiny. I lifted my face to the sun and felt its warm rays on my skin. It was indeed a new world now; the old had gone but remained fixed firmly in my thoughts. Looking at my family as they spread our lunch out over the big blue and black checked beach blanket I felt guilty, I had others to live for now. It was not just my dreams and aspirations I had to consider, but their happiness and stability as well. The kids were calling now, urging me to come along so we could start our lunch together as a family, my family, yes mine, something that I had dreamed of during those hard war years, something that had kept me centered on those cold dark stormy nights on the bridge while we kept a watchful eye over our convoy and ship. My feet automatically started to plod over the hot white sand towards my family. My children were eagerly anticipating ice-creams after their meal as a dessert so hastened my arrival with beaming faces. I smiled at Liz and she smiled back . . .

Whenever I could I would take Elizabeth, Tina and Shaun on drives into the countryside where windblown long brown grass covered the land around us, where green grass covered the hills and red, black and white sands covered long dune filled beaches . . . Above all this was a long white cloud, sometimes filled with life giving rain and at other times it allowed the sun to cast its rays beneficently upon the land below . . . *This then, was the land of our dreams . . .*

\* \* \*

Our days in Arrow Road, Auckland, were not always filled with sunshine, when it rained, it rained and rained and rained. On these days I would take the kids with me if I went to see clients and contacts. Not far from us at a house in Takapuna a surprise awaited Shaun on a business call I had to make. In the basement that had been turned into a playroom they had built an entire Wild West town complete with plastic 1/32 scale cowboys with horses, carriages and townsfolk on a diorama. And on the hillside behind the town Indians waited amongst the rocks and trees. Shaun was in his element and played and played with the family's boys and the cowboy town. And on the television, what should come on, the Milky Bar Kid promoting Milky Bars, *'The Milky Bar Kid is strong and tough and only the best is good enough . . .'* I reckoned that little ditty would stay with my young son for a long time . . . It was a good thing most of my clients had children because toys were always available for them to play with, including dolls for Tina and a garage with Matchbox cars for Shaun. So while I chatted with clients over tea and coffee Tina, in her tartan skirt and white blouse with bow, would be happily playing with some dolls and Shaun next to her zooming cars across a carpet . . .

\* \* \*

We hadn't decided to enlarge our family and when we found
out Elizabeth was pregnant we couldn't have been happier. Tina
and Shaun were thrilled at the prospect of welcoming a new
member into our family and couldn't wait for the little urchin
to make its arrival. Burnt toast and lukewarm tea arrived with
regularity at our bedside in the hopes that somehow by doing this
it would hasten the baby's arrival. While Elizabeth was pregnant
with our new baby I would take Tina and Shaun out with me
so I could to give her a well deserved break. We also instituted
the *fish & chips on Friday* law with *Fanta* soda pop so Elizabeth
wouldn't have to slave in the kitchen preparing evening meals.
This law was also brought into effect on Saturday and during the
week the further along she was. Of course it wasn't always fish we
had in batter; there were muscles and oysters as well. The best
fish & chips can be found in New Zealand, no other country in
the world can boast such excellence in this fried fare. Sausages
dipped in batter then deep fried are a delicacy and the best
can be found in sea-side antipodean towns like Takapuna. My
favorite fish & chip store was near the beach and the other one
was near Arrow Road. At the bottom I would turn left for one
hundred yards, then right for another one hundred and fifty
yards to the shopping centre where our barber was. Elizabeth
would always take Shaun there for a haircut. The barber would
put a padded board across the armrests of his big barber's
chair then secure a bib sheet around him to catch the hairs.
When Liz couldn't make the walk down with him I would pop
him down quickly in the car during my lunch break. They also
sold stamps there and had a little toy store for the kids. Toward
the beach was Jack Reed, our doctor. Jack was Scottish and
was recommended by Lou Armitage. He was a blue blooded
tallish man with a very good reputation in the community. If
the children were ill he would call in with his black bag to see
them, and after three weeks from our first meeting we became

very good friends with both him and his wife. One very hot day Shaun came down with severe stomach pains, I took him to Jack and after examining him, he said, "Go and get him an ice cold bottle of Coca Cola to drink . . . leave it open a little while so it goes flat . . . then let him sip it . . ."

I did what the doctor ordered and after an hour or so Shaun was as good as new. After that episode Jack often visited us, especially as Elizabeth's pregnancy progressed, making sure everything was well with both mother and baby. Jack would also make house visits if the children had high temperatures. He was a very intelligent methodical man who made sure his patients were well taken care of . . .

\* \* \*

When Elizabeth was close to term Jack Reed suggested we book her into the hospital at Takapuna so there would be no complications. Just before Liz went into hospital I brought home a doll for Tina. There would be no rushing my beautiful wife to hospital as had been the case when Shaun was born. It was a week before our new son arrived and I now realized I had the family I always wanted at last – and that the sacrifices those men had made had all been for this moment in time when a new generation could live without the heel of oppression crushing them. Sometimes I wondered, *'Did all those men have to die?'* I still had nightmares of bombers coming over and dropping their explosives on me, of the dead and dying, of my home and the place where I lived being turned into a smoldering ruin – then Mark made his entrance –Standing there holding my newborn son it finally dawned on me, I finally realized what life was all about, how we should not squander our short lives and somehow make them count in whatever manner we could. And that we should always remember the sacrifices of others . . . It was how much family mattered, how finding love mattered, how finding that one special person to share your life with truly mattered. Elizabeth, to me, shall always be that beautiful, attractive, vivacious young woman I met on that sunny summer's afternoon at Royston swimming pool; I had found my place in the world at last by her side. All men are equal in the eyes of God whatever race or religion they belong to. My new family had replaced my old one shattered by falling German bombs. No-one has the right to force or change the beliefs of others through threats or evil. Not even Hitler had the right to force an evil government on others. Ultimately, the price for his folly had been paid for in blood, both Germany's and the rest of the world's . . . I pondered over these past injustices and how they should be consigned to where they belonged, the *past* . . . and that man should make a new beginning using the foundations and lessons of war so that we should not make the same mistakes over and over again . . . *Because all life is sacred, and that no-one deserves to die at the behest of another* . . . These thoughts and many others flooded my mind as I stood there holding my newborn son . . . When I returned home to Arrow Road with Elizabeth and Mark, our babysitter and two young children were expectantly waiting for the new arrival to the Chapman clan . . . I was now the proud father of three beautiful children . . . and Elizabeth, she was their glowing and radiant mother . . .

\* \* \*

As time marched on the war and everything we stood against seemed inconsequential, things that don't and didn't really matter. On many occasions I would stand on our wooden deck at Arrow Road thinking about what we had stopped. The Japanese had been merciless and if they had got their way they would have taken both Australia and New Zealand by force. The populations of both countries would have been massacred, starved and enslaved. The old pillboxes on the coastlines would always remind me of what could have happened. The Germans were not immune from this merciless behavior either. If they had taken Britain the commonwealth would have crumbled and eventually the United States would have been the only country able to stand against them, but, without Britain as a forward operating base it is doubtful whether the nuclear program Germany had embarked upon would have been slowed down and ultimately stopped. In short order the Germans would have launched nuclear strikes from U-Boats against the United States and any country allied to them. Africa would have come under their domination and Russia would have had its major population centers destroyed. Japan and Germany would have divvied the world out between them. The world as we knew it then would have ceased to exist. The Allies had to sweep through Europe to destroy the German military machine as quickly as they could to cut off the head of the beast; they had no option . . . German inventiveness and willingness to utilize anything at their disposal made them one of the most dangerous foes the world had witnessed since the beginning of recorded history. Millions of people of Semitic origin were starved, gassed and slaughtered under German rule and occupation. If the Nazi war machine had triumphed this slaughter would have continued until every last person of Jewish decent was exterminated . . . But then again, it is doubtful any of us would be alive today if we had not won the war . . .

\* \* \*

On a Monday I had a meeting with Don Young and as per normal he gave me my list of clients to see for the week, there was a big project pending in Napier and he wanted me to go and sort everything out. I explained to him that Elizabeth and I had just had a new baby, Mark, a healthy beautiful bouncing boy who was keeping his mother very busy and I was looking after Tina and Shaun. Don said, "Well, take them along with you, we'll cover all the costs, they can have a little holiday . . ."

"Alright . . ." I answered . . . That evening when I returned home I told Elizabeth of the trip and Don suggesting I take the kids, she also thought it was a good idea and would give her a little break from taking care of them as well as our new baby. Tina and Shaun would stay at the house of the manager of our Napier branch, and because they also had children, there would be plenty for them to do. The manager had both boys and girls so Tina and Shaun would have no trouble fitting in . . . They were very excited when we told them they would be coming with me to Napier for a holiday and that we would be flying down . . . We got up at 4 am on the morning our flight was due to leave Mangere, it was still dark and both Tina and Shaun were still tired as Elizabeth ironed Shaun's shirt in the dining area next to the lounge. Elizabeth was not going to let her children leave until they were both pressed and clean. Mark was still asleep in his cot in our bedroom as I packed my bag. Tina and Shaun had their small brown cases to put extra clothes and toiletries in. It was still a little chilly so Liz ordered the children into warm clothing. Shaun had a brown suede sheepskin jacket which Elizabeth put on her six year old son and did up the buttons before he was allowed to leave the house to get into the car with his little case. I was a very proud dad as we drove off, Liz waving as we drove down the driveway. My children looked so smart when we left number one Arrow Road heading for Mangere Airport to catch our nine o'clock flight. Arriving at the airport we booked in our luggage and got on board the Fokker Friendship that would take us to Gisbon. The flight attendants all made a big fuss over Tina and Shaun who were bubbling with excitement in expectation of the flight ahead, the last time they had been in an aircraft was when we flew from Australia to Whenuapai . . . It was clear sunny skies all the way as we flew to Gisbon where we were met by the manager of our office there. After arriving at the office of Turnbull & Jones in Gisbon with the manager to discuss our new projects, Tina and Shaun went with his wife for some ice-cream. Business done, I hired a small private plane to take us to Napier for my meetings there. The kids were getting use to flying and treated it all as a little adventure; however, they had started to get on each other's nerves and began to squabble a little before we boarded the Cessna 172. Tina had still not forgiven Shaun for scalping two of her dolls and cutting fringes for her Barbie dolls . . . Flying in pretty much a straight line we headed down the coast to Napier, underneath us flashed white sandy beaches and forested woods. I forgot all about the kids in the back as I fixated on the beautiful scenery below. Every now and again the pilot would let me take the controls while he relaxed and double checked his maps. At one point we seemed to hit some turbulence because the plane rocked from side to side. Turning behind me to see if the children were alright I saw Tina and Shaun fighting in the back seat of the Cessna 172 as we flew on towards Napier. I hadn't heard them because both pilot and I had earphones on, initially I was a little cross with them but I smiled as I chastised them, the plane had rocked quite severely from side to side as they had roughhoused in the back seat, they had no fear of either the altitude we were flying at or the consternation of the pilot and the small size of the Cessna . . . *It reminded me of my brothers in our younger years, Ernie, Jimmy, Teddy and Alfie, of the warm summers we shared, of the adventures and mishaps, of mum and dad, and, of good old England* . . . I looked out the cockpit windows of the rocking Cessna, the future was uncertain and not cast in stone, because it is up to each one of us to shape it and mold it – Would mankind choose the right path, one filled with both light and goodness, I didn't know . . . but, whatever happened I would always know I had done my best . . . Uncle Percy O'Sullivan, Uncle Albert Chapman and millions of others like them had all lost their lives and their futures in petty international spats started by even pettier politicians, small inconsequential beings that were prepared to sacrifice millions on the burning pyre of their whims and fancies. But even so, we, the general populace of our planet, the Earth's citizenry, have a responsibility to make sure our loved ones' sacrifices were not in vain. For it is up to us to make sure those sacrifices counted – we owed at least that to them – I wondered what the future would hold for my children, would they be successful, would they live up to my expectations, would they realize the sacrifices so many had made so that they could live . . . I looked down at the forever changing landscape below, and thought, *'It's never too late to do something, even if we just try,'* for, no matter how bad things may seem, it is never hopeless and we can always rise above our failings and those of others . . . It just depends upon how much you put into pulling yourself out of the hole you find yourself in, for, while you still live, *there is always hope . . .*

The Beginning . . .

# AFTERWORD

*Every family has its problems, no less ours, but the thing about families is you accept them unconditionally and love them regardless. My father's family was split apart by the war; its members grew polarized and became estranged to one another. After hostilities ceased it was never the same again. I would hazard a guess that most families at that time in Britain's history experienced a similar disconnectedness . . . that one time lovers had their love shattered and torn asunder by the exigencies of that time, love that never again reached the pre-war pinnacles of feelings experienced by the men and women at war. Many came home to nothing, others just a fragmented existence with little or no future in store for them. I know my father experienced things that he would rather remain forgotten in the depths of his neural pathways. I have met many WW2 veterans and the thing the vast majority all have in common is their desire to let the memories remain undisturbed and hidden. But, personally I think it is important to consign those memories to paper, lest the lessons learnt are forgotten by humanity . . .*

*From the time I was born I would have nightmares of black bombers flying above dropping their loads of death and destruction. These dreams continued until I was about ten. Were they crystalline memory or did I pick up on deep seated emotions, hidden from all, from my father. I know my father was deeply affected by what happened to him during the war, the death and destruction, the city he grew up in aflame and populated by the dead . . . It took some persuasion on my part to get him working on 'Hopes of Victory', and many a time tears would be rolling down his cheeks as he put pen to paper and memories to voice . . .*

*I guess the bottom line is, we have to rise above the curve balls life throws at us, we have to rise above the failings of governments and the people around us to become beacons of light in this dim world we inhabit . . . we have to become the incorruptible statesmen, the conservationists, men and women of good conscience fighting for right and righting the wrongs perpetrated by those that care naught . . . In the end it is up to us, you and I, to make sure the world becomes a better place for future generations . . . Cdr. Shaun Chapman*

# Hopes of Glory

I sat on a stool in the local public house in Kuruman staring at the bottom of my beer mug. Times had been hard of late and money was tight. Maybe it was time to leave Kuruman for good? I turned to look at the soccer game playing on the television above the bar. Two Afrikaner policemen walked in. They strolled up to me. "You must be the king of Mothibistad?" one of them said. I looked at him and replied, "Then you must be its queen . . ." Liverpool scored a goal as I turned to face the screen – a heavy fist smacked me on the side of my face knocking my glasses to the floor and causing my beer mug to slip out of my hand. A heavy baton struck the back of my head. I tried to get off the stool but it was kicked away beneath me trapping my foot in its wooden foot rest. As I tumbled to the floor fist after fist was unleashed upon both my face and the back of my head by the two burly Afrikaner policemen. I fell to the floor and they proceeded to kick me in my chest and back, shouting, *"Ya, yo blixom Englesman!"*

They had murder on their mind as I tried to get up trying to block their kicks and punches with my arms. I managed to pick my glasses up as I stumbled to the door of the bar. They followed with even more physical abuse. All the while local Afrikaners jeered at me and praised my big burly assailants . . . The German I had been sitting with had called them, saying I was a *'K\*\*\*\*\* Boetie'* . . . I crawled to my car, a rambler station wagon. I tried to get the keys out of my pocket but another fist slammed into my face and another kick to my side took my breath away. Another kick hit my hand and the keys went flying. I crawled toward a ditch at the edge of the parking lot and tried to get in it and away from the flurry of punches and kicks and the beating these men were inflicting upon me . . . All seemed to go black . . . The kicking stopped and the Afrikaner policemen walked away laughing . . . I came back to my senses and crawled into the ditch . . . Above me I felt a presence, I mumbled incoherently to the shadow for help. The man just stood there and said, "For you Englander the war is not over . . ." He spat at me before turning around and walked off into the night. I heard a car start and pull away before I started to slip into unconsciousness, *'That's another fine mess you've got me into, Stanley . . .'* I thought.

*Let me tell you how I got here . . .*

# BIBLIOGRAPHY

Addison, E. G. The Knights Templars' History. New York; 1875.

Barber, Richard, The Knight and Chivalry. New York; 1982.

Barker, Thomas W. The Knights Templars in England. Tucson; 1963.

Bulfinch's Mythology, The Age of Chivalry and Legends of Charlemagne. London: 1900.

Gome, George Laurence, The King's Story Book. Westminster; 1897.

Goodenough, Simon, War Maps. London; 1983.

Hutchinson, Walter, Story of the British Nation. London; 1914.

James, Lawrence, Warrior Race A History of the British at War. London; 2002.

Jenner, Micheal, Ireland Through The Ages. London; 1996.

Mallory, Sir Thomas KNT. The Most Ancient and Famous History of the Renowned Prince Arthvr, King of Britaine. London; 1634.

Langmaid, Kenneth, Clear for Action! The Royal Navy in Defense and in Attack. London; 1970.

Lords Commissioners of the Admiralty, A Seaman's Pocket Book. London; 1943.

Mallory, Sir Thomas, Le Morte Darthur, Volume 2. London; 1469.

Mattern, Friedrich, UFOs: Nazi Secret Weapon. Toronto; 1972.

Mattingly, Garett, The Defeat of the Spanish Armada. London; 1959.

McCarthy, Justin, A Short History of Our Times. London; 1907.

Moncrieff, Ascott Robert Hope, Romance & Legend of Chivalry. London; 1846.

Monmouth, Geoffrey, The History of the Kings of Britain. London; 1969.

Morrison, G. W. & Whitely, J. S. Profile of the A4s. Poole; 1985.

Morton, H. V. Atlantic Meeting. London; 1943.

Odhams Press, The British People at War. London; 1942.

Pyle, Howard, The Story of King Arthur and His Knights. Norwalk; 1992.

Reader's Digest, The Past All Around Us. London; 1979.

Robinson, John J. Born in Blood. New York; 1989.

Shadbolt, Maurice, Reader's Digest: Guide to New Zealand. Sydney; 1993.

Stewart, W. K. Brown's Signalling: The International Code of Signals. Glasgow; 1941.

Younge, Charlotte M. The Caged Lion. London & New York; 1889.

# EPILOGUE

'Many times I would stand on the beach not too far from Arrow Road contemplating the blue Pacific waters, many times my thoughts would drift north to where a battle raged, a battle fought not in the cold Atlantic waters but one in the hot steamy jungles of Vietnam . . . It was a new war . . . and while we mowed our lawns, read our Sunday newspapers, ate our Sunday roast for lunch and consumed our apple pudding with cinnamon sprinkled over it, then sat down and relaxed in front of a Disney film in the afternoon, men, women and children died, being blown apart, shot or burnt to death with napalm and whatever else man's depraved nature could imagine and inflict upon others. Families were torn apart because of an ideology that some thought led to a better way of life, for they knew best . . . Yet, all this just led man on a pathway to further destruction, of a land, of primeval forests populated by creatures that knew naught of man and had done nothing to him. And in this turmoil where once a peaceful people had struggled to survive and raise their families on the meager subsistence they made from planting rice in water covered paddies, soldiers bled and died in the humid verdant expanse of the jungle as their life-blood left their soon to be corpses . . . and the indigenous peoples of the area paid with searing screaming pain as flesh peeled off napalm covered bodies . . . Yes, this was war in our modern age in all its hideousness, a lingering hurtful thorn embedded in the heel of humankind. An all-encompassing and self-inflicted pain wrought upon collective

humanity by autocrats, oligarchies, militocracies, dictatorships and bureaucracies . . . an unthinking kakistocracy that ruled a planet . . . born of ourselves. And all while those in positions of power continued to enjoy inflicting pain on others as they lived lives in their ivory towers, immersing themselves in a lust for power, money and luxuries, and those who had little continued to suffer. It didn't make sense to me. It seemed to me that the lessons of the last two major wars had not been learnt. And man continued to make the same mistakes over and over again . . .'
*Cdr. Stanley William Chapman*

# AUTHOR BIOGRAPHY

Shaun Chapman is a committed conservationist, chairman and founder of RAPTOR, an anti-poaching organization, and RockyfilmLtd., a visual media & film production company. He is the author of the Rocky adventure series, the Solar Princess series, James Spillaney's Casefiles and many other titles. 'Chapman's 2010 Theory of Alternating Crustal Displacement and the Torque Wrench Effect' is his brainchild and answers many scientific, mythological and theological questions asked by man for thousands of years. He was born in Wales and spent the rest of his life all over the Globe including the United States, New Zealand, Australia, Botswana, Lesotho and South Africa. He is a citizen of the Earth who has studied a vast spectrum from psychology, geology to pure and applied mathematics with a love of the martial arts, being a black belt in Goju-Ryu Karate and an exponent of both Kendo and Jeet Kune Do. At present he is focusing on a series of environmental education books for RAPTOR and a TV series for the same. He is also the editor of 'RAPTOR – Leader of the Earthwize Generation', an online environmental magazine.

# PHOTOGRAPHS

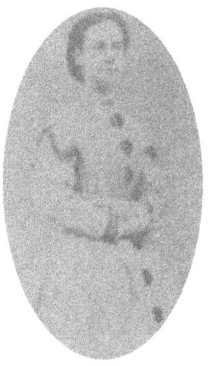

Eliza Ann Long, wife of George Langridge, and
my 2nd great-grandmother, born in Hampstead,
Middlesex, England in 1843, died in Toronto,
Ontario, Canada in November 1891.

George Langridge, my 2nd Great Grandfather, born in
Fletching, England, died April 1926 in Toronto, Canada.

Southwold Harbour, circa 1900.

Royston town center, circa 1900.

Saxmundham, Suffolk, with a donkey
buggy in the street, circa 1900.

Farnham Street in Saxmundham, Suffolk,
with a horse and buggy, circa 1900.

High Street in Saxmundham, circa 1910.

The road to Leiston Abbey.

St. Margaret's Church in Leiston where our
extended relatives, Rachel Mary Chapman (80), and
Sarah Chapman (92) (1816-1908), are buried.

A postcard from Leiston in Suffolk.

The train station at Leiston, Suffolk, circa 1910.

Left to right: Agnes Emily; George William Langridge
(Sr); Agnes Mabel Langridge (ne King); Kathleen Mabel.
At back: George William Langridge (Jr). Front row
left to right: Edith Mary; Florence Annie; Alice May.

'BRITAIN AT WAR' poster from August 5th 1914.

Daily Mirror headline with declaration
of war, Wednesday August 5th 1914.

Ernest Andrew Chapman, Royal Field Artillery, service
number: L/29187, astride 'Dolly' in quieter times.

Members of the Royal Field Artillery in
the stables during World War One.

Combatants of the 10<sup>th</sup> Roving
Battery, Royal Field Artillery.

A break from the front for the R.F.A., the old
hands show their stiff upper lip while others have
that thousand yard battle shocked stare.

World War One ends on Thursday, November
7th 1918 and the Armistice takes effect.

Revelers on a busy London street and
on a bus celebrating war's end.

Savy British Cemetery in Aisne, France,
where Pvt. Albert Chapman rests.

The grave stone of Pvt. Albert Chapman, #38158,
Gloucestershire Regiment, who died two months before
the war ended on 15th September 1918 aged 20.

Saxmundham station.

A truly Victorian family. Standing, left to right:
Alice May; Agnes Emily; George William Langridge
(Jr); Edith Mary; Kathleen Mabel. Seated, left to
right: George William Langridge (Sr); Alfred Ivors;
Albert King; Agnes Mabel Langridge (ne King).

George William Langridge (Jr), circa 1920.

St. John's Church in Saxmundham, just
a stone's throw from Leiston.

Plaque in St. John's Church in Saxmundham
bearing the names of parish members who died
in WWI, including Private Albert Chapman.

Stanley William Chapman, born November 30th
1924, being pushed in a stroller down Pudding Lane,
near Bow in London, in early 1925 by Elizabeth
Chapman (ne O'Sullivan), with proud father,
Ernest Andrew Chapman, walking alongside.

Ernest Andrew Chapman in the Austin he won
time and again in a raffle, circa 1934.

Ernest 'Ernie' Chapman aged 10.

Jessie O'Sullivan; Edward 'Teddy' Chapman,
age 5; Alfred 'Alfie' Chapman, age 4, on
holiday at the coast (circa 1937).

The O'Sullivans at the coast (circa 1937). Left to
Right: Mary O'Sullivan; Margaret Coughlin; Jessie
O'Sullivan; Grandmother Maria Coughlin-O'Sullivan
(ne Atkinson); Doreen O'Sullivan. Back row, left
to right: Daniel Coughlin; John O'Sullivan. Photo
taken by Elizabeth Chapman (ne O'Sullivan)

A4 Flying Scotsman, the engine that Ernest Andrew
Chapman drove before and after WWII.

Elizabeth Katherine Langridge &
David Langridge, circa 1937.

Mary Ann Postle (ne Cushion) and John Postle
outside their cottage in Burgh, Norfolk, circa 1938.

Great-grandparents of Elizabeth & David Langridge,
Mary Ann Postle (ne Cushion) & John Postle seated
outside their cottage in Burgh, Norfolk, circa 1938.

Left to right: John Postle; Iris Lillian Langridge
(ne Everett); Iris' mother Harriet Elizabeth
Everett (ne Postle); Grandmother of Iris,
Mary Ann Postle & David Langridge.

The book that turned a nation to hatred and pushed the
world to war, MEIN KAMPF, written by Adolf Hitler.

'War Declared' by Britain and France as Germany's
blitzkrieg stormed into the Low Countries and
took Holland, Belgium and Poland, having
already annexed Austria and others.

The attack on Britain begins in 1939 as bombs fall on
London setting it on fire and destroying much of it.

A Heinkel 1-11 like the one that strafed Stanley
William Chapman as he walked through the shunting
yards in London to take his father, Ernest Andrew
Chapman, lunch just before the sirens went off.

Tilbury docks in London under
attack by German bombers.

A Heinkel 1-11 begins its bombing run
over the River Thames in London.

A woman member of the ARP protects her son
as the bombs begin to explode during a German
daylight bombing mission over London.

The only truly safe place from German bombs,
the London Underground, where the citizens of
London reserved spaces for their family members
in order to get a good night's sleep and be off
the uncomfortable tracks during the Blitz.

London burns . . .

Alfie & Teddy Chapman in Caerwent in Wales after
being evacuated from London. The photo was taken by
Stanley on his visit there before joining the Royal Navy.

A convoy heads west across the Atlantic for
Newfoundland, Canada and the United States.

The convoy westward bound.

The Atlantic starts to bite the convoy, making it
difficult for the wolf-packs to fire their torpedoes.

HMS Sweetbriar (K209) making
headway through heavy seas.

The 4.5 inch gun on the forecastle of the
Sweet 'B'. Left to right: Asdic operator on his
action station; Chief engineer from the engine
room; Engineer from the engine room & our
cook, all showing us their action stations.

Just another sea-cruise aboard HMS Sweetbriar (K209).
The pom-pom gun is directly behind Stanley William
Chapman on the left, and, left to right: the Sweet 'B's
band leader, 'Smitty' Williamson; another asdic operator;
and yet another asdic operator at the edge of the photo.

Our Atlantic convoy under the watchful eye
of a Sunderland flying boat looking out for
U-Boats . . . *Stanley William Chapman*

One wrong word said at the wrong time and
place could cause many a life lost at sea.

Sunny skies over the Sweet 'B' as she cuts
through Mediterranean waters.

A Gibraltar street scene, taken by Stanley William
Chapman with his little box Brownie camera.

A worn photograph that has been in my wallet
since 1944. On the right is James 'Jimmy' Chapman
in Egypt with the 8th Army. On the left is a pal of
Jimmy's from his unit . . . *Stanley William Chapman*

Another careless word and another
ship sinks beneath the waves . . .

On patrol, HMS Arethusa, Ernie's ship,
seeking a German battle-group.

The German intelligence machinery gathered little
bits of information such as careless talk in public
places; newspaper articles; shipping manifests; loose
lips at the docks and in bars, anything, in order
to build up a picture of shipping movements.

The Sweet 'B' ready for battle at D-Day.

A troop ship being escorted to Juno beach
by HMS Sweetbriar at D-Day.

Lines of landing craft heading to
the beaches at D-Day, 1944.

HMS Rodney on its way to pound German
Positions at Juno beach near Caen.

B-26 Marauders with black & white D-Day stripes
on wings and fuselage inbound for continental
Europe to support the Allied assault in Normandy
fly over US, British and Canadian forces below.

The USS Nevada (BB-36) fires on German shore
gun emplacements and positions at D-Day.

HMS Warspite hits back at the Germans
at Normandy on D-Day.

HMS Sweetbriar (K209) with a
starboard beam sea running.

The war in Europe is over.

'Daily Mirror' headlines VE-Day.

After World War 2 in the garden at Buntingford
and just before my war against the communists
started . . . *Stanley William Chapman*

Berlin Airlift: C-47s at Tempelhof Airport
in Berlin being unloaded.

Supplies ready to be loaded and ferried to Berlin.

C-47s and C-54s at Tempelhof airport on concrete
staging areas once used by German fighter aircraft.

'Blockade Ends' . . . Airlift and the US
Navy wins against communist Russia.

Ernest Andrew Chapman and Elizabeth Chapman
(ne O'Sullivan) out bowling one Sunday in Royston.

Edward 'Teddy' Chapman, ringed, in his Marines
passing out photograph with the rest of the men
in his unit before heading off to the Far East.

Left: 'Teddy' in Malaya at camp during the Malaya
Emergency in 1957. Right: Unnamed Marine.

Elizabeth Katherine Langridge lazing on a
beach one summer in the middle 1950s.

Drama group in Royston putting on a Paris style show
with the Can-Can. Late 1950s with Elizabeth on the right.

Elizabeth Katherine Langridge at the beach with
Stanley William Chapman (taking photo).

An English rose, Elizabeth Katherine Langridge.

Elizabeth Katherine, now Chapman, on her
wedding day in Royston, Hertfordshire.

The wedding reception at the Banyers in Royston.
Left to right: Judy Croft, soon to be Langridge;
George William Langridge (Jr); Elizabeth Katherine
Chapman (ne Langridge); Stanley William
Chapman. Standing behind is Bob Nelson in the
center and other waiters from the Banyers.

Elizabeth Katherine Chapman in the
garden of 68 Orchard Road, Royston.

Elizabeth and our dog one Christmas day at our home near Arrington outside Royston before the birth of our first child, Tina . . . *Stanley William Chapman*

Elizabeth Katherine Chapman holding
Tina Louise Chapman in her arms in the
garden of 68 Orchard Road in May.

Stanley William Chapman holding an
irrepressible Tina Louise Chapman in the
house near Arrington one winter's day.

Stanley William Chapman pushing Tina
Louise Chapman in the pram on the coast
near Portmadoc in North Wales.

Elizabeth Katherine Chapman with newborn son, Shaun Chapman, at home in the Welsh hills and vales of Wales.

RMS Orion being nudged from her berth at the docks near Battersea power station taking the 'English Family Chapman' on a voyage to the other side of the world.

The Orion heading up the Thames
into the English Channel.

Looking from the stern of the Orion as
she heads down the Suez Canal.

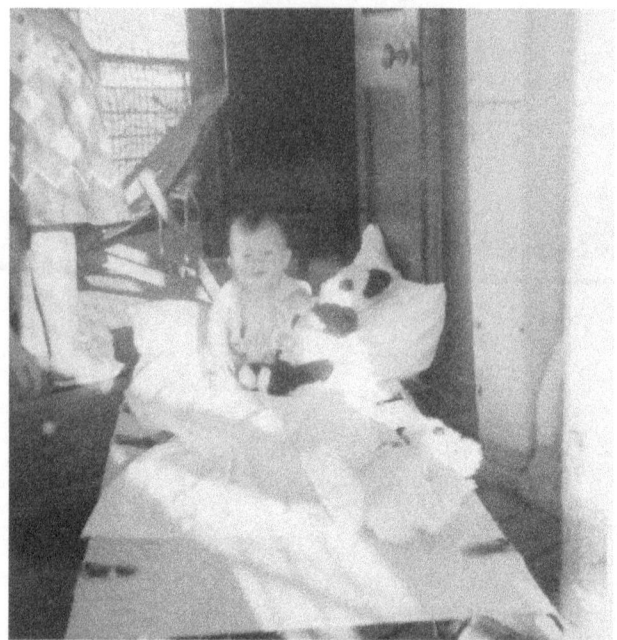

A young Shaun Chapman at five and a half months in
the sick bay of the Orion after dysentery spread through
the ship after the port of Beira. Mr. Panda is laying
next to him while Teddy is at the bottom of the cot and
Elizabeth Katherine Chapman stands on the left.

The Orion entering Sydney harbor.

Elizabeth Katherine Chapman holding Tina
Louise at Sydney Zoo before continuing
on to Brisbane in the Orion.

The 'English Family Chapman' enjoying Queensland's
beautiful un-spoilt beaches and blue clear skies. Left
to right: Tina, Elizabeth, Stanley & Shaun Chapman.

Shaun's 1st birthday party in Clontarf near Brisbane, Australia. Left to right: Tina, Michael, Joyce, Shaun and Raymond.

Bath-time for Tina and Shaun in Clontarf, Queensland, Australia.

Stanley & Elizabeth Chapman enjoying a
meal in the restaurant of the Redcliffe Hotel
with the manager of Redcliffe H.G. Palmers
& his wife near Brisbane, Australia.

Stanley & Elizabeth at a function in the Redcliffe
Hotel with its owner and the manager of H.G. Palmers,
Redcliffe, his wife and daughter from left to right.

Uncle Lou Armitage after giving Shaun and Tina a
ride around his garden in a wheelbarrow in Forrest
Hill, Auckland, New Zealand, in October.

Tina with Mr. Panda and Shaun at our first house
in Auckland, 270 East Coast Road, Forrest Hill.

Tina & Shaun in a black car in Auckland. Tina at two
and three quarter years of age, and Shaun 18 months old.

Our first Christmas in New Zealand at 270 East
Coast Road, Forrest Hill, Auckland, New Zealand.

Shaun playing with a Mercedes at our
house on East Coast Road.

Tina playing with her doll and Shaun playing
with his plastic Hellcat and a Volkswagen on
the small porch at 270 East Coast Road.

Shaun at two and a half years of age on his
tricycle at 270 East Coast Road in Auckland.

Shaun & Tina on their tricycles on the drive
in front of our house on East Coast Road.

Our young neighbor Catherine with Shaun in
the front garden of 270 East Coast Road.

Still on their bikes, Tina and Shaun.

Left to right: Tina, Shaun & Elizabeth in the
back garden of our house in East Coast Road.

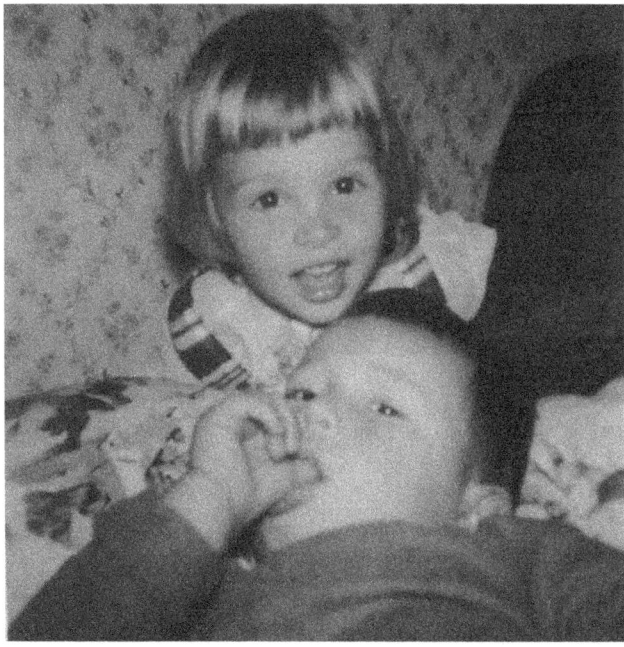

Tina and Shaun just before bedtime at East Coast Road.

Our beautiful little daughter, Tina, with
her trike . . . *Stanley William Chapman*

Our little angel, Shaun, asleep at 270 East Coast
Road, Auckland . . . *Stanley William Chapman*

Our children playing in their wheelbarrow
at the back of our East Coast Road house in
Auckland . . . *Stanley William Chapman*

Our new house, number one Arrow
Road, Forrest Hill, Auckland.

My beautiful wife Elizabeth standing in front of our new Holden in front of our new house, number one Arrow Road, Forrest Hill . . . *Stanley William Chapman*

The white glistening un-spoilt sands of Whangaporoa were a cornucopia of heavenly-like delights for our two young children and a pleasant place for us to relax and unwind. I took the photo while Elizabeth, Shaun & Tina posed . . . *Stanley William Chapman*

Stanley oversees Tina & Shaun holding the hose
with neighborhood friends at Arrow Road.

Shaun & Muffy on the deck at Arrow Road. 'Muffy' was
thrown out of the left side window of the car in front of
us as I was driving down Shore Road with Tina & Shaun
in the back seat. They screamed at me to stop. I jumped
out and picked up the little kitten. She became an
inseparable part of our family . . . *Stanley William Chapman*

Tina holding Muffy and Shaun, tickling Muffy's
paws, looking very nonplussed at Arrow Road.

Tina & Shaun in front of the family photographer
who used a plate camera with a black cloth
over his head of which Shaun was very curious,
wondering what exactly he was doing under there.
He used a puppet to make the children smile.

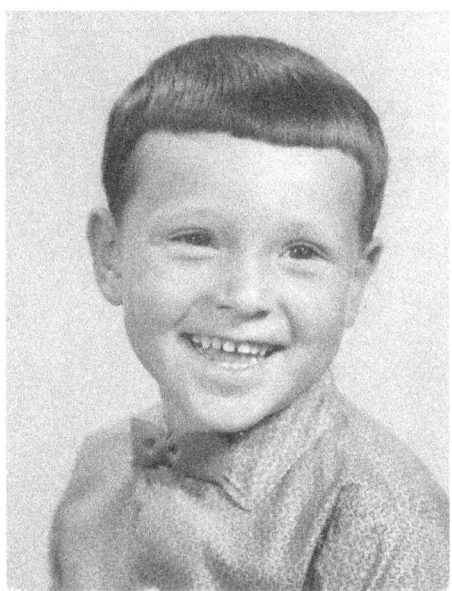

A portrait of our young son, Shaun Chapman, age 4 years old. The inscription on the back reads, "To Mum, I thought you might like to have this . . . Love Elizabeth"

A portrait of my beautiful wife Elizabeth at Arrow Road taken by our professional photographer . . . *Stanley William Chapman*

'Me' in the wheelbarrow taking a well deserved break
from mowing, raking, digging, sowing & clearing our
garden at Arrow Road . . . *Stanley William Chapman*

Taken at Whareporoa guest house with
Tina & Shaun on 'Gin' and me holding
the reins . . . *Stanley William Chapman*

Shaun with 'Teddy' at school in our orange tent.
Inscription on the back of the photo reads: "The
people next door put the fence up. We need one
down the other side now. Am going to disguise
it with trees, shrubs eventually. We bought 2
more trees, 3 shrubs yesterday . . . Elizabeth"

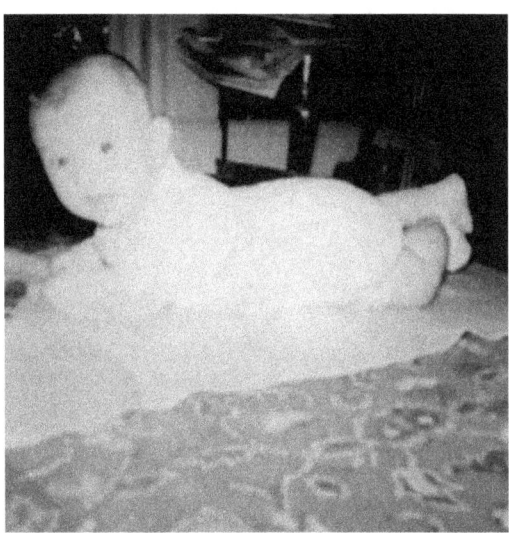

The newest addition to our family, Mark
Chapman, playing on his blanket at Aunty
Dor's house in Kumeu in the living room.

Taken at Aunty Dor's farm in Kumeu. Third from left: Simon Mason. Dogs from left: Mitzy & Bruno, Simon's dog. Tina & cowboy Shaun leaning against the gate, with their new friends staying at the guest house. The babysitter is at the back pushing Mark in a pram.

Shaun playing cricket with Stanley, out of frame and bowling, as Doreen Mason and Tina look on one Christmas at Arrow Road.

Shaun & Tina playing in their paddling pool in
the back garden of our house in Arrow Road
with Forrest Hill Primary School's rugby field
up past the embankment behind them.

Shaun, Mark & Tina Chapman at family portrait time
with the photographer's puppet making them all smile
at the same time and looking in the same direction.

Tina Chapman, at 7 years of age, on the bench and deck I built at number one Arrow Road in Forrest Hill . . . *Stanley William Chapman*

Shaun on the bench of our deck at 6 years of age in May.

Tina looking very pretty while Shaun sticks his
tongue out on the back step of Arrow Road.

Shaun having a whale of a time with his new
train-set and brick tunnel in the lounge at
Arrow Road while Tina and friend look on.

*Cdr. Stanley William Chapman, Legion d'Honneur*
*'Et exaltatus fueris ut aquila, quasi leo rugiet . . .'*
*(Soar like an eagle, roar like a lion . . .)*

CPSIA information can be obtained
at www.ICGtesting.com
Printed in the USA
BVHW030031120220
572049BV00003BA/22/J